Dynasties

ALSO AVAILABLE FROM ECLIPSE PRESS

Dynasties

Great Thoroughbred Stallions

BY

EDWARD L. BOWEN

FOREWORD BY

WILLIAM S. FARISH

ECLIPSE PRESS

Essex, Connecticut

ECLIPSE PRESS

An imprint of The Globe Pequot Publishing Group, Inc.
64 South Main St.
Essex, CT 06426
www.GlobePequot.com

Distributed by NATIONAL BOOK NETWORK

British Library Cataloguing in Publication Information available

Library of Congress Cataloging-in-Publication Data available

ISBN 978-1-4930-9047-1 (paperback)
ISBN 978-1-4930-7938-4 (ebook)

Contents

Cover: *Nearco* by Richard Stone Reeves

Foreword

ong before Lane's End Farm was established, the breeding of Thoroughbreds had become an overwhelming interest for me. In developing a racing stable and then Lane's End Farm, I have been fortunate enough to devote a considerable part of my professional time, and personal energies, toward breeding, raising, selling, and racing Thoroughbreds.

Over the years, I have been lucky enough to be involved with some highly memorable stallions. For example, I was fortunate to co-breed the leading sire Danzig; Warner Jones and I went into partnership on the young horse Raja Baba, the first stallion I "hung my hat on," and saw him become a leading sire. More recently, Lane's End had the gratifying experience of breeding and selling A.P. Indy and then bringing him back as a Horse of the Year to launch a highly successful stud career at his birthplace, where his half-brother, Summer Squall, also stands. Then, too, Dixieland Band, one of those little sons of Northern Dancer, has been a consistently successful stallion. On the other hand, it was only late in the career of Pleasant Colony that it worked out for him to stand

briefly at Lane's End, and so we were able to initiate some long-term breeding designs for the future that had been only theoretically possible before his arrival.

During those fortunate years, however, there were also horses whose careers were either baffling, or plain disappointing. I cannot explain why so many good racing sons of Bold Ruler would have failed as stallions. The same can be said of the sons of Alydar, sire of our Lane's End stallion Alysheba — a champion racehorse that did not rise to the top as a stallion. Manila, from the Northern Dancer sire line, was another recent stallion whose lack of success I just cannot explain, although, looking back, maybe he should have stood in Europe.

These examples remind us that no patterns in Thoroughbred breeding will turn out as expected all the time. I have been asked, however, whether I have strong opinions about what makes the best stallion prospects, and I certainly do. The horses I look for have to have demonstrated at least grade I miler-performance. I also am looking for horses that have classic performance and pedigree rather than pure speed in both categories.

I then look at conformation and try to avoid a stallion that does not have a lot of bone or good conformation. Our racetracks are so tough on horses, and we are seeing fewer and fewer starts per horse because of it. Pedigree, of course, is possibly the most important part of the package. I look for a sire line that is proven, but that is not to say that at times I will not reach out and take a chance on a line that looks like it could work.

I would not say it is any tougher now than it used to be to find horses with the preferred characteristics, although it might be more competitive to acquire them. You do have to look overseas more than before, because so many of our best broodmares have been sold abroad. Kingmambo is an example. You could say he is an American horse (as a son of Mr. Prospector), but he competed in Europe. One thing about Kingmambo that fascinated me was that his three grade I mile victories were run in extremely heavy going, and he would win with a flourish, with a whole lot left. I believe horses winning at a mile over the deep courses of Europe, uphill and downhill, actually show that they have enough stamina for a mile and an eighth or a mile and a quarter over here. To take this thought further, I believe a top miler in Europe is more likely to get classic horses here than that same horse would in Europe. I think the softer going creates greater demand for stamina, and I think in Europe that usually a horse that can get a mile and a quarter to a mile and a half is the best type of classic prospect for over there.

In Kingmambo's case, he was taking a great deal of stamina from his female side (his dam is the European champion miler Miesque, by Nureyev), and I thought his being by Mr. Prospector would mean he would get horses that would run well over here. Mr. Prospector can dominate so much. Kingmambo has done everything I hoped, and more.

As I think back over a number of years, several key events are very important. One, the success of the Nasrullah nick with Princequillo mares shaped my thinking. When a pattern like that exists, it is the breeder's goal to spot it in time to make use of it. Another key was Northern Dancer. I remember Joe Thomas of Windfields Farm saying, "This horse will change the perception of what a classic horse can look like." He was a small, close-coupled horse whose line has gotten good horses of all sizes. Some of the line, however, have experienced fertility problems.

Another illustration of how difficult it is to have hard and fast rules is the Raise a Native line. Raise a Native was not sound enough to race beyond two, but over the generations this line seems to get sounder. His great son Mr. Prospector got basically sound horses, even when they were not correct! A pattern like that is counter to a lot of expectations.

I believe the sire and the dam are equally important, and the fact that some sires stamp their foals does not change the importance of the mare. A mare does not have to put her stamp on her foals in order for her to have an influence on their abilities.

We all look for sires that can produce good runners. Next is the question of whether his sons will also be good sires. It seems that by the time you can assess whether a stallion is going to be a sire of sires, he is well along in his life. In Alydar's case, the pattern seemed to develop that his sons were not getting it done, and that continued. On the other hand, that pattern also seemed to be true of Danzig, but then his sons began to get top horses, so everyone wanted a Danzig stallion! We went out of our way to get Belong to Me, and I believe he will be a very good sire.

These are examples of how difficult what we all are trying to do really is. Breeders are not dealing in certainties, but percentages. That's why I look for horses that are correct, had at least grade I speed at a mile, and have good bone. I believe that's the high-percentage approach.

— *William S. Farish*
Lane's End Farm, Versailles, Kentucky

Introduction

ere lies the fleetest runner the American Turf has ever known, and one of the gamest and most generous of horses." This inscription, in lasting Barre granite, graces the gravestone of the horse named Domino. The stone lies within easy view of such motorists who know to pause along Huffman Mill Pike outside Lexington, Kentucky, to think again about the entire, complex issue of man and the Thoroughbred.

"Fleet," we know; that's an easy concept. The horse, by Nature's own decree, after all, was a creature who used his speed to evade his enemies. The attributes of gameness and generosity are something else. They are a bit more of man's making, or so we compliment ourselves in wanting to believe, and therein lies the sweet mystery of the racehorse. The Thoroughbred is bred to run, to race, and so the quality of being "game" is something this creature understands, because that is what we have sought for more than 300 years. The will and determination to turn away others, to be "generous" in his striving to win the race, are hallmarks of this breed's competitive fire.

The Thoroughbred is exalted among those multi-generational partnerships by which man has been awed and challenged by Nature, while at the same time perhaps a bit pompous in the assumption that we can shape it according to our own longings. Man has relied on creative human imagination to summon this mythic figure. Yet, the trade-off for the horse is that he, not we, remains the master. Mankind pours over his stud books, his production records, his print-outs, but what the entire exercise seeks — the superior runner of races — remains the province of caprice. As man sees himself as Nature's partner, so might the horse — and the horse is right.

The excellence of individuals described in these pages is easily seen as the ultimate success in the shaping of a breed of competitive animal which has fascinated, and uplifted, through recent ages. What could seem a more logical pattern than a grand runner of one era passing along his racing class to his sons, and they to the next generation, and so on through a dynasty of reverberating genetic reliability?

We might be smug in addressing the unbeaten Nearco, complimenting those who shaped his ancestry and managed his production record with such acumen that, six decades later, the chorus of his sire line raises the song of Northern Dancer, Nijinsky II, Danzig, Sadler's Wells, Halo, Seattle Slew, and A.P. Indy. Yet, how do we deal with the knowledge that Nearco's vaunted ancestor Phalaris — arguably the seminal individual of the century — was a bit of an oddity within his own realm? He was used in the stud of Lord Derby in part because he did not fetch the asking price of 5,000 pounds in the tumult of World War I and its immediate aftermath. (How much do we shape our destiny, and how much doth destiny shape — and laugh at — us?)

We might easily see in Bull Lea a prime example of wise matching of European stock with families longer associated with America. After all, he led the sire list five times and gave us the wondrous succession of champions that included Citation, Armed, Coaltown, Twilight Tear, Real Delight, Two Lea, and Bewitch. Great triumph in the knowledgeable sowing and reaping of genetics? How then did it happen that his sons disappointed gravely in the stud, while his daughters were prized matrons?

What do we learn from High Time, the intensely inbred foal of 1916 who won but a single race, then soared to the top of the sire list, only to fade quickly as influence for future generations? Even Bold Ruler, whose proud record seemed so much a logical extension of his exalted pedigree, in the end posed a riddle. How was it that, after he had sired so many truly brilliant racehorses, it was the thin thread stemming from one of his lesser sons that filtered through two generations and burst forth as the source of a Seattle Slew, while most of the other lines faded meekly?

A summary of sire lines of the 20th Century — both those which lasted and those that burst brightly and faded instantly — is a paradox: A repeating series of singular tales. Breeders have raced through the stud book like broken field runners — justifying one decision this way and another decision that way, but with price and availability constant leavening. Theories and ideals abound. A good stallion prospect is one that has a good pedigree and was a good, sound racehorse, achieving at a high level. Racing provides plenty of tests to show us the way. Naturally, one would prefer a classic winner as a sire prospect, certainly above an apparent sprinter that was not sound enough to go on. Well, of course, except for a Danzig, or a Raise a Native, limited by injury to three or four starts, all of them sprints. Concepts are frequently shattered. Turn-to represented the Royal Charger branch of the Nearco line, a branch looked upon as lacking in stamina. So, in speed-oriented America, Turn-to launched a sequence which sent Sir Ivor back to win the most exalted of the English classics and herald an era of American-bred success in Europe.

What we address in these pages is a selection of stallions which, briefly or for several generations, appeared on the top line of some of the top horses of their generations. This concept of a "sire line," like that of a "female family" (or bottom line), can beguile us into oversimplifying genetics. We understand that each of the antecedents in a pedigree has the potential to influence successive generations. Yet, the straight line, sire or female, is something we can grasp, can get our arms around figuratively. To try to absorb all the intermingling of other ancestors would create a zigzag pattern similar to the paths of certain chess pieces. Should we identify one genetic possibility

Introduction

as the "bishop-path" for example? No, the sire line (top line or tail male) and the female family (bottom line or tail female) are so much more readily grasped.

There is also something socially comfortable about a sire line. It reflects a concept that we tend to live, at least in Western civilization. Consciously, or not, we have always thought, and been taught, in terms of "sire" lines. We have no recollection of any Sunday School teacher, when addressing all those Biblical "Begats," having paused to counsel, "remember, the mothers were just as important — possibly more so, because the female controls the mitochondria, don't forget."

Ruling dynasties tended to think in terms of men and sons in the main, although more than a few history chapters dealt with times when a daughter emerged as a queen — deadly or benign. Modern social attitudes continue to reinforce the "sire line" concept. The author was surprised that when a son was born after two daughters, there was a strong presumption among acquaintances, ladies as well as men, that it was somehow more exciting that the baby was a boy. That a son "to carry on the name" was somehow to be more cherished than another daughter was undoubtedly a surface reaction on their part, not intended insult to anyone's daughters. Still, the very fact that for several thousand years, wives have generally taken husbands' names creates an intellectual and emotional familiarity with "sire lines." Whether, on balance, this custom — with all its gender-sensitive ramifications on egos — has served civilization best is subject to debate. Fortunately, however, that question is not within the scope of this book!

So, in looking at Thoroughbred history in the 20th Century in terms of sires and sons and grandsons, etc., we recognize that the straight line tells only part of the genetic tale. It is a part of that tale, however, that is familiar and appealing. The image of a great stallion standing atop a distinguished patriarchy summons the majesty of the Thoroughbred, just as the thought of female families summons appreciation for another kind of strength.

Addressing sires lines also recognizes the inequality in the numbers game that gives a stallion hundreds of more offspring than a mare. (Is it not amusing, then, that in so many cases the lasting presence over more than a couple of generations often is the province of the daughters, as stallions disappear as "sires of sires" and remain important only as sires of broodmares?)

A word about the selection process is in order. While many of the horses and lines included were obvious choices, some reflect a storyteller's prerogative. To include a Challenger II and omit a Count Fleet or a Pharamond II, for example, reflects a search for a variety in the type of history and the geography of the subjects. One hopes the horses included, collectively, illustrate a wide range of sire line sagas.

That mankind has not belled the cat of Nature is no detriment. Indeed, the mysteries of the Turf are as much a part of its wonder as are the tenets and the decisions which seem sage in aftermath. A look back at a century of outstanding stallions is, per force, a story of guesswork as well as wisdom, of expectations met and dashed, of predictability and random hits. As we cross over into another century, one might suspect that the history of its great Thoroughbred sires will be much the same. That is our expectation — and hope.

Edward L. Bowen,
Lexington, Kentucky, 2000

EARLY
20th CENTURY
STALLIONS

Commando

At the end of the Gay Nineties, when the 19th Century gave way to the 20th, a portion of the pride and prowess of the American Turf stemmed from the saga of Domino. That this sire line survives and flourishes a century later is illustrative of the whims of Nature insofar as Thoroughbred breeding is concerned.

Domino was a child of the racing gods, beloved as "the black whirlwind," a standard for pure speed by which several generations of colts were measured — and usually seen as wanting. As a sire prospect, one could hardly ask for more, but Domino died after siring only twenty foals and his best son, Commando, got only twenty-seven. This apparent prescription for a sire line's speedy disappearance was exacerbated by the circumstance of Commando's great son Colin proving a shy breeder. Yet, at the dawn of the 21st Century, we have former leading sire Broad Brush and his Breeders' Cup Classic winner Concern amply carrying on the tenuous torch that has burned since 1893.

Domino was bred by Major Barak Thomas, who at the age of fifty left a career of various posts in and out of government service and became one of the first Lexington horsemen to devote most of his time to Thoroughbreds. Racehorses had been deeply burned into the psyche of Kentuckians for

some time, of course, but for the most part Thoroughbred breeding was but one of many enterprises for agriculturists of the day. Domino was foaled in 1891 at Thomas' Hira Villa Farm. The Major was prone to honor horses by naming farms for them. His original farm, Dixiana, was named for the mare Dixie, who had produced his flying colt Herzog. When he sold Dixiana, he replaced it with a property he named Hira Villa, the matron Hira being the dam of another crack runner the Major had bred, namely Himyar.

Domino was a son of Himyar and was foaled from Mannie Gray, an Enquirer mare who went back on the bottom side to a son of the great 19th Century stallion and sixteen-time leading sire Lexington. Domino was sent to New York, where Thomas' yearlings were consigned, and caught the eye of Foxhall Keene, who bought him for $3,000. The sale average was $895, which might suggest that Domino was among the standouts at the old Tattersalls layout on 55th Street and Seventh Avenue. Black whirlwinds are in the eye of the beholder, however, and Keene's father, James R. Keene, had not favored the colt. Domino came to race in the elder Keene's white silks, with blue polka dots, because the Keenes, *pere et fils*, merged their stables when the colt was two.

James Keene was an English-born American

who put flesh and blood to the concept of the glissando — racing up and down the scales of financial success like the most nimble-fingered harpist. He wanted to be, and became, a millionaire, lost one fortune to a plan to corner the Chicago grain market, then found sugar a sweeter commodity, and was on his way to a larger fortune.

On the Turf, Keene established Castleton Farm, today a Standardbred farm and still one of the handsomest of the Bluegrass, with its stately rock walls suggesting the equine royalty within its boundaries. In addressing Keene's good luck in the matter of which horses came under his ownership, the former editor of *The Blood-Horse*, the late Kent Hollingsworth, got off one of his best riffs: "It has been said that opportunity knocks but once, and then softly. Opportunity rattled Keene's door as a constant irritant, occasionally breaking through. Great horses were thrust upon him."[1]

Someone else's judgment brought him Domino, and such later Keene horses as Commando and Colin were produced or taken in reluctantly, as well. The Keenes bred 113 stakes winners in just under two decades. The dozen and a half distinguished horses James Keene either bred or raced over a longer period included Spendthrift, Kingston, Sysonby, Celt, Sweep, and Pennant.

Domino dashed unbeaten through a spectacular two-year-old season of nine races in 1893. His earnings of $170,790 stood as a juvenile record for nearly four decades, until Top Flight earned $219,000 in 1931. At three and four, Domino proved unequal to such horses as Henry of Navarre and Clifford at distances much beyond a mile, but he won ten of his sixteen starts in those years. With a career mark of nineteen wins in twenty-five starts, he had earnings of $193,550, which stood as a record until the advent of Man o' War.

That a horse of extreme speed and limited stamina enjoyed such star status — and was destined for such lasting influence — as early as the 1890s might be instructive to modern horsemen. Successive generations of American breeders have fallen into self-flagellation rites. While apparently unable to keep themselves from breeding for speed, they assume the guilt of overemphasizing it as a uniquely American fault, and a recent one at that. In fact, emphasis on speed and early maturing two-year-olds is more than a century old. Domino, for example, earned $48,885 for winning the Futurity at two in 1893; the Belmont Stakes that year was worth $5,310 to the winner, the Kentucky Derby $4,090, the Suburban Handicap $17,750.

Indeed, Domino's own breeder was quoted by Hollingsworth as articulating a difficult balance as applicable to our eras of Northern Dancer and Mr. Prospector as to his own: "Give me speed. Of course, a horse must have stamina and weight-carrying ability, but if he lacks speed, he is of no account absolutely. It will not do to breed for speed to the neglect of everything else…At the same time, speed is very, very necessary."

The importance of speed was apparent not only to Major Thomas as the 19th Century played out. An essay by the noted Turf historian John (Salvator) Hervey reviews the march of change from the time when four-mile heats had been in vogue, relatively few decades earlier. Hervey authored an essay which appeared in *The Thoroughbred Record* and also served as an appendix to *Gallant Fox: A Memoir*, a remarkable volume both written by and privately published by William Woodward Sr. on the career of his 1930 Triple Crown winner, Gallant Fox.

Hervey observed in his essay: "Structurally, the most important of all equine proportions, especially in the race horse, are those of relative height and length. As is well known, the old-time four-

		Alarm, 1869	Eclipse / Maud
	Himyar, 1875		
DOMINO, br, 1891		Hira, 1864	Lexington / Hegira
		Enquirer, 1867	Leamington / Linda
	Mannie Gray, 1874		
COMMANDO, b h, 1898		Lizzie G., 1867	War Dance / Mare by Lecompte
		The Peer, 1855	Melbourne / Cinizelli
	Darebin, 1878		
		Lurline, 1869	Traducer / Mermaid
EMMA C., br, 1892		Flood, 1877	Norfolk / Hennie Farrow
	Guenn, 1883		
		Glendew, 1876	Glengarry / Glenrose

1st dam: Emma C., b, 1892-1907. Bred by J.B. Haggin (Ky). Unraced. Dam of 3 named foals, 2 rnrs, 2 wnrs, 1 sw.
  1898: COMMANDO, b c, by Domino. Bred by J.R. Keene (Ky). Raced 2 yrs, 9 sts, 7 wins, $58,196. Won Belmont S, Great Trial S, Brighton Junior S, Carlton S, Montauk S, Zephyr S; 2nd Second Matron S. Sire of 37 foals, 10 sw.
  1899: Telescope, b c, by Horoscope. Unraced.
  1900: Barren.
  1901: Barren.
  1902: Barren.
  1903: Barren.
  1904: Foal died.
  1905: Barren.
  1906: Barren.
  1907: Lyndin, br c, by Disguise. Raced 3 yrs in Eng, 15 sts, 1 win, $584. Sent to Bel 1911.

mile race horse was almost invariably longer than he was high. This was even the case with animals that were themselves very tall for their period. They were, as the saying went, 'long and low,' with marked bodily length and comparatively short legs. Such was, indeed, the preferred conformation. But with the gradual retrocession of long-distance races, there evolved a different structure — one in average height far superior to the former type, short-bodied and long-legged. This conformation may be said to be now prevalent. Many horsemen, including those of experience and reputation, dislike long-bodied horses, while few if any are adverse to the shortest of bodies. There

has been, in the words of the German philosopher Nietzsche, 'a transvaluation of values.'…{also} 'Perfection' {now} calls for exactly the same height at both the withers and the croup."

Of Domino's early death, the veterinarian Edward Hagyard later recalled that overfeeding of grain and corn was common at the time and that spinal meningitis had resulted in that particular case. The noted Dr. Hagyard was unable to save Domino, and so the horse slid into legend, as well as history, as forty or so gathered for his burial.

Commando, best among Domino's scarce produce, was out of a big, coarse mare named Emma C., by Darebin, he an Australian import of James

14

Ben Ali Haggin's and a proven weight-carrier and stayer. The combination apparently boosted the Domino stamina quotient, without deleterious effect on the sire line's speed. Commando, a Keene homebred, was a large, heavy sort, but was ready for action by late spring of his two-year-old season, 1900. Future Hall of Fame trainer James Rowe Sr. sent him out six times at two, and he won five. Keene's dislike of the dam had prompted him to leave Commando out of the Futurity's early payments, but Commando did win the Great Trial Stakes, which at $20,000 was another of the biggest juvenile races of the day. At three, Commando debuted successfully in the Belmont Stakes, then run at one and three-eighths miles; won another race, then broke down in the Lawrence Realization. He had won seven of nine and earned $58,196.

Castleton Farm stallions were routinely galloped under saddle for the twelve-mile round trip to and from Lexington. The health-inducing intent of this practice was betrayed in the case of Commando, who picked up a rock in a hoof, leading to tetanus.

The Hagyard family of veterinarians, and the surviving Hagyard-Davidson-McGee firm of today, became well-known for their part in the huge advances of veterinary research. In caring for the Domino-line sires, though, Dr. Edward Hagyard found himself in an era of insufficient tools. Commando's was "the most violent" case of the malady Hagyard had seen, he lamented, and the horse was dead within forty-eight hours. Commando was seven years old.

Commando's twenty-seven foals included an amazing concentration of important sons: Colin and Peter Pan were not only great racehorses but became influential stallions; Celt led the sire list; and unraced Ultimus also became an influence at stud.

Let's take these horses in order. Colin was that rarest of dreams, an unbeaten racehorse. The 1905 foal from Pastorella, by Springfield, ran fifteen times and won them all. At two in 1907, Rowe sent him out twelve times in the Keene colors, and his tapestry of triumphs included the Futurity, Great Trial, and Grand Union Hotel Stakes. At three he added three more wins. After his debut in the Withers, fog shrouded his performance in the Belmont Stakes. The rumors that swirled about his condition were just as thick, some going so far as to say that he won the classic with two bowed tendons. Whatever degree of exaggeration was attendant to the event, Colin did stay unbeaten by defeating Fair Play by a head. A later victory sent him to stud with earnings of $181,610.

Given his sire's and grandsire's fates at stud, Colin provided the line with good news in that he lived to the age of twenty-seven. The bad news was that he had limited fertility, getting only eighty-one foals in twenty-three crops. Thus relatively few horses inherited any of the genes of Colin, and none inherited his brilliance. The stallion got eleven stakes winners (fourteen percent), and while On Watch (broodmare sire of Stymie) and Jock were of good class, there were no champions among them. The key link to the present started through another stakes winner by Colin, namely Neddie, sire of moderate stakes winner Good Goods. It was with Good Goods' son, Alsab, that brilliance burst back into the picture.

By 1940, the bloodline's lack of fashion was such that Kentucky horseman Tom Piatt got only $700 when he sold Alsab as a yearling. Named for and racing for Albert Sabbath (technically in his wife's name), Alsab raced through a career that still ranks him with Stymie, Carry Back, and John Henry among historic poor-boy-makes-good sagas. He was the champion two-year-old of 1941, champion three-year-old of 1942, beat Whirlaway twice in three meetings at three, won twenty-five of fifty-one races, and earned $350,015.

Bargain-basement colts with bargain-basement pedigrees are not the hottest sire prospects. Alsab was better than most, getting sixteen stakes winners (six percent) of which the best included juvenile filly champion Myrtle Charm and $191,700-earner Armageddon. Bred and raced by Captain Harry Guggenheim's burgeoning Cain Hoy Stable, Armageddon lost sight in one eye when hit by a sharp stone during the running of the 1951 Champagne Stakes, but came from behind to win the race, anyway. The son of a Sir Gallahad III mare, Fighting Lady, Armageddon added the Withers, Peter Pan, and two other stakes as a one-eyed three-year-old.

The descent from Colin had settled into the pattern of one moderately good son per generation. Armageddon sired only seven stakes winners (five percent), and the anointed among them was Battle Joined, a quick two-year-old who won the Saratoga Special in 1961 and yet stayed well enough to win the one and five-eighths-mile Lawrence Realization the next year. Battle Joined (out of Ethel Walker, by Revoked) got thirteen stakes winners (seven percent), none of lasting note save for Ack Ack, who similarly showed plenty of speed but trained on to get one and a quarter miles.

Ack Ack won the 1969 Derby Trial for Guggenheim, but the owner, while keen to win the classics, had the patience to keep him out of the Majestic Prince/Arts and Letters frays of the Kentucky Derby and Preakness. Ack Ack (out of Fast Turn, by Turn-to) added the Withers and Arlington Classic for trainer Frank Bonsal. Guggenheim dispersed most of his horses in 1969, but retained Ack Ack and sent him to California trainer Charlie Whittingham. At four, the horse

Commando

won a pair of West Coast stakes. After Ack Ack had won once at five, Guggenheim died, and the animal was sold to E. E. (Buddy) Fogelson and his wife, the actress Greer Garson.

Whittingham had perceived that Ack Ack's reputation for seven-furlong and mile speed did not truly define him, and he set about stretching him out. By year's end, he had won seven of eight starts, and Whittingham had proved correct when Ack Ack carried 134 pounds to victory in the one and a quarter-mile Hollywood Gold Cup. He became the first horse voted Horse of the Year on the basis of a California-only campaign and went down in history as the first to win that honor under the Eclipse Award structure inaugurated in 1971. Ack Ack won nineteen of twenty-seven races and earned $636,641.

By the time Battle Joined had become the sire of a Horse of the Year, he had been sent from Kentucky to Colorado, but Ack Ack's potential at stud was of another ilk. He settled in at Claiborne Farm, whose owners, the Hancock family, had been standing leading sires since Celt (a son of Commando) led the list in 1921. Ack Ack sired fifty-five stakes winners, and the old Colin sire line got out from under the one-horse per generation survival motif — but not by far. Ack Ack's son Youth was a wonderful racehorse, winning the French Derby (Prix du Jockey-Club) and then adding dashing triumphs in the Canadian and Washington, D.C., Internationals. Alas, Youth was a virtual failure at stud, but the "virtual" (as opposed to "total") was earned by Teenoso, who gave the line added glory by winning the historic Epsom Derby in 1983. (Ack Ack also became the broodmare sire of the 1997 Epsom Derby winner, Benny the Dip, underscoring again that Charlie Whittingham had it right when he figured there was something besides speed lurking there.)

The strength of the lengthy sire-line descent from Domino-Commando-Colin today lies with Broad Brush, a son of Ack Ack. Broad Brush proved a bit of a character, as when he raced to the outside fence in the stretch turn of the Pennsylvania Derby and still won the race. He also won eleven other stakes, including the Santa Anita Handicap, Suburban Handicap, and Wood Memorial, and was third in the Kentucky Derby and Preakness. Broad Brush (out of Hay Patcher, by Hoist the Flag), won fourteen of twenty-seven races and earned $2,656,793 for owner-breeder Robert Meyerhoff, before going to stud in Kentucky at Gainesway Farm. He wasted little time in assuring that he would get at least his requisite good son when Meyerhoff's homebred Concern won the Breeders' Cup Classic in 1994.

So, ten generations after Domino, the tale of "the black whirlwind" still lengthens in the telling.

Peter Pan, et al.

Returning to other sons of Commando, we find that Peter Pan, a foal of 1904, was a vehicle through which the bloodline was embraced by another of the dominant stables of the early 20th Century, that of Harry Payne Whitney. The breeder of 192 stakes winners purchased Peter Pan for $38,000 to top the dispersal of the Castleton stock after James R. Keene's death in 1913. (Colin brought $30,000, Celt $20,000.) Whichever way the auction had gone, Peter Pan was assured a good home, for the underbidder was Colonel E. R. Bradley. This was still about a decade before Bradley really had his guns aligned for his Idle Hour Stock Farm, however, while Whitney was several steps ahead of him. The sale took place three days after Peter Pan's son Pennant had won the Futurity, becoming the fifth Keene-bred in the last five years to win the premier two-year-old event.

As a runner in Keene's colors, the homebred Peter Pan (out of a Hermit mare who was one of several distinguished matrons named Cinderella) had won ten of seventeen races and earned $115,450 in 1906-7. At two, he took the Hopeful under 130 pounds and three other races, and at three his best scores were in the Belmont Stakes, Brooklyn Derby, and Standard Stakes. Peter Pan was certainly not as good a racehorse as Colin, but proved a better sire. The aforementioned Pennant was one of Peter Pan's forty-eight stakes winners (twenty percent), the others including champions Tryster and Prudery, plus Black Toney.

Pennant, like many of the Keene horses, represented an American sire line crossed with imported blood. His dam was the English mare Royal Rose, by Royal Hampton. Pennant was foaled in 1911 and, racing being temporarily curtailed by anti-gambling legislation in New York, Keene sold all his yearlings from that crop. Bradley thought he was buying them all on behalf of a fellow named W. A. Prime, but the Prime rate of paying was more or less nil, and Bradley was stuck with the lot. Well, that was not a bad way to be stuck, for out of the melee he emerged with Black Toney, another son of Peter Pan and founder of a wealthy vein of the resilient sire line.

Bradley resold some of the Keene yearlings, including Pennant, for whom Whitney paid $1,700. Pennant went on to win nine of twelve races and earn $25,315. With racing in New York having resumed in 1913, Pennant won two prep races and the Futurity (run that year at Saratoga), an all-conquering short season duplicated more than sixty years later by Seattle Slew. Pennant won his comeback race at three, but broke down in the process. Since Whitney had purchased the sire, Peter Pan, he was in no hurry to introduce even a Futurity winner by that stallion into his breeding operation. Pennant was given plenty of time and returned to action at five. He was given no prep, but thrown right into the Brooklyn Handicap. The bettors had faith in trainer James Rowe and made the horse the favorite. Pennant was beaten for the first time, but his second to Friar Rock, while finishing ahead of Roamer, was testimony to his class, as well as to Rowe's preparation. Pennant won five of his seven remaining starts at five and six, adding several high-class stakes victories.

Whitney had a concentration of Peter Pan and Broomstick fillies[2], so as a son of Peter Pan, Pennant had only a portion of the farm's best mares available to him. What to do with him was further complicated by his own racing record indicating that he was by nature a miler, while Broomstick was also seen as less an influence for stamina than speed. It was a frequent circumstance among the best breeding operations: An intent to breed for the classics, but with success so often wrought by horses with great speed that it took a concerted effort to leaven speed with staying influences.

Nonetheless, Pennant became a fine sire, with thirty-nine stakes winners (sixteen percent) including the Preakness winner Dauber, Futurity winner Bunting, Kentucky Oaks winner Mary Jane, steeplechase champion Jolly Roger, and Brooklyn winner The Chief, among others. It was for one son, Equipoise, however, that he would be most remembered and revered. Equipoise was out of Swinging, who was by Broomstick, but of an imported female family of presumed staying influence.

In Equipoise, the physical being combined with a charisma and place in history that made him one of the best-loved racers by those who knew him. The author became aware, for example, of how distinguished racing official Jimmy Kilroe treasured the memory of Equipoise, although knowing many great horses over many years. Abram S. Hewitt addressed this subject in *Sire Lines*: "Some colts arouse a degree of loyalty and enthusiasm among their supporters which defies understanding…The horse becomes a folk hero and survives triumph and disaster alike better than any statesman can achieve."

Equipoise's conformation and presence inspired Turf historian John (Salvator) Hervey to a written soliloquy about "a living harmony in horseflesh, an embodiment of rhythm and modulation, of point and counterpoint, that sung to the eye and made music to the heart." The public loved Equipoise too, but while such phrases might have come easily for Hervey, most fans contented themselves with a more readily memorized nickname, "The Chocolate Soldier." (His grandsire, Peter Pan, had been named for a Broadway play, and in Equipoise's day, Oscar Straus' operetta *The Chocolate Soldier* was enjoying one of its sequence of revivals on Broadway.)

Harry Payne Whitney died late in Equipoise's two-year-old campaign, so the young colt's victory in the Pimlico Futurity served as a gripping introduction to the sport for his son, Cornelius Vanderbilt Whitney. C. V. Whitney had so many other interests, including politics, air travel, and movies, that he did not immediately throw into the Turf the energies his father had, but he decided to continue the Whitney stable. With time, he became as dedicated to the sport as his forebears.

The Pimlico Futurity found Equipoise gaining revenge on rival Twenty Grand for a loss in another struggle, the Kentucky Jockey Club Stakes. The two races cemented the image of the 1930 juveniles as among the best crop ever, it also including Jamestown and Mate. Equipoise developed a quarter crack, which hampered him throughout the remainder of his racing days, but the ailment contributed to his reputation for gameness. He raced on through seven, his great moments including a world-record mile and handicap victories under high weights. Equipoise won twenty-nine of fifty-one starts and earned $338,610.

If the class shown in some of his ancestry was embodied in Equipoise, so, too, was the lamentable pattern of shortened lives there to haunt him. The Chocolate Soldier served but four seasons at the C. V. Whitney Farm in Kentucky before dying of an intestinal infection.

With so many of his relatives populating C. V. Whitney's broodmare band, much of his success came with mares owned by other breeders. In Greentree Stable's Shut Out, he sired a colt good enough to win the Kentucky Derby, Belmont, and Travers in 1942, the year Equipoise topped the sire list. Equipoise's nine stakes winners (twelve percent) also included the Jockey Club Gold Cup victor Bolingbroke, Coaching Club American Oaks winner and champion Level Best, plus Attention and Swing and Sway.

Shut Out sired the champion filly Evening Out, plus such redoubtable runners as One Hitter, Social Outcast, and Hall of Fame. The final two were geldings, and One Hitter was not a success at stud. The sire line flamed again in the early 1960s, when Carry Back (whose sire, Saggy, was by the Equipoise horse Swing and Sway) won the Derby, Preakness, and a plethora of other races, commanding his own public affection with his dashing stretch runs. Carry Back's stud career, however, flickered only dimly.

In addition to Pennant, Peter Pan (son of Commando) sired Black Toney. This was not a great boost to Peter Pan's standing as a sire of racehorses, but as a sire of sires it was of considerable importance.

Black Toney did not fit the pattern of Domino blood on an English mare. He was, in fact, out of Belgravia, whose sire, Ben Brush, represented another vaunted American sire line. Ben Brush, the leading sire of 1909, ranked along with Domino and Fair Play among the progenitors of "American" sire lines prominent in the early days of the century. Still, the influence of English blood in Black Toney's genetic portfolio needs be recognized in the fact that his second dam, Bonnie Gal, was by Galopin, sire of the great St. Simon.

Black Toney was another product of the James R. Keene stud. He, like Pennant, was a foal of 1911 (a year after the farm proper had been sold to David Look) and, as cited above, wound up in Bradley's possession after the Kentucky marksman had purchased the Keene yearling crop with an eye to re-sell. Black Toney was apparently bid in on Bradley's own account for $1,600, or $100 less than the price Whitney paid for Pennant. From time to time, a hundred dollars would hardly be enough to make Bradley blink, for here was a high roller of the truest stripe — a self-made entrepreneur who once bragged to Congress that he was a gambling man by profession and who operated the swank Palm Beach Club as well as turning out Kentucky Derby winners at Idle Hour Stock Farm in Lexington.

Black Toney had won a dozen races from thirty-seven starts when Bradley put him to stud, following the 1915 season. Black Toney was fifth behind Pennant in the Futurity at two and won the one and three-sixteenths-mile Independence Handicap at Latonia in Kentucky at three. Bradley recognized that, in those days, New York was the true testing ground of the American racehorse and decided to keep Black Toney at home as a four-year-old, perhaps giving some insight into the colt's status in the mind of his own stable.

After a season at stud, Black Toney returned to win one of three races. Thus, his final racing talley read forty starts, thirteen wins, and earnings of $13,565 — hardly an indication of his promise as a stallion. But more than seventy years later, Black Toney's likeness in a bronze decorative still graces the stallion barn where he spent his post-racing years. (The core of the old Idle Hour became Darby Dan Farm after Bradley's death.)

Colonel Bradley bought into the idea of American sire lines and stylish English broodmare families. (His greatest contribution perhaps was the importation of La Troienne, a mare of lasting importance.) In selecting fillies for the stud, he believed in speed, even if it was exhibited only in training. No gambler wins every hand, of course: Bradley also chose to do away with an early foal from La Troienne, and, when he headed the Fair Grounds track in New Orleans, he once backed a Marx Brothers-like scheme to fit racehorses with goggles for running over muddy tracks.

Bradley's faith in Black Toney, however, was more than well-served. The stallion got forty stakes winners (a distinguished eighteen percent). The best included these outstanding runners:

• **Bimelech**, unbeaten two-year-old champion of 1939, stunning loser in the Kentucky Derby, but thereafter winner of the Preakness and Belmont and an important stallion.

• **Black Servant**, Blue Grass Stakes winner and Kentucky Derby runner-up and sire of the mighty runner and sire Blue Larkspur (sire of Myrtlewood, Blue Delight, Bloodroot).

• **Black Gold**, romanticized winner of the Golden Anniversary Kentucky Derby of 1924.

• **Brokers Tip**, winner of the 1933 Kentucky Derby as a maiden and survivor of a famous stretch duel with Head Play when jockeys as well as horses battled each other.

• **Black Helen** and **Big Hurry**, among the sto-

Commando

ried brood from the aforementioned mare La Troienne.

• **Balladier**, leading two-year-old of 1934. Balladier sired the brilliant racehorse and major sire Double Jay.

Double Jay was an important stallion at Claiborne Farm in Paris, Kentucky, which was founded by Arthur B. Hancock Sr., enhanced by his son, A. B. (Bull) Jr., and has been kept in the forefront of 21st Century international breeding operations under the third-generation management of Seth Hancock. As is illustrated below, the Hancocks over various generations — equine and human — were among those who respected and best utilized the scions of Domino-Commando.

Celt

Returning to the origins of this section, we find that Commando was also the sire of Celt. A 1905 foal, Celt was from the mare Maid of Erin, by Amphion, and thus another example of the cross of Domino blood and English mares. Since Celt was foaled in the same Castleton Stud crop as Colin, he had little chance for stardom, but he made the most of his limited opportunities. In his first start, he was beaten handily by his more famed stablemate, but then won the Junior Champion Stakes. At three, Celt gave Colin a wide berth. He won his first start, then prolonged the agony of Fair Play, who had been long suffering under Colin's rule. Celt defeated both Fair Play and King James in the ten-furlong Brooklyn Handicap, and took to stud a short racing record of three wins in four starts with earnings of $28,965.

Early in the next decade, at the eve of the brief demise of New York racing, Arthur B. Hancock Sr. leased Celt to stand at his Ellerslie Stud in Virginia. After two seasons, Hancock wanted to extend the lease, but Keene took the horse back to stand again at Castleton following the 1912 season. Keene died the next year, and Hancock went back to the same well, paying $20,000 to purchase Celt.

Although out of an English mare, Celt did not have much in the way of stout influences from the distaff quarter. Despite his own important win at one and a quarter miles, his reputation as a stallion was more for good two-year-olds than for classic runners. He died in 1919, two years before leading the general sire list. Celt sired thirty stakes winners (fifteen percent), including Futurity Stakes winner Dunboyne. Of more lasting fame, however, was a daughter, Marguerite, who made only one start but who became the dam of 1930 Triple Crown winner Gallant Fox, as well as other important winners Fighting Fox, Petee-Wrack, and Foxbrough.

Ultimus

The corny lyric to the country song "I'm My Own Grandpa" has never been consummated in Thoroughbred breeding, at least to the knowledge of the author. Absent such a phenomenon, another of Commando's sons can claim to have been party to one of the most extreme examples of inbreeding of the 20th Century. The Commando stallion Ultimus was the sire of High Time, about which author Hewitt surmised, "was probably as intensely inbred as any Thoroughbred since the early 19th Century, when it was fashionable to breed the great sire Sir Archy to his own daughters." Ultimus himself was closely inbred to Domino: His sire, Commando, of course, was by Domino, and Ultimus' dam, Running Stream, was also by Domino. In 1915, Ultimus was bred to Noonday, whose sire was, yes, none other than Domino! Thus, Domino was three of the seven

sires in the first three generations of High Time's pedigree — not exactly "my own grandpa," but "my mama's daddy was both my daddy's granddaddies!"

Ultimus was "a promising, even sensational yearling,"[3] but never raced. High Time was very fast, but was a bleeder and could not carry his speed as far as most races, even sprints, require. He won a single race from seven starts. If one were to set out the supposed criteria for a promising sire-son coupling, having one win among the two would hardly bode well for success. Yet High Time got the superb champion Sarazen, led the general sire list in 1928, and three times sent out more two-year-old winners than any other stallion. High Time sired thirty-seven stakes winners (thirteen percent).

A case could be made that Ultimus deserves to rank with Alibhai among the best unraced horses in North America in the 20th Century, at least if measured by stud success. He sired twenty-six stakes winners for a healthy twenty-one percent, and he was also something of a sire of sires. In addition to High Time, Ultimus sired the successful stallions Supremus, Stimulus, and Infinite. In 1933, that trio and High Time all ranked among the top ten on the sire list.

The twenty stakes winners (six percent) by Supremus included Hal Price Headley's champion filly and Blue Hen matron Alcibiades; the thirty-nine stakes winners (nine percent) by Stimulus included the 1940s champion filly Beaugay as well as Miss Dolphin (dam of Olympia) and the important broodmare Risque. Another sire by Ultimus was Luke McLuke, whose fifteen stakes winners (twelve percent) included champions Anita Peabody and Nellie Morse. Some double dipping of Domino clearly had its merits. ❖

Star Shoot

Star Shoot was the first stallion to lead the North American sire list as many as five years during the 20th Century. He established this elite status between 1911 and 1919, and when the century ended, the only additional members were Bull Lea, Nasrullah, and Bold Ruler.

Star Shoot emanated from one distinguished breeding operation and later graced two others across the Atlantic, all three bespeaking family traditions still carried on today. He was a product of the Eyrefield Lodge of Ireland, where the Loder family had set into motion more than a century of participation in the Turf — extending to the present time, when the family's involvement includes David Loder's training for a division of the Maktoum family's two-year-olds in France.

Star Shoot's dam was the Hermit mare Astrology, and it could well be interpreted that a bit of help was sent by whatever stars are assigned to oversee matters of the Thoroughbred world. His breeder, Major Eustace Loder, stopped by to check on the sick youngster en route to a day in the hunting field in the spring of 1898, and he left despairing of seeing the little fellow alive again. The foal by 1893 English Triple Crown winner Isinglass, however, came under the coddling wisdom and determination of the stud groom, "Eyrefield Dan"

McNally. That fine fellow took the colt into a tack room, wrapped him fore and aft in so many blankets that he could hardly move, and placed him before a roaring fireplace. While McNally, as was his wont, entertained other Eyrefield staff with his store of stories, the Isinglass—Astrology foal struggled through his fever.

Star Shoot survived to join the Loder string and became his master's first good horse on the flat, winning three nice stakes from eight races at two in 1900. (Ahead for Major Loder lay the breeding and racing of the great, three-time classic winner Pretty Polly, as well as winning the Epsom Derby of 1906 with the astute, 300-guinea purchase Spearmint.)

Star Shoot developed a wind problem and made only a pair of starts at three, and, thus, had a career mark of ten starts, three wins, and the equivalent of about $24,000 in earnings. The English and Irish of the day tended to assume that any wind condition could infect future generations if the animal were used for breeding. So, they sought to do the square thing by the Thoroughbred breed when they encountered such a situation, i.e., they sold the poor beast abroad.

In the case of Star Shoot, there was another reason to suspect England could be a sunnier place if the animal were dispatched to some distant shore. Conventional wisdom among those who followed the Bruce Lowe Family system was that many generations of results indicated that Family No. 9 was not likely to produce any important stallions. (The system assigned numbers to families based on the number of English classic winners descended from foundation females.) Star Shoot represented this family.

He was imported into the United States by John Hanning, who sold him to the partnership of Catesby Woodford and Ezekiel Clay. Woodford and Clay owned Runnymede Farm in Kentucky and for a time owned Miss Woodford, the first American Thoroughbred to earn $100,000. They also bred and sold the great Hanover, four-time leading American sire in the 1890s. Inasmuch as, in the year 2000, Runnymede is operated by descendant Catesby Clay, the ongoing story of the family as Thoroughbred breeders has now graced three centuries.

Star Shoot stood at Runnymede for a decade, then was sold to yet another lasting Thoroughbred family dynasty. The buyer, in 1912, was John E. Madden, a remarkably versatile horseman who excelled as breeder, trainer, owner, wheeler-dealer, and farmer. Madden bred five Kentucky Derby winners at his Hamburg Place outside Lexington, and the current master of Hamburg, grandson Preston Madden, added a sixth when he bred and sold 1987 Derby winner Alysheba.

According to Joe Palmer[1], "There is little chance of exaggerating Star Shoot's success as a stallion. His first foals came to the races in 1905. In 1908, he was among the 20 leading sires, and he stayed there through 1923. The five years in which Star Shoot led the list were 1911, 1912, 1916, 1917, and 1919. He also was seven times the leader in number of 2-year-old winners and in 1916 set a remarkable record for the era when 27 juveniles from one crop were winners."

Star Shoot shared the burden of Bruce Lowe Family No. 9 with a contemporary American stallion — Fair Play, sire of Man o' War. (With a decent "sire" family behind them, these two might really have achieved something.) In 1920, the best sons of Star Shoot and Fair Play squared off in a match at Windsor, Ontario. Star Shoot was represented by Sir Barton; Fair Play, by Man o' War. The latter, of course, won handily and handsomely, but Sir Barton was also a truly distinguished runner, having become the first to win what later was revered as the American Triple Crown — the (1919) Kentucky Derby, Preakness, and Belmont Stakes.

The blithe assertion that Sir Barton was Star Shoot's best son perhaps needs tempering, for no less an expert than John E. Madden himself declared that another Star Shoot colt, Grey Lag, was the best among the 182 stakes winners he bred. Since Madden had been co-breeder of Sir Barton with Vivian Gooch, one must conclude that Madden counted Grey Lag as the better of the pair. Grey Lag was regarded as the best horse in America at three, four, and five (1921-23).

As sires, neither Sir Barton nor Grey Lag was distinguished. Sir Barton got the Kentucky Oaks winner Easter Stockings, but little else, and wound up at a U.S. Army Remount Station in Wyoming, and Grey Lag was a shy breeder. In all, Star Shoot sired sixty-one stakes winners (thirteen percent), and the best of the others included Audacious, Uncle, Nimbus, and Fairy Wand. Uncle was the most important sire among Star Shoot's get, for he sired the Kentucky Derby winner Old Rosebud as well as the notable producer and lasting influence Uncle's Lassie (dam of Derby winner Clyde Van Dusen and matron Betty Derr).

While the sons as a whole did not breed on especially well, Star Shoot's daughters sent him to

		Sterling, 1868	Oxford Whisper
	Isonomy, 1875		
		Isola Bella, 1868	Stockwell Isoline
ISINGLASS, b, 1890			
		Wenlock, 1869	Lord Clifden Mineral
	Dead Lock, 1878		
		Malpractice, 1864	Chevalier d'Industrie The Dutchman's Daughter
STAR SHOOT (GB), **ch h,** **1898**			
		Newminster, 1848	Touchstone Beeswing
	Hermit, 1864		
		Seclusion, 1857	Tadmor Miss Sellon
ASTROLOGY, ch, 1887			
		Brother to Stafford, 1860	Young Melbourne Mare by Gameboy
	Stella, 1879		
		Mare by, 1861	Toxophilite Maid of Masham

1st dam: Astrology, ch, 1887-1910. Bred by Mr. H. Chaplin (Eng). Raced 1 yr in Eng, 5 sts, 0 wins, $122. 3rd Molyneux S. Dam of 13 named foals, 11 rnrs, 7 wnrs, 2 sw.

1891: Foal died.

1892: TELESCOPE, b c, by Horoscope. Raced 5 yrs in Eng, 26 sts, 7 wins, $18,371. Won Manchester November H, Northamptonshire S, Prince of Wales' Nursery Plate; 2nd St. Leger S, Great Yorkshire H, Liverpool Spring Cup; 3rd Astley S, Lewes H.

1893: Barren.

1894: Star Chamber, b f, by Tyrant. Raced 5 yrs in Eng and Ire, 30 sts, 4 wins, $2,273.

1895: Star and Garter II, b c, by Suspender. Raced 3 yrs in Eng and Ire, 19 sts, 4 wins, $1,548.

1896: Ch c, by St. Angelo.

1897: St. Celestra, b f, by St. Angelo. Raced 3 yrs in Eng, 8 sts, 2 wins, $973.

1898: STAR SHOOT, ch c, by Isinglass. Bred by Capt. E. Loder (Eng). Raced 2 yrs in Eng and Ire, 10 sts, 3 wins, $34,314. Won National Breeders' Produce S, Hurst Park Foal Plate, British Dominion Two-Year-Old Race; 2nd Summer Breeders' Foal Plate; 3rd Middlepark Plate, New S, Champagne S. Sent to USA 1901. Sire.

1899: Startling, b f, by Laveno. Raced 2 yrs in Eng and Ire, 20 sts, 2 wins, $1,134. 3rd Irish Oaks. Dam of 16 foals, 10 rnrs, 7 wnrs, including **Starfinch** (in Eng).

1900: Barren.

1901: Foal died.

1902: L'Etoile, ch f, by Isinglass. Raced 1 yr in Eng, 1 st, 0 wins, $0. Dam of 7 foals, 5 rnrs, 5 wnrs, including **ECOUEN** (in Fr), **ESTREES** (in Fr), **Prince Eugene** (in Fr).

1903: Zadkiel, ch c, by Gallinule. Raced 2 yrs in Eng and Ire, 8 sts, 1 win, $156.

1904: Astrophel, b c, by Florizel II. Raced 1 yr in Ire, 2 sts, 0 wins, $0.

1905: Auspicious, ch f, by Gallinule. Unraced. Dam of 3 foals, 2 rnrs, 2 wnrs, including **WASHING DAY** (in Eng), **AUGUR** (in Eng).

1906: Astrologer, b g, by Laveno. Raced 2 yrs in Eng and Ire, 11 sts, 0 wins, $24.

1907: Camstra, b f, by Laveno. Unraced.

1908: Barren.

1909: Astor, ch g, by Admirable Crichton. Raced 1 yr in Eng, 5 sts, 0 wins, $0.

1910: Barren.

the top of the broodmare sire list and produced such good horses as Mars, Clock Tower, and the champion Man o' War colt Crusader.

In 1919, or twenty-one years after he had dodged death before a fireplace in Ireland, Star Shoot succumbed to pneumonia and was buried in the graveyard at Hamburg Place in Kentucky.

Broomstick and Sweep

Another sire line whose legacy crossed the century line was that of Ben Brush. A foal of 1893, Ben Brush was America's leading sire of 1909, and his sons Broomstick and Sweep led the list a combined total of five times in the first quarter of the 20th Century.

Ben Brush also was bred by Woodford and Clay and sported a distinguished Kentucky ancestry. His sire, Bramble, had been the best older horse in America in 1879 and was himself a son of Bonnie Scotland, the leading sire of 1880 and 1882. Ben Brush's dam, Roseville, by Reform, was a full sister to an early Kentucky Derby winner, Azra (1892). Ben Brush was sold at the Runnymede yearling sale for $1,200 to the partnership of Eugene Leigh and Ed Brown. This was a duo destined to lasting fame. Leigh was a farm and racehorse owner who lived on a financial edge, eventually falling off, but dusted himself off and enjoyed later success in the States and abroad as the trainer of the French horse Epinard. Brown, noted as one of the wealthiest black men in racing, was known as Brown Dick and became a Hall of Fame trainer.

Ben Brush, whom Brown named for the superintendent of the Gravesend track in Brooklyn (neat way to get stalls), won the first five races of his two-year-old season. The Brooklyn butcher shop owners who gained fame on the racetrack as the Dwyer Brothers had owned and raced Bramble as their first champion. They were impressed enough to buy the son, Ben Brush, who went on to win thirteen of sixteen races that year. The Dwyer Brothers possessed the same surname and some common genes, one presumes, but they were no more of a piece in other ways than Rolls and Royce. After Ben Brush's two-year-old season, the high-rolling Mike split with the penurious Phil, and the colt raced thereafter in Mike Dwyer's white silks with gold trim. Thusly accoutered, Ben Brush at three and four won the Kentucky Derby

and Suburban Handicap and was retired with a career record of twenty-five wins in forty starts and earnings of $65,522.

He was sold to James R. Keene, whose Castleton Stud would produce so many significant animals that the purchase of a leading sire — from a distant perspective — seems a conspicuous excess. After Keene's death in 1913, Ben Brush was sold to Senator Johnson Camden and lived until the age of twenty-five, when he was chloroformed to preclude undue suffering.

Ben Brush's greatest son at stud was Broomstick, who not only led the sire list in 1913, 1914, and 1915, but ranked in the top ten for seventeen consecutive years. Broomstick was yet another horse connected to the ubiquitous Keene. While a considerable portion of Keene's Thoroughbred career involved an inability to bring misguided instincts to fruition, Broomstick was one that got away — even from the lucky master. The Galliard mare Elf was chosen for culling by Keene, against the wishes of Keene's farm manager, Foxhall Daingerfield. Veterinarians — lacking at the time such tools as palpation or ultrasound — disputed Daingerfield's sense that she was in foal, and the mare was sent to auction in New York. Colonel Milton Young, a prominent commercial breeder, bought Elf for $250 and sent her back to his McGrathiana Stud in Kentucky. The 1901 Ben Brush foal she produced to prove Daingerfield right was thus foaled about two miles from whence the mare came, i.e., Castleton. The following year, the Ben Brush—Elf colt, to be named Broomstick, was sold in a draft of Young yearlings to Captain Samuel Brown, a Pittsburgh coal millionaire who also was a member of The Jockey Club, majority stockholder in Churchill Downs, and soon to be owner of the Kentucky Association track in Lexington.

		Bonnie Scotland, 1853	Iago Queen Mary
	Bramble, 1875		
		Ivy Leaf, 1864	Australian Bay Flower
BEN BRUSH, b, 1893			
		Reform, 1870	Leamington Stolen Kisses
	Roseville, 1888		
		Albia, 1881	**Alarm** Elastic
SWEEP, br h, 1907			
		Himyar, 1875	**Alarm** Hira
	Domino, 1891		
		Mannie Gray, 1874	Enquirer Lizzie G.
PINK DOMINO, b/br, 1897			
		Beaudesert, 1877	Sterling Sea Gull
	Belle Rose, 1889		
		Monte Rosa, 1882	Craig Miller Hedge Rose

1st dam: Pink Domino, dk b/br, 1897-1914. Bred by J.R. and F.P. Keene (Ky). Unraced. Dam of 9 named foals, 8 rnrs, 6 wnrs, 2 sw.

1902: Intrigue, br f, by Kingston. Raced 3 yrs, 32 sts, 0 wins, $0. Dam of 14 foals, 8 runners, 7 wnrs, including **SCHEMER**, **MURPHY**, **Intrigante**.

1903: Curiosity, ch f, by Voter. Raced 1 yr, 3 sts, 0 wins, $0. Dam of 4 foals, 2 rnrs, 2 wnrs, including **NOVELTY**.

1904: PHILANDER, b g, by Ben Brush. Raced 3 yrs, 36 sts, 4 wins, $8,605. Won Election Day H; 2nd Westminster H, Kings County H, Montague S; 3rd Edgemere S.

1905: Barren.

1906: Selectman, b c, by Voter. Raced 1 yr, 13 sts, 3 wins, $5,715. 2nd Champagne S, Nursery H, National Stallion S; 3rd United States Hotel S.

1907: SWEEP, br c, by Ben Brush. Bred by J.R. Keene (Ky). Raced 2 yrs, 13 sts, 9 wins, $63,948. Won Belmont S, Lawrence Realization, Futurity S, National Stallion Race, Carlton S; 2nd Hopeful S, Saratoga Special; 3rd Brooklyn Derby, Great Trial S. Sire of 395 foals, 46 sw, 1.33 AEI.

1908: Sweepaway, br f, by Wild Mint. Raced 2 yrs, 12 sts, 3 wins, $1,805. 3rd Spinaway S. Dam of 3 foals, 1 rnr, 1 wnr. Granddam of **PLAYDALE**.

1909: Barren.

1910: Cabaret, br g, by Delhi. Raced 2 yrs in Eng, 16 sts, 2 wins, $2,647. 2nd Exeter S, Park Nursery H; 3rd White Rose S.

1911: Barren.

1912: Pierette, b f, by Ben Brush. Unraced.

1913: Barren.

1914: Swan Song, br f, by Ben Brush. Raced 1 yr, 7 sts, 2 wins, $1,318. Dam of 4 foals, 3 rnrs, 3 wnrs.

Broomstick was a smallish colt, but he came out battling, winning three stakes, including the important Great American, in his first three outings. He did not win again in six later starts at two, and, while he won eleven of thirty races at three and four, he only on rare occasions could hop up and beat any of the best of his contemporaries. (That was exceptional company, including Keene's great Sysonby as well as Beldame, Ort Wells, and Irish Lad.) Broomstick won a total of fourteen of thirty-nine races and earned $74,730.

Modern-day horsemen — used to seeing Lyphard, Mr. Prospector, Danzig, Deputy Minister, and Storm Cat atop sire lists — will not find it difficult to understand that the very best proven racehorses of one period do not necessarily become the best stallions of the next. Nevertheless, the success of Broomstick defies easy placement into a pattern. In a sport in which the average of the breed long has been set at about three percent stakes winners and where a stallion that gets ten percent is counted as exceptional, Broomstick proceeded to sire a gaudy twenty-five percent stakes winners from foals — sixty-nine of 280.

Broomstick was retired to Brown's Senorita Stud in Kentucky by the end of 1905, but Brown died the following year. As would be true four decades later in the case of Colonel E. R. Bradley, the surviving brother, burdened with estate duties, found it prudent to dispose of this Thoroughbred business, so a sale was set for late 1908. It happened that one of the top breeders of the day, Harry Payne Whitney, had purchased a colt from Broomstick's first crop. By the time Brown's horses were on the block in Lexington in 1908, trainer A. J. Joyner was sufficiently impressed with the youngster that he implored Whitney to go for the young stallion and any of his get available. One might have his/her own opinions about the propriety of trying colts sufficiently in the fall of their yearling year to develop much of an assessment, but it was a propitious development for the stud career of Broomstick.

The colt demonstrably below the best of his time as a runner was snapped up by Whitney for $7,250, topping the sale of Brown's horses. Standing at Whitney's farms, in New Jersey and later in Lexington, Broomstick sent out a procession of distinguished runners. They included Whisk Broom II and Regret. Whisk Broom II in 1913 won the three races long renowned as the New York Handicap Triple, i.e., the Metropolitan, Suburban, and Brooklyn, a sweep repeated in the next eighty-seven years only by Tom Fool, Kelso, and Fit to Fight. From 1915 until 1980, Regret was distinguished as the only filly to win the Kentucky Derby and was a proven champion whose participation in that race did much to

move it from regional into national importance. Others sired by Broomstick included another Kentucky Derby winner, Meridian; English Two Thousand Guineas winner Sweeper; Cudgel, Wildair, Bostonian, Dr. Clark, and Tippity Witchet.

Broomstick sired his last stakes winner, Slapstick, when he was twenty-eight, and went on to live to thirty years of age.

Six years after Broomstick was foaled to the credit of another breeder, James R. Keene became the breeder of another future leading sire, Sweep, also by Ben Brush. Sweep was from the Domino mare Pink Domino and thus represented a popular Castleton cross. It worked the other way, too, Domino blood on Ben Brush mares. (The thought has often occurred, and does again, that there is no other nick quite so good — nor less mysterious — as Quality on Class, and vice versa.)

Sweep won the most important two-year-old race of his time, the Futurity, and came back the next spring to win the classic Belmont Stakes. He also added the Lawrence Realization and might generally be presumed to have been the best three-year-old of 1910. In two seasons, he won nine of thirteen races and earned $63,948.

The 1913 Madison Square Garden sale following Keene's death sent various significant animals out to continue making history. Sweep went for $17,500. He was purchased by a triumvirate of Kentucky breeders, namely, Kinzea Stone, John Barbee, and J. C. Carrick. He was sent to Barbee's Glen-Helen Stud, which in that same decade enjoyed an oblique distinction as the home of the broodmare band of Samuel D. Riddle — before he bought Man o' War and set up his own domain at Faraway Farm.

Before his death at Glen-Helen in 1931 at the age of twenty-four, Sweep sired a total of twenty crops. He got forty-eight stakes winners, or twelve percent

— a sterling mark if one does him the courtesy of not judging it against that of Broomstick. Sweep led the sire list in 1918 and again in 1925. He went Broomstick one better, for Sweep became part of a three-generation dynasty of leading sires: He, son of leading sire Ben Brush, led the sire list and then sired The Porter, himself the leading sire of 1937.

The Porter, bred by David Stevenson and foaled in 1915, was renowned for his courage, despite his diminutive size. He won twenty-six of fifty-four races and earned $73,866, campaigning for most of his five seasons for E. B. McLean. He stood at McLean's farm in Leesburg, Virginia, until purchased at auction for $27,000 in 1931 by John Hay Whitney, who moved him to Kentucky. The Porter's thirty-three stakes winners (eleven percent) included Santa Anita Handicap winner Rosemont, Santa Anita Derby winner Porter's

Star Shoot

Cap, Futurity and Champagne winner Porter's Mite, Suburban Handicap winner Aneroid, and Saratoga Handicap winner Haltal. Among individuals who kept this line going into the second half of the century, Rosemont (sire of thirteen stakes winners) became the sire of 1950s distaff champion Bed o' Roses, plus Thinking Cap, Rich Tradition, and so on, and Haltal (sire of ten stakes winners) got the good filly Marta.

As a broodmare sire, Sweep twice led the list, in 1937 and in 1941, which coincided with the two years of distinction only he has achieved — maternal grandsire of two Triple Crown winners, War Admiral and Whirlaway, respectively. Sweep's place in the pedigree of War Admiral was especially significant in assuring that remnants of the old Ben Brush legacy would filter through to modern times. ❖

Fair Play

Fair Play's place in American racing lore would have been secure with the siring of Man o' War alone, for that was a horse for the ages. Man o' War thrilled American sports fans in the first quarter of the 20th Century, and at the conclusion of that 100-year span of history was still voted the best horse it had produced, on various ballots of racing folk.

Fair Play did a great deal more than sire Man o' War, however. He was the first stallion in North America to sire six runners that earned as much as $100,000 each, reminding that well into the middle of the century, a six-figure Thoroughbred earner was still a mark of high achievement. Fair Play led the sire list three times in the 1920s.

At the conclusion of his racing career, Fair Play had prompted his distinguished breeder-owner, August Belmont II, to proclaim that the stylish chestnut colt was the best he had ever bred. Belmont predicted he would outstrip the other good stallions he had stood, among them Rock Sand and Hastings. Fair Play fit a common pattern among great stallions in having been a good race-horse without having been hailed as a truly great one. Indeed, he was born into such a rich American foal crop that he was not necessarily even the second best of his generation, for he arrived in 1905, the same year Colin and Celt were foaled into the

Castleton Stud operation of James R. Keene.

Fair Play was a son of Hastings, a horse of irascible spirit who nonetheless excelled as a racer and was himself the leading sire of 1902 and 1908. Hastings was by 1879 Belmont Stakes winner Spendthrift and out of the Tomahawk (or Blue Ruin) mare Cinderella, she also the dam of Kentucky Derby winner Plaudit.

The late Abe Hewitt, a scholarly horseman who wrote the book *Sire Lines* for *The Blood-Horse* in the 1970s, attributed to Cinderella the "overdose" of a "fiendish temper" for which Hastings became known. Literary allusion would have been better served, perhaps, had she been named Wicked Stepsister, rather than Cinderella.

In a nicer touch for history, Hastings met up with a young lad named Louis Feustel when the horse was in training at the Nursery Stud on Long Island. Nursery Stud had been established by August Belmont I, who had launched the family's connection to the best in racing, both from a sportsman's and an administrator's level. Feustel was destined to be the trainer of Hasting's immortal grandson, Man o' War, but when he encountered Hastings for the first time, he saw more of the "fiendish" than the friendly. At about ten or eleven, Feustel, a neighborhood kid, went to work at Nursery. Some time later, when it was deemed

		Australian, 1858	West Australian Emilia
	Spendthrift, 1876		
HASTINGS, br, 1893		Aerolite, 1861	Lexington Florine
		Tomahawk, 1863	King Tom Mincemeat
	Cinderella, 1885		
FAIR PLAY, ch h, 1905		Manna, 1874	Brown Bread Tartlet
		Doncaster, 1870	Stockwell Marigold
	Bend Or, 1877		
FAIRY GOLD, ch, 1896		Rouge Rose, 1865	Thormanby Ellen Horne
		Galliard, 1880	Galopin Mavis
	Dame Masham, 1889		
		Pauline, 1883	Hermit Lady Masham

1st dam: Fairy Gold, ch, 1896-1919. Bred by R. Swanwick (Eng). Unraced. Dam of 11 named foals, 6 rnrs, 6 wnrs, 4 sw. Sent to USA 1903.

1901: St. Lucre, b f, by St. Serf. Unraced. Granddam of **ABJER, CORRIDA, GOYA II, DARK LEGEND, KENTUCKY CARDINAL, Zacaweista**.

1902: Gold Measure, ch c, by Florizel II. Unraced. Sire.

1903: Barren.

1904: Foal died.

1905: **FAIR PLAY**, ch c, by Hastings. Bred by August Belmont (Ky). Raced 2 yrs, 26 sts, 10 wins, $86,950. Won Lawrence Realization, Jerome H, Flash S, Montauk S, Municipal H, First Special H, Coney Island Jockey Club S, Brooklyn Derby; 2nd Belmont S, Withers S, Brooklyn H, Hopeful S, September S, Oriental H, Matron S, Produce S, Belmont Park Autumn Race; 3rd Suburban H, Nursery S, United States Hotel S. Sire of 262 foals, 47 sw, 2.82 AEI.

1906: Golden View, ch f, by Hastings. Raced 1 yr, 6 sts, 1 win, $670. Dam of 7 foals, 4 rnrs, 4 wnrs.

1908: Fargone, ch f, by Octagon. Unraced.

1909: Golden Rock, b c, by Rock Sand. Unraced.

1910: **Farrier**, b c, by Hastings. Raced 1 yr, 10 sts, 2 wins, $1,140. 2nd Spring Brewery S.

1911: **FLITTERGOLD**, b c, by Hastings. Raced 7 yrs, 150 sts, 29 wins, $24,492. Won Old Bay H, Royal Blue H, Chesterbrook H; 2nd Havre de Grace H, Belvidere H, Philadelphia H, Fox Hill H, Autumn Highweight H, Harford H, Laurel H; 3rd Long Beach H, Woodbury H, Glenmore H, Havre de Grace H, Fox Hill H, Old Bay H, Pimlico Fall Serial H, Chesterbrook H. Sire.

1912: Barren.

1913: **FRIAR ROCK**, ch c, by Rock Sand. Raced 2 yrs, 21 sts, 9 wins, $20,365. Won Belmont S, Brooklyn H, Suburban H, Saratoga Cup, Adirondack H, Whirl S; 3rd Saratoga H, Withers S, Saratoga Special. Sire.

1914: Barren.

1915: Barren.

1916: Barren.

1917: **FAIR GAIN**, ch c, by Vulcain. Raced 2 yrs, 54 sts, 8 wins, $20,225. Won International H; 2nd Queen's Hotel Cup H; 3rd Hamilton Cup H. Sire.

1918: Treasure Fair, ch f, by Ferole. Unraced.

---

proper to increase his duties, he was learning the ropes of galloping horses and getting along all right until he was put to exercising Hastings, who ran off with him for a couple of miles.

August Belmont II is one of those breeders of yore who are examples of what is usually called "breeding for the classics." In this country, the traditional definition of "the classics" is restricted to the Kentucky Derby, Preakness Stakes, and Belmont Stakes, all spring three-year-old races and today ranging from one and three-sixteenths miles to one and a half miles. In connection to the highest ambitions of breeders, however, an approach like Belmont's could probably also be interpolated today to embrace such races as the Travers, Jockey Club Gold Cup, Breeders' Cup Classic, and a top few of the handicaps on dirt, although they are not "classics" per se.

Proponents of this approach are sometimes, fairly or unfairly, presumed to have insufficient appreciation for speed in their horses. Belmont's approach did not make this mistake. He may have put stamina first, but he realized that a truly successful horse was one that had sufficient speed as well. Author-horseman Hewitt tells that around 1920, when William Woodward Sr. was seeking to lay a foundation for what would become the great Belair Stud breeding operation (Gallant Fox, Omaha, Vagrancy, Nashua, among others), Belmont counseled him: "Billy, breed stoutness! When you get one that has some speed, you have a very good horse!" (One might quibble that the progeny of late 20th Century stallions such as Northern Dancer, Danzig, and Mr. Prospector support the argument that a higher-percentage philosophy would be: "Breed speed. When you get one that can also stay, you have a very good horse!")

In the case of Hastings, Belmont was apparently willing to gamble that the speed he saw early on was, in fact, accompanied by the potential for stoutness, to be proved later, and he was correct to some degree. Hastings was bred by Dr. J. D. Neet, and Belmont paid $37,000 for the horse as a two-year-old in 1895. At three, Hastings was a rival of Ben Brush, as well as of Handspring, and he scored in a top sprint, the Toboggan, and a classic, the one and three-eighths-mile Belmont Stakes. At four, however, his speed was seen as his hallmark, more than stamina, and in his successful stud career he was regarded more a source of speed than staying power.

In 1904, Hastings' book included Fairy Gold, who had won the Woodcote Stakes, an important spring race for two-year-old fillies in England. Fairy Gold was by the great stallion Bend Or, sire of the unbeaten English Triple Crown winner Ormonde and thus also a distant name in the ancestry of the Teddy line. The Hastings—Fairy Gold colt, foaled in 1905, was Fair Play. Fairy Gold's five stakes winners also included the top-class Friar Rock.

Fair Play was a sharp two-year-old, but neither he nor anyone else had an answer for Colin. The Belmont stable was not shy about seeking that answer, for three of Fair Play's seven losses at two were to the unbeaten James R. Keene superstar. Fair Play won three races, including the Montauk Stakes and Saratoga's Flash Stakes. At three, the tilting at windmills continued, and finally came close to a success. Colin beat Fair Play by two lengths in the Withers, but in the Belmont Stakes, Fair Play got to within a neck of ending the other colt's unbeaten status. Colin is widely believed to have been beset by some degree of unsoundness at that time, but the closeness of the finish was thought by many to be attributable to Colin's rider, Joe Notter, becoming overconfident, or confused in the foggy day. Colin made but one more start, retiring unbeaten in fifteen races.

Any thought that the way was now clear for Fair Play to dominate was pulled up short by the result of the Brooklyn Handicap. Celt, like Fair Play, had been overshadowed by stablemate Colin, something along the lines of Calumet's Citation and Coaltown of a later day. Celt took advantage of his opportunity to become first string and defeated Fair Play while giving him seven pounds in the Brooklyn.

Mercifully, from Fair Play's vantage point, Celt, too, was then retired. Fair Play still had quality competition, but he won seven of his remaining eleven

Fair Play

races at three, including the Brooklyn Derby, Lawrence Realization, and Jerome. The Keene stable was not the sort of outfit to slink into the shadows just because a couple of brilliant homebreds had left the races. Keene still had the older Ballot around, and he defeated Fair Play in the Suburban Handicap.

Fair Play had set at least one track record and was no doubt a high-class racer, although Hewitt judged that "it is doubtful he was within 10 pounds of Colin." Reformists of the time were assailing racing because of its link to gambling, and eventually succeeded in shutting down the sport in New York and many other states. Some of the best Eastern stables sent their strings to England even before the curtain was lowered, and it was there that Fair Play campaigned at four. It is easy to presume that, as he got older, the irascible aspects of the Hastings blood grew more pronounced, for he failed to place in any of his six races. His one acceptable effort was in the Coronation Cup, and even then he finished no better than sixth.

Belmont's belief in the colt as a sire prospect was not erased by that woeful campaign, and Fair Play was installed as a stallion at Nursery Stud in Kentucky with a record of thirty-two starts, ten wins, and fourteen placings, as well as earnings of $86,950. American sportsmen for some two centuries had looked to Europe, especially England, for the stock to establish and then to nurture the American Thoroughbred. Belmont's investments had included a major one when he purchased English Triple Crown winner Rock Sand for $125,000 in 1906. When Fair Play went to stud, Nursery was standing six stallions and it was not an era when breeders were avid in promoting their stallions for outside mares. Thus, Fair Play had sufficient competition at his own homestead that he got only six foals in his first crop, but he was still a young horse when the homebred Rock Sand fillies began to come back to Nursery Stud as broodmares. The cross of those two bloodlines proved highly significant. The six horses by Fair Play which earned $100,000 or more each were Man o' War, Display, Mad Hatter, Chance Shot, Chance Play, and Mad Play. Each of these except Display had Rock Sand blood on his dam's side. All told, Fair Play sired forty-seven stakes winners, an exceptional eighteen percent, and headed the American sire list in 1920, 1924, and 1927. Man o' War's brilliance at two also carried the sire to the top of the juvenile sire list in 1919, and he led the broodmare sire list in 1938.

(Rock Sand, the genetic ally of Fair Play, was a son of Sainfoin—Roquebrune, by St. Simon. In addition to his prowess as a sire of broodmares, Rock Sand sired the English St. Leger winner Tracery as well as Fair Play's half-brother, the accomplished distance horse Friar Rock. Sons of Friar Rock included Pilate, in turn the sire of the brilliant racehorse and sire Eight Thirty as well as the Belmont Stakes winner and champion Phalanx.)

After August Belmont II's death in 1924, the breeding stock and weanlings were acquired by Joseph E. Widener, and the yearlings and racing stock were purchased by a partnership of two gentlemen destined to be remembered more for their influence on statesmanship than the Turf. One was W. Averell Harriman, a racing man and member of The Jockey Club who later separated himself from the sport when he commenced a distinguished political career that included important advisory and diplomatic roles to a succession of presidents as well as governorship of New York. His partner was George Herbert Walker, grandfather of former President George Bush and great-grandfather of governors George W. and Jeb Bush.

The Harriman-Walker stable was known as Log Cabin. Although the partnership broke up soon over different philosophies — Harriman interested in developing and campaigning horses and Walker more enamored of quicker action — the success of the Belmont acquisition was significant. Among the horses thus acquired was Chance Play, a Fair Play yearling out of Quelle Chance, by Ethelbert. Chance Play was a stakes winner at two and three, then was regarded as the best horse in America in 1927 when he won six handicaps, including the Toboggan, Saratoga Cup, and Jockey Club Gold Cup. He was one among the third generation of his sire line to lead 20th Century sire lists when he topped all stallions for the year 1935, and he repeated in 1944, despite standing in upstate New York for a portion of his stud career. Chance Play got only twenty-three stakes winners (seven percent), including juvenile filly champion Now What, Jockey Club Gold Cup and Arlington Classic winner Pot o' Luck, Futurity winner Some Chance, plus Good Gamble, Grand Slam, and Psychic Bid. Chance Play's younger full brother, a weanling when Widener bought him from the Belmont estate, was Chance Shot, winner of the Belmont Stakes and Withers Stakes in 1927 and later sire of twenty-two stakes winners (nine percent).

We suspect that one could be in company rather well versed on Thoroughbred history and still be able to stump them with the cocktail party zinger: "Besides Man o' War and Chance Play, what other son of Fair Play led the sire list?" The answer is Chatterton, something of a Millard Fillmore among once pre-eminent stallions. Chatterton was one more Fair Play from a Rock Sand mare, Chit Chat, and was a foal of 1919. He touched distinguished American breeding operations and stables, but his career hardly read like a typical leading sire's. Bred by Belmont, he was sold to and raced by Frank J. Kelley. In *The Bloodstock Breeders' Review* of 1932, Neil Newman described Chatterton as "always more or less winded" and stated that "nine furlongs was about his limit." Chatterton won fifteen of thirty-two races at three and four and earned $26,565. His best wins included a sort of hostelry triple on the Kentucky circuit, as he won the Phoenix Hotel and Lafayette Hotel Handicaps, and the Louisville Hotel, in addition to the Falls City and Latonia Autumn. He entered stud in California, where Kelley had established a farm at Warm Springs, but the owner died the following year and his son arranged for Chatterton to stand at Claiborne Farm. A. B. Hancock Sr. liked the horse well enough not only to stand him but later to buy him. Chatterton sired the outstanding 1920s juvenile filly Current and then, for the prominent Belair Stud of William Woodward Sr. (a recently added Claiborne patron), Chatterton got the sterling Faireno. Faireno's half-dozen stakes victories in 1932 included the Belmont Stakes, Hawthorne Handicap, Saratoga Handicap, and Lawrence Realization. Ironically, the year Faireno's wins elevated Chatterton to the status as leader on the sire list, Hancock had perhaps waned in his thought that this was a horse for Claiborne. Chatterton that year was leased to Stuyvesant Peabody, who stood him at his Arrowbrook Farm in Illinois. After Faireno's big year, the stallion was returned to Claiborne, but later was diagnosed to be suffering from an incurable kidney ailment and was euthanized on July 14, 1933. Chatterton sired only eleven stakes winners (five percent), and his chapters to the Fair Play saga were soon more or less forgotten.

After Widener purchased the breeding stock from the August Belmont II estate, he held what might best be described as a reduction sale, disposing of sixty-seven animals while keeping eighteen. Widener bid $423,400 for those retained and sold the others for a total of $358,600. He went to $100,000 to retain Fair Play, then age twenty, but the price was cheap when reckoned in a personal way, inasmuch as it was the moment when Widener's son finally learned to share the father's love of the Thoroughbred.

In a personal memoir published some years later, Peter A. B. Widener recounted with some contrition that his indifference to horse racing as a young man had been a source of sadness for his father and tension between them. Then, when he and his young bride acceded out of "curiosity" to his father's urging that they attend the Belmont auction, "We came home with a new enthusiasm. The course of our lives had been changed by a golden horse. The horse was the grand old man of the American turf, Fair Play, sire of Man o' War. I'll never forget him as he stood in the sale ring. The bright Kentucky sun streamed down upon him, burnishing his chestnut sides as if with gilt. He looked a king…The energy of the twenty-year-old horse, his royal impatience, got me. Then, too, it was a touching thing to see how well-loved he was. Members of the many families that had had a hand in the raising and training of Fair Play wept openly as the great horse was auctioned off…"

True to the inspiration of their Fair Play afternoon, Mr. and Mrs. P. A. B. Widener II contributed importantly to the sport over many years. Polynesian, the 1945 Preakness winner and later sire of the internationally renowned Native Dancer, raced for Mrs. Widener, as did the French-raced Native Dancer colt Dan Cupid, sire of the great Sea-Bird.

Also witnessing the sale of Fair Play was young Marion du Pont (afterward Scott), who attended with her father. A pioneering lady of the show ring, Miss du Pont that day was struck by the Thoroughbred and by Fair Play in particular. Her long and distinguished career as a breeder would be marked by a willful devotion to utilizing the blood of Fair Play and Man o' War, despite their inevitable recession into distant generations of pedigrees. Her English Grand National Steeplechase winner Battleship was by Man o' War, and her great broodmare Accra (dam of Neji, Mongo, etc.) traced to Man o' War and was inbred closely to Fair Play.

Mentioned above was the Fair Play colt Display, one of the $100,000-earners by the sire, but the one which was not out of a Rock Sand mare. Display was a 1923 foal from Cicuta, by Nassovian. He was bred and raced by Walter J. Salmon Sr. of Mereworth Farm. Display became known as an "Iron Horse" during the 1920s, winning twenty-three of 103 races and earning $256,326. He ran from 1925 through 1930 and raced against his kinsman Chance Play, beating him on occasion, while weighted some pounds below him. His dozen stakes wins from two through six included the 1926 Preakness Stakes and Latonia Championship and, later, the Pimlico Cup and Hawthorne Gold Cup.

Display sired only four percent stakes winners (eleven), but one of them was the great Discovery. Purchased from Mereworth by a young Alfred G. Vanderbilt as his first major purchase, Discovery was a weight-carrying marvel through the middle 1930s and was retired to his master's Sagamore Farm in Maryland. Discovery, grandson of Fair Play, sired twenty-five stakes winners (eight percent), including the tough old gelding Find as well as champion Conniver. With Discovery, the route of Fair Play's ongoing presence veered off into the distaff side, for the Sagamore stallion became the broodmare sire of two of the most important race-horses and stallions of the century: Native Dancer and Bold Ruler! (These two are dealt with in separate chapters of their own in this volume.)

Man o' War

To address Fair Play's greatest distinction, we backtrack to Man o' War. In his own time, and in passing years, Man o' War was the stuff of legends, ironies, and glory. He was to supplant Fair Play and all else as the best horse bred by August Belmont II, but the breeder, who held the rank of Major, was tied up overseas dealing with supplies during the Allies' World War I effort. Belmont also was sinking a great deal of his personal fortunes into the Cape Cod Canal, whose eventual contribution to American commerce came too late to do its mastermind much good. These factors led him to the decision to sell his yearling crop in 1918. After conjuring with the idea of withholding Man o' War, he at length decided to include the big, leggy son of Mahubah, she a modest winner from a modest family, but another daughter of Rock Sand.

The Pennsylvania and Maryland sportsman Samuel D. Riddle bought Man o' War for $5,000 at Saratoga and turned him over to Louis Feustel, the one-time employee of Nursery Stud and combatant with Hastings. Man o' War swept through two seasons with twenty victories in twenty-one starts. His lone defeat came in the 1919 Sanford Memorial, when he got into so much traffic so many times that even he could not quite get to Upset at the finish. This defeat introduced a key ingredient to Saratoga's image as a place where odd things befall great horses — at short prices.

Man o' War won nine of ten races at two, carried 130 pounds six consecutive times, and rounded off his campaign by winning the Futurity under 127 pounds. Because Riddle for most of his career was against pushing a colt to run one and a quarter miles at three as early as the Kentucky Derby was run, Man o' War did not compete in that event. Indeed, he never ran in the state of Kentucky, which was his birthplace and would become his kingdom. (It would require a room full of racing novices for one to get far using those circumstances as a cocktail party quiz.) So, Man o' War made his three-year-old debut in the Preakness, and it launched a campaign of eleven wins in eleven starts that season, also including the Belmont Stakes. Each race in that streak somehow was invested of some compelling brilliance: Five American or world records were set from one mile to one and five-eighths miles. Margins ranged up to a reported (guessed) 100 lengths, weights carried ranged up to 138 pounds, giving thirty or so to rival horses. In his greatest trial, Man o' War was challenged by John P. Grier for most of the Dwyer, but in the end he pulled away adroitly. In his showdown against the older Sir Barton — winner of the 1919 Kentucky Derby, Preakness, and Belmont — Man o' War so subjugated the other star that Sir Barton's owner was left muttering "what a marvel" in tribute to his insolent adversary.

At the dawn of the Roaring Twenties, also known as the Golden Age of Sport — a time of Babe Ruth and Jack Dempsey, Bobby Jones, and Red Grange — Man o' War was horse racing's magnificent contribution to America's post-war emergence.

Man o' War brought to Riddle and his family's Faraway Farm (after initial service at a nearby Kentucky farm) his record of twenty wins in twenty-one starts and unprecedented earnings of $249,465. He lived to the age of thirty and was buried amid a panoply of unprecedented respect and sentiment for one of his species.

For most of his last one and a half decades, Man

o' War had been accompanied by one Will Harbut, a black gentleman who was equal parts expert horseman, orator, and public relations genius. The rich, the famous, the powerful, and the meek trekked to Lexington to pay homage or stare in awe and curiosity. At Faraway, they all could be treated to eloquence as Harbut posed "Big Red" for one spiel or another, ending with the forceful conclusion "he wuz de mostest hoss that ever wuz."

Riddle's approach to management of a stallion hardly set a standard similar to that of his horse. Still, his lasting reputation for having precluded Man o' War an opportunity to be bred to good mares has been exaggerated. Harry Scott, whose father managed Faraway Farm for a time, recalled that Riddle was ambivalent about the need for quality in mares: At times, he would take the attitude that Man o' War was so great that the quality of his mares was incidental, while at other times he would side-step a request for a breeding season by pronouncing the mare in question not good enough for Man o' War. Nevertheless, Riddle must have recognized in the spring of 1921 that he personally did not have all the quality in a broodmare band that Man o' War might deserve, and a brace of mares was purchased abroad either on his account or in the name of Walter Jeffords Sr., a rising sportsman whose wife was Mrs. Riddle's niece.

Man o' War began turning out champions early and while the rate of his accomplishments at stud waned statistically midway in his career he sired his most important son, War Admiral, when he was sixteen. Man o' War's sons also included the champion Crusader, Kentucky Derby winner Clyde Van Dusen, the flashy War Relic, English Grand National Steeplechase winner Battleship, and such high-class fillies as Bateau, Edith Cavell, and Frilette. In all, he sired sixty-four stakes win-

ners (seventeen percent), and he led the sire list in 1926. He also excelled as a broodmare sire, for his daughters produced eight champions among 128 stakes winners.

War Admiral was unlike his sire in looks, being a small, dark colt from the Sweep mare Brushup. Scott recalled that Riddle was so displeased with the little foal of 1934 that he offered to give him to Jeffords; the nephew-in-law liked War Admiral, but turned down the offer, perhaps fearing more family strife than the deal was worth would be generated should the little colt become a star.

Thus, sixteen years after Man o' War last raced, War Admiral began racing in Riddle's familiar colors. The owner was even prevailed upon to waive his rule against running in the Kentucky Derby, and thus War Admiral was able to become the fourth Triple Crown winner, sweeping the three classics in 1937. He was trained by George Conway, who had been a Feustel assistant in the days of Big Red. Horse of the Year and division championship balloting had begun in 1936, and War Admiral became the second winner of the highest annual honor in racing. At four, he proved a noble weight-carrier as well as a brilliant speedster and stayer and won nine of eleven races. Just as Man o' War was the victim of one famous defeat, War Admiral's loss to Seabiscuit in the 1938 Pimlico Special became as oft-mentioned a performance in his past as any of his victories.

War Admiral won twenty-one of twenty-six career starts and earned $273,240. He was a complete stallion, leading the general sire list, in 1945; the two-year-old sire list, in 1948; and the broodmare sire list, in 1962 and 1964. His forty stakes winners (eleven percent) included the remarkable filly Busher, Horse of the Year at three in 1945, and Blue Peter, champion two-year-old male of 1948. Colonel E. R. Bradley and later Ogden Phipps thrived in crossing War Admiral with the female family of La Troienne, and War Admiral's lasting place in the bottom half of important pedigrees was presaged by the performance of daughters on the racetrack. His rugged racemares included Searching, a prolific Blue Hen; Busanda, dam of Buckpasser; and Iron Maiden, dam of Derby winner Iron Liege and second dam of Derby winner Swaps.

Seen from the narrow context which generally frames this volume, that of a stallion's tail male line, the wonderful heritage of Hastings-Fair Play-Man o' War could not maintain its degree of prominence enjoyed through the first half of the century. Nevertheless, the state of the sire line as the 21st Century breaks is very far from a subject to create regretful nostalgia. Much of its present security traces through another of Riddle's homebred Man o' War colts, War Relic.

A foal of 1938 (sired when Man o' War was twenty), War Relic was inbred to both Belmont's Fairy Gold and Rock Sand, each appearing twice in the third generation of his ancestry. War Relic was not a top-class horse, but he scored some notable victories against good horses while receiving significant weight concessions. These included his win over Whirlaway when War Relic's rider, Ted Atkinson, befuddled the stretch-running champion by slowing the early pace on War Relic and sauntering home in the Narragansett Special. War Relic won nine of twenty races at three and four and earned $89,495. Statistically, his total of fourteen stakes winners was not impressive, for they accounted for only five percent of his foals. Within that small arsenal, however, was considerable firepower.

Like Man o' War and War Admiral, War Relic secured his name in some lasting female families. His son Battlefield was not only the champion two-year-old male of 1950, but became the broodmare sire of the 1969 Horse of the Year, Arts and Letters. War Relic's son Relic jousted early in 1948 with Citation and, while that was unrewarding on general principles, Relic did sire the versatile runner and successful stallion and leading broodmare sire Olden Times. Relic was exported to France, and his thirty-three stakes winners (nine percent) also included the 1956 French Two Thousand Guineas winner Buisson Ardent and 1960 Sussex Stakes winner Venture. Buisson Ardent became a major sire, and another Relic colt, El Relicario, runner-up to Buisson Ardent in the French Guineas, became the broodmare sire of the important handicapper and stamina influence Vigors. Relic probably is best known, however, as the sire of the mare Relance, she a French heroine as the dam of three important winners, Relko (Epsom Derby), Match II, and Reliance II.

Most prominent of the branches of the Fair Play-Man o' War sire line as it descends through War Relic is that of Intent. A 1948 War Relic colt from Liz F., by Bubbling Over, Intent raced for the Brookfield Farm of Harry Z. Isaacs, who named most of his runners with names which, like his own, began with the letter I.

Intent won the Santa Anita Maturity (later renamed the Charles H. Strub Stakes) and one and three-quarters-mile San Juan Capistrano, but also had the lick to win the Lakes and Flowers at seven furlongs, and he begot the brilliant sprinter and miler Intentionally. After being sold by Isaacs to W. L. McKnight's fledgling Tartan Farms of Florida, Intentionally ended his career by getting one and one-eighth miles successfully and went to stud.

Intentionally sired Tartan's champion sprinting filly Ta Wee, whose son Great Above sired the 1994 Horse of the Year, Holy Bull. Intentionally's twenty stakes winners (eleven percent) also

Fair Play

included major stakes winner and classics-placed In Reality, a versatile runner for Tartan client, the Frances Genter Stable. In Reality, four generations removed in the male line from Man o' War, did much to secure the line in recent years and for the immediate future. (He also figures on the bottom side of the pedigree of Derby winner and rising sire Unbridled.)

In Reality's eighty-one stakes winners (fifteen percent) include Known Fact, winner of the English Two Thousand Guineas (on the disqualification of Nureyev) and sire of important winners here and abroad. Another son of In Reality is the now-pensioned Valid Appeal, who, along with such sons as World Appeal extended the line's importance to Florida. In Reality also sired Relaunch, a consistent sire of important winners who for some reason never enjoyed a fashion status commensurate with his success. Relaunch sired the Jockey Club Gold Cup winner Waquoit, the Breeders' Cup Classic winner Skywalker (in turn sire of handicap champion Bertrando), Breeders' Cup Distaff winner One Dreamer, and Metropolitan Handicap winner Honour and Glory.

Some six decades after War Relic's birth, his branch of Fair Play/Man o' War sire line descent achieved another high point with the emergence of Tiznow (by Cee's Tizzy, a son of Relaunch, he by In Reality). Tiznow was Horse of the Year in 2000 and won consecutive Breeders' Cup Classics. He was a successful sire, but the sire line has not been strong afterward. ❖

Sir Gallahad III

Sir Gallahad III is a key marker in a sire line which has authored a prolonged prominence across centuries and oceans. The line remains important even today, although in less abundance than in earlier times. Depending upon one's age, national origin, or specific interests, this line today perhaps is again more familiar not as the Sir Gallahad III line, but as the Teddy sire line. Teddy was the sire of Sir Gallahad III, and important recent contributions trace from another son of Teddy, Sun Teddy — down to Damascus and Private Account. However, some historians might be more comfortable in naming the sire line after Ormonde, or even his own great sire, Bend Or. Bend Or, in turn, was by Doncaster, whose sire, Stockwell, was revered in England as "the Emperor of stallions." Stockwell descended from the Sir Hercules branch of the ubiquitous brigade of the Eclipse sire line.

As would be expected, the importance of this bloodline weaves in and out of pedigrees in all manner of links and combinations. Patriarchs of the line sired many important daughters as well as sons. Addressing it as merely a "sire line" no more describes its actual impact than would describing Michael Jordan as "a handy defender." For purpose of this present volume, however, we will address the male line descent most prominently.

Sir Gallahad III helped introduce a branch of this noble line to the United States, and he was followed in something of a non sequitur by his kinsmen. Full brother Bull Dog and their sire, Teddy, were imported well after Sir Gallahad III's arrival.

Illustrative of the enormous quality of this bloodline is the fact that Sir Gallahad III occupied a generational place card in both the descent and ancestry of separate Triple Crown-winning doubles. His paternal ancestor on the top line was the unbeaten Ormonde, whose sixteen career victories embraced the 1886 English Triple Crown — Two Thousand Guineas, Epsom Derby, and St. Leger. Just as American horsemen of the 1990s saw in Cigar the reality that great horses are not guaranteed immortality at stud, those who revered Ormonde in England more than 100 years ago were saddened to learn that he had been found to be a "roarer." A wind condition was looked upon by English sportsmen of the day as something akin to leprosy, and Ormonde was exported to Argentina, eventually winding up in California.

Whether the fear of contaminating future generations was the Duke of Westminster's entire motive for shipping Ormonde to distant shores is not certain, however. By that time, the horse had suffered through a severe illness which would limit his fertility for the rest of his life. Maybe the

TEDDY, **b, 1913**	Ajax, 1901	Flying Fox, 1896	Orme Vampire
		Amie, 1893	Clamart Alice
	Rondeau, 1900	Bay Ronald, 1893	Hampton Black Duchess
		Doremi, 1894	Bend Or Lady Emily
PLUCKY LIEGE, **b, 1912**	Spearmint, 1903	Carbine, 1885	Musket Mersey
		Maid of the Mint, 1897	Minting Warble
	Concertina, 1896	St. Simon, 1881	Galopin St. Angela
		Comic Song, 1884	Petrarch Frivolity

SIR GALLAHAD III (Fr), b h, 1920

1st dam: PLUCKY LIEGE, b, 1912-1938. Bred by Lord Michelham (Eng). Raced 2 yrs in Eng, 13 sts, 4 wins, $8,813. Dam of 12 named foals, 12 rnrs, 12 wnrs, 9 sw.

 1919: **Marguerite de Valois**, b f, by Teddy. Raced 2 yrs in Fr and Spain, 17 sts, 2 wins, $4,468. 3rd Prix Spearmint, Prix Solange. Dam of 8 foals, 6 rnrs, 5 wnrs, including **HOSTILITY** ($19,730), **Cascapedia** ($10,790), **Cleves** ($4,450), **Sardana** (in Eng). Granddam of **ALONZO, MISLEADER, ANTAGONISM, Munition, Devil's Luck, Navarre**.

 1920: **SIR GALLAHAD III**, b c, by Teddy. Bred by J.D. Cohn (Fr). Raced 3 yrs in Fr and Eng, 24 sts, 11 wins, $114,304. Won Poule d'Essai des Poulains, Prix Boïard, Prix Edgard de La Charme, Prix Jacques Le Marois, Prix Daphnis (twice), Lincolnshire H, Prix Eclipse, Prix du Petit-Couvert; 2nd Prix Royal Oak, Prix des Sablons, Prix du Gros Chene; 3rd Prix du Jockey Club, Prix du Petit-Couvert. Sent to USA 1925. Sire of 566 foals, 60 sw, 2.13 AEI.

 1921: **NOOR JAHAN**, b f, by Teddy. Raced 2 yrs in Fr, 17 sts, 3 wins, $11,435. Won Prix de la Reine-Mathilde; 2nd Prix Mackenzie-Grieves; 3rd Prix du Rond-Point.

 1922: **CHIVALRY**, b c, by Good Luck. Raced 1 yr in Fr, 9 sts, 2 wins, $6,514. Won Prix de l'Ete; 2nd Prix de Pinceloup.

 1923: Barren.

 1924: **Noble Lady**, b/br f, by Teddy. Raced 2 yrs in Fr, 7 sts, 2 wins, $5,529. 3rd Prix d'Arenberg.

 1925: Slipped.

 1926: **ELSA DE BRABANT**, b/br f, by Teddy. Raced 1 yr in Fr, 4 sts, 1 win, $2,345. Won Prix Yacowlef.

 1927: **BULL DOG**, b/br c, by Teddy. Raced 2 yrs in Fr, 8 sts, 2 wins, $8,205. Won Prix Daphnis, Prix la Fleche d'Or; 2nd Prix Robert Papin. Sire of 345 foals, 52 sw, AEI 2.36. Sent to USA 1931.

 1928: **QUATRE BRAS II**, b c, by Teddy. Raced 5 yrs in Fr and NA, 47 sts, 8 wins, $12,605. Won Prix Yacowlef; 2nd Houston H, Christmas H, Lone Star H, New Year's H; 3rd Champlain H, Texas H. Sire of 130 foals, 8 sw, 1.24 AEI. Died 1944.

 1929: Diane de Poitiers, dk b f, by Aethelstan II. Raced 1 yr, 11 sts, 1 win, $1,175. Dam of 9 foals, 9 rnrs, 7 wnrs.

 1930: Barren.

 1931: **ADMIRAL DRAKE**, br c, by Craig an Eran. Raced 3 yrs in Fr, Bel, Ger, and Eng, 26 sts, 5 wins, $95,741. Won Gran Prix de Paris, Grand International d'Ostende, Prix Biennal; 2nd Grand International d'Ostende, Poule d'Essai des Poulains, Gran Prix de Berlin; Prix du Jockey Club. Sire.

 1932: Barren.

 1933: **BEL AETHEL**, dk b c, by Aethelstan II. Raced 2 yrs in Fr and Eng, 7 sts, 3 wins, $11,655. Won Prix Daru; 2nd Prix Edgard de La Charme, 3rd Gold Vase. Sire of 76 foals, 5 sw, 1.07 AEI. Died 1943.

 1934: Barren.

 1935: **BOIS ROUSSEL**, br c, by Vatout. Raced 1 yr in Eng and Fr, 3 sts, 2 wins, $51,214. Champion 3yo colt in Eng. Won Derby S, Prix Juigne; 3rd Grand Prix de Paris. Sire.

 1936: Barren.

 1937: Foal died.

Duke was cashing in under the guise of protecting the British Thoroughbred. At any rate, the fact that a stallion destined to be a poor foal-getter had begotten a key son in the sire chain prior to his malady might be counted a compensating bit of luck. Ormonde's son, Orme, a major winner, sired Flying Fox in his own first year at stud. Flying Fox was inbred to Galopin 3 x 2 and proved an irascible sort, but nonetheless emulated the grandsire by winning the English Triple Crown, in 1899. The Duke of Westminster died late that year, with Ormonde and Flying Fox having made him the only man to breed and own two English Triple Crown winners. (Also descending from this sire line would be Gallant Fox and his son Omaha, which made William Woodward Sr. the first breeder and owner of two Triple Crown winners in the United States.)

Following the Duke of Westminster's death, his horses in training were sold at auction, and the French breeder Edmond Blanc was reported to have occasioned as many snickers as plaudits when he bid a world-record price of 37,500 guineas (approximately $190,000) to acquire Flying Fox. Primogeniture had strong support among European peerage of the human kind, and, while it could not have been purposeful in the outlook of horses, Flying Fox followed the pattern of his sire and grandsire in begetting his most important son in his first crop. This was Ajax, and here the tale begins, albeit obliquely, to bring together this noble line of Thoroughbred with the career of one William Woodward Sr.

To explain the link, we must digress to a story involving Maryland aristocracy, a black man named Andrew Jackson, and two Captain Hancocks.

The Squire of Belair

William Woodward Sr. was one of the most important figures in American racing of the first half of the 20th Century. Like August Belmont II before him, he was to the Turf equal parts sportsman, breeder-owner, organizational leader, and benefactor. He served as chairman of The Jockey Club in the United States and was instrumental in

the elimination of the Jersey Act, by which England's Jockey Club had precluded many American strains from acceptance in England as true Thoroughbreds.

In that complicated parquet of image/reality which Americans embrace under the name of "nostalgia," Woodward can be cast as the ultimate Victorian, traditionalist, and aristocrat, while at the same time meriting salute as a true agriculturist. Woodward bred and raced two Triple Crown winners in the name of Belair Stud, brought a succession of other distinguished runners to the American racing scene, left a surpassing champion in the hands his son, and imbued a lasting interest in the sport in various descendants.

It all began with a boyhood idyll.

Woodward left behind a remarkable record, recollections collated and written late in his life which trace his interest and participation in the sport and the many parts of life which racing touched. He began one of his carefully preserved manuscripts:

I think my love of Thoroughbred horses and racing came to me first about 1887, when I was 11 years old. In those days, my father used to take me every Decoration Day, May 30, to Jerome Park, which was about nine miles from our house in 51st Street, New York City. My father was very proud of his carriage horses and 'turn-out,' as were all the well-known people of New York City at that time, and I can see him now sitting in the Duke with me at his side. A Duke was a large Victoria (carriage) swung on C springs, and occasionally a rumble was used in the rear for the groom, but in driving to Jerome Park, it being a considerable distance, the rumble was removed

Sir Gallahad III

and two men sat on the box. We would arrive there in time for lunch and on the way out there would be numerous drags with their fine teams which would be going along with us. It made a gala sight and a pleasant holiday.

The first race that I really remember was the Belmont Stakes of 1888, in which Sir Dixon, the winner, and Prince Royal provided a stirring contest. I remember the colors and the whole scene. It was run in glorious sunshine.

Even before a boyhood "love" of the sport, there had been curiosity about racing, and with an English angle, as well. This, too, was associated with his father, and it began at breakfast as Woodward writes in a private memoir of the English stable he maintained for a quarter of a century prior to his death in 1953:

My first inspiration to race in England came to me in 1884 or 1885. My father, who had always been interested in various sports, was at breakfast one morning with my mother, my sister, and myself, and I remember him saying, 'Pierre Lorillard is the first American to have won the English Derby.' Mr. Lorillard won it with Iroquois in 1881.

The remark made an impression on me, and I made up my mind (not knowing if I could ever own a race horse or hardly what a race horse was) to be the second American to win the Derby

More immediate tasks, and goals, were placed before young Woodward, and it was some time before he was able to translate such delicious childhood impulses into an avocation. His father died in 1889. Young Woodward followed horse racing as a youth while at Groton and Harvard and then traveled to England in 1901 and became secretary to Joseph Choate, the United States ambassador to England. While no doubt hoeing to a fine and stringent line of employment, Woodward found time for horseback riding with his boss and for renewing an association with English racecourses which he had visited during earlier summers. He would wager a few pence on the biggest contests: "Those were almost classic days in English racing, the days of Sceptre, Ard Patrick, William the Third, Rock Sand, Ballantrae, and many others — hence the basis for my love."

Woodward returned to the United States in 1903 and went about a business career, rising to chair the Hanover National Bank. Career and family came first, but racing was never out of his thoughts and ambitions. When rumblings of so-called reform articulated a threat to the very existence of racing in New York and elsewhere, young Woodward conceived of a participation in the sport which would be geared toward "saving" the American Thoroughbred. The crisis in American racing would come and pass, but Woodward's dreams of the Turf were not diminished.

An uncle was the owner of Belair, a wondrous mansion in Maryland which dated from past glories of Maryland governors and their stables of fine horses. Well before he inherited Belair, William Woodward Sr. launched in rather ramshackle form the fleshing out of those vague ambitions from childhood:

I was at Belair with my uncle and found out about a bunch of Gov. Bowie's mares which had been in possession of his son, who had died. I bought three of them at $100 apiece. They were well-bred and in good condition. Bringing them to Belair, I needed some stalls for them and built three stalls at a cost of $100, for which my uncle made me pay — and he was quite right. The mares were all in foal, and I realized that by spring it would be necessary to have a stallion. Our old Negro, Andrew Jackson, who had been a jockey for Gov. Bowie, told me there was a stallion by the name of Capt. Hancock (Eolus—Belle d'Or, by Rayon d'Or) that was standing as a county stallion at a barn in Collington, and he could be bought. I went to see him with some friends, and he looked like a bag of bones. But he had four legs and the necessary anatomy to serve my mares, and I bought him for $60. So Belair Stud started with an expenditure of $360.

I took Capt. Hancock to Belair and told Andrew that he had inveigled me into purchasing the horse and it was now up to him to get him into shape. He was exceedingly faithful in doing so, and two months later the horse looked like an Arab — sleek and beautiful.

There was another Captain Hancock already connected here. This was Captain Richard Hancock, a Confederate who had served with Stonewall Jackson and had been injured and taken in by a Virginia family. A daughter of that household married Captain Hancock and they stayed on in Virginia, where he began the family's enduring connection to Thoroughbred racing, at Ellerslie Stud. Eolus, sire of the equine Capt. Hancock of later years, was a handsome young stallion whom Captain Hancock had coveted but could not afford. The stallion passed into a Black Beauty existence as a buggy horse and was finally tracked down on

Captain Hancock's behalf by a black groom. Eolus was the first of the Hancock family's important Thoroughbred stallions — the ranks of which have become virtually an innumerable caravan with the likes of Celt, Sir Gallahad III, Blenheim II, Nasrullah, Princequillo, Double Jay, Bold Ruler, Buckpasser, Secretariat, Round Table, Damascus, Nijinsky II, Danzig, and Mr. Prospector!

The family of Governor Oden Bowie figured prominently in all of this. Bowie, who was instrumental in the creation of Pimlico and the Preakness Stakes, was one of the the gubernatorial Maryland families which had owned Belair itself, and it was Bowie who had been asked to dispose of Eolus because the owner who had raced the horse lacked an interest in breeding. As noted above, Woodward's first collection of three mares sprang from the Bowie family's breeding operation.

All these factors came together in a positive way when the equine Capt. Hancock sired Aile d'Or out of one of Woodward's first three $100 mares. Aile d'Or became the first winner for Woodward and in time foaled his first stakes winner, the 1920 Toboggan Handicap victor Lion d'Or. In those early days, Woodward chose to race his horses in the name of a very good friend, P. A. Clark ("He was a good judge of a horse's conformation"), and it was this same good fellow who abetted Woodward in another purchase of lasting consequences:

In 1914, I had a bit of great good fortune. It was during the days of World War I when the Germans were marching on Paris, and I was exceedingly busy in New York with no time to spare and rarely went up to Newport, where my family was spending the summer. But one Sunday I was there for 24 hours and Phil Clark and I were reading the newspapers under the

Sir Gallahad III

trees that morning. I saw a short paragraph in the *New York Times* that M. Edmond Blanc, who then owned the greatest stud in France, was selling a number of his horses at Cheri's sales in Paris on Monday, the following day, and they were listed. I said to Clark there were five by Ajax that I would love to buy. He said, 'Why not buy them?' I said, 'It seems quite impossible as they're to be sold in about 20 hours from now, in Paris.'

He suggested that he ask George Blumenthal of Lazard Freres to cable his partner, Michael Lazard, who was a French racing man, to buy them for me.

Woodward agreed, and the message was duly sent, with instructions that the total should not exceed $7,500 and that no individual would be purchased for more than $3,750. The instructions were to buy as many of the five as possible, under these restrictions, and Woodward was initially delighted to learn that the entire group of five had been purchased for him at the top price for one — $3,750.

The bad news was that, because of an effort to preserve French bloodstock, the authorities would not allow any but the yearling to be exported. Woodward's was not a career in which insurmountable road blocks were a dominant motif, but, he recalled years later, "I tried hard to get them out (of France), but to no avail." By Woodward's plaintive retelling nearly forty years later, four of his prized Ajax purchases spent four years in Normandy at the farm of Jules Jariel, who fed them no grain during those fretful days. Even so, their fate was better than that of the yearling which, Woodward recalled "was sent over on a wretched little ship from Bordeaux," and after a storm at sea she was found dead one

morning on the "galley stove, to which place she apparently had been washed."

By the time the others arrived at Belair, Woodward was there to greet them four years later and was astounded at their condition. He prescribed a routine of gradually returning them to health, treating them gently as riding horses, and skipped the breeding shed for a year. The four mares arrived with a variety of offspring, and one of them was a yearling filly by Durbar II. Out of the mare La Flambee, the filly was given the name Flambette and won the Coaching Club American Oaks. ("I was one of the founders of that race, and always liked to have a starter.") Flambette eventually became the second dam of Woodward's 1935 Triple Crown winner, Omaha, and, indeed, the early, precipitous purchase of the five Ajax fillies and mares was among the key moments in establishing a broodmare band which produced a lasting distinction for Woodward's Belair Stud — so named after he inherited the great Maryland property from his uncle.

Ajax, Teddy, Sir Gallahad III

Readers by now may be excused for flipping back to the start of this chapter and pondering when they are, in fact, to be in the presence of the title horse, Sir Gallahad III. Woodward's fascination with the get of Ajax is one link, for Sir Gallahad III was a son of Ajax' son Teddy. Moreover, Woodward was one of the partnership which purchased Sir Gallahad III for $125,000 and brought him to stand in America. Woodward noted wryly the coincidence that his first stallion was named Capt. Hancock. The family of the human Captain Hancock would become Woodward's lasting ally. Captain Hancock's son, Arthur B. Hancock Sr., married a

Kentucky girl who inherited land in Paris, Kentucky, and he created Claiborne Stud there. For a time, he operated both Ellerslie in Virginia and Claiborne in Kentucky. Claiborne eventually became the Hancock's one domain, and Woodward became a long-time client, not only having his foals born there (then sent to Belair after weaning), but returning a continuing succession of accomplished homebred racehorses back to stud at Claiborne.

In order to acquire Sir Gallahad III, Arthur B. Hancock Sr. recruited not only Woodward as a partner. He also brought in R. A. Fairbairn and the well-known Chicago merchant Marshall Field. They bought the horse from Captain Jefferson Davis Cohn, who, like Woodward, had bought into a good thing (Teddy) in 1914.

In addition to the draft of Ajax fillies and mares which Woodward bought on a Newport whim, horses sold hurriedly by Blanc in those World War I days included the rest of his yearlings that same year. One of them was the colt who would be named Teddy, and Ajax was his sire, too. Ajax was an unbeaten Flying Fox colt whose five races included the French Derby and Grand Prix de Paris of 1904.

The sire line described above, that of Bend Or, Ormonde, Orme, and Flying Fox, thus had soldiered on into the 20th Century. In addition to the prowess of Flying Fox's son Ajax, the latter's son Teddy had won six of his eight races in Spain and France over the disrupted landscape of World War I European racing. Teddy, which cost Cohn only the equivalent of about $1,000 when purchased from Blanc, went to stud in 1918. His son Sir Gallahad III was foaled in 1920. Sir Gallahad III raced in England and France, winning eleven of twenty-four starts and approximately $41,945 in purses converted to the American dollar. He

chanced into a vintage crop, or at least one that was perceived to be such, as European racing righted itself after the interruptions of the war. Massine, Le Capucin, and Epinard also were foaled in 1920, and Sir Gallahad III was not capable of much stardom in that company.

In the book *Sire Lines*, author Abe Hewitt conjectured that Sir Gallahad III's record of finishing well back a few times and then winning indicated that Cohn was not above manipulating form for a betting coup. Thus, the record of Sir Gallahad III might have been better, or, on the other hand, worse — subject to the agenda of his owner. As it were, he did plenty to justify one of the largest importation prices of the time and he achieved the status of classic winner by taking the one-mile Poule d'Essai des Poulains (French Two Thousand Guineas). He was tried repeatedly at distances that seemed beyond him, being asked to race one and a half miles in the French Derby and one and seven-eighths miles in the Grand Prix de Paris and Prix Royal-Oak. He showed enough class to run third, beaten two necks by Le Capucin, in the French Derby. Then, faced with the one and seven-eighths miles of the Grand Prix de Paris, Sir Gallahad III might have wished those who had set him on the task would go jump in the lake. Unable to orchestrate that eventuality, he did the next best thing; the colt dumped his rider during a false start and jumped into the infield lake himself. The race went on without him.

That a future four-time leading American sire would baptize himself with such lack of dignity was made up for when he won the one-mile Lincolnshire in England as a four-year-old in 1924. He got in at 117 pounds; Epinard was assigned a steadying 140, but did not run. Later, in a two-horse race over six and a half furlongs at St. Cloud, Sir Gallahad III received eleven pounds from the noble

Sir Gallahad III

internationalist Epinard and upset him by a short neck in a thrilling dash. According to *The Bloodstock Breeders' Review* of 1924, Cohn turned down an offer from the United States of nearly $200,000, something he would not always be flush enough to consider. Under the management standards of the day, it was announced that Sir Gallahad III would be bred in his first year to eight of Cohn's mares and eight outside mares. The fee was set at the equivalent of about $1,200.

These figures are repeated here because they appeared in a contemporary account in a prestigious journal. However, turning down nearly $200,000 to earn less than $10,000 in fees the first year does not seem to add up. Whatever Cohn's deals, and decisions, were in 1924, he sold Sir Gallahad III to the Claiborne partnership for $125,000 after the horse had stood one year in France.

While the author would not as a generality deny the oft-stated illusion that European classic winners, proven at longer distances, were more popular as imports in earlier eras than they are today, the acquisition of Sir Gallahad III is a reminder that speed in a sire prospect has long been cherished. Sir Gallahad III failed in the ultimate tests of the European racehorse, and yet A. B. Hancock Sr. saw in him a beguiling combination of sprint/miler speed along with enough class and courage to place in the longer classics. This pattern would be demonstrated by significant imports over succeeding eras, Nasrullah and Blushing Groom coming quickly to mind as examples.

Sir Gallahad III's first book at Claiborne included the Celt mare Marguerite, whom William Woodward Sr. had purchased from Hancock. The resulting foal was Gallant Fox, who carried Woodward's Belair colors of white, with red polka dots, on a sublime tour of the American Triple Crown and a succession of other major races in 1930.

Woodward authored a privately published book, *Gallant Fox: A Memoir*, in which the proud owner-breeder, could not resist a comparison with Man o' War: "Now, looking back with prejudice and affection, it is possible that neither 'had anything' on the other; but that will never be determined — it is unnecessary. They are both among the greatest of horses — that is sufficient."

It will be recalled that far back in the sire line of Sir Gallahad III were two English Triple Crown winners, Ormonde and Flying Fox, separated by one generation in the form of Orme. Gallant Fox came home to Claiborne and quickly went that duo one better, siring Omaha to complete a sire-son Triple Crown in this country. Like Gallant Fox, Omaha was trained by Sunny Jim Fitzsimmons, and five years after the Fox's 1930 Triple Crown sweep, Omaha duplicated the Triple. Omaha also was a Woodward homebred, and he was an arch example of the influence of the early Woodward acquisitions of mares. His dam, Flambino, by Wrack, was out of the CCA Oaks winner Flambette, she from La Flambee, one of the original draft of Ajax fillies and mares. Since Ajax was also Sir Gallahad III's grandsire on the top side, Omaha was thus inbred to Ajax 4 x 4.

At stud, Gallant Fox was something of an enigma. His early crops turned out spectacular stars, and yet his prowess waned, and eventually he had a record of only nineteen stakes winners, or six percent from foals. The good ones, however, gave Woodward many gratifications in his seeking of the great, traditional prizes, both here and abroad. Omaha was in Gallant Fox's first crop, and in the second crop were Granville and Flares. Granville won the Belmont Stakes and a sequence of other major races at three in 1936 and, as balloting for championships had come into vogue that year, he had the distinction of being the first recipient of a certified Horse of the Year honor.

Granville was out of Gravita, whose sire, the unraced Sarmatian, had been a forlorn yearling who arrived at Belair four years after the purchase of the Edmond Blanc horses. Sarmatian was by Sardanapale, and his dam was Mousse Des Bois, one of the daughters of Ajax Woodward first read about in the *New York Times* of 1914.

Flares was by Gallant Fox and out of Flambino and thus was a full brother to Omaha and yet another dividend from the Blanc purchase. He avenged his older brother's defeat in the Ascot Gold Cup and was a highlight in the extraordinary career of the Woodward stable abroad. Woodward's childhood musing on becoming the second American to win the Epsom Derby took hold and was pursued with a bull dog's determination, but also with an astute businessman's and horseman's planning and knowledge. Beginning in 1928, Woodward for the rest of his life would send a few yearlings — almost always two — to Freemason Lodge, the yard of the Newmarket, England, trainer Captain (later Sir) Cecil Boyd-Rochfort. The collated copies of many years of exchanged letters and wires between owner and trainer bespeak a relationship of mutual respect and sympathy. As the years rolled by without a Derby win, but with high hopes often raised, it was Woodward who frequently provided support and optimism for the future when Boyd-Rochfort admitted to being devastated by the turn of events.

Woodward was a New York banker by trade, but he must have spent a goodish bit of time on his weekends really studying his weanlings and yearlings at Belair. Each year, he had extensive reasons to give Boyd-Rochfort for why he selected the youngsters he did for England. In one instance, he spoke enthusiastically of having placed one colt in the most hilly paddock at Belair and was pleased to see the way the youngster came roaring down the hill to the gate — evoking hopes for a colt that would handle the alarming descent at Tattenham Corner, which has undone many an Epsom Derby colt.

While the Holy Grail of Epsom eluded Woodward, he and Boyd-Rochfort enjoyed remarkable and sustained success. Woodward won four English classics: two St. Legers with Boswell and Black Tarquin, the Oaks with Hycilla, and the One Thousand Guineas with Brown Betty. His Prince Simon lost photo finishes in both the Two Thousand Guineas and Epsom Derby; Woodward horses ran up a strong string of wins in other important stakes; and his Foxbrough was the top-weighted two-year-old of 1938.

The Ascot Gold Cup's two-mile status was still intact in those days, and the race was a frequent goal for the best classic colts in their following year. In sending an American Triple Crown winner, Omaha, to try for the event, Woodward set a sporting standard seldom matched. Omaha was edged in a storied Ascot Gold Cup duel with the brave filly Quashed in 1936, but Flares avenged the defeat two years later in a blanket finish over Buckleigh and Senor.

While Woodward seldom traveled to England to see his horses run, an early Derby hope was too much for him to resist. In 1931, the colt Sir Andrew's attempt at the Derby was the centerpiece of a lengthy voyage to England and on to France. Sir Andrew was by Sir Gallahad III and out of Gravitate, who would prove to be the second dam of Granville. Woodward, apparently traveling alone, kept a rich diary. His entries constitute rare insight into various aspects of busi-

Sir Gallahad III

ness and social life, in addition to racing, for he spoke of many things — of dancing girls and luncheons, and currencies and kings.

There were shopping expeditions for Chippendale and Waterford pieces, a whirlwind round of lunches at country houses of the likes of Lord Rosebery, Lord Derby, and Lord Granard, a chance to look over others' art collections — and note with satisfaction that they did not always match his collection of Herrings. He made trips from his Ritz headquarters out to Freemason Lodge, of course, and kept abreast of things at home. One entry noted that he had received news that his two-year-old Faireno had "won the Victoria Plate at Toronto — pleasant reading for the breakfast table."

At a dinner at Buckingham Palace, Woodward was surprised by the rapidity with which courses were served and removed, and pleased by how kind King George V was during an organized one-on-one conversation. Woodward noted wryly that the King referred to his colt as "St. Andrew" rather than Sir Andrew, and he did not correct His Majesty to explain that the horse was named for the black man Andrew Jackson. Sir Andrew ran fairly well, but got shuffled back in traffic and could not challenge. (The colt did win two prestigious races that year, the Newmarket Stakes and Prince of Wales's Stakes, and was one of eight stakes winners in England and France for Sir Gallahad III.)

Woodward stayed on abroad after Epsom and at one point extricated himself from the pleasantries of the trip and huddled with leaders of four of the top five banks in England. The conversation among these international captains of finance centered on the various ways the Allies might deal with Germany's debt, as the post World War I recovery of Europe was a festering worry. Woodward, the lone American present, mused, "Is it not an interesting commentary that the nation who had no place in the jealousies that started the war, but gave willingly of its possessions and men, and that settled the war by its strength, should be asked to pay for the war?" Woodward made no mention of a fellow named Hitler, but seemed to harbor a foreboding about the possibilities for the future: "The sooner this thing is settled, the better. The outlook is unpleasant."

In a more jubilant vein, during the brief Paris soiree of this journey, Woodward attended the Folies Bergère with a collection of swells and could not help noting of the chorus: "Very little clothes on them — one marvelous little dancer."

To return to Sir Gallahad III, we recall that he launched his stud career in this country by siring a Triple Crown winner in his first crop. This set a pace no stallion could maintain, but Sir Gallahad III did sire two later Derby winners, spread over the next decade and a half. Neither was a champion, but each added to the lore of the Derby. In 1940, the Sir Gallahad III colt Gallahadion scored at 35-1 at the expense of the previously unbeaten Bimelech. Gallahadion raced for Ethel V. Mars, whose Milky Way Stable carried the name of one of the more famous of the Mars family's candy bars. In 1945, another Sir Gallahad III colt, Hoop, Jr., sired when Sir Gallahad III was twenty-one, won the Derby and became forever known as the first horse owned by the remarkable horseman Fred W. Hooper. (January 1, 2000, marked the dawn of the third century in which Mr. Hooper has participated, he having been born near the tail end of the 19th Century.) To this day, no stallion has sired more than three Derby winners, and only Falsetto, Virgil, and Bull Lea rank with Sir Gallahad III in that measure.

Another classic victory by a Sir Gallahad III colt

also had an unusual twist. This involved High Quest, who was owned by Brookmeade Stable and was allowed to defeat his own stablemate, Cavalcade, in the 1934 Preakness, even though Cavalcade was coming off a win in the Kentucky Derby. This may sound like the ultimate expression of the sporting credo of "Let the best horse win," but probably is more an indication that, at that time, the Triple Crown as an entity still was not the dominant factor it is today.

Sir Gallahad III first led the American sire list in 1930, when his son Gallant Fox set a one-year earnings record of $308,275. He led the list again in 1933, 1934, and 1940. In all, he sired sixty-five stakes winners (twelve percent). In addition to those named, they included the Belair Stable distaff champion Vagrancy; the Jockey Club Gold Cup and Travers winner Fenelon, also a distinguished handicapper at four; Gallant Sir, winner of the Latonia Championship, which for a time ranked perhaps just below the classics in importance; Hadagal, Tintagel, and Good Morning.

As we shall presently see, Sir Gallahad III's lasting influence was more a product of his being a sire of successful broodmares by the dozen than being a sire of stallions. Nevertheless, some of his sons transferred the line's prowess with notable success. Gallant Fox, for all his early success, did not figure prominently in extended success, but one of his full brothers, Fighting Fox, did. Fighting Fox was Marguerite's second of three stakes-winning Sir Gallahad III colts. A foal of 1935, he loomed briefly as a possible classic colt in the spring of 1938, when he won the Wood Memorial, and he proved a solid handicap horse later. (The Derby of 1938 was won by Lawrin, a son of another Sir Gallahad III horse, Insco, who also accounted for the champion filly Inscoelda among thirteen stakes winners.)

Fighting Fox's eighteen stakes winners included the 1945 champion three-year-old Fighting Step, the good stakes filly and producer Bonnie Beryl, and 1952 handicap champion Crafty Admiral. Earner of just under $500,000 when such a figure was exalted, Crafty Admiral carried on the line admirably if not brilliantly. Crafty Admiral's twenty-six stakes winners comprised only seven percent of his foals, but one of them, Admiral's Voyage — while generally a disappointment — became the broodmare sire of the marvelous stallion Danzig. Moreover, Crafty Admiral himself is also the broodmare sire of Triple Crown winner Affirmed, who gave Sir Gallahad III a lingering waft of Triple Crown glory four decades after a son and grandson had taken turns at center stage.

Another son of Sir Gallahad III who kept the flame alive at stud was Roman. A foal of 1937, Roman linked the fundamentally European lines of Teddy/Sir Gallahad III, Spearmint, and St. Simon with a female family tracing quickly to American sires such as Ultimus (son of Commando) and Sweep. His second dam, Look Up, was inbred 3 x 4 to the consummate American speed influence, Domino.

Roman was atypical of Sir Gallahad III, who, as author Hewitt put it, "got middle distance performers in profusion." Roman came out early in his two-year-old season, won several spring stakes, and was not asked to face the best of his crop late in the year. At three, he showed brilliant speed sprinting and stretched far enough to win the Jerome and Laurel Stakes at one mile each. He tried going with Bimelech early in the Kentucky Derby, perhaps setting up the favorite to fall to Gallahadion, by Sir Gallahad III, in the stretch. At four, Roman won a series of sprints against good opposition, his campaign reaching a climax when he won the Fall Highweight under 140 pounds.

Sir Gallahad III

Although Roman's breeder and owner, Joseph E. Widener, put primary emphasis on the classics, he stood the horse at his Elmendorf Farm. Within a decade, Widener had died and the farm changed hands a time or two. When Elmendorf's farm manager, Lou Doherty, left to establish his own operation in the early 1950s, The Stallion Station, Roman was moved to that establishment. He was a mainstay at The Stallion Station, which Doherty ran in association with Harold Snowden. Roman twice led the sire list in number of two-year-old winners and twice led the list of juveniles in earnings. He sired fifty-four stakes winners, thirteen percent, and while speed was the hallmark of many of them, he got a share of high-class middle distance horses. These included Hasty Road, winner of the Preakness and Widener Handicap after a championship juvenile season; Romanita, also a champion at two and then winner of the Monmouth Oaks; as well as Roman Patrol, Cosmic Missile, and Queen Hopeful (granddam of New York Handicap Triple winner Fit to Fight). Roman Line followed Hasty Road as Roman's second Kentucky Derby runner-up.

Inexorably, however, it was the daughters that reached out farther than sons in continuing influence. Roman's daughters included the Blue Hen Pocahontas (Tom Rolfe, Chieftain, among others) and Roman Zephyr (Roman Brother). Hasty Road in turn sired the notable producer Broadway and also Lady Golconda, dam of the great Forego. Given that Lady Golconda went back, top and bottom, to full brothers Sir Gallahad III and Bull Dog, Forego's career might give breeders of a certain age to ponder before an evening fireplace on "what if I had crossed that mare of mine with..."

Followers of pedigrees and/or the feminist movement can be excused if by now they wonder whether this chapter should be hurled into the above referenced fireplace. When, they wonder, will it be acknowledged that Sir Gallahad III's dam was Plucky Liege, arguably the greatest producer of sons in international Thoroughbred breeding in the 20th Century?

The answer to this fair question is that more details on Sir Gallahad III's sire (Teddy), dam (Plucky Liege), and full brother (Bull Dog) are savored in another chapter, on Bull Dog's remarkable son Bull Lea. Before we leave Sir Gallahad III, though, it must be dwelt upon that, with this power of a singular female behind him — coincidentally or not — Sir Gallahad III was even more prominent as a broodmare sire than as a sire. He, in fact, led the broodmare sire list for ten consecutive years (1943-1952). He also led once before, in 1939, and once later, in 1955, for a total of twelve times atop the list, unmatched by any other stallion. His son Roman led the broodmare sire list in 1965, and the aforementioned brother Bull Dog led the broodmare sire list three times.

Several of Sir Gallahad III's daughters were good stakes winners themselves and then generated even more success as producers over generations, these including Betty Derr, Escutcheon, and Vagrancy. The 183 stakes winners produced from Sir Gallahad III's daughters included such important matrons as Alablue, Rare Perfume, Nothirdchance, Judy-Rae, and Iron Maiden. Other stakes winners out of Sir Gallahad III mares included Challedon, Jet Pilot, Gallorette, Battle Morn, Royal Native, and Revoked.

Sir Gallahad III died at the age of twenty-nine in 1949. ❖

Challenger II

For the most part, stallions who led the American sire list during the 20th Century constituted a parade of animals that stood at least a part of their careers in Kentucky. A break in this pattern took place in 1939, when Challenger II led the list. He reigned from Maryland, which, like Virginia and New York and some other Eastern Seaboard states, had a particularly proud history in racing from Colonial times. In 1971, Maryland was again home of the leader, in the form of the great Northern Dancer. More recently, What a Pleasure, Dr. Fager, and Buckaroo have been based in Florida and have led national lists.

That Challenger II was available for importation to America as young as three was, in part, a result of archaic rules pertaining to England's classic races. He was a foal of 1927, and in that time the rules of eligibility still called for all engagements to be cancelled upon the death of the owner. Lord Dewar, of a well-known whiskey dynasty, had purchased Challenger II from his breeder, the National Stud, for 5,000 guineas; Dewar passed away on April 11, 1930, as trainer Fred Darling had been preparing the unbeaten colt for a potential classic bid. Lord Dewar was a bachelor, but had a ready lieutenant in a nephew, John A. Dewar, to whom he bequeathed his hors-

es. The rule was abandoned for horses one year younger than Challenger II, but the old strictures still prevailed for his crop.

Challenger II had won his only two races at two, the Richmond Stakes and Clearwell Stakes, earning the equivalent of about $11,000, and was assessed at 127 pounds on the Free Handicap. This placed him third, two pounds below leader Diolite and one pound above Blenheim II, who won the Derby the following year. Challenger II was by Swynford, sire of Blenheim II's sire, Blandford. Both Challenger II and Blenheim II were destined to become leading sires in this country.

C. J. FitzGerald was best known in racing as an official, but he filled the role of bloodstock agent in the acquisition of Challenger II. As FitzGerald recorded for *American Race Horses* of 1939:

I was commissioned by Messrs. William L. Brann and Robert S. Castle in 1929 to buy them a 3-year-old of racing quality whose individuality and bloodlines would warrant his place at the head of the stud they expected to establish in Maryland.

On my next trip to Europe, I looked the field over but found nothing available that suited me. As you know, it is a diffi-

		Isinglass, 1890	**Isonomy** Dead Lock
	John o' Gaunt, 1901		
		La Fleche, 1889	St. Simon Quiver
SWYNFORD, br, 1907			
		Tristan, 1878	Hermit Thrift
	Canterbury Pilgrim, 1893		
CHALLENGER II (GB), b h, 1927		Pilgrimage, 1875	The Palmer Lady Audley
		Gallinule, 1884	**Isonomy** Moorhen
	Great Sport, 1910		
		Gondolette, 1902	Loved One Dongola
SWORD PLAY, br, 1921			
		Royal Realm, 1905	Persimmon Sand Blast
	Flash of Steel, 1913		
		Flaming Vixen, 1907	Flying Fox Amphora

1st dam: Sword Play, b, 1921-1945. Bred by National Stud (Eng). Raced 2 yrs in Eng, 17 sts, 4 wins, $3,801. Dam of 12 named foals, 8 rnrs, 7 wnrs, 4 sw.

1926: EN GARDE, br g, by Spion Kop. Raced 7 yrs in Eng, 39 sts, 6 wins, $16,918. Won Chester Vase, Berkshire Foal Plate; 2nd Great Foal S; 3rd John Porter S, Belgrave S.

1927: CHALLENGER II, b c, by Swynford. Bred by National Stud (Eng). Raced 2 yrs in Eng and NA, 18 sts, 2 wins, $10,973. Won Clearwell S, Richmond S. Sent to USA 1930. Sire of 315 foals, 34 sw, 2.09 AEI.

1928: Nushirawan, b c, by Solario. Raced 4 yrs in Eng, 11 sts, 0 wins, $0.

1929: La Rixe, br f, by Phalaris. Winner in India.

1930: Sword Craft, b g, by Warden of the Marches. Raced 4 yrs in Eng and NA, 44 sts, 4 wins, $2,934.

1931: Barren.

1932: Foal died.

1933: Trustaway, b f, by Fairway. Unraced.

1934: Barren.

1935: Long Drove, br g, by Cameronian. Unraced.

1936: Thrust, b f, by Fairway. Unraced. Dam of 8 foals, 5 rnrs, 2 wnrs, including **Match Point** (in Eng). Granddam of **FLYING FRIENDSHIP**, **Deuce II**, **Fellermelad**.

1937: Kozuka, br f, by Easton. Raced 2 yrs in Eng, 11 sts, 1 win, $745. Dam of 10 foals, 8 rnrs, 5 wnrs. Granddam of **My Sandra**.

1938: POISE, b g, by Fair Trial. Raced 5 yrs in Eng, 23 sts, 5 wins, $6,122. Champion 2yo in Eng. Won Saxham S, Wood Ditton S, Weston's Yard H, Back End S; 2nd July Cup, Westbury H.

1939: Sword Knot, br f, by Trimdon. Raced 1 yr in Ire, 9 sts, 1 win, $496. Dam of 11 foals, 8 rnrs, 5 wnrs, including **STEEL FLASH** ($27,352), **NICKY NOOK**, **SWORD FLASH**, **Trinity**, **Sailor's Knot**. Granddam of **Bright Nick**.

1940: br c, by Morland.

1941: Barren.

1942: Sword of Honor, br g, by Fair Trial. Unraced.

1943: RAPIER, b c, by Fairhaven. Raced 3 yrs in Eng, 23 sts, 4 wins, $6,598. Won Bogside H, Studley Royal H; 2nd Ayrshire H, Beeswing H, Roseberry S.

cult matter to buy a good 3-year-old with engagements in either England or France.

I had met Lord Dewar and had seen his Challenger win the Clearwell Stakes in superb style after being boxed in, a furlong from home...The colt was then two and the critics were acclaiming him as a coming Derby winner...Unfortunately, the fine old sportsman died within a few months. As the colt's nomination for the Derby and other races were voided by the death of the owner, I was prompted to secure the son of Swynford for my

American clients.

In my opinion, the blood of Swynford, coming through such a fine type, would be most helpful to American families with their predilection for speed.

FitzGerald noted that the younger Dewar asked 15,000 pounds for the colt, but the American agent stated a limit of 10,000 pounds, and the lesser offer was accepted.

The American owners were newcomers to the game and were anxious to have Challenger II ready for summer's Arlington Classic. That Chicago race had been inaugurated the year before and, with a purse of some $60,000 to the winner, had become an instant addition to the targets of the better three-year-olds. (Blue Larkspur had won the first one and, as matters transpired, Triple Crown winner Gallant Fox won the 1930 running for which Challenger II was intended.)

Within twenty-four hours of the sale, and while Challenger II was still in Darling's yard, however, there occurred an accident which if timed earlier would likely have scotched the Dewar deal. Barbed wire does not figure prominently in the image of the great English training gallops, but apparently there was some of this harsh material in a hedge at Beckhampton, and Challenger II got into a contest with it. FitzGerald's letter described the incident as the colt having "hurt himself seriously on his way home from the Beckhampton gallops" and that it left the right hock "terribly lacerated and apparently ruined." *The Blood-Horse* of 1949, in reviewing Challenger II's life, gave a different version: "While playing in a paddock, he kicked into some hidden barbed wire in a hedge, seriously injured a tendon in his right hind leg."

At any rate, the hock was badly injured, and all hope of the Arlington Classic was immediately dashed. Challenger II remained in England for several months before eventual importation. The Agua Caliente Handicap then became a chief target, and he turned in some impressive works at Bowie. He was clocked once breezing four furlongs in :46 3/5 and later worked a full one and a quarter miles in 2:07 under a custom of the day. He did not get to start in the Caliente, however. He did get to the races in this country, but in eight starts at four he never gained a part of any purse, causing FitzGerald to muse in retrospect that allowing him an entire year to recover from his injury might have been wise. Thus, the future leading sire had a career record of two wins in ten starts, and his English earnings total remained all that was attached to his scoresheet.

Trying to make a sire out of a colt who failed to place in eight starts in front of his new constituency is no high-percentage proposition in the best of circumstances. Take him to a regional market and breed him basically to eight or ten of your own mares, and you might just as well hide him behind a hedgerow — with or without barbed wire. Challenger II, however, overcame this formula.

His original racing owner, Lord Dewar, had been known as an excellent after-dinner speaker. One of what *The Bloodstock Breeders' Review* described as "sparkling epigrams (which) came trippingly from his tongue" and received a wide publicity was: "Four-fifths of the perjury of the world is expended on tombstones." Another was: "Samson was the first advertiser. He took two columns and brought down the house."

As it happened, Challenger II's new owners were real advertising men, and good ones. William Leavitt Brann had a New York ad agency and was credited with creating the famous mail-order catalogue of one of his accounts, Montgomery Ward & Co.[1] Brann retired in 1928

Challenger II

and formed a partnership with Robert S. Castle, who had been head of Montgomery Ward's advertising department and thus worked closely with him. The two started Branncastle Stable and built Branncastle Farm in Frederick County, Maryland. Brann described himself and Castle as "two tired and retired businessmen who turned to racing and breeding for recreation," the pair thus heeding a siren song oft-repeated over the years, to the general betterment of the Turf.

Although Challenger II by and large started with only farm-owned mares, FitzGerald did take credit for calling the colt to the attention of other breeders, including William Woodward Sr., who patronized him at least to some degree. Challenger II's runners paved his way into the consciousness of top breeders, and he sired at least thirty foals in each of the first three years of the 1940s, but in those days the distance from Kentucky's bountiful broodmare communes remained a detriment.

Challenger II had a few nice stakes winners in his first several crops. Then in the 1936 crop came Brann's and Castle's homebred Challedon. Brann later bought out Castle and renamed the property Glade Valley Farm. (The latter-day Glade Valley was established at a nearby location.) Challedon endeared himself to the hearts of Marylanders. He won the state's pride and joy, the Preakness, engendering such emotion that fans altered the time-honored "Maryland, My Maryland," with a new version, "Challedon, My Challedon."

Voting for championships and Horse of the Year began in 1936. In 1939 and 1940, Challedon became the first horse to be named Horse of the Year twice. Challedon won a total of seventeen stakes, and they came young and old and coast to coast in a career spanning ages two through six. At

two, he won the Pimlico Futurity and two lesser stakes and at three, in addition to the Preakness, his winning races included the Hawthorne Gold Cup, Pimlico Special, and Narragansett Special. One of his victories over Johnstown in 1939 came in the Arlington Classic, so Brann had a delayed triumph in what he had once envisioned as the first big target for Challedon's sire.

Challedon won a second Pimlico Special at four in 1940, when his travels also took him to the West Coast for a victory in the Hollywood Gold Cup. He won twenty of forty-four races and earned $334,685. After Challedon had been at stud for several years, Brann sold him for $250,000 to Ira Drymon, who later syndicated him to a group of Kentuckians. Challedon sired only five percent stakes winners, thirteen in all, but several had some distinction. They included the crack steeplechasers Ancestor and Policeman Day; the high-class Donor, whose earnings of $367,560 were remarkable for the 1940s; and the popular and durable New Orleans campaigner Tenacious.

In his crops of 1942 and 1943, Challenger II sired two distaff champions: the top older filly or mare of 1946 and the best three-year-old filly of the same year. The first was Gallorette and the second was Bridal Flower.

Gallorette was bred by Hall of Fame trainer Preston Burch from the mare Gallette, whose dam was the distinguished Belair Stud mare Flambette (also second dam of Triple Crown winner Omaha).

Brann and Burch had a multi-year foal-swap arrangement with Challenger II and Gallette which presaged a later deal whereby the Chenery family got a Bold Ruler—Somethingroyal colt named Secretariat and the Phipps family got something-less-royal.

Racing for Brann, Gallorette was a female version of Challedon in durability. She won twenty-one of seventy-two races from two through six, jousted successfully from time to time with the likes of Stymie, and earned a total of $445,535. That total stood for some time as the record for any filly or mare. Gallorette's soundness, class, courage, and consistent efforts when facing males time after time made her such a heroine that the American Trainers Association voted her the best distaffer over the first half of the 20th Century. (In that poll, conducted via Delaware Park — itself a champion of distaff racing — breeder Burch modestly declined to place her first on his personal ballot.)

Brann, the old ad man, cashed in on Gallorette as he had on Challedon. He sold the mare for $125,000 to Marie Moore. Mrs. Moore bred the mare to the steeplechaser Lovely Night, and the resultant filly, Mlle. Lorette, won Pimlico's stakes named for the dam, the Gallorette Stakes of 1954. Gallorette's other stakes winner was Courbette, by Native Dancer, and her subsequent descendants include Irish St. Leger winner White Gloves II and classic-placed Dancing Moss. More recent descendants from the family of Gallorette include Irish champion Minstrella and her graded stakes-winning daughter Colonial Minstrel; Canadian champion Charlie Barley; and Greenwood Lake, who won the 1999 grade I Champagne.

Challenger II's other filly champion of 1946, Bridal Flower, underscored the status which the stallion eventually achieved nationally.

This filly was bred by Colonel E. R. Bradley, owner of the vaunted Idle Hour Stock Farm of Kentucky, and was from Big Hurry, one of the daughters of the great Idle Hour mare La Troienne.

Challenger II's other stakes winners included the good sire Errard, as well as Hollywood Gold Cup winner Challenge Me, Escadru, Pictor, Victory Morn, and The Schemer (dam of distaff champion Conniver).

Challenger II was in declining health by the summer of 1948. He had several cases of colic and late in the year had heart failure as well. He died on December 23 that year at the age of twenty-one.

A Swynford Era

In addition to Challenger II and Blenheim II, son and grandson of Swynford, other important stallions from that line during the middle decades of the 20th Century included St. Germans. The latter was the sire of Kentucky Derby winners Twenty Grand and Bold Venture, as well as of handicap champion Devil Diver. Bold Venture, in turn, sired the Triple Crown winner Assault and another Derby-Belmont winner, Middleground.

Swynford was a product of the historic breeding operation of Lord Derby in England and was by John o' Gaunt and out of the Epsom Oaks winner Canterbury Pilgrim. Swynford's early training indicated a headstrong colt and led to suspicions that he would confound his pedigree by failing to stay. He eventually settled down in the hands of the great trainer George Lambton and put matters right by winning the longest of the English classics, the one and three-quarter-mile St. Leger in the racing autumn of 1910. At four, Swynford defeated consistent rival Lemberg in the Princess of Wales' Stakes and Eclipse Stakes before suffering a fetlock injury serious enough that his survival for stud was not immediately a sure thing. Lambton later was quoted by Abe Hewitt[2] as opining that Swynford was the best horse he ever trained, better even than Hyperion. Swynford was consistently a leading sire, led the English list in 1923, and got six classic winners — five fillies and the Derby winner Sansovino.

Challenger II, son of Swynford, was from modest forebears up close. His dam, Sword Play, was only a moderate winner and was by Great Sport, whom Hewitt called "a proven stud failure." The same was said of Royal Realm, broodmare sire of Sword Play. Nor was Flash of Steel, the second dam of Challenger II, much beyond ordinary. The third dam, however, was Flaming Vixen, by (English) Triple Crown winner Flying Fox and out of a sister to the good sprinter and sire Sundridge.

Swynford's son St. Germans matured slowly, in the general pattern of the sire's get, and he was second in Sansovino's Derby to give the stallion a one-two finish. St. Germans won at one and three-quarter miles later at three and the following year won the one and one-half-mile Coronation Cup and two and one-eighth-mile Doncaster Cup for his breeder, Lord Astor. St. Germans' record had about it the look of a plodder by American standards. Thus, Greentree Stud's importation of the horse could have been eyed as a slavish devotion to the concept of breeding for the classics rather than recognition of the

Challenger II

realities of the sport in this country. Nevertheless, St. Germans, as stated above, sired Twenty Grand (Derby and Belmont), Bold Venture (Derby and Preakness), Devil Diver, and The Rhymer among twenty-three stakes winners (thirteen percent). He was the leading sire in America in 1931.

St. Germans cast a shadow over his sons, however. He himself was not gifted with high fertility, and his son Twenty Grand was sterile; Devil Diver was a failure at stud; Bold Venture was successful, but his own great son Assault was sterile, and Bold Venture's other Derby-Belmont winner, Middleground, averaged fewer than ten foals per year.

The Rhymer, another son of St. Germans, fared better. This Widener Handicap winner sired the high-class handicap horse Vertex, who, in turn, sired Kentucky Derby winner Lucky Debonair and juvenile champion Top Knight (another victim of virtual sterility). Lucky Debonair was moderately successful at stud and got the Irish Sweeps Derby winner Malacate. ❖

Blenheim II

During the spring of 1977, Lord Carnarvon was undergoing a brief flurry of fame extending beyond that which was permanently his due — as the breeder of an Epsom Derby winner, raconteur extraordinaire, father of the Queen's racing manager, and as an English Lord replete with an 18th-Century castle — Highclere — and an Edwardian manner.

This added fame was connected to the Treasures of Tutankhamun, which were touring North America and fostering a resurgence of interest in a long-dead Egyptian pharaoh with a famously spiffy tomb. An earlier wave of interest had greeted the 1922 discovery and excavation of that tomb by an archeological venture financed by Lord Carnarvon's late father. Both in personal conversations and in appearances on late-night American television, Carnarvon indicated his realization that more than a little of the fascination came from oft-told tales of an ancient curse unleashed by violation of the tomb. His standard, coy reply to the inevitable question was, "I don't believe and I don't disbelieve. Certainly there have been many curious things…I keep an open mind."

The Sixth Earl of Carnarvon proved such a gifted storyteller that two volumes of his rollicking reminiscences were published by Weidenfeld and Nicolson of London about this time, to wit, *No*

Regrets: Memoirs of the Earl of Carnarvon, and *Ermine Tales: More Memoirs of the Earl of Carnarvon*. He was a dashing little fellow with a ready smile that emblazoned an impressive squadron of teeth, the glint of which was, however, not up to the sparkle of his eye. He delighted in recalling tales in which he was something less than the hero, but, true to his upbringing, he could pop instantly into a pose, with cigar or rifle in hand, that bespoke a fully grounded self-confidence.

It was as the breeder of Blenheim II that Lord Carnarvon made a major contribution to American racing and breeding, as well as to the beloved Turf of his native land. He also got a bit back from the Americans, for as early as the late 1930s he had the sagacity to raid the Saratoga sales and take home some nice, profitable winners — three decades before American-breds were frequently winning the best races abroad.

Blenheim II was a son of the great stallion Blandford. In one of the few passages which refute the title *No Regrets*, Lord Carnarvon wrote about why he did not wind up the owner of Blandford. In 1920, when Blandford was a yearling, Carnarvon was a young British Army officer who then had the sort of junior title of his family, Lord Porchester, and was known by the chummy nickname "Porchey." He recalled that trainer R. C.

		John o' Gaunt, 1901	**Isinglass** La Fleche
	Swynford, 1907	Canterbury Pilgrim, 1893	Tristan Pilgrimage
BLANDFORD, br, 1919		White Eagle, 1905	Gallinule Merry Gal
	Blanche, 1912	Black Cherry, 1892	Bendigo Black Duchess
BLENHEIM II (GB), br h, 1927		Desmond, 1896	St. Simon L'Abbesse de Jouarre
	Charles O'Malley, 1907	Goody Two-Shoes, 1899	**Isinglass** Sandal
MALVA, b, 1919		Robert le Diable, 1899	Ayrshire Rose Bay
	Wild Arum, 1911	Marlicacea, 1902	Martagon Flitters

1st dam: Malva, b, 1919-1941. Bred by Lord Carnarvon (Eng). Unraced. Dam of 9 named foals, 9 rnrs, 8 wnrs, 4 sw.

1924: Deltos, b g, by Volta. Raced 2 yrs in Eng, 19 sts, 3 wins, $4,667. Sent to India 1927.

1925: **FRANKLY**, ch f, by Franklin. Raced 2 yrs in Eng, 13 sts, 1 win, $4,818. Won Warwickshire Breeders' Foal Plate S. Dam of 4 foals, 1 rnr, 1 wnr, **OPEN WARFARE**. Granddam of **SUMMERTIME, BATTENED DOWN, ALEXANDER, MULBERRY HARBOUR, Moneria, Syndey Street**.

1926: Not bred.

1927: **BLENHEIM II**, br c, by Blandford. Bred by Lord Carnarvon (Eng). Raced 2 yrs in Eng, 10 sts, 5 wins, $73,309. Won Derby S, Hopeful S, New S; 2nd Challenge S, Middle Park S, Sandown Park Stud Produce S. Sent to USA 1937. Sire of 536 foals, 61 sw, 2.49 AEI. Died 1958.

1928: Foal died.

1929: Barren.

1930: **KING SALMON**, b c, by Salmon-Trout. Raced 3 yrs in Eng, 19 sts, 4 wins, $73,823. Won Eclipse S, Coronation S, Great Yorkshire S, Sandown Park Stud Produce S; 2nd Gordon S, Epsom Derby, Newmarket S, Two Thousand Guineas; 3rd July S. Sire.

1931: Lily of the Valley, b f, by Tetratema. Raced 1 yr in Eng, 5 sts, 1 win, $712. Dam of 10 foals, 3 rnrs, 2 wnrs, including **FLEUR DE LYS**. Granddam of **PROSPER, UBI, Magic Fair**. Sent to USA 1941.

1933: **HIS GRACE**, b c, by Blandford. Raced 2 yrs in Eng, 25 sts, 6 wins, $41,361. Won Royal Standard S, Coronation Cup, Duke of Cambridge H, Lowther S; 2nd Eclipse S, Hardwicke S; 3rd Newmarket S, Jockey Club S, Atlantic S. Sire.

1934: Barren.

1935: Blue Lotus, b/br f, by Cameronian. Raced 1 yr in Eng, 3 sts, 0 wins, $0. Dam of 8 foals, 8 rnrs, 4 wnrs.

1936: B c, by Trimdon.

1937: Rufigi, b c, by Easton. Raced 3 yrs, 11 sts, 1 win, $1,750. Sire.

1938: Barren.

1939: Slipped foal.

1940: Good Cheer, b c, by Felicitation. Raced 2 yrs in Eng, 9 sts, 1 win, $613. Sent to Brz 1943.

(Dick) Dawson told him that he and his brother, Sam, had purchased a Swynford colt bred by the National Stud. The colt was entered for the Newmarket December sale. Dawson suggested to Porchester that the colt would not sell for a very high price. Abe Hewitt, in *Sire Lines*, claimed that the colt had some apparent faults: (1) He had been harassed by work horses that broke into his paddock and nearly killed him; (2) He had straight and short pasterns.

Carnarvon told Dick Dawson to go up to 2,000 guineas for the colt, and Dawson averred that far less would buy him. When the bidding lagged, as expected, Dawson assumed he was buying the colt on behalf of his friend, Porchester. Brother Sam Dawson, however, cajoled, or coerced, his sibling into taking the position that he was buying back the colt for the pair rather than let him go for less than 1,000 guineas. Carnarvon's first set of memoirs could not be accused of understating the importance of this turn of events: "My whole life would have taken on a completely different hue had this tragedy not occurred."

(The records indicate that Dawson had not owned the colt prior to the auction, so Carnarvon's account might have a bit of extra spice for flavor.)

Whether Hewitt's description of poor conformation identified the inevitable or not, Blandford bowed in both front legs after his second race at three and was retired with three wins in four starts. He had not been made eligible for the Epsom Derby by the National Stud, which bred him, but he did win the Princess of Wales's Stakes at one and a half miles in July of 1922.

The Dawsons sent Blandford to their Cloghran Stud, and he led the English sire list three times and sired four Epsom Derby winners within seven years, including the 1935 English Triple Crown winner, Bahram. Moreover, he sired Brantome, who won the French Two Thousand Guineas as well as the French St. Leger and Prix de l'Arc de Triomphe.

Trainer Dawson had recorded a trial in which he had Blandford as a two-year-old in June of 1921 give twenty-three pounds to a filly named Malva. A daughter of Charles O'Malley, Malva was a nice winner at three, and Lord Carnarvon regarded her as his best young broodmare prospect in the middle 1920s. At that time, he was struggling to work out a plan to enable him to maintain Highclere, which had been left to him by his father's death not many months after the discovery of the King Tut tomb. (It was not always easy in the face of estate duties, but he succeeded in saving his beloved home.)

Carnarvon ponied up the 148 guineas to breed Malva to Blandford, whom he had tried to buy. The resulting foal, a colt born in 1927, was named Blenheim II after the home of the Dukes of Marlborough, where Sir Winston Churchill happened to be born, and the site of some Carnarvon weekend revelries. (The colt was known in England as Blenheim. He became Blenheim II in this country because there already was another Blandford colt named Blenheim over here. This was a 1928 foal from Flying Squadron, who had been imported *in utero*.) Carnarvon concluded that it would be wise to sell the Blandford—Malva colt, and in the Newmarket July sale, the colt was purchased for 4,100 guineas for the account of the Aga Khan.

The Aga Khan of Blenheim II's day was the grandfather of the present Aga Khan. The family's tradition in racing was somewhat ordained by the "old" Aga's education about the Turf from childhood. Religious leader of millions of Ismaili Muslims, the Aga in 1952 published a recollection in which he reminisced that, late in the 19th Century, "...I remember as a child our whole family was almost in mourning and despair at the death of the great jockey Fred Archer. Names such as Ormonde and St. Simon were household words in our family."

Some years later, in 1921, His Highness wrote, a pivotal event took place. He was dining in a house in London, and was seated next to a sister-in-law of the great trainer George Lambton. This personage, a Mrs. Asquith, suggested that the Aga, then in his forties, get in touch with her sister's husband and pursue the idea of starting his own stable:

"It was like a trigger being drawn on a cannon. What was pent up from childhood, and would never have come out, suddenly became an irresistible mental storm." The Aga Khan thus launched into one of the most successful of all racing and breeding operations. By the time of his death in 1957, he had raced five winners of the English Derby, matching the record of Lord Egremont.[1] Of his Derby winners, Blenheim II and his son Mahmoud both were destined to become leading sires in the United States. (Insofar as the Aga's influence on America, his having bred Nasrullah, Khaled, Alibhai, and Gallant Man perhaps surpassed the importance even of his Derby winners.)

The Aga Khan's son, Prince Aly Khan, was a serious horseman and insightful internationalist. His reputation as a playboy, however, presumably was what prompted His Highness to skip over him and name a grandson as his successor. Thus, the present Aga Khan was anointed as a young man. This Aga rallied to the challenge of maintaining the farflung French and Irish breeding and racing operations, and has turned out a dizzying succession of classic winners whose influence has been important in international breeding. The Aga Khan, for example, is the breeder of the 1999 American Turf champion Daylami, and he purchased, raced, and exported Blushing Groom, one of the most important international stallions of the 1980s and 1990s.

At two in 1929, Blenheim II won four of seven starts. He had come along quickly enough to have three races before the Royal Ascot meeting, at which he triumphed in the New Stakes, then an important event. He was rested until September, after which he added a win in the Hopeful Stakes and experienced narrow defeats in the Champagne and Middle Park Stakes. He was weighted three pounds below the best on the Free Handicap, which was led by Diolite, Press Gang, and Challenger II (also destined to lead the American sire list).

Blenheim II

The following spring, Dawson brought out Blenheim II for the Greenham Plate, in which the horse was prominent for a bit and then fell back. Next was the Two Thousand Guineas, in which he finished fourth. The Aga Khan's stable rider, Michael Beary, preferred Rustom Pasha, and the Aga agreed that this was his best Derby hope.

With Harry Wragg aboard, however, it was the 18-1 Blenheim II who came with a strong run to master Iliad and Diolite and win by a length. *The Bloodstock Breeders' Review* of 1930 recounted how the Epsom crowd gave "a striking demonstration of enthusiasm when the Aga Khan, hat in hand, and laughing like a happy school boy, led the colt through a lane of humanity to the unsaddling enclosure, when he was presently summoned to the presence of the King and Queen."

Lord Carnarvon wrote of standing with the Aga during the running: "They were 150 yards from home when Wragg shot Blenheim into the lead, and with my heart thumping with excitement, I cheered Blenheim home. But the Aga, who was very short-sighted, could only see his colors in the lead and started yelling at the top of his voice, 'Rustom wins. Rustom wins.' 'No, he doesn't, you bloody fool. Blenheim wins.' "

Carnarvon took the moment of high glee to ask whether, as breeder of this fine colt, he might qualify for an annual season gratis. The Aga Khan stated firmly that the breeder could pay the same price as anyone else. It had been worth a try, and, after all, "the spirit of the occasion brooked no sense of hurt. I was thrilled and wildly excited at having had the luck to breed a Derby winner, even if I no longer owned him."

The Derby proved to be the last start for Blenheim II, who injured himself while training for the Eclipse Stakes and never recovered completely. He was sent to France to enter stud with a record of five wins in ten starts and earnings equating to about $71,000. He got three stakes winners in his first crop, including the top-ranked French two-year-old of 1934, Pampeiro. In the second crop came the Aga Khan's spectacular Derby winner Mahmoud, as well as Wyndham (sire of the successful American-based stallion Windy City II, who got Blue Norther, Restless Wind, Old Pueblo, etc.). In his third crop, Blenheim II sired Donatello II for the noted Italian horseman Federico Tesio. Donatello II lost only once, in the Grand Prix de Paris, and he sired the great stayer Alycidon, who proved a rare phenomenon in modern times by being a stellar Cup horse who also became the leading sire of flat runners. Another important son of Donatello II was the Guineas and Derby winner Crepello.

Less noted at the time was the arrival of a Blenheim II filly named Mumtaz Begum, who would gain lasting fame as the dam of Nasrullah and the second dam of Royal Charger.

As early as 1933, negotiations with the Aga Khan for the sale of Blenheim II had been ongoing. Marion du Pont, who had become enamored of Thoroughbreds when she saw Fair Play sold as an aged stallion [refer to Star Shoot chapter], was at the time married to the American movie actor Randolph Scott. Mrs. Scott and her brother, William du Pont Jr., considered putting together a syndicate to buy Blenheim II, but the deal was not completed.

In 1936, Arthur B. Hancock Sr. of Claiborne Farm came into the picture. During the months of negotiations through an agent, the sons and daughters of the horse were raising his stock. Blue Bear won the French One Thousand Guineas that spring and then when Mahmoud set a record in winning the Derby, the price rose to $250,000. The Aga Khan's announcement that Blenheim II had been sold generated some criticism in the press. Not only were Europeans chagrined any time they lost such a distinguished animal, but mare owners who had booked to the horse for 1937 and 1938 felt ill-treated. The Aga Khan's response which appeared in the *Daily Telegraph* emphasized that the contracts to breed to the horse always had stipulated that they were valid only so long as he continued to own Blenheim II, and he appended that "...no one is a greater or more loyal supporter of British blood-stock and racing, and all that it means."

Blenheim II arrived at Claiborne Farm, where he stood for the rest of his life. Hancock was the head of the syndicate, although the owner with the greatest percentage was Warren Wright Sr., owner of Calumet Farm. Wright took one-quarter of the horse, and one-eighth each was acquired by Hancock, Mrs. Scott, du Pont, John Hay Whitney, John D. Hertz, and Robert Fairbairn.

Suitably, Wright and Calumet got the first great dividend. In his first season in Kentucky, Blenheim II's mates included the Sweep mare Dustwhirl, who the following spring foaled Whirlaway. A classy little colt with a long tail and a penchant for running wide on the turns, Whirlaway was coerced into being a professional racehorse in time to sweep the Triple Crown in 1941. Blenheim II led the American sire list that year. Whirlaway repeated as Horse of the Year as a handicapper in 1942. The horse revered as "Mr. Longtail" was greeted by adoring citizenry of Lexington, Kentucky, when he returned triumphantly to stud at Calumet as the greatest money earner of all time. He had won thirty-two of sixty races and earned $561,161. He was the first horse to earn a half-million dollars, and in the next decade Calumet's Citation would be the first to earn a full million. Whirlaway was later leased to Marcel Boussac and spent the last years of his

Blenheim II

life in France. He was not an outstanding stallion, but did get the Coaching Club American Oaks winner Scattered and the important producer Rock Drill among eighteen stakes winners.

If we take into account his record in both Europe and America, Blenheim II sired sixty-one stakes winners (eleven percent). Jet Pilot in 1947 became his second Kentucky Derby winner, following Whirlaway, to add to his Epsom Derby winner Mahmoud. Others among Blenheim II's best included the high-class Calumet fillies A Gleam and Mar-Kell, along with Free America, Bryan G. (sire of Cicada), Battle Morn, Risque Rouge, Fervent, and Thumbs Up. Mrs. Scott received a major dividend late in Blenheim II's days. In 1951, when he was twenty-four, Blenheim II sired a colt which Mrs. Scott gave the responsibility of taking the name Saratoga to the races. Foaled in 1952, the sleek Saratoga stood the burden nobly, winning a half-dozen stakes and testing Nashua in both the Flamingo and Preakness of 1955.

In addition to Mumtaz Begum, daughters which lent distinction to Blenheim II as a broodmare sire included Easy Lass, dam of Calumet champion Coaltown. Blenheim II mares produced a total of more than 120 stakes winners.

Blenheim II died at Claiborne at the age of thirty-one in 1958.

Mahmoud

The author has seen few old race films as startlingly impressive as that of Mahmoud's Epsom Derby. The view of the early stretch run seems to show a gray projectile bursting toward the leaders in a manner that is very much like the corresponding view of Whirlaway's Kentucky Derby rally. Even knowing that several furlongs still face the field from that point at Epsom, those close at hand as that 1936 Epsom classic unfolded before them must have sensed that the race was all over at that stage.

Nevertheless, Mahmoud apparently was not viewed as a particularly outstanding Derby winner nor his crop an outstanding one. He was bred in France by the Aga Khan and sent to English trainer Frank Butters after he failed to meet his reserve at the Deauville yearling sale. Like his sire Blenheim II, Mahmoud ran ten times in two seasons. He won four races and earned the equivalent of about $74,000. Mahmoud would have had eleven starts but for the circumstance of his supposed debut, when thirteen of the sixteen riders raced off and completed the course, only to find it had been a false start. Most of the trainers declined to send their animals out again, so the sixteen-horse field was reduced to four.

Mahmoud had a tendency to get away slowly, but he did win three of five starts at two, including the Richmond and Champagne Stakes. He was ranked one pound behind the Aga's Bala Hissar among English-raced two-year-olds of 1935.

At three, Mahmoud was fifth in his first start, then lost by only a short head to Pay Up in an excellent performance in the Two Thousand Guineas. Next came his showcase performance in the Derby. He was ridden at Epsom by Charlie Smirke, who was far from trainer Butters' favorite character. In fact, author Hewitt recalled that Butters had told him he only put Smirke on the colt because he felt Mahmoud was inferior to the Aga Khan's Taj Akbar over the one and a half miles. Butters put the great Sir Gordon Richards on the supposed better colt, but Charlie got the last smirk.

Mahmoud won his Derby by three lengths over the rallying, but non-threatening Taj Akbar, and his time of 2:33 4/5 over exceptionally hard going bettered by one-fifth of a second the previous Derby record set by Hyperion. Mahmoud's record, though matched, was not lowered at Epsom for a long time, or until Lammtarra won the Derby in 2:32 1/5 in 1995. (Several wartime Derbys were run faster, but the race was held then at Newmarket.)

Mahmoud was upset in his next race, the St. James's Palace at Royal Ascot, then finished third in the St. Leger after having had a slight setback in training with a heel sore. He was then retired to stud.

Although Nasrullah was by Nearco, he and Mahmoud had much in common in their pedigrees. The flying filly Mumtaz Mahal was the second dam of each: Mahmoud was by Blenheim II and out of Mah Mahal, while Nasrullah's dam, Mumtaz Begum, was by Blenheim II and out of Mumtaz Mahal.

In his four seasons at stud in Ireland, Mahmoud's statistics were not exceptional, but he did get two fine fillies. One was the Irish Guineas and Irish Oaks winner Majideh (later the dam of Gallant Man and Masaka), and the other was Donatella III, the top two-year-old filly of her year (1941) in Italy (and eventually the dam of eight stakes winners).

In 1940, Mahmoud followed his sire to Kentucky. Again, this occasioned shock and dismay on the part of English and Europeans. Not only did the Aga Khan send Mahmoud away, but in that same year he disposed of his 1935 English Triple Crown winner, Bahram, also sold to the United States. Mahmoud was purchased for a reported $85,000 by C. V. Whitney and sent to his farm outside Lexington.

If the human heritage tracking the horse and his sire had been marked by a Lord here and an Imam there, Mahmoud found himself delivered unto no less an exalted master. Cornelius Vanderbilt Whitney, like Mahmoud himself, was the son and grandson of noteworthy males. His grandfather, William Collins Whitney, had created the family connection to racing and among his good works was helping renovate Saratoga. The next generation was Harry Payne Whitney, among the most successful breeders in history.

C. V. Whitney's first big day as an owner was well-chronicled, and would be brought up in virtually every profile ever written about him in the sporting press over sixty-plus years. He was the young, and perhaps bewildered, owner of Equipoise, who won an epic battle with Twenty Grand in the 1930 Pimlico Futurity not many days after Harry Payne Whitney's death. Here was young Whitney rooting home a new star against his Aunt Helen's Twenty Grand. (The latter raced for the Greentree Stud, begun by Harry Payne Whitney's brother, Payne Whitney, and his wife, Helen Hay; yes, they liked the name of Payne in that family.) C. V. Whitney's mother was a great-great-granddaughter of another tycoon, Commodore Cornelius Vanderbilt.

C. V. Whitney led the nation's owners annually through 1934, but, for the most part, this involved horses already designed by his father. The young owner was exceptionally busy in other pursuits and ambitions. During World War I, he had been, at eighteen, one of the Army's youngest flight instructors, and by the time of the next war he had become a founder, and chairman, of Pan American Airways. He and a cousin, John Hay Whitney, also backed David O. Selznick's color motion pictures, including *Gone With The Wind*.

Whitney also took a run at public office, making an unsuccessful bid for Congress as a Democrat from a New York district. Later, he was a decorated Colonel in World War II and wrote the operation of the raid on Ploesti. He got some experience in political service, after all, in appointed

Blenheim II

positions as Assistant Secretary of the Air Force and Undersecretary of Commerce for President Truman as well as serving in diplomatic postings to England, Spain, Luxembourg, and Italy.

It was no surprise then, when in 1937, Whitney sold his racing stable. "He was never seen on a racecourse before his father's death," sniffed *The Bloodstock Breeders' Review* of 1937, "and stud books and pedigree charts were as Sanskrit to him." (This apparently was not quite true. Whitney years later enjoyed telling of deputizing for his father when Whiskery won the 1927 Kentucky Derby, then later that evening back at the Lexington farm encountering a group of grooms who had brought the queenly Derby winner Regret out to serenade her in front of a bonfire.) Whether the rumors that Whitney tried and was unable to come to a deal to sell his Kentucky farm and bloodstock were accurate or not, the happy conclusion was that the treasure of Whitney mares was not lost to the family. Two years later, there he was with a change of heart, and after the purchase and importation of Mahmoud it is doubtful that his devotion to the game came under much question.

Until he dispersed about eight years before his death in 1992, Whitney was the epitome of the racing sportsman born of his era. He bred a total of 176 stakes winners, most of which he raced. They included Counterpoint, First Flight, Silver Spoon, Fisherman, Career Boy, and Silver Buck. Tall and erect, Whitney could certainly give Lord Carnarvon a run insofar as making the mundane act of smoking appear something of a fashion/personality statement. Whitney, called incongruously "Uncle Sonny" by some of his family, had a way of holding his cigarette between two fingers, palm turned slightly outward and upward, while he spoke in a pleasing, personalized, Eastern-cum-English accent. His widow, Marylou, long ago mastered the feminine version of similarly confident demeanor — although of late with a vocal distaste for smoking — and, as the breeder of Catinca, has shown in recent years more than a little of the family pedigree destiny as well. (As do most of Mrs. Whitney's horses, Catinca traces to a grand Whitney family, in this case the family of Silver Spoon.)

Mahmoud and Bahram were the sixteenth and seventeenth Epsom Derby winners to that time who had set out for North America, and, it being wartime, Mahmoud almost joined the two others among them who did not make it. Mrs. Whitney recounted for *The Blood-Horse* the version her husband had told her: "Sonny tells the story that when they were bringing Mahmoud over, they got ready to sail from England and had 40 documents. But the ship's captain said, 'I can't take that horse; you don't have the proper papers.' So, they put him in some sort of shed and the boat left without him. Then it was torpedoed!"

Mahmoud came over safely on another vessel. His first American-sired foals came to the races in 1944, and he quickly began multiplying his total of stakes winners left abroad. Hewitt in *Sire Lines* went so far as to say that "Mahmoud was a very good sire for the American racing program, with its fast, dirt tracks and emphasis on short to middle-distance racing. He was at best an indifferent sire for Europe, where racing is on the turf, and the emphasis is on (longer) racing."

Like many generalizations, this one might be picked apart by examples, such as The Axe II, who raced briefly abroad and then at home specialized in the longer, grass races such as he would have faced if he remained abroad in maturity. One of the more precocious of the Mahmouds was

Whitney's First Flight, who whipped other two-year-old fillies in three important stakes and then took on colts in the Futurity. The ancestral Mumtaz Mahal would clearly have been proud of the Whitney filly's victory over I Will and the future Kentucky Derby winner Jet Pilot, and First Flight was voted champion of her age and sex for 1946. She also helped Mahmoud lead the sire list that year. First Flight stretched out well enough to win the Monmouth Oaks at three, then reverted to terroristic sprinting to defeat males in the Fall Highweight Handicap at four.

Mahmoud sired seventy stakes winners here and abroad, for an excellent mark of seventeen percent. Others among his best included the co-champion two-year-old colt Oil Capitol, plus Adile, Alabama, Billings, Cohoes, Eurasia, Mameluke, Mount Marcy, Mr. Trouble, General Staff, Idolater, Jeep, Polamia, Magic Forest, Maharajah, Olympic Zenith, Recce, Snow Goose, Vulcan's Forge, and Yildiz. Mahmoud lived to the age of twenty-nine.

Hewitt's idea of Mahmoud's suitability to this country was certainly given credibility by the sire's total of sixty-three sons and daughters being ranked on the Experimental Free Handicap for two-year-olds. Still, there were some among Mahmoud's get that demonstrated considerable stamina. His son Mr. Trouble finished third in the Kentucky Derby and then sired the dam of Epsom Derby winner Sir Ivor. The Greentree-bred Mahmoud colt Cohoes capped his career by winning the Brooklyn Handicap, and his five stakes victories also included the Grand Union Hotel, the Sysonby, and Whitney. Cohoes was not an outstanding sire statistically, but he got the gifted Quadrangle, winner of the Belmont Stakes, Travers Stakes, and Lawrence Realization, among

others, for Paul Mellon's Rokeby Stable. Cohoes also sired the remarkable producer Miss Swapsco.

The Axe II, the Mahmoud colt which Greentree initially raced abroad, was from the La Troienne family, as was Cohoes. The Axe II had a campaign at five in 1963 that might have netted a grass course championship but for Mongo's sensational win over Kelso in the Washington, D.C., International. The Axe II placed second in voting, having won grass stakes from West to East and throughout the year — the Arcadia, San Luis Rey, Lindheimer, Man o' War, and Canadian Championship. The Axe II had a modicum of success in prolonging the Blenheim II/Mahmoud tale as a male line subject. His good stakes-winning sons included Al Hattab and Hatchet Man. Al Hattab got forty-four stakes winners and became the broodmare sire of 1994 Horse of the Year Holy Bull and 1991 Horse of the Year Black Tie Affair.

The quality of his daughters would inevitably slant the lingering legacy of Mahmoud toward the distaff side. The graceful scenes of Kentucky pastures through the 1950s tended to be stamped with the name of the jovial photographer "Skeets" Meadors and often had a sprinkling of gray mares. It was easy to fall into the presumption that any such mare bore testimony to the influence of Mahmoud. Not all the Mahmoud mares, of course, were gray. One that was not was the chestnut Almahmoud — revered as the second dam of Halo and Northern Dancer! One particularly notable Mahmoud daughter that was gray was named Grey Flight — revered as one of the few mares to produce nine stakes winners!

Even the Derby-winning son of a Derby winner could hardly ask for a better legacy than to be remembered as the sire of Almahmoud and Grey Flight. ❖

THE GREAT
MELTING POT

Hyperion

yperion had a richly jeweled pedigree, but he was a smallish colt, so little as a yearling that a special feed trough had to be provided. His breeder, the 17th Lord Derby, was said to be so discouraged at the colt's failure to grow into something more prepossessing that he considered gelding him. Hyperion was long-bodied and short-legged, and author Abe Hewitt dared state what photos suggested, that, at least at two, he was a bit ewe-necked.

This seemingly imperfect combination, however, was invested of power and elegance. There was also that inward ingredient that in horses corresponds to the differences which, to name one human endeavor, place one individual in the Royal Academy and another doodling on the corner. In another era, a great-grandson named Northern Dancer would make short-and-stout the uniform of the day. Likewise, Hyperion's size would denote power and a sturdy constitution. He was a good two-year-old, a classic winner, an adequate stayer, and he was to lead the English sire list six times and launch a veritable United Nations project of sons and daughters across the globe.

As can be the case with a great horse, the supposed deviation from perfection was subsumed by a satisfying whole. Adrian Scrope, who for years was in daily attendance of Hyperion as manager of Lord Derby's studs, said of the stallion: "His length of quarter and the perfect conformation of his hind legs were amongst his most notable attributes; but it was in his head and expression that his unique personality was apparent, and it was this reflection of character that eluded all the artists who painted him."

Author and horseman Abram S. Hewitt conjectured in his book *Sire Lines* that the acquisition of Hyperion's third dam, Gondolette, for the Derby stud in 1912 was made with a view of providing a vehicle for inbreeding to the mare Pilgrimage, winner of the One Thousand and Two Thousand Guineas. The Derby stud was in the hands of the 17th Earl of Derby, whose father had purchased property formerly owned by the Duchess of Montrose. This ended a twenty-five-year hiatus from the Turf [1] of a family whose distant ancestor had lent his name to the greatest of English races, the Epsom Derby. Pilgrimage was the dam of Derby winner Jeddah and Oaks winner Canterbury Pilgrim, and the latter had endeared herself to the Derby program by producing its outstanding stallions Swynford and Chaucer. Pilgrimage also had foaled Loved One, sire of Gondolette.

Gondolette's link to Hyperion was the foal she was carrying at the time, a filly by the sire Minoru, who apparently was never patronized by

Lord Derby. This filly was named Serenissima, who managed three wins amid the limited opportunities of World War I racing.

With Serenissima, inbreeding to Pilgrimage was accomplished through her mating with Chaucer, son of the great St. Simon and grandson of the targeted mare. The Chaucer—Serenissima foal in question here was Selene. Chaucer was a smallish sort, and Selene was tiny, so much so that she was not kept eligible for the classics. Selene, however, belied the thought that her size would stop her, for she won eight of eleven races at two and was rated England's best of her age and gender. The next year, she again won eight of eleven races, including the Park Hill Stakes over one and three-quarters miles.

Selene became one of the great mares of the century. She produced Hyperion as well as the Phalaris colts Sickle and Pharamond II, both of which were destined to be important stallions in the United States. From Sickle's male line descended Native Dancer, and all that was to follow in the brigade of Raise a Native, Mr. Prospector, Exclusive Native, Affirmed, Alydar, Sea-Bird, Sharpen Up, Diesis, and others.

From Pharamond II's male line came Menow, Tom Fool, Buckpasser, Silver Charm, and their own attendant glories. Selene also foaled the important South American sire Hunter's Moon. Her daughters included All Moonshine, dam of the successful Nearco stallion Mossborough.

Hyperion was another pearl in the brood of Selene. The little chestnut, with four white socks, was sired by Gainsborough, an English Triple Crown winner and successful sire. Gainsborough, in turn, was by Bayardo, a brilliant racehorse who also sired another Triple Crown winner, Gay Crusader. (Even taking into account the disruption of English racing during the wartime days of Gay Crusader and Gainsborough, for a stallion to sire Triple Crown winners in successive crops created an exceptional standard.)

While inbreeding proponents nod knowingly about all this, those who reckon that several generations of quality also might have something to do with success, regardless of in- or out-breeding, could also raise their hands for attention. Hyperion, indeed, was by Sustained Class out of Brilliance.

The erstwhile runtish scalpel candidate was recognized by trainer George Lambton as the muscular sort of two-year-old that would need heavy training. Hyperion made his first start in May, and he won three of his five races as a juvenile of 1932. Initially, he was fourth in a field of nineteen, then won the New Stakes in record time, dead-heated for a win in the Prince of Wales's Stakes (at Goodwood), was third against good company in the Boscawen Stakes, and concluded with a victory in the Dewhurst. His form was not given particular flattery by the Free Handicap, which was topped by the filly Manitoba (the Boscawen winner) at 127 pounds to his 126.

At three, however, Hyperion became one of the bellwethers of the great brigade of horses in the black silks and white cap of Lord Derby. Hyperion was still only 15 hands, 1 1/2 inches, but he proved to be a powerful force with which to reckon. He won each of his four races: the Chester Vase, Epsom Derby, Prince of Wales's Stakes (Ascot), and St. Leger. In the beloved Derby, he set a record of 2:34, scoring easily by four lengths. His next two races were run at one and five-eighths miles and one and three-quarters miles, so he embodied that wonderful, but rare, combination of high-class winning speed at two and classic endurance at three.

George Lambton had been associated with Lord Derby for nearly forty years, but in the winter of

		Bay Ronald, 1893	Hampton Black Duchess
	Bayardo, 1906		
GAINSBOROUGH, b, 1915		Galicia, 1898	**Galopin** Isoletta
		St. Frusquin, 1893	**St. Simon** Isabel
	Rosedrop, 1907		
HYPERION, ch h, April 18, 1930		Rosaline, 1901	Trenton Rosalys
		St. Simon, 1881	**Galopin** St. Angela
	Chaucer, 1900		
SELENE, b, 1919		Canterbury Pilgrim, 1893	Tristan Pilgrimage
		Minoru, 1906	Cyllene Mother Siegel
	Serenissima, 1913		
		Gondolette, 1902	Loved One Dongola

1st dam: SELENE, b, 1919-1942. Bred by Lord Derby (Eng). Raced 2 yrs in Eng, 22 sts, 16 wins, $71,299. Won Nassau S, Houghton S, Park Hill S, Cheveley Park S, Rous Memorial S, Hardwicke S, Knowsley Dinner S, Eglinton S, Liverpool Autumn Cup. Dam of 14 named foals, 12 rnrs, 10 wnrs, 6 sw.

1924: SICKLE, br c, by Phalaris. Raced 2 yrs in Eng, 10 sts, 3 wins, $19,986. Won Prince of Wales's S, Mersey S; 2nd New S, July S, Middle Park S; 3rd Champagne S, Two Thousand Guineas. Sent to USA 1929. Sire of 297 foals, 43 sw, 2.25 AEI.

1925: PHARAMOND II, br c, by Phalaris. Raced 2 yrs in Eng, 11 sts, 1 win, $19,198. Won Middle Park S; 2nd Lancashire Breeders' Produce S; 3rd Windsor Castle S. Sent to USA 1928. Sire of 399 foals, 35 sw, 1.86 AEI.

1926: HUNTER'S MOON, b c, by Hurry On. Raced 2 yrs in Eng, 8 sts, 3 wins, $24,522. Won Newmarket S, Gratwicke Produce S; 3rd Prince of Wales's S. Sire in Arg.

1927: Salamis, b c, by Phalaris. Raced 1 yr in Eng, 5 sts, 0 wins, $48.

1928: GUISCARD, b g, by Gay Crusader. Raced 5 yrs in Eng, 35 sts, 9 wins, $18,921. Won Queen's Prize; 2nd Chester Cup S (twice); 3rd Goodwood H, Churchill S.

1929: Barren.

1930: HYPERION, ch c, by Gainsborough. Bred by Lord Derby (Eng). Raced 3 yrs in Eng, 13 sts, 9 wins, $124,073. Champion 3yo colt in Eng. Won Epsom Derby, Chester Vase, St. Leger, Prince of Wales' (twice), Dewhurst S, New S, March S; 2nd Dullingham S; 3rd Ascot Gold Cup, Boscawen Post S. Sire in Eng of 497 foals, 109 sw, 2.25 AEI.

1931: Foal died.

1932: Coronal, ch f, by Coronach. Raced 2 yrs in Eng, 11 sts, 1 win, $3,676. 3rd Falmouth S, Coronation S, Lingfield Autumn Oaks. Granddam of **LADY MIDGE**, **Beyond the Moss**, **The Champ**.

1933: Barren.

1934: Hecate, b f, by Felstead. Unraced. Dam of 5 foals, 2 rnrs, 2 wnrs, including **DOWNRUSH**.

1935: Foal died.

1936: NIGHT SHIFT, b f, by Trimdon. Raced 1 yr in Eng, 3 sts, 1 win, $5,256. Won Yorkshire Oaks.

1937: Moon Priestess, b f, by Dastur. Raced 2 yrs in Eng, 6 sts, 0 wins, $0. Dam of 7 foals, 5 rnrs, 1 wnr, **Sabaean** (in Eng).

1938: Moonlight Run, ch c, by Bobsleigh. Raced 2 yrs in Eng, 6 sts, 1 win, $932. Sire of 108 foals, 3 sw, 0.77 AEI.

1939: Barren.

1940: New Moon, ch f, by Solfo. Unraced. Dam of 9 foals, 8 rnrs, 8 wnrs, including **HERVINE**, **NEW MOVE**, **TURN A PENNY**, **Moon Game** (in Eng), **Moongate** (in Eng). Granddam of **PRINCE MOON**, **INITIAL**, **Treasure Island**, **New One**. Died 1959.

1941: All Moonshine, ch f, by Bobsleigh. Raced 2 yrs in Eng, 7 sts, 1 win, $1,271. Dam of 13 foals, 11 rnrs, 8 wnrs, including **EYEWASH** ($5,698), **MOSSBOROUGH**, **All My Eye** (in Eng). Granddam of **EPIDENDRUM**, **VARINIA**, **COLLYRIA**, **SIJUI**, **AMFISSA**, **Ken's Pago**, **Rising Dawn**, **Mythical II**, **Fiddlededee**, **Kamok**, **Orbit**.

1942: Shooting Star, b f, by Bold Archer. Raced 2 yrs in Eng, 12 sts, 1 win, $957.

1933-34, his Lordship concluded that the trainer's health was such that he should name a successor. Lambton disagreed and stomped out, although he later was said to have reconciled with Lord Derby while also proving his own point by living, and training, for another decade. Lord Derby did not exactly recede to the sidelines of the Turf, either. Colledge Leader was named the new trainer, and he had mixed results with Hyperion at four.

Hyperion won the March Stakes at ten furlongs, carrying 138 pounds and winning by a neck from Angelico (118) with the high-class Felicitation third. Next, he added the one and a half-mile Burwell Stakes by three-quarters of a length from King Salmon, with both under 136. This last race was not up to his regular brilliance, and perhaps his loss in heavy going in the two and a half-mile Ascot Gold Cup was predictable. Hyperion had handled Felicitation in the St. Leger the year before, but in the Gold Cup the other horse made the running in a way that severely tested all who chased, and Hyperion could not come to terms with him. Lord Derby colt's was beaten by nearly ten lengths and even lost second place to Thor II near the finish.

Great horses fire great emotions in the hearts of those who are represented by them, and feel responsible for them. Lord Derby and Leader shrank from the thought that Hyperion — glorious, brave little Hyperion — should go off to retirement with the tut-tut of defeat the last expression to follow him. Many years later, his descendant Nijinsky II engendered similar emotion in owner and trainer (Charles Engelhard and Vincent O'Brien) when he lost the Prix de l'Arc de Triomphe, which was to have sent him off to stud unbeaten. Both horses were given one more run, in that sweet human thought that they "deserved" to retire in triumph. Hyperion lost the Dullingham Stakes of 1934, just as Nijinsky II lost the Champion Stakes of 1970. Happily, neither's stud career was demonstrably inhibited by losing two races in succession, for they both became stallions of great importance and great longevity.

In Hyperion's final start, he faced only one horse, but he was carrying 142 pounds to the other runner's 113. The three-year-old Caithness, with wily jockey Harry Wragg playing a waiting game, had enough left that when Tommy Weston brought Hyperion alongside, the outsider shot back in front and won by a head.

Thus, Hyperion was retired to an honored place in the Derby stud with a record of nine wins in thirteen starts and earnings of $124,073.

The statistics of Hyperion's career at stud are lavish. He led the English/Irish sire list six times, topping the list in 1940, 1941, 1942, 1945, 1946, and 1954. (Modern stallion Sadler's Wells has surpassed Hyperion's feat, leading the English/Irish sire list nine times since 1990.) A lengthy research project conducted at *The Blood-Horse* in 1984 settled on his career numbers as 527 foals, 347 winners (sixty-six percent), and 118 stakes winners (twenty-two percent). This extraordinary number, and percentage, of stakes winners, indeed the entire study, embraced England, Ireland, Italy, France, North America, Brazil, South Africa, Argentina, Venezuela, Malaysia, India, Germany, and Belgium.

Hyperion lived until the age of thirty. The 17th Lord Derby died in 1948, and his son continued the stud although without the success of his forebear. Hyperion was spirited away to Yorkshire during non-breeding seasons during World War II since Newmarket was closer to presumed German air-raid targets. By and large, however, he stood his entire career at Lord Derby's Woodlands until being euthanized because of laminitis at his advanced age, in 1960.

Hyperion was of such a gentle nature that, while still under Leader's care, as recalled by his old friend, stud manager Adrian Scrope, the trainer chanced upon his young children in the horse's stall, playing

Hyperion

a great game of flinging his bedding back and forth across him while they ducked down in hiding on either side of the Derby winner. Hyperion was not annoyed and stood quietly for these highjinks, although Leader put an abrupt stop to the game and perhaps took some time settling his nerves over the imagined scene had Lord Derby sauntered past.

As would be expected, those connected to the horse had deep personal regard for him. The 18th Lord Derby once recalled from years before, "The first time I saw Hyperion was with my father and George Lambton when he was a yearling. I remember Lambton remarking that he was the most beautifully made little horse he had ever seen and would undoubtedly win the Pony Derby. It was, of course, said in jest, but it was quite obvious then that he was already getting a great affection for Hyperion."

Scrope recalled for David Hedges in a 1988 interview for *The Blood-Horse* that Hyperion as a stallion "was an angel to deal with, though he...refused to have his teeth dressed, and they were never attended to. We would have had to put him on the floor to do it, and it was too risky in those days." Scrope had often noticed Hyperion liked to look at airplanes and that he tended to cock his head when he looked up at them. He attributed to the artist John Skeaping the discovery from observing the horse's preserved skeleton that Hyperion had fractured a small bone in his head, possibly at birth, and that the cocking of his head was a result of being deaf in one ear."

Turf writers took him to their hearts, as well. John Hislop wrote in *The Observer* that the horse was somewhat eccentric and "would stop and stand still for half an hour or more, but George Lambton would never have him touched, allowing him to wait until he felt like moving on."

Hislop (afterward the breeder and owner of a grand horse of his own in Brigadier Gerard) once wrote that "Hyperion, besides being an individualist, was very fond of George Lambton. Before the (Ascot) Gold Cup, Hyperion caught sight of Lambton in his wheel chair — he had been seriously ill — at the entrance to the parade ring and the lad in charge had some difficulty in getting Hyperion to leave his old friend."

The Hyperions Come to America

Affection for a horse, of course, is augmented if he provides great moments for those in his wake. Certainly, many of the world's breeders and owners came to have reason to adore Hyperion, even though they might have dwelt thousands of miles from him and never knew any of his endearing individual qualities.

Looking at Hyperion's offspring from the standpoint of earnings at the racecourse, we find at the top with 36,225 pounds, the colt Aureole. As winner of the King George VI and Queen Elizabeth Stakes and runner-up in the Derby for the young Queen Elizabeth II, Aureole himself was well beloved among the English sporting public. Earlier, the Hyperion filly Sun Chariot had won the One Thousand Guineas, Oaks, and St. Leger for Her Majesty's father, during the strife of World War II. She was one of seven English classic winners by Hyperion, and the stallion also got the American classic winner Pensive, winner of the Kentucky Derby and Preakness Stakes for Calumet Farm in 1944. Pensive was the only star among the four Hyperions that won stakes in this country.

As the name identified with a sire line, Hyperion's influence in North America was significant and came through far more than a single son.

Commando

Foaled in 1898, Commando (above) was the best racing son of "the black whirlwind" Domino. Unfortunately, Commando died at the age of seven, but not before siring the unbeaten Colin (left). Modern descendant Broad Brush (below) was leading sire in 1994.

Star Shoot

Star Shoot (top) became the first stallion to lead the North American sire list five times during the 20th Century. On the racetrack, he was represented by Sir Barton (above), the first Triple Crown winner. Sweep (right), a son of Ben Brush, was a two-time leading sire in the early part of the 20th Century.

Fair Play

Fair Play (left), although best-known as the sire of the immortal Man o' War (below), was the first stallion in North America to sire six $100,000 earners, and he led the sire list three times. Man o' War sired numerous champions, but his best was 1937 Triple Crown winner War Admiral (bottom).

Fair Play

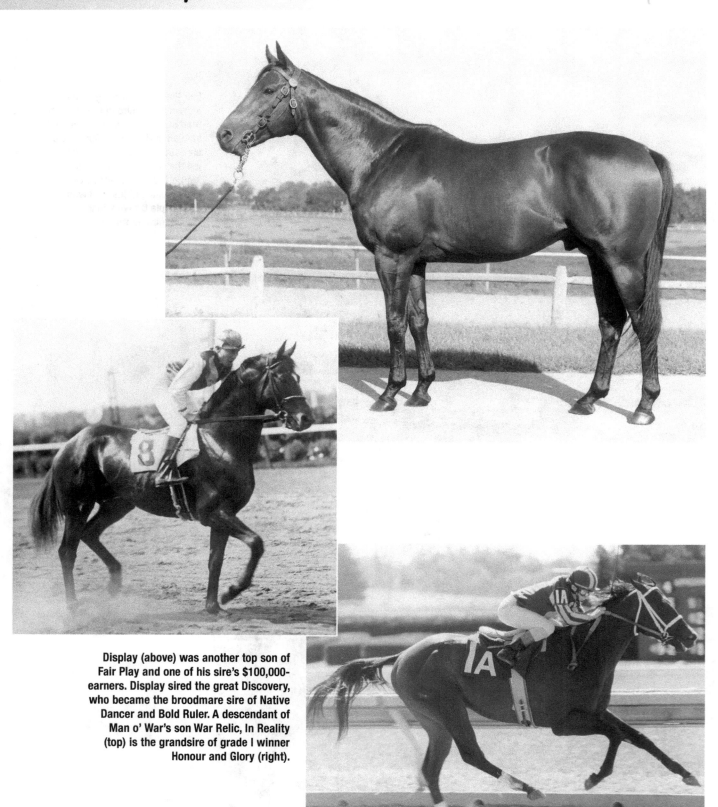

Display (above) was another top son of Fair Play and one of his sire's $100,000-earners. Display sired the great Discovery, who became the broodmare sire of Native Dancer and Bold Ruler. A descendant of Man o' War's son War Relic, In Reality (top) is the grandsire of grade I winner Honour and Glory (right).

Sir Gallahad III

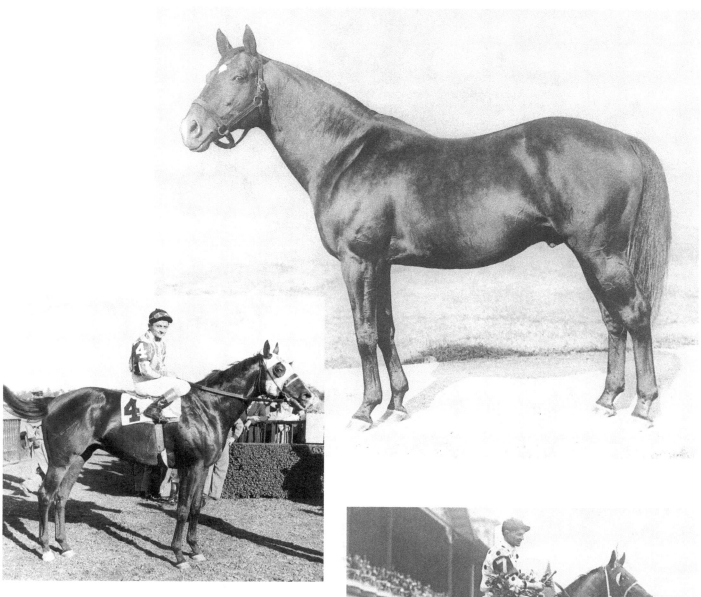

Sir Gallahad III (top) was imported by A. B. Hancock Sr. and other prominent horsemen to stand at Hancock's Claiborne Farm. Gallant Fox (right), a son of Sir Gallahad III, captured the 1930 Triple Crown, then later sired 1935 Triple Crown winner Omaha. Another son of Sir Gallahad III, Roman (above), was well-represented as a broodmare sire through his daughters, including the outstanding producer Pocahontas.

Challenger II

Challenger II (top) reigned as leading sire from Maryland when his son, Challedon (right), triumphed in the Preakness. Gallorette (above), a champion daughter of Challenger II, is the ancestress of Irish champion Minstrella and Canadian champion Charlie Barley.

Blenheim II

Blenheim II (top) won the Epsom Derby and later sired the English Derby winner Mahmoud (right). Both became influential stallions in the United States. A member of Blenheim's first American crop, Whirlaway (above) won the 1941 Triple Crown and was named Horse of the Year.

Hyperion

Hyperion (above) is considered one of England's greatest sires of the 20th Century and led the English sire list six times. Khaled (left), a son of Hyperion, became an important sire in California. His best-known offspring was Swaps, who won the 1955 Kentucky Derby. Arc de Triomphe winner Vaguely Noble (below) descends from Hyperion's son Aureole.

Heliopolis

From the first crop of Hyperion, foaled in 1936, Heliopolis was from the Swynford mare Drift, also dam of the One Thousand Guineas winner Tide-way. Heliopolis was inbred to the mare Canterbury Pilgrim. As Hewitt noted in *Sire Lines*, "This pattern of inbreeding to outstanding mares, rather than the usual inbreeding to stallions, occurred repeatedly in the pedigrees of Lord Derby's stud." Inbreeding to superior females has been preached and practiced since then by various others.

Heliopolis won once in four races at two, but earned his way briefly into the classic scene of 1939 by winning the Chester Vase. He was third behind Blue Peter in the Derby and thereafter was not tested against the best of his age, winning three stakes at one and a half miles later at three. He merely placed from three starts at four. Winner of five races in fourteen starts to earn $73,495, Heliopolis was not a horse Lord Derby needed for his own stud, but on pedigree and grade-II ability he was certainly a good prospect for someone else.

C. B. Shaffer, who had imported Bull Dog to his Coldstream Stud in Kentucky and bred Bull Lea by him, stepped in to purchase another overseas prospect. He bought Heliopolis for a reported $20,000, or one-fourth what he was said to have paid for Bull Dog.

Heliopolis led the American sire list in 1950 and again in 1954. He sired fifty-three stakes winners (fifteen percent), and there was plenty of class among them. They included the champion fillies Grecian Queen, Berlo, Parlo, and Aunt Jinny. (Parlo was an ancestress of Arts and Letters, and Aunt Jinny was a half-sister to Tom Fool). His other fillies included Princess Turia, Athene, Gay Grecque, and Imacomin.

The best of Heliopolis' sons included High Gun, who won the 1954 Belmont Stakes for King Ranch and was champion three-year-old that year and champion handicapper at four when he defeated Nashua in the Sysonby. Helioscope was almost of championship quality and had sterling wins over High Gun in the Suburban and Monmouth Handicaps, and another Heliopolis colt, Summer Tan, topped the 1954 Experimental Free Handicap over Nashua and was a superb campaigner at three and four. Others among Heliopolis' better sons included Ace Admiral, Globemaster, Greek Ship, Greek Song, and Olympia. Of this list, only Olympia truly excelled as a sire. Greek Song did get the Preakness winner Greek Money, Oil Royalty, and Waltz Song among eighteen stakes winners, and Summer Tan had some success, but Helioscope was a disappointment and High Gun was infertile.

Olympia had enough speed to win a Quarter Horse race and high-stakes bet for owner Fred Hooper, and he wheeled into Churchill Downs as favorite for the Kentucky Derby of 1949. He also wheeled for home in front at 4-5, but faded to sixth behind another grandson of Hyperion in Ponder, son of Pensive. Olympia served a long and distinguished career at stud, getting forty stakes winners (twelve percent). There were some good ones among them to be sure, and certainly his speed, leavened by the stamina of his background, seemed to make him a logical horse for this country. His get included the wonderful sprinter Decathlon, the Jersey Derby winner Creme dela Creme, plus Pia Star, Talent Show, Greek Game, Alhambra, My Portrait, the distaff champion Pucker Up, and the steeplechase champion Top Bid. These did not reproduce their own quality in the stud, however.

Hyperion

Khaled

Readers of *The Blood-Horse* first learned of a fellow named Rex Ellsworth when the Arizona native traveled to Lexington in a truck in 1933. The lanky Mormon cowboy was looking for some inexpensive stock to haul back West. At that point he would not have been seen as a sort who in later years would be dickering over horse deals — one at a time or in packages — with the office of the Aga Khan, nor winning the Kentucky Derby and Horse of the Year (with Swaps) and the Prix de l'Arc de Triomphe (Prince Royal II). Nevertheless, Ellsworth filled all these roles in subsequent years, abetted in many cases by his friend and trainer, Meshach Tenney. Sadly, Ellsworth was accused of neglect of horses at one stage years later, but his contributions to the Turf included leading the breeders' list in earnings in 1962 and 1963 and in races won in 1973-76, inclusive. In addition to Swaps, he bred or raced Olden Times, Candy Spots, and Terrang; as breeder of Bushel-n-Peck he is not so far removed from today's scene, inasmuch as that mare is the dam of the first Breeders' Cup Classic winner and current stallion, Wild Again.

Ellsworth and Tenney, with their lanky frames adorned in cowboy hats and bluejeans, seemed to enjoy their image as iconoclasts of the backstretch, although they dressed in suits and ties for afternoons in the clubhouse. Tenney slept in the barn with Swaps when they shipped to the Derby in 1955, and after Candy Spots won the 1963 Preakness, Tenney turned a hose on the colt to bathe him while casually talking to reporters. He also once posed seated in a Western saddle aboard the high-class stakes horse (and sire) Olden Times.

Ellsworth and Tenney made a point of demonstrating that, as ranchers first and Thoroughbred horsemen second, they treated horses as working stock. The author once saw Tenney flip the shank on Olden Times to put him into a correct pose for a conformation photo. Ellsworth arrived a few minutes later, and Tenney reported the photo had been accomplished. "How was he standing?" the owner asked, whereupon, Tenney flipped the shank again, briefly inspected his charge's stance, and said, "Like that." (Were these guys really that good, or simply confident that a small knot of reporters at Churchill Downs was not much schooled on posing cowponies?)

In Hyperion's son Khaled, Ellsworth acquired for his Chino, California, ranch perhaps the best stallion to have remained in California for lengthy service. Iconoclast or not, Ellsworth represented a combination of economics, personal agenda, image, and management style that contrived to keep a stallion in the state long after the horse had established himself in the upper echelons of popular success. No combination has arisen to dictate a similar stud career in the state since then.

If one chooses to see Ellsworth as a maverick, it follows in a sense that it was appropriate for his foil to be the Aga Khan. His Highness was a bit of a maverick in a way, too. According to *Sire Lines*, many Europeans breeders resented the pattern of the Aga Khan of the day (grandfather of the present Aga) selling off so much outstanding or potentially outstanding breeding stock. Lord Derby allegedly was so affronted by this traffic out of Europe, in fact, that he chose not to make his stallions available to the Aga Khan's mares. This policy denied Hyperion access to some of the best mares of the time, so only by purchasing Khaled's dam while she was carrying the foal did the Aga Khan become the breeder of record of one of Hyperion's distinguished sons.

The mare in question was Eclair, who had won

the Leicester Oaks and several other races and elicited some support as the best three-year-old filly in England in 1933. Eclair was by Ethnarch, a decent son of the great flyer and pedigree influence, The Tetrarch. Eclair's dam, Black Ray, eventually would become the fourth dam of the great horse and leading sire Mill Reef. Eclair was purchased by the Aga Khan at Newmarket in December of 1942.

She was in foal to Hyperion at the time and the following year produced the colt to be named Khaled. At two, Khaled was unbeaten in three races, the last of which was the Middle Park Stakes. Since the Middle Park has been one of the very best juvenile races for a very long time, it might seem likely that an unbeaten winner of the race would inhabit the upper marks of the Free Handicap for two-year-olds in England. Khaled, however, was rated no better than sixth on the handicap in a year in which the top colts had not been sent out against each other sufficiently to establish much confidence in their relative merits.

At three in 1947, Khaled won his first race, the Column Produce Stakes, but was heard to make the noise associated with being "gone in the wind." Nevertheless, he carried on. He was second to Happy Knight in the Two Thousand Guineas in his first defeat, then in the Derby he fell back to be unplaced after racing prominently for more than a mile. Dropped back to a mile, Khaled won the St. James's Palace Stakes, then was well beaten at one and a quarter miles in the Eclipse Stakes. Khaled thus had a record of five wins in eight races, for earnings of $29,725. That completed his racing days, or so it seemed.

Author Hewitt recalled meeting Ellsworth before the Westerner was to travel to England looking for a stallion prospect. When asked about the top prospects that might be available among youngish stallions in England or Ireland, Hewitt placed Khaled as second choice. His first was Nasrullah! Ellsworth by that time had become successful enough that a $100,000 price tag did not dissuade him, but anything far above that figure posed a problem. Khaled was priced at $160,000, so the intrepid cowboy used his $100,000 as a down payment and went home to arrange the remainder. Khaled stood a season in Ireland before being imported.

As straightforwardly as the foregoing facts of Khaled have all been reported over the years, certain things do not seem to make sense. For example, Hewitt recalled that Ellsworth inquired about the wind affliction, to which Prince Aly Khan supposedly replied, "I'm afraid that goes with him." Why then, would Ellsworth strain his personal finances to purchase a horse that would not be imported until after he had stood a year at stud, and then put him back in training in California?

Regardless of the motivation, the record is clear that after Khaled arrived in California following the 1947 breeding season, he was put back in training. He ran three times in January of 1948, winning once in allowance company. He stood the 1948 season at stud, was returned to training once again, and finished last in a race on December 28. Thus, his record for the months between the end of the 1947 breeding season and the end of calendar year 1948 read: one ocean voyage, two brief campaigns as a racehorse, thirty-seven foals conceived.

Khaled sired forty-five foals in his second California-sired crop, and their mark of twenty-six winners at two came within one of Star Shoot's record of the time of twenty-seven from his 1914 foal crop. The fact that Khaled sired forty-five foals in a year in the 1950s might seem to place Ellsworth well ahead of his time insofar as book size, but then again, Star Shoot sired fifty-two foals in a crop as early as 1914.

Khaled's success came early, and often. First was Correspondent, a $207,292-earner who won the Hollywood Gold Cup (and sired only three stakes winners, but one was 1961 Belmont Stakes winner Sherluck). Then, in 1952, the Khaled—Iron Reward colt to be known as Swaps was foaled in California, the same year Nashua was foaled in Kentucky.

With Tenney training the Ellsworth colt, Swaps proved a promising two-year-old, then won the Santa Anita Derby the next winter. Sent to Kentucky, Swaps turned back the vaunted Nashua to win the Derby. The Triple Crown was not as big a deal then as it would become, and Ellsworth and Tenney followed by only one year the pattern of a California-based colt winning the Derby and then immediately going back West, bypassing the Preakness and Belmont. Determine, the 1954 Derby winner, was a Kentucky-bred but was owned by Californian Andy Crevolin.

Swaps beat older horses in the Californian and remained unbeaten at three until he faced Nashua in a heralded match race that summer in Chicago. Nashua's six and a half-length victory was hardly official before the rumors that Swaps was unsound reverberated, apparently having been hidden successfully beforehand. One of many events billed as a Race of the Century thus joined several of the others in being inconclusive.

At four, Swaps joined the great horses of American racing. He won eight of ten races from coast to coast, set or equaled world records with disdainful regularity, carried 130 pounds up to one and five-eighths miles, and was the clear choice as Horse of the Year. Ironically, when he suffered a life-threatening leg fracture during a workout that autumn, it was Sunny Jim Fitzsimmons, trainer of rival Nashua, who lent Tenney a stall sling to help support the colt's weight and get him through the crisis.

John W. Galbreath of Darby Dan Farm and his wife had come calling and bought a half-interest in Swaps for $1 million. Ellsworth, who had scratched around to sow $160,000 into Khaled, had reaped $848,900 with Swaps, had sold half of him for a near-record price, and still owned the other half. He had the thought of standing the horse in alternate years in California, then Kentucky, but the Galbreaths came with another $1 million to buy out his interest so they could install the horse safely in Kentucky.

Swaps had an unusual stallion record. His early crops were sensational: Brilliant filly champions Affectionately and Primonetta, Kentucky Derby-Belmont winner and champion Chateaugay, and Wood Memorial winner and classics contender No Robbery. Then, the parade faded. Eventually, he had a record of thirty-five stakes winners, or only eight percent. He was fashionable enough at one time that the Phipps family bred Glamour to him and got the filly Intriguing, she the dam of the champion filly and major broodmare Numbered Account. Numbered Account foaled Private Account, and Intriguing also foaled the dam of Woodman. Thus Swaps' appearance in pedigrees is assured for some time, but not as a savior of the Hyperion line on the top side.

After Swaps, Khaled kept up a steady stream of major winners, eventually siring sixty-one stakes winners (twelve percent). Even before Swaps had emerged, Calumet Farm bred the top-class Khaled filly A Glitter, winner of the 1958 Coaching Club American Oaks. Other of Khaled's best runners included California Kid, Candy Dish (dam of Candy Spots), Corn Off the

Cob, El Drag, Going Abroad, Hillary (sire of Kentucky Derby runner-up Hill Rise), Linmold, New Policy, Physician, Prince Khaled, and Terrang. Again, though, the line's success as a producer of stallions was short lived. Khaled was the broodmare sire of seventy-two stakes winners, and his daughter Track Medal was a Greentree Stud mare who produced four major winners, including Outing Class.

Alibhai

Alibhai was a Hyperion colt whose dam, the fine race mare Teresina, by Tracery, was purchased for the Aga Khan from the historic Sledmere Stud in Yorkshire. George Lambton, who had trained Hyperion at two and three, bought the mare for the Aga.

Foaled in 1938, Alibhai was purchased from the Aga Khan by movie mogul Louis B. Mayer of Metro-Goldwyn-Mayer. The Hollywood potentate was getting into racing on a large scale and, presumably, felt buying from a potentate of another order made sense. Alibhai showed brilliant speed in training, but bowed in both front legs. Mayer turned down Abe Hewitt's offer of $5,000 to take the cripple off his hands and placed Alibhai in the stud, either too naive to recognize the odds against an unraced horse or too stubborn to succumb to them. Smart, or lucky, Mayer five years later accepted an offer not of $5,000 but of $500,000 from the same, humbled Hewitt, acting that time in the company of Leslie Combs II. One of the key figures in the modern organization of stallion syndication, Combs took the horse to Kentucky to his Spendthrift Farm.

Alibhai became the *beau ideal* among breeders with a dream. The unraced horse sired fifty-four stakes winners (fourteen percent), and they included the Kentucky Derby winner Determine,

the two-time Widener Handicap winner Bardstown (a Calumet Farm homebred from the great filly Twilight Tear), the half-million-dollar earner On Trust, the high-class three-year-old and handicap horse Traffic Judge, plus Solidarity, Your Host, Honeys Alibi, Sharpsburg, Hasseyampa, Mr. Consistency, Chevation, and Cover Up.

Alibhai's best racing daughters included the champion older filly Bornastar, the Delaware Handicap winner Flower Bowl (dam of Graustark and Bowl of Flowers), and Lurline B. (dam of four stakes winners).

While the Alibhai branch of the Hyperion sire line did not proliferate over many generations, several of his sons did make marks at stud. Your Host, for example, sired the five-time Horse of the Year Kelso, the great gelding of the 1960s. Determine, a Kentucky Derby winner, got another Derby winner in Decidedly and a juvenile champion in Warfare (in turn, sire of grass champion Assagai). Traffic Judge was something of an international success although siring only twenty-two stakes winners (seven percent); these included the extraordinary broodmare Best in Show, the crack two-year-old Delta Judge, and the Hopeful winner Traffic. Delta Judge, in turn, sired Mississippi Mud, the dam of Dixieland Band, as well as the distaff champion Proud Delta in this country.

A commercial listing does not necessarily tell the entire picture about the Hyperion line's status as a tail-male entity today, but it is a telling feature of *The Blood-Horse Stallion Register* of 2000 that only two entered stallions are listed under his sire-line ancestry: Traffic Judge's grandson Deputed Testamony, winner of the Preakness; and Green Forest's son Forest Gazelle, he six generations removed from Hyperion through the branch of Stardust.

Worldwide Influence

Hyperion

As mentioned above, Hyperion did have one outstanding racehorse in this country. This was Pensive, the 1944 Kentucky Derby winner, who, in turn, begot the 1949 Derby winner, Ponder. Completing an unusual trio of Derby-winning generations, Ponder then sired the 1956 Kentucky Derby winner, Needles. As a broodmare sire, Hyperion's place in this country is illustrated by his having sired Hydroplane II, dam of the great Citation, as well as Lady Angela, dam of Nearctic — he, in turn, the sire of Northern Dancer. Thus, here and abroad, Hyperion's place as a distant ancestor of shimmering glory is safe.

As the head of a sire line, Hyperion's name also reverberated around the rest of the Thoroughbred world. His best sons at home, as stated earlier, included Queen Elizabeth's Aureole. After his distinguished racing career, Aureole sired the Epsom Derby winner St. Paddy and Prix de l'Arc de Triomphe winner St. Crespin. Aureole's other sons included Vienna, and that name also brings the influence of Hyperion back to American shores. Vienna was the sire of Vaguely Noble, one of the most important international influences of his day — but one that seems to have been a one-generation phenomenon insofar as his male descent. Vaguely Noble was an exceptional two-year-old and then at three in 1968 climaxed his racing career with a smashing victory over the brilliant Sir Ivor in the Prix de l'Arc de Triomphe. The Vienna colt was owned in part by Texan Nelson Bunker Hunt, and was imported to Kentucky. Vaguely Noble stood at Gainesway Farm, where John R. Gaines in the 1960s laid the groundwork for one of the most prominent of international breeding operations. Gaines also stood such top stallions as Blushing Groom, Lyphard, and Riverman, before selling the farm to the internationalist Graham Beck of South Africa.

Vaguely Noble was a sire of a list of important winners. The greatest included his daughter Dahlia, a champion in England, Ireland, Canada, and the United States and in the year 2000 a thirty-year-old, revered and successful retired broodmare. Sons of Vaguely Noble were more noble than vague — Epsom Derby winner Empery, Hall of Famer Exceller, Jockey Club Gold Cup winner Lemhi Gold, plus Royal and Regal, Mississipian, Ace of Aces, Gay Mecene, and others. To a degree reminiscent of Bull Lea, however, the brilliant sons of the racecourse receded meekly into history without comparable success as stallions.

Another of Hyperion's noteworthy sons in his native England was Owen Tudor, winner of the 1941 English Derby and 1942 Ascot Gold Cup. Owen Tudor, whose dam was the Pharos mare Mary Tudor II, a Guineas winner in France, was never higher than seventh on the English sire list. Nevertheless, he was one of the best of the Hyperion stallions, playing a role in the sire line which was strong for some time.

Owen Tudor's best horses included Tudor Minstrel and Abernant, both descending in their female families from the vaunted Lady Josephine/Mumtaz Mahal line. Tudor Minstrel and Abernant were regarded as two of the swiftest of modern English horses. Tudor Minstrel's sons included the somewhat delicate colt Tomy Lee, who was imported and won the Kentucky Derby of 1959 in a blood-letting duel with Sword Dancer through the stretch. Tomy Lee proved virtually sterile after being acquired for stud in Kentucky. Also among Tudor Minstrel's forty-four stakes winners (nine percent) to excel in this country were What a Treat, champion three-year-old filly of 1965, and Poona II, winner of the 1955 Santa Anita Handicap. Another son, King of the Tudors, got the Arlington-Washington Futurity winner Golden Ruler and the Frizette winner Tudor Queen. Sing Sing, Tudor Melody (sire of Kashmir II), and Tudor Grey also were among sons of Tudor Minstrel to achieve some success at stud.

Just as Tudor Minstrel was a Two Thousand Guineas winner that sired a Kentucky Derby winner, his sire Owen Tudor was capable of getting stayers as well as sprinters and milers. Another of Owen Tudor's sons was the French Derby winner Right Royal, and he also got the hardy Tudor Era, who in this country was disqualified from victory in the one and a half-mile Washington, D.C., International and won the Man o' War Handicap.

To illustrate Hyperion's worldwide influence further, we will summarize one example based in Australia and another stemming from Argentina.

Star Kingdom, who became a dominant stallion in Australia, was a son of Stardust. Stardust was a 1937 colt by Hyperion and finished second in such divergent tests as the Two Thousand Guineas and St. Leger. His son Star King was a once-beaten two-year-old and a stakes winner at three. He was well-respected for his short head defeat by the flying Abernant in the National Produce Stakes at two.

Sent to Australia, Star King was renamed Star Kingdom because a horse with his original name already was ensconced in the country. Star Kingdom led the sire list in Australia five times before his death in 1967, and his legion of high-class stakes horses included the revered Todman and the imported Noholme II. There the story again comes back to America, for Noholme II was another exceptional success for the Hyperion sire line in this country. He got fifty-five stakes winners (eleven percent), including the handicap champion Nodouble and the sprint

champion Shecky Greene. Shecky Greene sired the French Guineas winner and champion Green Forest, he, in turn, the sire of Paul Mellon's English-Irish filly champion Forest Flower.

Nodouble, son of Star Kingdom's son Noholme II, got a total of ninety-one stakes winners for an impressive fourteen percent. If they tended not to be brilliant horses they had enough collective quality to place Nodouble atop the American sire list of 1981. The Nodoubles included Overskate, Double Discount, and Skillful Joy. Apropos of this global clan, the Nodouble filly Mairzy Doates ventured to Tokyo and won the Japan Cup.

Among the various sons of Hyperion sent to South America to achieve success for the sire line was Aristophanes, a 1948 foal out of Commotion, by Mieuxce. Aristophanes' son Forli was so brilliant that A. B. (Bull) Hancock Jr., master of Claiborne Farm, put together a syndicate to bring him to this country. Forli arrived in 1967 and was sent to masterful trainer Charlie Whittingham. Whittingham moved up many a horse over his career, but there was not much room to improve off Forli's record in his native country. The classy chestnut out of Trevisa, by Advocate, had won all his seven races in Argentina, including what is known as the Quadruple Crown. This involves the three classic equivalents, plus the Carlos Pelligrini, against older horses.

If there was any blot on Forli, it was that a couple of his victories had been slower and less commanding than expected, and his stable made the explanation of worms one time and being off his feed the other. One of his owners — who had pledged never to sell the hero out of Argentina — claimed that negative reports on these races moved, or maddened, him to tears and encouraged the decision to sell the horse.

Bull Hancock was not turning out copy for

Buenos Aires publications we feel certain, but he was the beneficiary of this change of heart. In this country, Forli certainly indicated that any chink in his armor might well have been caused by the problems cited by the stable. He won the 1967 Coronado Stakes in his debut in California, then added an exhibition victory before being sent to Arlington in Chicago for the Citation Handicap. Alas, he was injured and finished second to Dominar. Forli, grandson of Hyperion, was sent to Claiborne with nine wins in ten races.

Forli had to be kept in a stall for more than two months before being turned out at Claiborne. The author happened to be showing some South American visitors around the Bluegrass the morning the horse was released for the first time, and we watched in helpless trepidation. Hancock had posted several men around the paddock to wave and shout Forli away from the fence, especially the corners of the paddock, but after a few tentative steps, the horse confounded all precautions. Forli dashed between his shouting protectors and attempted to leap the fence cleanly. While Hancock and the rest watched with hearts in throats, Forli tumbled to the ground on the other side. He rolled over, nearly reaching the next paddock fence and drawing the rapt attention of new neighbor Sir Gaylord, who perhaps was trying to put into horse talk the concept that "We don't do it that way; just wait, and they will lead you to the barn when it's time."

Forli proved a very successful sire, his sixty stakes winners (nine percent) including several which wrought success in Europe, such as Posse, Thatch, Home Guard, Gay Fandango, and Punctilio. His best son was Forego, who had championship sprinting speed but could stay as well, as he paraded through three consecutive Horse of the Year campaigns of the 1970s. Forego stamped himself as one of the great racehorses of history, his signature triumph perhaps being his charge from far back to win the 1976 Marlboro Cup under 137 pounds. Forego, however, was a gelding; moreover, for Forli's other top American-raced sons, such as Intrepid Hero, Key to Content, and Forceten, fashionable success at stud was elusive.

As a broodmare sire, Forli fared well. He was the sire of Tuerta, the dam of Claiborne's ill-fated Swale, winner of the Kentucky Derby and Belmont Stakes. Forli was crossed with the potent female family of Rough Shod II and got the wonderful mare Special, dam of Nureyev and second dam of Sadler's Wells.

Thus, Forli did not for long enhance his legacy in terms of a sire line in America, but like the great Hyperion himself — as broodmare sire of Nearctic, and others — he became a lasting name in the pedigrees of great stallions from another angle. ❖

Bull Lea

"Daddy disappeared for several days," Tyson Gilpin recalled with a laugh one day early in the year 2000. The Virginia horseman, affable and knowledgeable, was thinking back nearly seventy years to a bit of family adventure. "We were touring Europe. I was ten or eleven. Daddy had the whole family in a seven-passenger Buick: Wife, kids, mother-in-law, and a nurse. We had a full boat."

The Gilpins of Virginia had visited Paris, then went on to Naples and Rome and back to Ostende. "Daddy" was Kenneth Gilpin, owner of Kentmere Farm in Virginia, and, in the midst of being a good family man on vacation, he could not resist hying off to meet with Captain Jefferson Davis Cohn and work out a horse deal. Cohn was the owner of Teddy and had bred and raced the sire's noted son, Sir Gallahad III, before selling him to America for $125,000. In 1931, when the Gilpin Buick rolled into his life, Cohn was reeling from losses in the stock market crash of 1929 and resulting worldwide depression.

According to Arthur Fitzgerald's history of the Prix de l'Arc de Triomphe[1], Cohn had inherited a fortune from a relative in Cologne and lived in London and then Paris. He owned a sort of gold mine in the mare Plucky Liege, and he eventually sought to convert his bloodstock into a fortune

saver. He sold his French farm, Haras de Bois Roussel, along with his breeding stock, to Leon Volterra in 1932. Thus, one major figure gave way to another of lasting fame on the French scene.

Cohn was already in a selling mode in 1931. Tyson Gilpin's father got in touch with F. Wallis Armstrong, owner of Meadowview Farm in New Jersey, and they purchased Teddy, who at that time was eighteen years old. Teddy was sent to stud at Kentmere, where, Tyson Gilpin recalled, the horse was lunged every day for exercise because he had been handled in such an indulgent manner that he had become rather wild if turned loose. At Kentmere, this international patriarch was housed in a "converted garage, and backyard" rather than in a more conventional, open paddock.

If the Teddy bloodline had been a human family, it would bespeak a common immigrant experience of the younger members establishing themselves in the New World and then sending back to Europe for the beloved parents. By 1931, Teddy's son Sir Gallahad III had burst onto the scene in the United States as the sire of 1930 Triple Crown winner Gallant Fox. Teddy himself had led the French sire list in 1923 and had been second several times as well as ranking second once in Italy. Sir Gallahad III was out of Plucky Liege, and a younger full brother, Bull Dog, had been sold by

		Ajax, 1901	Flying Fox Amie
	Teddy, 1913		
		Rondeau, 1900	Bay Ronald Doremi
BULL DOG, b/br, 1927			
		Spearmint, 1903	Carbine Maid of the Mint
	Plucky Liege, 1912		
		Concertina, 1896	St. Simon Comic Song
BULL LEA, br h, April 5, 1935			
		Voter, 1894	Friar's Balsam Mavoureen
	Ballot, 1904		
		Cerito, 1888	Lowland Chief Merry Dance
ROSE LEAVES, br, 1916			
		Trenton, 1881	Musket Frailty
	Colonial, 1897		
		Thankful Blossom, 1891	Paradox The Apple

1st dam: Rose Leaves, br, 1916-1939. Bred by W.O. Parmer (Ky). Unraced. Dam of 10 named foals, 10 rnrs, 7 wnrs, 6 sw.

1920: RUDDY, b c, by McGee. Raced 8 yrs, 174 sts, 12 wins, $11,413. Won Rainbow Selling S.

1921: No report received.

1922: No report received.

1923: ESPINO, br c, by Negofol. Raced 3 yrs, 37 sts, 9 wins, $56,310. Won Saratoga Cup, Lawrence Realization S; 2nd Belmont S, Champagne S, Huron H, Jockey Club Gold Cup; 3rd Walden H, Oceanus H, Wood S, Dwyer S, Withers S, Brookdale H, Saratoga Cup. Sire.

1924: BOIS DE ROSE, b/br c, by Negofol. Raced 3 yrs, 31 sts, 3 wins, $20,450. Won Empire City Derby; 2nd Belmont S, Junior Champion S; 3rd Dwyer S, Withers S. Sire.

1925: Barren.

1926: Ch f, by My Play.

1927: Pan of Roses, b f, by Peter Pan. Raced 1 yr, 10 sts, 0 wins, $0. Dam of 9 foals, 9 rnrs, 8 wnrs.

1928: B c, by Pot au Feu.

1929: Slipped.

1930: Dead foal.

1931: Ch c, by Pot au Feu. Died 1932.

1932: NECTARINE, dk b f, by Bull Dog. Raced 3 yrs, 26 sts, 11 wins, $10,265. Won Miami Beach H; 3rd Joseph Mclennan Memorial H. Dam of 8 foals, 7 rnrs, 7 wnrs, including **APPLE-**

KNOCKER ($55,475), **Pindus** ($31,200). Granddam of **YING AND YANG**, **PASSADO**, **Cavort**, **Fresh Meadow**, **Sweet Woman**.

1933: Swift Rose, ch f, by Lord Swift. Raced 1 yr, 2 sts, 0 wins, $0. Dam of 7 foals, 7 rnrs, 3 wnrs. Granddam of **Hesarocket**.

1934: Slipped.

1935: BULL LEA, br c, by Bull Dog. Bred by Coldstream Farm (Ky). Raced 3 yrs, 27 sts, 10 wins, $94,825. Widener H, Autumn H, Blue Grass S, James C. Thorton Memorial H, Kenner S, Pimlico H; 2nd Champagne S, Hopeful S, Classic S, Continental H, Narragansett Special, Potomac H, Mclennan Memorial H; 3rd Saratoga Special, Aquidneck H. Sire of 377 foals, 58 sw, 4.37 AEI. Died 1964.

1936: Ten Carat, ch c, by Jean Valjean. Raced 1 yr, 2 sts, 0 wins, $0. Sire.

1937: Summer Time, br f, by Bull Dog. Raced 3 yrs, 15 sts, 1 win, $1,480. Dam of 9 foals, 8 rnrs, 8 wnrs, including **Unification** ($24,015). Granddam of **ROYAL LIVING**, **RILEY**, **STEVE'S LARK**, **BLUE BALLAD**, **Hail Navy**.

1938: Barren.

1939: DOGPATCH, br c, by Bull Dog. Raced 5 yrs, 62 sts, 13 wins, $38,828. Won Shevlin S; 2nd Babylon H, Del Mar H, Walter Connolly H; 3rd Speed H, Breeders' Futurity. Sire of 115 foals, 14 sw, 1.15 AEI.

Cohn after the colt's three-year-old campaign of 1930 for a reported $80,000. Bull Dog had arrived at Coldstream Stud in Kentucky. Thus, Teddy already had two noted sons at stud here when he arrived in this country, and the family was to grow stronger. In the case of Bull Dog, it was he who sired the title horse of this chapter, the five-time leading sire Bull Lea.

Teddy died of a twisted colon in the summer of 1936, having served five seasons in the United States. All told, he sired sixty-five stakes winners internationally (eighteen percent). He was a successful sire for the sales ring in this country and after importation sired thirteen of his stakes winners here. As we shall review later, two of them telescoped his influence: Case Ace, who was to be the broodmare sire of the great stallion Raise a Native, and Sun Teddy, from whom the male line re-emerged in the forms of Damascus, Private Account, and others.

In the 1930s, however, Teddy and his sons were very much a European bloodline. While Sir Gallahad III might have been presumed by Americans to have been his most brilliant son, Teddy was also the sire of the Italian colt Ortello, who won the Prix de l'Arc de Triomphe in France in its tenth running, in 1929. Ortello resulted from a season given free by Cohn to the owner of a mare who had failed to get in foal the previous year.[2]

Another of Teddy's sons who authored something of a European counterpart to the Sir Gallahad III and Bull Dog classic influences in this country was the colt Aethelstan. From this branch came, in tail-male descent, the two-time Arc winner Tantieme, his son Tanerko, and the latter's high-class colt, 1963 Epsom Derby winner Relko. In 1962, this element surfaced in perhaps an unwelcome way at Laurel, not many miles from Teddy's former Kentmere home, when Tantieme's son Match II outran the great Kelso in the Washington, D.C., International.

The saga of Teddy also is inseparable from those of two of the greatest of all mares. One was La Troienne, a daughter of Teddy who was not much of a racemare but founded a female family in this country to which trace more than 800 stakes winners (and counting) in tail-female

alone. The other mare was Plucky Liege, she the dam of Teddy's multiple leading-sire sons Sir Gallahad III and Bull Dog — and much else. Thus, of perhaps the two greatest broodmares of the 20th Century, Teddy was father to one and consort to the other.

Plucky Liege's influence does not match the saturation of La Troienne, in the daughter-to-granddaughter-to-great-granddaughter scenario. Insofar as the imprint on the breed by one mare's first generation descent — her own foals — Plucky Liege, however, need not bow to anyone. Her foals, as stated, included Sir Gallahad III and Bull Dog, who between them led the American sire list five times and the broodmare sire list fifteen times. These were her precocious sons. By other sires, Plucky Liege also foaled Bois Roussel, winner of the English Derby, and Admiral Drake, winner of the Grand Prix de Paris (at a time it ranked as at least equal to the French Derby). There were also two other stakes winners, for a total of six. Of Plucky Liege's later developing sons, Bois Roussel led the English sire list once and sired St. Leger winner Tehran (he, in turn, the sire of champion Tulyar), Arc winner Migoli (sire of Gallant Man), and others. Admiral Drake became a leading sire in France and got the Epsom Derby-Grand Prix de Paris winner Phil Drake.

To put Plucky Liege's record into a modern context, it might do well to fantasize for the moment that two leading sires in America — one a three-time leader and the other a one-time leader — as well as an English Derby winner with some success at stud, and one more group I European winner and good sire, were all produced from one mare. So, imagine, for example, that Danzig, Broad Brush, Generous, and In the Wings were all from the same dam!

Now, you have a feel for Plucky Liege.

Bull Lea

Bulls and Roses

Because Bull Dog was a full brother to Sir Gallahad III, he came under close scrutiny early. He was a foal of 1927 and thus made his debut at two before Gallant Fox had emerged to emblazon the older brother's name as a sire, but Sir Gallahad III had a reputation as a rather brilliant racehorse. Bull Dog ran three times for breeder-owner Cohn at two, failing to win but finishing second in the important Prix Robert Papin. At three in 1930, Bull Dog won two decent stakes races from five starts, but showed he was not up to classic form. His wins came in the Prix Daphnis at Le Tremblay and the Prix Fleche d'Or at Le Touquet.

Each was run over a mile at a course somewhat below the status of the top Paris or Deauville venues.

Winner of two of eight races and earner of the equivalent of $7,765, Bull Dog was purchased for $80,000 and placed at stud at C. B. Shaffer's Coldstream outside Lexington. Author Hewitt declared in *Sire Lines* that "there can be very little doubt that Bull Dog was a better sire than Sir Gallahad III." This passage is startling to encounter. Bull Dog did sire a higher percentage of stakes winners, fifteen percent to twelve percent, but there was no Triple Crown winner among them, and no Kentucky Derby winner, and he led the sire list only once (1943) to his brother's four times.

Still, the fifty-two stakes winners by Bull Dog included not only the great sire-in-the-making Bull Lea, but also the good sire Johns Joy, plus Occupation, Occupy, Our Boots, The Doge, and major producers Miss Dogwood, Miss Ferdinand, and Miss Mommy. Bull Dog led the broodmare sire list three times, and the eighty-eight stakes winners from his daughters included Horse of the Year Tom Fool and Derby winner Dark Star, plus Royal Coinage, Rough'n Tumble, Aunt Jinny, Decathlon,

Imbros, Three Rings, Donut King, and others.

Bull Lea was bred by Coldstream and was included in its consignment to the Saratoga yearling sale of 1936. The Bull Dog colt was from Rose Leaves, an unplaced Ballot mare. The generations in this family darted quickly back in time. Rose Leaves was nineteen when she foaled Bull Lea, just as she had been foaled from the nineteen-year-old Colonial. Thus, the yearling appearing in the second third of the 20th Century was the grandson of a mare foaled in the 19th.

Rose Leaves had already produced four stakes winners, of which two, Espino and Bois de Rose, had seemed to prefer long distances and both had been runners-up in the Belmont Stakes.

The Bull Dog—Rose Leaves colt was one of the more attractive lots at Saratoga and brought $14,000, third-highest price paid at the Spa auction that year. The Calumet Farm of Warren Wright Sr. was the buyer, topping by $400 the last bid by Ethel V. Mars of Milky Way Stable. Mrs. Mars was not easy to dissuade, as she paid $18,000 for the top-priced number at the sale, but in the case of the Bull Dog colt it was the baking powder man (Wright of Calumet™) over the candy lady (Mars of Mars™ candies). That year at the races, Mrs. Mars followed Isabel Dodge Sloane of Brookmeade Stable in becoming the second lady to top the owner's list in American racing. Wright, who had converted his father's Kentucky Standardbred Farm, Calumet, into a Thoroughbred operation and had already raced the star filly Nellie Flag, would not top the owners list for another five years. Once Calumet got the hang of it, however, it would not let go, as Wright and his widow Lucille (later Mrs. Gene Markey) topped the list a dozen times from 1941 through 1961.

Much of Calumet's stardom came from sons

and daughters of that Bull Dog—Rose Leaves colt. Named Bull Lea, he was not quite a champion as a racehorse, but he was virtually unequaled as a stallion. Turned over to trainer F. J. Kearns (who pre-dated Ben A. Jones and son Jimmy in the Calumet shedrow), Bull Lea won at second asking in the summer of 1937 in Chicago. He later placed in Saratoga's Special and Hopeful and was being aimed for the top juvenile race of the era, the Belmont Futurity. He finished second in the Champagne, which then was run before the Futurity, but came up slightly lame and had to miss the bigger fixture.

In the spring of 1938, Bull Lea came out at Keeneland. It would not be long before the sight of Calumet's devil red and blue silks would take on special, sentimental meaning to the fans at the Lexington, Kentucky track, and Bull Lea had his role in building that foundation of pride and good feeling. In the Blue Grass Stakes, he carried the silks home in front of already established colors, the Headley family silks flown by Menow, the champion two-year-old of the previous year. The Kentucky Derby was next, and Bull Lea was second choice to Fighting Fox (son of Sir Gallahad III), but the two "cousins" both finished unplaced. The race was won by Lawrin, whose trainer, Ben Jones, would one day declare that the secret to success for Calumet was breed all the mares to Bull Lea and send them to himself to train! Bull Lea for his sophomore season was ranked fifth best among his male contemporaries.

The next winter, Bull Lea won at one and a quarter miles in good company to put behind him — partially at least — the suspicion wrought in the Derby that the distance was a bit beyond him. The occasion was the Widener Handicap, then the biggest trophy for older horses during the fashionable South Florida winter racing season. Bull Lea

defeated Stagehand, from whom he received seven pounds. At the time, the race was the biggest yet won by Calumet and gave bright hopes for a fine four-year-old season for Bull Lea, but ankle trouble flared and he was soon sent to Calumet to stud. In addition to the Blue Grass and Widener, Bull Lea had won the J. C. Thornton Memorial, Kenner Stakes, Pimlico Handicap, and Autumn Stakes. He placed in nine additional stakes. In addition to those already named, they included the Arlington Classic, Potomac, and McLennan. He won ten of twenty-seven races and earned $94,825.

It was later in that year, 1939, that Wright, the button-down Chicago tycoon, hired as his private trainer Ben Jones, a different sort of Midwesterner who had ventured from his Missouri farm upbringing to train racehorses on both sides of the Mexican-U.S. border.

Bull Lea would earn a little statue of himself in the Calumet cemetery, and he set about it early. His first crop was something akin to a wave of class; perhaps that should be plural, but the early Bull Leas came to the fore not all at once but in sequence. The first good ones by the medium-sized brown horse were fillies, specifically Durazna, the champion two-year-old distaffer of 1943, and Twilight Tear, a truly great race filly. Twilight Tear won fourteen of seventeen races for Calumet and Jones in 1944, defeated older male champion Devil Diver in the Pimlico Special, and made off with Horse of the Year honors. Also in the first crop was Armed, who was gelded, used for a time as a lead pony, and generally took his time in becoming America's best racehorse. This project was completed by 1947, in which year Armed won eleven of seventeen starts and became his sire's second Horse of the Year. Durazna, Twilight Tear, and Armed were three champions whose titles were spread over five years, but they all were in the first crop of Bull Lea!

The year Armed was older champion and Horse of the Year, the champion two-year-old colt and filly were younger foals by Bull Lea, born in his fifth crop in 1945. The filly was Bewitch, who at the conclusion of her career ranked as the greatest money-earning distaffer of all time with $462,605. The colt was Citation, who at the conclusion of his career ranked as the first million-dollar earner in history and fifty years later ranks in the top three of the century whenever any panel puts its mind to such cogitation.

Ben Jones and his son and assistant Jimmy never needed much time to sort out how Citation ranked. Their opinions were ready, and clear, such as "Citation was the best horse I ever saw, probably the best horse anyone ever saw," and "Citation could run down any horse he could see." Unlike any other trainer in history except Sunny Jim Fitzsimmons, the Joneses could even sit back and split hairs about which was the greater of the two Triple Crown winners they handled. Again, Citation had pride of place. Said Jimmy some years ago: "I always say you don't compare a horse like Citation to Whirlaway; you don't even compare them."

Citation won twenty-seven of twenty-nine races at two and three. His three-year-old campaign of nineteen wins in twenty starts was a masterpiece never equaled before or since. He defeated top older horses in the winter of his three-year-old season and dashed speedy stablemate Coaltown (a champion rising) in the Kentucky Derby, en route to a facile Triple Crown. For added emphasis of his superiority, he tucked the Jersey Stakes in among the three Triple Crown races that spring. He next went to Chicago to continue his mastery, then returned to New York, where he won the one-mile

Bull Lea

Sysonby at midweek and the two-mile Jockey Club Gold Cup that very Saturday!

Coaltown was possessed of such speed that Keeneland horsemen in the spring of 1948 conjectured that he might be able to lower the colors of Citation. Under the logistics then in place, Ben Jones had had Coaltown under his supervision while Citation during that phase was attributed to son Jimmy (although the colt appeared under Ben's name for the Triple Crown). Father Ben was injudicious in his declarations that Citation was by far the better, but, years later, Jimmy conceded that there came a point in that Derby of many springs ago where Coaltown was so far in front as to implant the fleeting fear that "the old man had conned me." Jockey Eddie Arcaro and Citation quickly abolished any fear of a Jonesian rift, as they came to, and passed, Coaltown to win handily.

Arcaro had become Citation's rider several races earlier, after jockey Al Snider had been lost in a boating expedition off Florida. In his first start on the colt he would spend years calling the greatest he rode, Arcaro found himself trailing in the mud in the Chesapeake Trial and, since this was just a prep for a prep, he did not persevere with Citation although he later said the colt could have won if driven to do so. The only other defeat Citation had during his first two campaigns came in the 1947 Washington Park Futurity. Calumet figured rather strongly that it could finish first, second, and third, so the riders were warned not to rough up their mounts so long as things were going to plan. The filly Bewitch got off to an early lead and, although Citation made up five lengths in the stretch, he finished a length behind her. Jockey Steve Brooks expressed confidence that his mount could have won, had he been pressed to do so.

So, arguably Citation had the quality to have

been undefeated in twenty-nine starts at two and three. One wonders what the riders who "allowed" him to lose would have done had some clairvoyant suggested to them the place in history they were about to inhabit. On the other hand, one can also conjecture as to whether even the Joneses and Wright could have made themselves campaign Citation in quite the way they did if they had been enduring the expanding pressure of an unbeaten career.

At any rate, Citation developed an osselet and the ankle malady cost him his entire four-year-old season. He came back at five and won his first outing, increasing his winning streak over several years to sixteen races. This figure was of much interest years later, in 1996, when Cigar ran his own string to sixteen straight wins, but could not get the seventeenth. Citation at five and six was only "a shell of what he had been," lamented Jimmy Jones. Nonetheless, that shell still constituted a powerful racehorse. Owner Wright was anxious that Citation reach $1 million in career earnings. This was not a monetary greed — Wright had plenty of money — but the millionaire level was a status, a trophy as it were, that no Thoroughbred ever had achieved. Wright died before Citation reached the goal, but the widow instructed the Joneses to carry on, and Citation made it in high style, by winning the Hollywood Gold Cup in the summer of 1951. He then was sent home to stud at Calumet, with a record of thirty-two wins in forty-five starts and earnings of $1,085,760.

Illustrative of Bull Lea's prowess, when Citation was on the shelf, Coaltown filled in to earn Horse of the Year honors at four in 1949. He won twelve of fifteen that year in the best season of an overall career of twenty-three victories from thirty-nine starts and earnings of $415,675. He thus became the fourth Horse of the Year for Bull

Lea in six years: Twilight Tear, 1944; Armed, 1947; Citation, 1948; Coaltown, 1949.

Bull Lea first led the sire list in 1947, and he repeated in 1948 and again in 1949. (One doubts that the term "threepeat" occurred either to Wright or the Joneses.) Heliopolis and Count Fleet crowded in to lead the lists in 1950 and 1951, respectively. Then Bull Lea re-assumed the crown to lead in 1952 and 1953. This completed his five years atop the list. At that time, only Star Shoot among 20th Century sires had led the list so often. Later, Nasrullah matched the five-time status and then Bold Ruler led for a total of eight times.

The year 1952 coincided with the second Derby victor for Bull Lea, in the fleet Calumet homebred Hill Gail. Even after he would no longer be statistically the leading sire, Bull Lea continued to turn out major runners. In 1957, he got his third Derby winner to reach a number only three other stallions have attained and none has surpassed. This was Iron Liege, and therein lies an unusual set of tales. In 1954, when *Sports Illustrated* was but a fledgling itself, the birth of Iron Liege was subject of a photographic assignment to be updated with his progress over the next few years. By the time the foal crop of 1954 was getting geared into heavy Kentucky Derby preparation by the Jones boys, however, yet another Bull Lea colt had eclipsed the status of Iron Liege. This was Gen. Duke, and so brilliant was he during the winter of 1957 that there were murmurs — furtive perhaps — wafting from Florida press boxes that he might compare with Citation himself. After swapping victories at Hialeah with the fleet Bold Ruler, Gen. Duke doused his rival and various others in the Florida Derby with a run that matched the world record of 1:46 4/5 for one and one-eighth miles.

Bull Lea

Before the Derby, though, Gen. Duke was having foot problems, and on the eve of the race, he had to be scratched. So extraordinary was that crop of three-year-olds, however, that those left to contest the Roses were seen — at the time and thereafter — to comprise one of the greatest of Derby fields. The stars were Bold Ruler, Gallant Man, and Round Table. Iron Liege, left as the seemingly forlorn back-up to Gen. Duke, beat them all. Born to an artist's camera, Iron Liege just tripped a mechanical one in time to win at 8-1, a nose in front of Gallant Man. This was the race in which one of the great jockeys of all time assured himself a lifetime of maddening interview questions: Bill Shoemaker on Gallant Man mistook the sixteenth pole for the finish line and rose in his irons for one heartbeat. Did it cost him the win? Many say yes, but then most didn't even notice the instant of uncertainty. Regardless, Calumet and the Joneses wore the roses again.

The National Museum of Racing launched its Hall of Fame in 1955, and before the decade was out, both Joneses were accepted during the initial flurry of elections. In the horse categories, Bull Lea did a fine job helping populate the Hall. His seven sons and daughters enshrined in the Saratoga institution are Armed, Bewitch, Citation, Coaltown, Real Delight, Twilight Tear, and Two Lea.

A Harsh Reality

Bull Lea was, justifiably, the darling of the Bluegrass. There developed, however, a somber pattern that seemed difficult to accept, but could not be ignored. His sons, even the best ones at the racetrack, were consistently disappointing at stud. Citation was the greatest of his champions, and even he could not escape the smell of failure. This was odd, for in his first crop, foaled in 1953,

Citation got Calumet Farm's Fabius, winner over Needles in the Preakness, runner-up to the same colt in the Derby, and third behind him in the Belmont. That first crop by Citation also included Beyond, a Calumet homebred that dead-heated with stablemate Princess Turia in the Acorn Stakes, plus two lesser stakes winners. In his fourth crop, Citation got the filly champion and eventual Hall of Famer Silver Spoon for the C. V. Whitney Stable, as well as Watch Your Step, winner over Intentionally and Restless Wind in the Sapling Stakes. So, early on, Citation sired a crack two-year-old, a classic winner, a champion filly. This was failure?

There were several cosmetic factors against Citation, and they were paradoxical. On the one hand, a half-dozen years had passed between his imperial three-year-old form and the appearance of his first runners; on the other, lingering sweet memories of his greatness at three perhaps instilled in some horsemen unrealistic expectations. The numbers, though, were the culprit. While Silver Spoon, Fabius, Beyond, and Watch Your Step might seem a pretty strong early showing, there was not much else. Citation lived to 1970 and stood at Calumet the entire time, but got only a dozen stakes winners — an anemic four percent.

Coaltown was not nearly so good a stallion; he never sired a single stakes winner. There was more to this depressing litany of sons of Bull Lea. Faultless, his 1947 Preakness winner, got a few nice stakes winners, but only five percent; Mark-Ye-Well, a durable son who earned over a half-million in a more penurious era, sired three stakes winners and was sent off to Scandinavia; Alerted earned over $400,000 and got but two stakes winners; the fine handicapper Yorky earned $307,130, then sired only a single stakes winner, the same number gotten by American Derby and Travers winner Beau Prince; Jockey Club Gold Cup winner Level Lea sired one stakes winner, and Derby winner Iron Liege sired none prior to his being sent to France and later Japan. (Iron Liege's contemporary, Gen. Duke, became a wobbler and died without being able to enter stud.) The other Derby winner, Hill Gail, statistically did little to counter this trend, but had an unusual career. His only stakes winner in this country was the high-class filly Smashing Gail, but Hill Gail was exported and zoomed briefly into stardom abroad when a son, Martial, won the Two Thousand Guineas for owner Reginald Webster in 1960. Hill Gail did linger in pedigrees of various group winners.

One of Bull Lea's lesser stakes-winning sons, Bull Page, emerged as the sire of Canadian Triple Crown winner New Providence and the additional Queen's Plate winner Flaming Page among nineteen stakes winners (seven percent). Flaming Page, however, soon did him the favor of transferring his chance for lasting fame into the broodmare sire category as she became the dam of the great racehorse and stallion Nijinsky II and second dam of another classic winner, The Minstrel — by which time Bull Page had been sent to Western Canada.

It will be no surprise to readers that Bull Lea's continuing influence was not as a sire of sires, but as a broodmare sire. In addition to those wonderful colts, he got a brace of champion fillies. Besides the aforementioned Durazna, Twilight Tear, and Bewitch, there was Real Delight, as close a thing to Twilight Tear at three as could be imagined; the durable handicap mare Two Lea (both for Calumet), and Alfred Vanderbilt's Next Move — bringing Bull Lea's

number of champions to nine. Other good race mares by Bull Lea included Good Blood, Amoret, Rosewood, Harriet Sue, Twosy, Miz Clementine, and Miss Arlette.

A goodly number of the best Bull Lea fillies at the racetrack joined the widespread ranks of his daughters that were successful broodmares. Bull Lea led the broodmare sire list (in the tradition of sire and "uncle") four times in succession — 1958-61. The first year was particularly significant, for 1958 — one year after he sired his third Derby winner — marked the emergence of Tim Tam to give Bull Lea a Derby winner as a grandsire. Tim Tam was from the champion Bull Lea mare Two Lea and gave Calumet the seventh of its eight Derby winners. (Tim Tam followed Iron Liege as the second credited to trainer Jimmy Jones, after father Ben had set the record with six.)

Bull Lea's daughters produced a total of 105 stakes winners, also including Quadrangle, Idun, Leallah, A Gleam, Bramalea, Barbizon, and Bardstown. The great Calumet stallion died at twenty-nine in 1964. An even two decades later, he cropped up as the broodmare sire of another classic winner, when Gate Dancer, out of the aged Bull Lea mare Sun Gate, won the 1984 Preakness Stakes. Nearly fifty years after a sale at Saratoga, Bull Lea still would have his say.

On Teddy and the Road to Damascus

To return to Bull Lea's paternal grandsire Teddy, his stay in America gave rise to the line identified today with Damascus and Private Account. In 1933, the Sun Briar mare Sunmelia foaled the Teddy colt Sun Teddy, who won the Arlington and Saranac Handicaps of 1936 en route to a career record of eight wins in eighteen starts and earnings of $24,000. Sun Teddy got only six stakes winners (five percent), but one of them was Sun Again, a Calumet Farm homebred from the Stimulus mare Hug Again (dam also of the high-class Fervent and Arrogate).

Sun Again won the Arlington Futurity of 1941 and came back at four and five to add seven additional stakes, including the Dixie, Equipoise, and McLennan. He won fifteen of thirty-four starts and earned $154,375. Having shown a degree of precocity, plus staying ability, he graduated to a successful career at stud which saw him get thirty stakes winners (nine percent). Among them were the Calumet Farm distaff champion Wistful, the sprint champion White Skies, plus Sunshine Nell, and Palestinian, who placed in all three Triple Crown events in 1949. Another nice Sun Again colt was Brookmeade Stable's Sunglow, who in 1951 won the Widener Handicap over Three Rings and County Delight. Sunglow won a total of a half-dozen good stakes during a career of nine wins in forty-five starts and earnings of $168,275. He also finished third in an early Washington, D.C., International won by Worden II, and fourth in the Kentucky Derby of Middleground. Sunglow stood at historic Mereworth Farm in Kentucky and, for the most part, was an indifferent sire, getting only six stakes winners (five percent). One of them, however, was a 1956 foal from an unraced By Jimminy mare. The foal was bred and raced by Isabel Dodge Sloane's Brookmeade Stable. A stylish little chestnut with more than a touch of white, he was given a name suggested by that of his dam. She was Highland Fling; he was Sword Dancer.

At three in 1959, Sword Dancer earned his way into the better element among the racing sons of the Teddy sire line, an upper crust embracing Gallant Fox, Omaha, Citation, Coaltown, Armed, and Gen. Duke. He was edged by Tomy Lee in as

fiercely run a Kentucky Derby as the rules allow, then won the Metropolitan Handicap, Belmont Stakes, Travers, and other top stakes. That fall, he teamed with Eddie Arcaro to win a renewal of the Woodward Stakes against a field which rivaled that to be won by a son, Damascus, nearly a decade later. Damascus had to beat Buckpasser and Dr. Fager to win his Woodward of 1967. Sword Dancer had to follow Arcaro's courageous decision to slither along the rail and run down Hillsdale and Round Table to win his Woodward in 1959. A repeat win over Round Table in the Jockey Club Gold Cup secured Sword Dancer Horse of the Year honors. Trainer Elliott Burch had him back at four to win a second Woodward, plus the Suburban and Grey Lag, in a campaign which found him scuffling with a crack handicap division including Bald Eagle, First Landing, and On-and-On. Sword Dancer then went to stud at John W. Galbreath's Darby Dan Farm with a record of fifteen wins in thirty-nine starts and earnings of $829,610.

Prolific success was never the hallmark of this branch of the Teddy descent. Sword Dancer went to extremes in the motif of only a few, but what a few. He got only fifteen stakes winners (five percent), but two of them gave him champions in consecutive years: Lady Pitt, champion three-year-old filly of 1966, and Damascus, three-year-old colt champion and Horse of the Year in 1967.

The great horse Damascus introduces into this branch of the Teddy tale a stable using the white silks with red dots made famous by William Woodward Sr. Woodward had been one of the owners and beneficiaries of the Teddy stallion Sir Gallahad III [refer to that chapter]. After Woodward's death in 1953, the Belair operation was inherited by his only son, William Jr. The

90

younger Woodward thus took into his ownership the 1954 juvenile champion and 1955 Horse of the Year Nashua. Upon William Jr.'s death late in 1955, the Belair horses were dispersed and a family tradition dating from near the turn of the century suddenly was set adrift.

Another of Woodward's children, Edith, had been the one most enthralled by the father's serious and joyous avocation of Thoroughbred racing. Edith had married Tom Bancroft, who was in the textile business, and she and her mother, Mrs. William Woodward Sr., revived the white and polka-dot silks for the small partnership they created. Woodward had boarded his mares at Claiborne Farm, but, apparently wanting a separate identity of her own, Mrs. Bancroft sent her small broodmare band to John A. Bell III's Jonabell Farm. One of them was Kerala, a My Babu mare which Bull Hancock had purchased for Mrs. Bancroft for $9,600 as a yearling in the 1959 Keeneland summer consignment of Duval Headley. The mare did not race. Bred to Sword Dancer in 1963, she foaled Damascus at Jonabell the following spring.

Damascus, inbred somewhat distantly to Phalaris and the great mare Selene, was turned over to trainer Frank Whiteley Jr., later renowned as trainer of Forego and Ruffian and already having a championship under his belt with Tom Rolfe. Damascus was a nice two-year-old late in the year and developed into a classic three-year-old. He was upset in the Kentucky Derby, but won the Preakness and Belmont. He then won the American Derby, added a twenty-two-length victory in the Travers Stakes, and beat older horses in the Aqueduct Stakes.

The 1967 Woodward was one of those races when all the elements come together in perfection, or nearly so. The author could not let this one go off without his physical presence, and with three oth-

ers of similar thought drove all night in a two-door Mustang from Lexington, Kentucky, to New York City. For a first trip to the Big Apple, Lauren Bacall on Broadway (*Cactus Flower*), and Damascus, Buckpasser, and Dr. Fager at the Big A (as Aqueduct was known) would be difficult to top.

In the paddock before the race, Buckpasser's owner, Ogden Phipps, likened the showdown to the 1957 Trenton Handicap, in which his mother's Bold Ruler defeated Gallant Man and Round Table. Buckpasser's trainer, Eddie Neloy, joked that it was not as big as a race at Suffolk Downs he remembered that meant fifteen thousand to him if he won.

Dr. Fager's trainer, John Nerud, had once sent a longshot out with Bold Ruler to soften him up for Gallant Man's winning charge in the Belmont Stakes. Now, with a congenital front-runner — and such a brilliant one — in Tartan Stable's Dr. Fager, the rabbit was on the other foot, so to speak. Both rival camps had their own rabbits: Neloy sent Great Power to assure a swift pace on Buckpasser's behalf, and Whiteley sent Hedevar as Damascus' lieutenant. The riders of the pacemakers set out whooping and hollering, and the already headstrong Dr. Fager rushed madly into the lead. In the stretch, Damascus came with such a startling run that he swept away to win by ten lengths, Buckpasser second, a weary Dr. Fager third.

As so often happens in such showdowns, it had not been as definitive as one could hope. The Phipps-Neloy combine was hardly noted for making excuses, but Buckpasser was too great a colt for a ten-length beating by any three-year-old not to give some degree of credence to the fears that he was not 100 percent. Even with that proviso, however, Damascus' effort had been extraordinary, and when he turned in a similar sweep to the front to win the Jockey Club Gold Cup, he had secured a Horse of the Year title to match his sire's. Not to belabor the point, but he became the seventh in the Teddy sire line to achieve this honor and, had voting commenced six years before it did, Gallant Fox and Omaha would likely have added two more to that honor roll.

At four, Damascus swapped outstanding one and a quarter-mile handicap victories with Dr. Fager, who took his turn as Horse of the Year. In the Suburban Handicap, without Hedevar's help, Damascus was third behind the other colt, carrying 133 pounds and giving the winner one pound. In the Brooklyn Handicap, Hedevar was there to goad Dr. Fager early, and Damascus came along to win in 1:59 1/5. That time he was getting five pounds. Damascus was retired at the end of the year with twenty-one wins from thirty-two starts and earnings of $1,176,781. He beat his sire into the Hall of Fame by three years, being inducted in 1974. *The Blood-Horse* panel ranked him sixteenth among horses of the 20th Century.

Although Mrs. Bancroft (who was too ill by then to attend Damascus' races) had established a connection to Jonabell Farm, Damascus went to Claiborne, as the family colts had done for years. He lived to the age of thirty-one and died there in 1995, six years after being pensioned because of declining fertility. Damascus was a very good sire, getting seventy-one stakes winners (nine percent). He did not get the truly big horse, although several of his colts seemed poised for major stardom from time to time. His Ogygian, for example, was brilliant in the old Tartan silks worn by Dr. Fager, winning the Futurity and the Dwyer; Time for a Change upset Devil's Bag in the Flamingo; Private Account won the Widener and Gulfstream Park Handicaps and the Jim Dandy; Desert Wine won the Hollywood Gold Cup and was second in the Kentucky Derby; Crusader Sword won the Hopeful; Judger took the Florida Derby and Blue Grass Stakes; and Belted Earl was a champion sprinter in Ireland. Mrs. Bancroft's sons, Thomas and William, racing as Pen-Y-Bryn Stable and using the old Belair silks, bred and raced a good son of Damascus in Highland Blade. This colt won the Marlboro Cup and Brooklyn Handicap and was second in one of the Woodward-Bancroft family's traditional strongholds, the Belmont Stakes.

Good stallions get good mares, and so their chances to be good broodmare sires are high, although by no means certain. Damascus, like many of his male relatives, became an important broodmare sire, his daughters having foaled more than 135 stakes winners to date. These include Chilukki, the champion two-year-old filly of 1999, plus Coronado's Quest, Shadeed, and Desert Stormer.

From the standpoint of extending the male line, the best son of Damascus was probably Private Account, a Phipps stable homebred. Private Account sired the wonderful Phipps filly Personal Ensign, who concluded her career unbeaten in thirteen starts when she swooped down the rain-soaked Churchill Downs stretch barely in time to catch Winning Colors in the 1988 Breeders' Cup Distaff. Private Account's sons at stud include Secret Hello, Personal Flag, and the high-class Private Terms, the last-named being sire of young stallions Afternoon Deelites and Soul of the Matter. Also among sons of Damascus, the aforementioned Time for a Change sired the champion colt Fly So Free. The latter is the sire of 1999 Hollywood Futurity winner Captain Steve. So, while the Teddy line, as with any sire sequence, has been augmented and diluted by the innumerable genetic tributaries which have joined it, the line remains extant into the 21st Century. ❖

Princecquillo

When Charismatic won the last Kentucky Derby of the 20th Century, much was made of the fact that only a few months before he had competed in a claiming race. Not too much of a typical rags-to-riches story applied here, however, for he was a son of a classic winner, Summer Squall, had various connections to Secretariat in his genetic make-up, and had been a highly prized weanling. Moreover, Charismatic raced for one of the most successful stables of his day and was in the barn of a Hall of Fame trainer. Then, too, he was dropped in for a $62,500 tag, far from the bottom of the pecking order.

The real rags-to-riches stories of the Turf were more along the lines of John Henry, a one-time $1,100 yearling that earned well over $6 million; or Carry Back, the shabbily bred little fellow who emerged as a Derby winner and public hero; or Stymie, dropped to $1,500 from more stylish beginnings, claimed for that figure, and later installed at the top of the earnings list.

None of these accomplished the one extra dimension of the $2,500-claim, Princequillo, in climbing also to the heights of fashion in international pedigrees. From that standpoint, we would not be confident of ever seeing Princequillo's story quite matched, although it would be an engrossing scenario to follow however often it might occur.

Any career earning the cliché "rags-to-riches" on the Turf can be expected to include either a combination of sage horsemanship and Lady Luck, or an all-out blitz by the latter. For the saga of Princequillo there also was room for that rampaging human trio: Ego, Pique, and Revenge.

Horatio Luro, who claimed Princequillo, was one of the Turf's most appealing characters. Tall, distinguished, handsome, Luro came from Argentina's Turf aristocracy, and had some Basque ancestry. Part of his upbringing was accomplished in Paris, and its specific lessons were avidly engulfed. If life's wanderings found Luro buffeted from time to time financially, he never wavered from his suave aura of outward self-confidence. He gave off the air of a playboy, and his interest in ladies might be said to have swung between appreciation of beauty and wealth — when a choice had to be made. He was courtly and gracious, as well, however, in a way that showed something stronger in his appreciation of women, and in time, Luro settled into a long marriage with his Frances. Meanwhile, no hint of the playboy marred his well-earned reputation as a superb horseman. He became known as one of the best on this side of the Atlantic at aiming a horse for a distant, important target, and delivering the animal at perfect pitch on the appointed day.

		Prince Palatine, 1908	Persimmon / Lady Lightfoot
	Rose Prince, 1919		
		Eglantine, 1906	Perth / Rose de Mai
PRINCE ROSE, b, 1928			
		Gay Crusader, 1914	Bayardo / Gay Laura
	Indolence, 1920		
		Barrier, 1910	Grey Leg / Bar the Way
PRINCEQUILLO (GB), b h, 1940			
		Tracery, 1909	Rock Sand / Topiary
	Papyrus, 1920		
		Miss Matty, 1914	Marcovil / Simonath
COSQUILLA (GB), b, 1933			
		White Eagle, 1905	Gallinule / Merry Gal
	Quick Thought, 1918		
		Mindful, 1913	Minoru / Noble Martha

1st dam: COSQUILLA, b, 1933-1953. Bred by Mrs. Cradock (Eng). Raced 3 yrs in Fr, 27 sts, 7 wins, $13,167. Won Prix de Chantilly, Prix Fille de l'Air; 2nd Grand Prix de Deauville, Prix Massine, Prix August Du Bos, Prix Dollar; 3rd Prix Joubert, Prix de Pomone. Dam of 7 named foals, 6 rnrs, 3 wnrs, 1 sw. Sent to USA 1946.

1940: PRINCEQUILLO, b c, by Prince Rose. Bred by L.L. Lawrence (Eng). Raced 3 yrs, 33 sts, 12 wins, $95,740. Won Jockey Club Gold Cup, Saratoga Cup, Saratoga H, Merchants' and Citizens' H, Questionnaire H, Old Rosebud H; 2nd Whitney S (twice); 3rd Dwyer S, Empire City H. Sire of 482 foals, 65 sw, 3.31 AEI. Died 1964.

1941: China Boy, b g, by Tai-Yang. Raced 1 yr in Eng, 4 sts, 0 wins, $0.

1942: B f, by Columbo. Died 1943.

1943: Barren.

1944: G.H.Q., b c, by War Lord. Raced 2 yrs in Eng and Fr, 11 sts, 1 win, $1,394.

1945: Barren.

1946: Lydia Languish II, b f, by Suzerain. Unraced. Dam of 9 foals, 9 rnrs, 7 wnrs. Granddam of **Bonge**. Sent to USA 1952.

1947: Royal Visitor, b c, by Donatello II. Raced 1 yr, 3 sts, 0 wins, $0. Sire.

1949: Rebee, ro g, by First Fiddle. Raced 5 yrs, 42 sts, 9 wins, $18,440.

1952: Persine, b f, by Heliodorus. Raced 2 yrs, 8 sts, 0 wins, $0.

The claiming of Princequillo and guiding him to success as a major horse competed in the Luro legend with various other accomplishments. These included winning the Santa Anita Handicap with Argentinian-bred Talon; importing and campaigning a series of other important South Americans (Argentinian-breds Miss Grillo and Rico Monte, among them); guiding One for All to international successes; and, the ultimate, winning two Kentucky Derbys with horses that had to be coaxed toward that spe-

cific excellence. In Decidedly, Luro had a Derby winner whose constitution would not stand much rough stuff, but had to have sufficient action to be fit enough. In Northern Dancer, he had a powerful little tiger, but one he felt was not inherently best suited for a race as long as one and a quarter miles. Luro tuned them both with precision.

Luro collaborated with America's most famous racing writer of the time, *Daily Racing Form*'s Joe Hirsch, on a book, *The Grand Senor*, published by

The Blood-Horse in 1989. Senor Luro was at least ninety when he passed away in 1991.

As Luro and Hirsch recounted, the germ of his connection to Princequillo began in late 1941. Luro and his partner-assistant Charlie Whittingham — another future Hall of Fame trainer — were in New York not long before Whittingham headed off for World War II. They had been traveling around the country with a small stable, and through a friend met Laudy Lawrence at a cocktail party at the Plaza. Lawrence had been Metro-Goldwyn-Mayer's main man in France, where he raced some horses, but with the wartime disruption of racing in Europe had brought some over to America. He proposed that Luro and Whittingham might want to lease a few to race. Thus, Luro traveled to Belmont Park to get his first look at a smallish colt who was a yearling at the time and had crossed submarine-riddled waters on a ship with his dam.

When Luro called Lawrence's office the next day to arrange the deal, he was told by the receptionist that Mr. Lawrence would not speak with him and did not know anyone named Luro. Enter Ego and Pique. Revenge was fiddling about, stage right, not ready for his entrance.

Some months later at a cocktail party in Palm Beach, Luro glimpsed the main chance again when the wealthy Audrey Emory, whom he knew, invited him to her new plantation in Charleston, South Carolina. She was on her way there, while Luro was soon to head out by car toward Toronto, where his small stable was being transferred after the South Florida season. Boone Hall in Charleston evoked images of *Gone With The Wind*, but Audrey apparently had more of a liking for Russian nobles than Rhett Butlers. She was at the time married to her second of that description, Prince Dimitri Djordjadze.

A wealthy lady with no racehorses was an affront to the young Luro's sense of propriety, and he soon interested the couple in being partners in some horses. It was an even deal — they to give him $5,000, he to spend it. Keeping $500 for expenses, he bought a couple of runners and, as so often was the case with Luro, they won some nice races, even when sent to the Saratoga meeting.

About that time, Luro miscalculated in running a horse in a claiming race, and the filly was taken. So, he had $2,500 and an empty stall, something racing secretary John Campbell did not need to tolerate for long at Saratoga. Reading the *Racing Form*, Luro spotted a colt, made inquiries, received some positive feedback, and went to look at the horse in the paddock. Lo and behold, he recognized that it was the colt Lawrence had shown him, so he made the quick decision to claim the colt for $2,500. Revenge had leapt to center stage.

The little colt had the attractive name of Princequillo and actually had started for as little as $1,500 in the past. With Luro at the controls on behalf of the Boone Hall connection, Princequillo wound up winning three of ten races at two. For all the speed, necessity, and vanity which surrounded the acquisition, Luro knew the colt was bred to improve with longer distances, and so he did.

In January of 1943, Luro was stabled at Tropical Park when the wartime Office of Price Administration ordered the track's owners to cease racing. (Princequillo won a six-furlong allowance race on January 6.) When Luro claimed Princequillo, the colt had been running in the name of Anthony Pelleteri, who apparently had leased him from Lawrence after the deal with Luro and Whittingham came to nothing. At any rate, Luro regarded Lawrence as the owner. With Tropical closed, it made sense to move his stable to Fair Grounds in New Orleans. Racing there was allowed to continue

Princequillo

because its ready access by trolley meant fans did not have to use precious gasoline. The sticky point was that Pelleteri at the time owned the racetrack.

Assured he was welcome, Luro used some of Prince Dimitri's farm gasoline coupons and shipped to Fair Grounds, where he was informed there was no stall. At Saratoga, he had briefly had $2,500, a stall, and no horse. Now he had a $2,500 horse and no stall.

Luro paid a dairy farmer to leave his herd out a couple of nights and let Princequillo stay in his barn, but in this specific case, being frightened by rats while in a cement-floor stall proved more bothersome than submarines in the Atlantic, and a leg filled.

Luro gave him two months off, apparently recognizing the tendon needed more time than he had given it at first. Still at Fair Grounds, he brought Princequillo back at six furlongs, and the colt was fourth and second in two efforts.

Back in New York, Princequillo continued his transformation from claimer to major winner. At one and one-sixteenth miles, Princequillo landed an allowance race at 9-1. In his first stakes test, he was fourth in the Peter Pan, then won another allowance race and was stepped up to one and five-eighths miles to win a handicap. He placed in two stakes, before getting a rest leading to the Saratoga meeting (run at Belmont Park because of the wartime restrictions). At one and a quarter miles, the claimer of a year before was now running against a Kentucky Derby winner, Shut Out, and a distinguished stayer, Bolingbroke. The latter beat him a nose in the Whitney. Then came the Saratoga Handicap, also at one and a quarter miles. Again receiving large chunks of weight from the older stars, Princequillo tracked the pace and then went right away to win by five lengths. The Saratoga Cup prescribed weight-for-age conditions, and the distance was up to one and three-quarter miles. At the finish, Princequillo just surged enough to regain the lead from Bolingbroke.

After losing in a hastily arranged trip for a big purse in Chicago, a chastened Luro rested the colt. In later years, Luro often would be quoted for his colorful description of being careful with a horse as "don't squeeze the lemon dry." Princequillo's trip to Chicago might well have been a key moment in developing that wisdom. Princequillo had a month break before the Jockey Club Gold Cup, then run at two miles. Princequillo chased Lawrence Realization winner Fairy Manhurst a long way, then darted to the lead, despite being on the rail where the mud was deep, and prevailed by two and a half lengths as Bolingbroke closed to be third.

Luro had some difficulty dealing with Prince Dimitri, and Princequillo's trainer of record through a lot of this and the next campaign was Dave Englander, although Luro apparently was intimately involved with every step. Englander had ridden in Argentina for Luro's father and had lent encouragement to claiming Princequillo because he recalled enough about the colt's dam, Cosquilla, to have a good impression of her.

At four, Princequillo was hampered by navicular problems. Nevertheless, he was able to add two more major wins from eight races, taking the one and five-eighths-mile Questionnaire Handicap and one and three-sixteenths-mile Merchants' and Citizens' Handicap. Hirsch felt Princequillo "may have run his best race" despite a loss in the Whitney that year, when he was beaten by only a half-length by the champion Devil Diver at level weights, with Bolingbroke trailing. Princequillo pulled up lame after the Saratoga Handicap that year and was through with racing. He had won twelve of thirty-three races and earned $96,550.

How Princequillo was accepted into the comfortable folds of the Hancock family as a young, unproven stallion, is subject to different interpretations. Luro told Hirsch that when he promoted the stallion to Arthur B. Hancock Sr., then running Claiborne Farm, he was met with resistance. Hancock said that Claiborne had enough sources of stamina in its stud barn that adding another would "over-balance" that aspect of pedigrees. Luro assured Hancock that Princequillo could have sped five furlongs in fifty-nine seconds at any time asked, and finally prevailed upon him to start Princequillo at the family's lesser division, Ellerslie Stud in Virginia, at $250 a season. Conversely, Hancock's son and successor, A. B. (Bull) Hancock Jr., recalled for *The Blood-Horse* in 1971 that after seeing Princequillo win the testing Saratoga Cup — and mindful that he had also won at six furlongs that year — he told his father: "This is one horse we've got to have."

At any rate, Princequillo entered stud at Ellerslie and was a difficult sell. Fortunately, Chris Chenery's farm was in Virginia, so he sent a mare (Hildene) and the staunch Claiborne patron William Woodward Sr. sent two, while the Hancocks sent four. From Princequillo's second crop, Chenery got the American champion Hill Prince, and Woodward got the English champion Prince Simon, who brought the owner to within a photo of his long-sought goal, the English Derby. Princequillo promptly graduated to the Hancock family's first-string stud barn at Claiborne in Kentucky.

The Misfit That Roared

Abram S. Hewitt in the book *Sire Lines* described Princequillo as "the wrong kind of horse in his racing record, backed by the wrong kind of pedigree for America." The wrong kind of race-horse meant one who thought a really good time was when races got beyond one and a half miles. As for the wrong kind of pedigree, Hewitt had much to choose from in justifying the description.

Princequillo was by Prince Rose—Cosquilla, by Papyrus. Broodmare sire Papyrus won the Epsom Derby, but was an indifferent sire. Cosquilla was a good filly who finished second in the one and five-eighths-mile Grand Prix de Deauville. Still, as Hewitt summarized it, "there was no high-class speed close up in 'Princequillo's' pedigree...His sire was a very good horse at twelve furlongs and more, but had a pedigree crammed with plodders. Also, Princequillo's first three dams were sired by proven failures and, apart from his dam, the mares in the family close up had no racing merit."

The sire, Prince Rose, was a representative of the St. Simon sire line, which has waxed and waned and re-emerged over more than a century. Prince Rose, however, was four generations removed from the noble founder. St. Simon, nine-time leader of the English sire list, was foaled in 1881, and his best son as a stallion was the Epsom Derby, St. Leger, and Ascot Gold Cup winner Persimmon. The latter sired Prince Palatine, who won the Ascot Gold Cup twice, as well as the St. Leger, Coronation Cup, and (short by such standards) the one and a quarter-mile Eclipse Stakes. Prince Palatine was a shy breeder, and those he got did not seem to be doing much. He was sold out of England, first to France and then to the United States, and he wound up dying in a fire at Xalapa Farm, not far from Claiborne. (During his time in this country, Prince Palatine got Blue Glass, dam of Unbreakable, sire of Polynesian, he, in turn, sire of Native Dancer [refer to separate chapter].)

Prince Palatine's key link to Princequillo, and a great deal more in the male line, was his son Rose Prince, winner of the two and a quarter-mile

Princecquillo

Cesarewitch in England. Rose Prince, who was conceived during Prince Palatine's French stay at stud, was out of a good family, his granddam being a dual classic winner in France. Crossed with the mare Indolence (by the generally disappointing sire Gay Crusader, an English Triple Crown winner), Rose Prince sired Prince Rose, who was to win sixteen of seventeen races in three years in the early 1930s. Prince Rose was dominant at two and three in Belgium, but Belgian form is regarded as far below English, French, or Irish form. Sent traveling to improve his image, he was third in France's Prix de l'Arc de Triomphe, which probably accomplished the aim. At four, Prince Rose won four more important races in Belgium and then returned to France to win the Prix du President de la Republique, now known as the Grand Prix de Saint-Cloud.

The Belgian government declared Prince Rose such a national treasure that for a time it prohibited his sale outside the country. The threat of invasion weakened this position, of course, and Laudy Lawrence was able to get the horse out of Belgium and stand him in France. There he bred Cosquilla to the horse, then sent the mare on to Ireland. Thus, Princequillo, son of a Belgian hero and a French mare was, out of expedience, an Irish-bred.

Prince Rose was killed by artillery fire in France at the age of sixteen, but he had made an extraordinary contribution. In addition to Princequillo, Prince Rose sired two other sons destined to create important sire lines: Prince Bio and Prince Chevalier.

Prince Bio sired two outstanding stallions in Prince Taj and Sicambre. The latter got the Belmont Stakes winner Celtic Ash, several European classic winners, the Washington, D.C., International winner Diatome, and the dam of the great Sea-Bird. This line's representation in the United States in recent years produced Play Fellow and Western Playboy, as well as the Brazilian import Siphon.

Prince Rose's son Prince Chevalier sired an Epsom Derby winner in Arctic Prince, a French Derby winner in Charlottesville, and a Prix de l'Arc de Triomphe winner in Soltikoff. In turn, sons of Prince Chevalier sired the Irish Derby winner Meadow Court, the Epsom Derby winner Charlottown, and the Epsom Derby runner-up Pretendre (in turn the sire of Kentucky Derby-Preakness winner Canonero II).

Princequillo, of course, is the son of Prince Rose about which we are most concerned here. He took his offbeat combination of qualities and became a great and lasting influence. He got sixty-five stakes winners (fourteen percent) before his death at twenty-four in 1964. Princequillo led the American sire list in 1957 and 1958, and the top end of his offspring could stand up against, or above, the best of many great stallions:

- *Round Table*, durable champion, Horse of the Year, one-time leading money earner.
- *Misty Morn*, three-year-old filly champion and later Broodmare of the Year.
- *Hill Prince*, Preakness winner, three-time champion, Horse of the Year.
- *Prince Simon*, champion three-year-old in England.
- *Dedicate*, a champion handicapper in this country.
- *Quill*, champion filly at two.
- *Prince John*, Garden State Stakes winner.
- *Tambourine*, Irish Derby winner.

Princequillo also sired three winners of the Coaching Club American Oaks — How, Cherokee Rose, and Quillo Queen — at a time it ranked perhaps as the country's top race for three-year-old fillies. Others that seemingly equate to grade I winners of today include Dotted Line, Firm Policy, Kingmaker, Crimea II, Princessnesian, Blue Prince, Rose Bower, Monarchy, and Whodunit. (As a bit of a footnote, one of his grandsons was Ole Bob Bowers, in turn, sire of the singular John Henry.)

Round Table

Princequillo's son Round Table has remained a standard of soundness and toughness which few horses, before or after him, have approached. A smallish colt from the Sir Cosmo mare Knight's Daughter, Round Table was a Claiborne-bred foaled in 1954, on the same evening as Bold Ruler. Round Table won stakes for the Hancocks at two, then the following winter, a majority interest was sold for a reported $145,000. It was 1957, the year A. B. Hancock Sr. passed away, and his son, Bull Hancock, recognized such a deal would be very helpful in paying estate taxes and keeping the farm strong. He kept enough shares to make sure Round Table retired to Claiborne if and when it was appropriate.

All the same, the experience of breeding, and selling a Round Table, sent Bull Hancock in search of a solution that would guard against letting future colts of his ilk get away. He first worked a deal with Howard B. Keck, who bought an interest in one foal crop, and then offered a similar deal to Canadian Bill Beasley. It was William Haggin Perry, however, who signed on to purchase a half-interest in each Claiborne crop based on twice the average price realized at the Keeneland and Saratoga summer yearling sales combined. This partnership lasted for the rest of their lives and produced a remarkable series of major winners for both, as well as for Hancock's surviving family.

Round Table, though, wore Oklahoma oilman Travis M. Kerr's silks to fame. He won forty-three of sixty-six races and retired as the all-time leading money earner, with $1,749,869. Round Table's one problem was with off going. Otherwise, trainer Willie Molter could switch him from dirt to turf at will and ship all over the country. Round Table won in major company carrying weights up to 136 pounds, won racing beyond one and a half miles, set several track records at one and a quarter miles, and blazed a mile in 1:33 2/5. Round Table won fifteen of twenty-two races at three, fourteen of twenty at four, and nine of fourteen at five. He was voted Horse of the Year and handicap champion at four in 1958 and was grass champion for three years, 1957-59.

Round Table was retired to Claiborne and lived to be thirty-three. Such was his status that Queen Elizabeth II altered her schedule when on a Kentucky visit in 1984 to visit the Claiborne pensioner, then thirty years old. Round Table died in 1987.

Although overshadowed by his neighbor across the Claiborne stud barn aisle, Bold Ruler, Round Table, too, became a very good sire. He got eighty-three stakes winners, a glossy twenty-one percent, and he led the American sire list in 1972. A considerable number of Round Table's best runners made their mark in Europe. His first crop included the English Two Thousand Guineas winner Baldric II, and then followed Apalachee, Cellini, Artaius, Brahms, Flirting Around, and Targowice (sire of the international champion mare All Along).

In this country, Round Table's best included the rugged grass mare Drumtop, plus Advocator, King Pellinore, King's Bishop, Duel, Bicker, Beau Brummel, He's a Smoothie, Illustrious (broodmare sire of Gold Beauty), Dancealot, Knightly Manner, Tell, Royal Glint, Table the Rumor, Upper Case, and Poker.

Round Table, as a sire, was thus marked by a great many high-class horses, but not many champions. He could be said never to have gotten "the big horse," while granting that is an indistinct description. His good son Poker has achieved late fame as the broodmare sire of Triple Crown winner Seattle Slew and Derby-Preakness winner Silver Charm. Similarly, Targowice sired All Along, while Apalachee has sired nearly sixty stakes winners, including K One King. Advocator, Knightly Manner, King's Bishop, Tell, and Flirting Around (sire of South African import Wolf Power) at one time each gave hints of extending this branch of the sire line, but it is far from strong in numbers today.

Prince John

The Princequillo colt Prince John was far from as accomplished a racehorse as Round Table and got considerably fewer stakes winners, but he was a better sire of sires, although his branch has weakened recently.

Most of the image builders in the Princequillo line were bays, like the sire. Prince John, however, was a bright chestnut with a lengthy triangle of white on his face. He was out of the mare Not Afraid and was bred by Mrs. John D. Hertz, in whose colors had raced the colt's broodmare sire, Count Fleet. The latter sired thirty-nine stakes winners (nine percent) and led the sire list in 1951, eight years after winning the Triple Crown. Count Fleet's best included two Horses of the Year in the early 1950s in Counterpoint and One Count, as well as the Kentucky Derby winner Count Turf. His fillies bred on better than the colts. They included the champion Kiss Me Kate, the good runner and producer Juliets Nurse (the 1966 Broodmare of the Year), and eventually the dams of 119 stakes winners — including Lamb

Princequillo

Chop, Quill, and the singular Kelso (five-time Horse of the Year). Count Fleet continued the decade-by-decade progression from great racehorse to leading sire to leading broodmare sire, topping the latter category in 1963.

The Princequillo—Not Afraid colt of 1953 was purchased as a yearling at Keeneland by Maxwell H. Gluck, who had acquired historic Elmendorf Farm in Kentucky. The horse's issue would prove rather helpful to the New York clothing tycoon's emergence as three-time leading breeder.

Prince John broke his maiden in his second start for trainer Walter Kelley, in August of 1955 at Saratoga. He had placed in the Sanford and Washington Park Futurity and run fourth in the Belmont Futurity by the time he lined up at one and one-sixteenth miles for the Garden State Stakes. Off at 24-1, Prince John tracked the early leaders, took command turning for home, and just held off Career Boy, winning by a nose. Needles, another staying sort with speed, was along for third.

In the Remsen at the same distance, though, he was second to Nail. Prince John was ranked at 124 pounds on the Experimental Free Handicap, two pounds below topweight Career Boy, while the co-champions in a competitive crop, Nail and Needles, were between them.

The following winter, disaster struck. Prince John broke loose from his handlers, ran off, and fractured a pedal bone. He never got back to the races, although he did not begin standing at stud until the next year, 1957. Prince John had won three of nine races and earned $212,818. He stood first at Elmendorf and later was moved to Leslie Combs II's Spendthrift Farm.

Among Prince John's fifty-five stakes winners (ten percent), the Greentree Stable homebred Stage Door Johnny accomplished what the sire hinted he might be able to achieve — develop late, thrive as distances stretched, and win a classic. Stage Door Johnny won the centennial running of the Belmont Stakes and then followed with a major stud career of his own. He got fifty-one stakes winners, but has not done much to extend the success of the sire line.

Prince John's other runners included the distaff champion Typecast; two juvenile champions Silent Screen and Protagonist; Coaching Club American Oaks winner Magazine; Irish St. Leger winner Transworld; the distance horse Jean-Pierre; and, in contrast, as quick and brilliant a filly as Deceit. Transworld is known today as the sire of a champion, but the champion is five-time steeplechase leader Lonesome Glory — not much of an addition to an ongoing sire line. Silent Screen had a degree of success, but again did not leave much to continue the sire line.

Among Prince John's sons that had more success as sires of sires were winners well below championship and/or classic status. Selari, Rash Prince, and Mandate were examples. Selari won the Grey Lag Handicap at four and got the $600,000-earner Great Contractor and a number of other nice runners. Again, though, there is little to remind of them among active stallions of today.

Prince John's status as a sire of sire was underscored by a star son who was among his first runners but not necessarily one of the best. This was Speak John, a member of Prince John's first crop. Speak John won the Del Mar Derby and Tropicana Hotel of Las Vegas Handicap at three in 1961. He then sired twenty-four stakes winners, including the juvenile filly champion Talking Picture and a pair named Hold Your Peace and

Verbatim who nobly upheld the history of the sire line. He also sired Thunder Puddles, in turn, the sire of Travers Stakes winner Thunder Rumble.

Hold Your Peace, who won the Arlington-Washington Futurity, placed in Riva Ridge's Kentucky Derby. He is the sire of Meadowlake, whose 1999 runners included the Champagne Stakes winner Greenwood Lake. Meadowlake's thirty-five stakes winners also include champion Meadow Star and the fleet Meafara. Hold Your Peace also sired the Breeders' Cup Juvenile winner Success Express.

Verbatim was a high-class colt who won six stakes at three and four, including the Gotham and Haskell. He never ascended to the high levels of fashion, but he turned out the marvelous filly champion Princess Rooney, the Belmont Stakes winner Summing (sire of champion Epitome), plus Alphabatim and Hopeful Word, among fifty-eight stakes winners. Even he, though, now appears to be sliding from the charts on the top line.

It will come as no surprise that a number of these animals were important broodmare sires. Princequillo's best, Round Table, became the broodmare sire of 124 stakes winners. Prince John mares have foaled 172 stakes winners, and he led the broodmare sire list three times. Speak John led it once, in 1985, when represented by Spend a Buck, and his daughters have foaled forty-nine stakes winners. Stage Door Johnny's daughters have foaled ninety-eight.

Princequillo, himself, outdid them all. He led the broodmare sire list eight times. His daughters foaled 170 stakes winners, and one of them was Secretariat. ❖

Rough'n Tumble

ough'n Tumble's sire line may linger, or it may fade, but he will always have a legion of successors in a non-genetic sense. Any successful Florida operation can be said to owe a little debt to Rough'n Tumble.

A few visionary, adventuresome horsemen in the 1950s launched an era in which Florida went from a backwater Thoroughbred breeding state to one of the rich sources of champions. They recognized advantages of the climate and the limestone soil, of Central Florida especially, but they needed some cooperation from equine genes. Rough'n Tumble was the key supplier thereof, and his running offspring gave supporting depth to the breakthrough success of the first national champion Florida-bred, Needles.

Rough'n Tumble went back in his male line to the 19th Century star Himyar, winner of fourteen of twenty-seven races and during the late 1870s regarded as the fastest horse in Kentucky and nearby states. Himyar was also the sire of Domino, whose legacy is addressed in the chapter on Commando in this volume. Rough'n Tumble, however, represented another branch descending from Himyar. In addition to Domino, Himyar's sons included the 1898 Kentucky Derby winner, Plaudit. In turn, Plaudit got the high-class King James, he the sire of Spur, a winner of the Withers and

Travers Stakes. Spur was owned during his stallion career by James Butler, a successful grocery man who built Empire City racetrack in New York.

Spur sired Sting, winner of the Metropolitan and Suburban Handicaps for Butler; Sting, in turn, sired Questionnaire. If Himyar was the high point on a horizontal graph of these horses, Questionnaire probably represented a upward blip toward him and above his closer-up male ancestors. Questionnaire got off slowly, winning only two of fourteen starts at two, but eventually won nineteen of forty-five from 1929-1933 and earned $89,611. His thirteen stakes triumphs included the Metropolitan, Brooklyn, Empire City, and Paumonok Handicaps, and at three he ran the champion Gallant Fox to a head in the one and five-eighths-mile Lawrence Realization.

Sting had stood in New York, in that era an out-of-the-way state in Thoroughbred breeding circles, but Questionnaire had the fortune of standing at Greentree Stud in Kentucky. He was a good sire, getting twenty-four stakes winners (nine percent), including the 1943 champion three-year-old filly Stefanita, the high-class runner and stallion Requested, plus Hash, Carolyn A., Wine List, and Third Degree.

Another son of Questionnaire was Free For All. Although he faded from memory because of a generally desultory stud record, Free For All appeared to be a potential champion in 1944 and early 1945. He was unbeaten in his first six races before breaking down while finishing fourth in the Derby Trial. Free For All must have engendered some of the excitement, followed by the kicked-in-the-stomach feeling associated with such later apparent Derby comets as Turn-to, Gen. Duke, Sir Gaylord, Graustark, Hoist the Flag, Timely Writer, and Dehere.

Free For All won the Arlington Futurity, Washington Park Futurity, and Hyde Park Stakes in dashing style while unbeaten in five starts at two. Meanwhile in the East, Pavot was winning everything, going unbeaten in eight races, including such prestigious events as the Futurity, Hopeful, and Grand Union Hotel. Nevertheless, a measure of the impression Free For All made was indicated by his being rated equal topweight with champion Pavot on the Experimental Free Handicap. Also, after he won his first start at three, he was regarded as the Kentucky Derby favorite, and his trainer, Burley Parke, secured a commitment from the star jockey Eddie Arcaro to ride him.

Starting with the Derby Trial, Free For All's fortune took a virtual free fall, although he was acquired for stud at a good location, the respected veterinarian Charles Hagyard's farm in Kentucky. There he suffered only slight injuries when struck by lightning, but aside from Rough'n Tumble, Free For All sired little of note, and by 1957 Hagyard consigned him to the Keeneland fall mixed sale. Rough'n Tumble had won the Santa Anita Derby six years before, but his rise as a sire was not yet recognizable, and Free For All brought only $5,700. He was purchased by W. D. Rorick of Kansas and eventually died in Colorado in 1964, by which year he was the grandsire of champion My Dear Girl (and of a foal to be named Dr. Fager).

The bright spot among Free For All's nine stakes winners (three percent) was Rough'n Tumble, who was bred by Hagyard from the mare Roused. The fact that Roused was by the leading sire and broodmare sire Bull Dog was possibly the only thing to recommend about the bottom half of the colt's pedigree. Roused was not a winner and had no other high-class foals, and her own dam, Rude Awakening, while stakes-placed, was by the moderate stallion Upset of defeating-Man o' War fame.

Harold and Frances Genter, relative newcomers to the Turf, had purchased a colt from Hagyard's consignment in 1948. The next summer, having gotten nothing from the summer sale, they visited Hagyard Farm and purchased the Free For All—Roused colt privately. The colt was small, even a bit scrawny. Sunshine Calvert, trainer for the Frances Genter Stable (as the couple's horses were identified) launched the colt's career in claiming company the following summer. Rough'n Tumble won for $7,000 first time out and jumped up in class to win the Primer Stakes in his second start. While he won no more at two, he was classy enough to finish third at 33-1 in Battlefield's Futurity.

Sent West, Rough'n Tumble battled with Phil D. in several early races and got the better of him in the key event for three-year-olds, the Santa Anita Derby. The Genter party (which included son-in-law Bentley Smith, an owner of stakes winners in the year 2000) sent the colt to Kentucky. They had little time to contemplate the Kentucky Derby, for Rough'n Tumble came up lame. The problem was a splint and, while it did not end his career as his sire's pre-Derby injury had, it put him out of the classics.

After treatment and rest, Rough'n Tumble was matched against the best three-year-olds and older horses in Chicago through the summer. He

		Sting, 1921	Spur / Gnat
	Questionnaire, 1927	Miss Puzzle, 1913	Disguise / Ruby Nethersole
FREE FOR ALL, br, 1942		Chicle, 1913	**Spearmint** / Lady Hamburg II
	Panay, 1934	Panasette, 1928	**Whisk Broom II** / Panasine
ROUGH'N TUMBLE, b h, 1948		Teddy, 1913	Ajax / Rondeau
	Bull Dog, 1927	Plucky Liege, 1912	**Spearmint** / Concertina
ROUSED, b, 1943		Upset, 1917	**Whisk Broom II** / Pankhurst
	Rude Awakening, 1936	Cushion, 1917	Nonpareil / Hassock

1st dam: Roused, b, 1943. Bred by Dr. Charles E. Hagyard (Ky). Raced 1 yr, 8 sts, 0 wins, $0. Dam of 9 named foals, 8 rnrs, 5 wnrs, 1 sw.

1948: ROUGH'N TUMBLE, b c, by Free For All. Bred by Dr. Charles E. Hagyard (Ky). Raced 2 yrs, 16 sts, 4 wins, $126,980. Won Santa Anita Derby, Primer S; 2nd Garden State S, Remsen H, Sheridan H; 3rd Futurity S, San Felipe S. Sire of 206 foals, 24 sw, 2.83 AEI. Died 1969.

1949: Hit the Deck, b c, by Free For All. Raced 8 yrs, 82 sts, 8 wins, $5,997.

1950: Bemidji, b c, by Free For All. Unraced.

1951: Whay-Thlay, b f, by Basileus II. Raced 1 yr, 5 sts, 0 wins, $0.

1952: Barren.

1953: Barren.

1954: Rumpled, dk b/br f, by Free For All. Raced 2 yrs, 18 sts, 3 wins, $5,600. Dam of 9 foals, 8 rnrs, 7 wnrs. Granddam of **PERSUADABLE, BUSTED, GRANADOS, Affair d'Honneur, Get the Axe, Knight of the Road, Big Duel.**

1955: Dead foal.

1956: Barren.

1957: Surrencified, ch f, by Mr. Busher. Raced 1 yr, 14 sts, 2 wins, $2,040. Dam of 8 foals, 7 rnrs, 5 wnrs. Granddam of **PISTOL WHITE.**

1958: Sufficiency, b f, by Helioscope. Raced 1 yr, 9 sts, 4 wins, $4,384. Dam of 8 foals, 8 rnrs, 7 wnrs, including **ROGER'S CHOICE** ($118,575). Granddam of **MADAM'S DARLING.**

1959: Barren.

1960: Full o' Beans, b f, by Traffic Judge. Raced 2 yrs, 18 sts, 0 wins, $2,075. Dam of 9 foals, 9 rnrs, 7 wnrs, including **Beanery** ($46,641). Granddam of **ROCKHILL NATIVE, PRON REGARD, SATIETY, TANTALYZING TODD, Silent Man, Thanks Eddie, Initial Encounter, Dorothea R.**

1961: Barren.

1962: B c, by Hail To Reason.

1963: Barren.

1964: Sleeping Child, dkb/br f, by Spy Song. Raced 1 yr, 1 st, 0 wins, $0. Dam of 5 foals, 3 rnrs, 2 wnrs. Granddam of **HOT DANCE, Ark.**

did not win again, but was second when Bernwood got a mile in a track-record 1:33 4/5 in the Sheridan Handicap. The distinguished To Market was farther back. Rough'n Tumble also ran a race which looked good in a sense on paper when beaten by only one and a half lengths by Hall of Fame, with Battlefield second, in the Arlington Classic. The bad news was that Rough'n Tumble finished sixth. He had won four of sixteen races and earned $126,980 at two and three.

Nagged by lameness, Rough'n Tumble never ran again after his three-year-old season, although the Genters and Calvert tried for two more years. By the end of 1953, Hagyard agreed to stand the horse at stud at his farm. At that same time, the O'Farrell brothers from Maryland, Tom and Joe, needed a stallion for their Windy Hills Farm, and Cromwell Bloodstock Agency put them in contact with Calvert and the Genters. A deal was struck whereby Rough'n Tumble would stand at Windy Hills as property of the Genters. (One can only guess that Hagyard was relieved.)

Rough'n Tumble first stood there in 1954. The next year, Joe O'Farrell was invited to inspect a farm in Ocala, Florida, and went home ready for a career change. Fellow Maryland horseman Bruce Campbell bought the farm with some associates, put Joe O'Farrell in charge, and changed the name from Dickey Stables to Ocala Stud. Rough'n Tumble was transferred to Ocala Stud and, in time, was purchased by the farm.

It was a time when any stakes winner was a big deal to a Florida operation. When Ragtime Cowboy, from Rough'n Tumble's first crop (foaled in 1955) won a steeplechase stakes at three, it was cause for excitement. Even better, his full sister Wedlock won a division of the Kentucky Oaks the following year. It mattered not to the Ocala Stud group that some of the first good Rough'n Tumbles were Maryland-breds. They had a sire on the rise, and their stated faith in his future was fervent; even so, it turned out to be understated.

Yes You Will, also from the second crop, won the $100,000 John B. Campbell, then the biggest handicap in Maryland, as well as the Carter Handicap in New York, and Bruce Campbell's Conestoga won the Campbell the next year among a brace of stakes. The biggest leap for Rough'n Tumble into the big time, though, was the Genter Stable's My Dear Girl, who had won the Gardenia Stakes and Frizette Stakes in 1959. She followed

1956 Kentucky Derby-Belmont winner Needles as the second champion from Florida.

Rough'n Tumble's stud fee had started at $250, and it was to rise to $10,000, a very high mark for his time, regardless of state. By the middle 1960s, Rough'n Tumbles were selling for as much as $70,000 at the Hialeah sale of two-year-old state-breds, less than a decade after this sale drew snickers.

Several Rough'n Tumbles generated Triple Crown talk, although he never got a classic winner. In 1965, the fashionable Bieber-Jacobs Stable had a nice Rough'n Tumble colt in Flag Raiser, who upset champion Bold Lad in the Wood Memorial and went on to the Kentucky Derby. He was eighth, but bounced back to win the Withers and various other stakes. By 1968, Charles W. Engelhard, the dominant yearling buyer of his time, had put a seal of approval on Rough'n Tumble and had a three-year-old by him named Alley Fighter. This colt won the Santa Anita Derby, but soon faded from the scene.

All this was pale compared to what had transpired by the end of 1968. W. L. McKnight, head of 3-M Corporation, had been among major investors to follow the Ocala Stud lead and locate a farm in Florida. In 1963, his Tartan Farm mare Aspidistra was sent to Rough'n Tumble and the following year foaled a big, rowdy sort of colt to be named Dr. Fager. Trained by Hall of Fame horseman John Nerud, Dr. Fager showed brilliant speed, but not equal brilliance in knowing how to use it.

He was among the best two-year-olds of 1966, but the next year, even after the colt defeated the crack Damascus in the Gotham Stakes at a mile, Nerud was too crafty to subject the headstrong front-runner to the Derby. (Ironically, that same year, another Tartan Farm-foaled colt, the Genter Stable's In Reality, was another of the top three-year-olds. He was one of what proved to be many exceptional foals from the Rough'n Tumble champion My Dear Girl. Calvert, too, bypassed the Derby, but ran In Reality in the Preakness, where he was second to Damascus. In the Jersey Derby, the son and grand-son of Rough'n Tumble ran and, paradoxically, both won, and both lost. Dr. Fager dominated In Reality, but fouled him early in the race and was disqualified, giving the other colt the official victory.)

By the autumn of 1967, Dr. Fager had added the Withers, Arlington Classic, and New Hampshire Sweepstakes, while Damascus had added the Belmont, Travers, and American Derby. When those two superb three-year-olds met in the Woodward, they were also facing the great older champion and defending Horse of the Year, Buckpasser. This crackling field, however, was joined by a pacemaker for each of Dr. Fager's foes, and they goaded him on a merry chase early. Damascus won by ten, Buckpasser was second, Dr. Fager exhausted.

The following year at four, however, Dr. Fager reigned, and he did so with a completeness only a few have even approached. He was not only champion older male and Horse of the Year, but also champion sprinter, and, to complete the sweep, Nerud ran him once on grass and he was champion on that surface in one poll, as well.

Dr. Fager and Damascus met twice at four, swapping smashing triumphs in historic races. Damascus won the Brooklyn Handicap, carrying 130 pounds to Dr. Fager's 135, but Dr. Fager had won the Suburban, carrying 132 to the other's 133. A pattern developed: When Damascus' pace-maker, Hedevar, ran in the race, Damascus won; otherwise, Dr. Fager won.

Dr. Fager also went West to win the Californian. In Chicago, he turned in one of racing's historic per-formances. Under 134 pounds in the Washington Park Handicap, he blazed a mile in a new world record, 1:32 1/5, a mark which survived for nearly three decades. Dr. Fager also carried 134 pounds to win the United Nations Handicap at one and three-sixteenths miles in his showcase on grass. Finally, he won the seven-furlong Vosburgh Handicap under 139 pounds, setting a track record that would stand thirty-one years. He had done it all, winning seven of eight races at four, and every performance deserved the often abused 1 and 1A adjective entry of "brilliant" and "sensational." Apparently, Dr. Fager knew one way of going, and that way was fast. Whatever thrill his speed achieved for his equine inner self, it surely did not exceed the thrill sum-moned in his human witnesses. *The Blood-Horse* panel voted him the sixth-best of the century.

Dr. Fager won eighteen of twenty-two races and earned $1,002,642. He went to stud at Tartan. He was a very good sire and might have proven a bet-ter one, but he died very young at twelve of a twist-ed intestine. He got thirty-five stakes winners (thir-teen percent), including the champion two-year-old filly Dearly Precious, the co-champion sprinter Dr. Patches, and the Canadian Horse of the Year L'Alezane. By 1977, *The Blood-Horse* had begun the ever-changing process and progress of incorporat-ing stallions' earnings in various major racing countries into sire statistics. Under that reality, the magazine historically lists Northern Dancer as the leading sire of 1977. *Daily Racing Form*, however, listed Dr. Fager as the leading sire that year, based on North American earnings.

Dr. Fager is the broodmare sire of ninety-eight stakes winners, but his sons did not contrive to further the sire line in lasting, numerical strength.

To return to Rough'n Tumble, we find that it has been his fate, as with so many other good stallions, that his best racing son did less to preserve the ongoing sire line than did a lesser horse. By and large, the Rough'n Tumble stallions were not outstanding sires. Dr. Fager was, of course, an exception, while the aforementioned Flag Raiser got Vencedor among his few stakes winners and Gunflint got nineteen stakes winners. There was another colt, however, one who joined Dr. Fager and In Reality in the memorable crop of foals born at Tartan Farm in 1964. This Rough'n Tumble colt was Minnesota Mac, named for the farm founder, McKnight (of Minnesota). Minnesota Mac was not in Dr. Fager's class, but in his crop. He won a single stakes, the $75,000 Chicagoan Handicap. In the stud, Minnesota Mac got only eighteen stakes winners (seven percent), but several of them had some impact. One was the grass course Eclipse Award winner Mac Diarmida, and another was the $500,000-plus earner Honey Fox. Of the eighteen, nine earned at least $200,000 each, such winnings still a very significant level for offspring of a stallion foaled in 1964.

The key, lasting link in the sire line to Minnesota Mac's sire, Rough'n Tumble, was Great Above. Minnesota Mac sired that colt from a mating with Dr. Fager's half-sister, the sprint champion Ta Wee (by Intentionally). Great Above was a good grade III sprint winner in New York and has sired thirty-seven stakes winners. His ace is the gray Holy Bull, who was spectacular as Horse of the Year in 1994. Holy Bull sired some fifty stakes winners, including Kentucky Derby winner Giacomo and juvenile champion Macho Uno. ❖

EUROPEAN ROOTS

Nearco

"Together with the late Lord Derby, Signor (Federico) Tesio had more influence on the breeding of the Thoroughbred than anyone else in my time." So testified Lord Rosebery in his address as president of England's Thoroughbred Breeders' Association at its annual meeting on December 7, 1954. A revered and successful breeder in his own right, Rosebery was commemorating the fact that Tesio had passed away during that year.

Nearco was beneficiary of the strategems of both these remarkably successful horsemen. His sire line was that of Phalaris, a product of Lord Derby's stud and author of an almost ubiquitous presence in the distant realms of pedigrees even today. Nearco's breeder was Tesio himself, the Italian breeder-owner-trainer whose success reached almost mythical status. This combination is appropriate, for Nearco's presence through the majority of the 20th Century was so pervasive that it is difficult to determine just how many chapters of a book on stallions need be assigned his issue.

As is true of Hyperion, Nearco's lore and legacy do not bespeak one of those sire lines which dangled generation after generation upon the emergence of one or two surviving sons. Tesio named his horses for artists, and Nearco slathered his potency upon the canvas of the Turf with lavish and enduring depth and breadth. Consider that Nearco's sons included the following great sires:

• **Nasrullah**, five-time leading American stallion, a leading English sire, and sire of such sons as Bold Ruler, Nashua, Never Bend, Red God, and Grey Sovereign — placing his name in tail male in the pedigrees of Secretariat, Seattle Slew, A.P. Indy, Mill Reef, Darshaan, Blushing Groom, Nashwan, and Caro.

• **Nearctic**, sire of the great stallion Northern Dancer and thus on the top line of the pedigrees of Nijinsky II, Danzig, Nureyev, Lyphard, Sadler's Wells, The Minstrel, Caerleon, Storm Bird, Storm Cat, Deputy Minister, Theatrical, Cigar, Peintre Celebre, Kahyasi, Montjeu, Danehill, and Green Dancer.

• **Royal Charger**, founder of a branch of the sire line that extended to Turn-to, Sir Gaylord, Hail to Reason, Sir Ivor, Roberto, Halo, and Sunday Silence.

• **Mossborough**, in turn the sire of Prix de l'Arc de Triomphe winner Ballymoss (sire of Epsom Derby winner Royal Palace), Cavan, and Noblesse, among others.

• **Dante**, Epsom Derby winner and sire of various major winners, including Toulouse Lautrec, from whom descend in tail male the North American champion Hawaii and his Epsom Derby-winning son Henbit.

• *Amerigo*, a major winner who died young but sired champion Fort Marcy, Politely, and so on.

Phalaris, grandsire of Nearco, was the prototype of the horse of speed which confounded a certain purist view to exert influence beyond all expectation. Lord Derby probably was more comfortable breeding a Derby winner to an Oaks winner, but in the sprinter Phalaris he harbored a stallion of startling potency. To what extent it was intent to do so is questionable.

Phalaris was by the Cyllene stallion Polymelus, who was a bit off top class, but won the Cambridgeshire and Champion Stakes. Arthur Hancock Sr. told Abe Hewitt that he had urged Henry Oxnard to purchase Polymelus when the horse came up for sale, but Oxnard went another route and got more or less nothing instead of a stallion with hidden excellence. Polymelus led the sire list in England five times. Among his get was Phalaris.

Phalaris was out of the mare Bromus, winner of only one race from ten starts and, at that time, the only winner from her dam. Cheery, dam of Bromus, was from the Springfield mare Sunrise. The owner of this lot at the time, J. H. Houldsworth, came under the spell of the best horse of his career in Springfield[1], and embarked upon a lengthy pattern of breeding Sunshine, granddam of Sunrise, and her brood to that stallion. By the time of Bromus, the twists and turns of such dedication created a filly inbred 2x3 to Springfield, or as it used to be stated, inbred with only two free generations.

What attracted Lord Derby's trainer, The Honorable George Lambton, and his bloodstock advisor, Walter Alston, to Bromus might be presumed to be in part Lambton's opinion — expressed from time to time — that the Derby stock, for all its success, was in need of some toughening strains. Whether a poor mare with a dull family highly inbred was exactly what they set out to find is unlikely, but in securing Bromus for Lord Derby they did their master a fine turn.

Phalaris, the 1913 Polymelus—Bromus, by Sainfoin, colt was not as good a two-year-old as might be suggested by the extraordinary speed he showed later. He was reckoned a dozen pounds off the top of the Free Handicap, and then at three he quickly showed that the classics were beyond him, being unplaced in the Craven Stakes and the Two Thousand Guineas. He eventually won three of seven races at age three.

At four, Phalaris came into full bloom, winning seven of his nine starts, most of them sprints. Oddly, he also walked over for The Whip, a race of just over two miles. However, he showed himself unable to get much distance in top company when he was unplaced under 126 pounds in the one and one-eighth-mile Cambridgeshire. Still in training at five, Phalaris won four of five races and carried 147 pounds in winning the Abingdon Plate of five furlongs. He also won the Lanwades Plate at seven furlongs under 141 pounds. Phalaris won sixteen of twenty-four races and earned the equivalent of about $27,000.

It has been often repeated that Lord Derby tried to sell Phalaris for 5,000 pounds, but finding no takers in the economics coinciding with the end of World War I, sent him home to stud. Hewitt quoted Lambton as saying, "I cannot say I really believed in him (as a sire prospect). However, he had absolutely first-class speed, an excellent constitution, and was up to very high weights. Furthermore, he had very good action and was as true as steel for as far as he could go." Such a description might put a nicely bred colt atop many bloodstock agents' predictions as top freshman sire today, but, again, it hardly seemed the sort of horse the 17th Lord Derby was looking toward to sire more classic winners.

		Polymelus, 1902	Cyllene / Maid Marian
	Phalaris, 1913		
PHAROS, b, 1920		Bromus, 1905	Sainfoin / Cheery
		Chaucer, 1900	**St. Simon** / Canterbury Pilgrim
	Scapa Flow, 1914		
NEARCO, br h, January 24, 1935		Anchora, 1905	Love Wisely / Eryholme
		Rabelais, 1900	**St. Simon** / Satirical
	Havresac II, 1915		
NOGARA, b, 1928		Hors Concours, 1906	Ajax / Simona
		Spearmint, 1903	Carbine / Maid of the Mint
	Catnip, 1910		
		Sibola, 1896	The Sailor Prince / Saluda

1st dam: NOGARA, b, 1928-1948. Bred by Federico Tesio (Italy). Raced 2 yrs in Italy, 18 sts, 14 wins. Champion 2 and 3yo filly in Italy. Won Premio Parioli, Premio Regina Elena, Premio Bimbi. Dam of 9 named foals, 8 rnrs, 7 wnrs, 6 sw.

1933: Nicoletto da Modena, b c, by Sagacity. Race record unavailable.

1934: Barren.

1935: NEARCO, br c, by Pharos. Bred by Federico Tesio (Italy). Raced 2 yrs in Italy, 8 sts, 8 wins. Champion 2 and 3yo colt in Italy. Won Criterium Nationale, Gran Criterium, Premio Chiusura, Premio Tevere, Gran Premio del Re, Gran Premio Di Milano, Grand Prix de Paris, Gran Premio Dell'Impero. Sire in Eng of 485 foals, 99 sw.

1936: Barren.

1937: Barren.

1938: NICCOLO DELL'ARCA, b c, by Coronach. Raced 2 yrs in Ger and Italy, 15 sts, 12 wins. Champion 3yo colt in Italy. Won Premio Bimbi, Premio Lazio, Premio d'Italia, Gran Criterium, Derby Italiano, Gran Premio del Fascia, St. Leger Italiano, Gran Premio di Milano, Premio Emanuele Filiberto, Premio Parioli, Grosser Preis der Reichhaupstadt. Sire.

1939: NICOLAUS, b c, by Solario. Raced 3 yrs in Italy, 26 sts, 9 wins. Won Premio Verbane; 3rd Gran Premio del Fascio, Premio San Gottardo. Sire.

1940: NAKAMURO, br c, by Cameronian. Raced 1 yr in Italy, 3 sts, 2 wins. Won Premio Principe Di Napoli, Premio Gian Giacomo Trivulzio; 2nd Derby Italiano. Sire.

1941: NERVESA, b f, by Ortello. Raced 1 yr in Italy, 4 sts, 1 win. Won Premio Di Diana; 2nd Premio Regina Elena; 3rd Premio Besana, Premio Emanuele Filiberto. Granddam of **TANAVAR, NOSSENT, PINTURISCHIO, NIGRETTA, MARVARAL, NARDINI, Nerone**.

1942: NICCOLO' D'AREZZO, b c, by Ortello. Raced 3 yrs in Italy, 15 sts, 2 wins. Won Premio Lecco; 2nd St. Leger Italiano, Premio Besana, Premio Sedrina. Sent to USA 1948. Sire. Died 1971.

1943: Barren.

1944: Barren.

1945: NAUCIDE, dk b c, by Bellini. Raced 2 yrs in Italy, 8 sts, 6 wins. Champion 2 and 3yo colt in Italy. Won Premio Volta, Premio Besnate, Premio Chiusura, Premio Ambrosiano; 2nd Premio Emanuele Filiberto, Premio Triennale Italiano; 3rd Derby Italiano. Sire.

1946: Barren.

1947: King of Tara, br c, by Torbido. Raced 1 yr in Eng, 4 sts, 0 wins, $154. 3rd Granville S.

1948: Barren.

Nevertheless, the speedy Phalaris led England's sire list in 1925 and again in 1928. He got the brilliant Fairway, the Derby winner Manna, plus Nearco's sire Pharos and two very good American stallions in Sickle and Pharamond II. Much of his success came with mares by Chaucer, which is not surprising since Chaucer was another Derby stallion. When one looks at the legacy of Nearco outlined above and then considers what else springs from Phalaris in the male line, a case can be made for the 20th Century being identified more with this stallion than any other: Phalaris' son Sickle led the sire list in the United States twice and to him in tail male traced Native Dancer; thus, the line of Raise a Native, Mr. Prospector, Alydar, and others, represents the sire line of Phalaris. Likewise, Phalaris' son Pharamond II was the sire of Menow, who begot Tom Fool, who begot Buckpasser to create another branch of lasting import.

Overseas, again in addition to Pharos, Phalaris got Fairway, sire of two Derby winners (Blue Peter and Watling Street) and a cog in branches that included Fair Trial, Court Martial, Petition, Great Nephew, Grundy, and Shergar, and eventually trickled down to Brigadier Gerard and thus to Lord At War.

Pharos and Fairway were full brothers, both being from the Chaucer mare Scapa Flow. They were inbred to St. Simon, sire of Chaucer and grandsire of Bromus. (Tesio was said to seek a concentration of St. Simon blood, as long as it was not too close; Nearco got more St. Simon blood from his dam's side.) Anchora, dam of Scapa Flow, caught Lambton's eye as another element of toughness for the wily horseman as she had run through the age of seven and up to twelve furlongs.

The crossing of a sprinter with more or less a family of plodders might easily be seen on the surface as combatting two failings, but in practice it is often the formula to create a horse with no viable talent — not enough speed, nor enough stamina to rise above mediocrity. In the case of Pharos, however, this combination produced a notable runner, and in Fairway it produced a St. Leger winner.

Pharos won six of nine races at two, but although he took the Chesham Stakes at Royal Ascot in June, Lambton did not campaign him against the best thereafter. Pharos suggested stamina limitations when he failed at a mile, and was rated ten pounds below the top on the Free Handicap.

At three, Pharos was aimed for the Derby only after Lambton discerned the 1923 English crop of three-year-olds was a desultory lot. In the Derby, he ran a fine race, leading a quarter-mile out and finishing second to Papyrus, beaten one and a half lengths. (Failing in the Epsom Derby was hardly a mark of disgrace for this tribe, for Nasrullah and later Blushing Groom also failed to get the trip successfully, but without apparent deleterious effects on their stud careers.)

Pharos never did win a race at one and a half miles, but he won in top company at one and a quarter miles, notably in the Champion Stakes at four. He won again at five and had a career record of fourteen wins from thirty starts and earnings of about $70,000. He stood three seasons at Lord Derby's Woodland Stud, getting the Guineas and Derby winner Cameronian and the St. Leger winner Firdaussi. He was then moved to France, but Lord Derby retained a number of seasons per year. In France, Pharos sired Nearco and Pharis, the latter unbeaten in three races, including the French Derby and Grand Prix de Paris. Pharis was to have challenged Blue Peter for the St. Leger, but the event was cancelled because of World War II.

The Tesio Touch

Nearco was in Pharos' 1935 crop and was out of Nogara, whose sire, Havresac II, led the Italian sire list eleven times. Nogara and her offspring represented one of the best bits of upward mobility which Tesio masterminded. Student of Mendel and a horseman of exceptional acumen though he was, Tesio was not a rich man. Thirty years into his racing and breeding career, he found it expeditious to take on as a partner, or money man apparently, the Marchese Mario Incisa della Rochetta. Tesio

Nearco

set himself the difficult regimen of maintaining a breeding operation on Lake Maggiore and a training stable some forty miles away at the racecourse in Milan. He marshalled this organization for more than fifty years before his death at age eighty-five in 1954.

Although he once spent as much as 5,000 pounds for a mare, Tesio loved a bargain in the rough. None was more delicious than Catnip, the Spearmint filly he acquired for seventy-five guineas at auction in England during World War I, in 1915. Catnip was consigned by Major Eustace Loder and had been a moderate winner at two. She was in foal to a horse called Cock-a-Hoop, whose status as a half-brother to the great Loder mare Pretty Polly did not raise his stud fee over eighteen pounds. Catnip, however, was out of a classic winner, her dam being the American-bred Sibola, by The Sailor Prince. Sibola had been taken to England by Pierre Lorillard, but was raced by Sir William Beresford when she won the English One Thousand Guineas. Sibola was later acquired by the Loder family.

It is scarcely of much import, but a matter of some nationalistic pride, that Sibola, great-granddam of Italy's great Nearco, descended from an American-based family of yore — that of the Cub Mare — and that the great American sires Sir Archy and Lexington appear in the distant ancestry.

Sibola's daughter Catnip produced for Tesio the filly Nogara, who won both the Italian equivalents of the One Thousand and Two Thousand Guineas. Nogara was an exceptional mare, producing three classic winners: Nearco, Niccolo Dell'Arca, and Nervesa. Niccolo Dell'Arca, who won the Italian Derby by twenty lengths, was one of the twenty-two winners of that country's classic which Tesio bred.

Nothing is so unlikely as an unbeaten racehorse, but Tesio bred them in multiples: Cavaliere d'Arpino (five races), Nearco (fourteen races), Ribot (sixteen races), and Braque (twelve races). Because the Italian foal crops numbered about 300 during much of Tesio's career, however, it took some wandering of his horses to prove the international quality of the partnership's stock. This was done in spectacular style by the likes of Donatello II (who returned a dividend to Lord Derby by siring his great stayer and stallion Alycidon), Botticelli, Tenerani, and, ultimately, Ribot, as well as Nearco.

Tesio put a positive spin on the economic desirability of selling his best and most fashionable horses to stand abroad. Having a stallion at home, he mused in his writings, would create a temptation to breed mares to him just because they were handy rather than because it was an optimum cross. Good thinking, when a Donatello II could sell abroad for 47,500 pounds and a Nearco for 60,000 pounds. Thus, Tesio frequently sent mares to France and England to be covered. (Ribot, maybe the best of the great Italian's work, was foaled in England.)

In 1937, Nearco dashed unbeaten through a two-year-old season of seven races, taking the best of Italy's juvenile races, such as the Criterium Nazionale, Gran Criterium, Premio Teveres, and Premio Chiusura. At three, he won the Premio Parioli (Italian Two Thousand Guineas) and Italian Derby, as well as the Gran Premio di Milano. These races tested him at a mile, one and a half miles, and one and seven-eighths miles, respectively. None was a problem.

Only six days after the one and seven-eighths-mile Milano, Nearco was in France to seek his international stamp of approval. The target was another one and seven-eighths-mile race, the Grand Prix de Paris, then the most prestigious of France's three-year-old races despite being outside the strict definition of the classics. The race brought out a field distinguished by recent classic performances. There were Bois Roussel, the Epsom Derby winner; Cillas, the French Derby winner and his runner-up Canot; and two brave fillies in Feerie, winner of both the French One Thousand Guineas and Oaks, and Ad Astra, runner-up in the French Oaks. Any thought that the Italian wonder would be outclassed was soon put aside, for Nearco came away under a hand ride in the final furlong to win by one and a half lengths from Canot, with Bois Roussel third.

The Grand Prix marked Nearco's fourteenth race and fourteenth victory. Despite his wonderful victories at nearly two miles, his taskmaster did not regard him as a true stayer. The sacred notebook kept by Tesio's wife adjudged Nearco as follows: "Beautifully balanced, of perfect size and great quality. Won all his fourteen races as soon as he was asked. Not a true stayer…won these longer races by his superb class and brilliant speed."

Heeding his alleged fear of misusing a home stallion, Tesio cashed in on Nearco. The brilliant colt was purchased for 60,000 pounds, a record at the time, by Martin Benson, a highly successful British bookmaker. Benson sent him to his Beech House Stud, which, befitting the times, was equipped with a bomb shelter. Nearco stood there throughout his career. He was euthanized at the Equine Research Station, Newmarket, at the age of twenty-two in 1957. He led the English sire list twice.

In his report on Nearco in the *The Bloodstock Breeders' Review* of 1957, Gerald McElligott wrote: "Beautifully proportioned, he stood just over 16 hands and was all quality. His temperament was ideal, and when I first knew him in Paris in 1938 he was inclined to be playful. When I visited his box, he was throwing his stable rubber about and catching it in his mouth. He proved to be what he looked, a genuine Thoroughbred, and transmitted his looks to many of his offspring."

Of Nearco's offspring, Nasrullah and Amerigo exhibited temperament described as anything from "mulish" to "disinclined to race" under the scrutiny of the annual Timeform publication *Race Horses*. Nasrullah was a wonderful sire, but quirks were noted in some of his best sons, including Nashua and Jaipur.

The leading earning sons by Nearco included the Derby winners Nimbus and Dante and the St. Leger winner Sayajirao as well as Hafiz II. While they were not failures at stud, they did not come up to the success of some of his lesser racehorses insofar as stallion performance was concerned, as is outlined above and elaborated on in succeeding chapters.

Nearco's distinguished daughters included the English Oaks winners Masaka and Neasham Belle, as well as Irish Oaks winner Noory. While his standing as a sire of sires predominates his ongoing fame, Nearco's status as a broodmare sire was illustrated by his position as maternal grandsire of the brilliant racehorse and stallion Vaguely Noble.

So revered was Nearco by the time of his demise that the international pedigree student K. Bobinski underwent a writer's version of contrition in addressing the subject for *The Bloodstock Breeders' Review* of 1957: "To all those who like myself have admired the perfect harmony of Nearco's body, who have enjoyed the poesy of his movements, the noble dignity of his look, who like myself have lived for many years under the magic spell of his name, and who like myself will find my narrative boring, my remarks superficial and my generalizations trivial, I offer my most humble apologies for not having risen to the occasion." ❖

Nasrullah

The late Bull Hancock stood a great many stallions during his tenure as head of Claiborne Farm, just as his father, A. B. Hancock Sr., had done before him and as son Seth Hancock has done for nearly three decades.

How a stallion winds up on a particular farm sometimes is a complicated matter, perhaps with a good deal of chance attached. The tide of economic force on occasion is as strong a component as genetic prescience. Given that a cliche runs that anywhere from one in ten stallions to one in twenty will really "make it" as a success, the Claiborne star rate over all three generations has been extraordinary. A. B. Sr. reached out to get the likes of Sir Gallahad III and Blenheim II; Bull fell for Double Jay, Princequillo, Nijinsky II, Damascus, and others; and Seth has recruited the likes of Secretariat, Mr. Prospector, and more recently Unbridled.

Some horses come to a farm more or less automatically, owned by long-term farm clients. From the farm's standpoint, this might seem a bit of good fortune one time, discomfiting the next. Even at the level at which Claiborne has operated for seventy years or so, there have probably been some squint-eyed reactions to horses in the Hancocks' paddocks. William Woodward Sr. had a knack for turning out classic winners to return to Claiborne,

but more than a few of them had European, stamina-oriented pedigrees that most Kentucky hard-boots would just as soon not have to go around promoting. Also, Bull Hancock over time hosted Whodunit, Nance's Lad, Pronto, and some other genetic reality checks.

It is unlikely that Bull Hancock ever needed more determination than the effort it took to acquire that solid gold Rolls-Royce named Nasrullah. From the standpoint of history, it might seem that anyone would have been panting over the prospects of Nasrullah, and, indeed, he did have some obvious gifts going for him. Those who would seek him early on for their breeding operations were also relying on some horseman's intuition, however, for Nasrullah was of such temperament that the phrases "mulish antics" and "spoilt child" found their way into expert commentary about his racing career.

Bull Hancock had as much respect for stamina in a racehorse as the next man, and he longed to win the Kentucky Derby with a horse in his own goldish Claiborne colors. He understood the importance of speed, as well, however. He had liked Princequillo when he noted that the horse won a six-furlong race the same year he won the one and three-quarter-mile Saratoga Cup. He loved Double Jay from the moment he saw him outrun

Education — after Education had convinced the young Hancock of that colt's own superb powers.

In the case of Nasrullah, there were pedigree and performance intrigues which warmed Hancock.

"I picked him out because he was the best 2-year-old of his year; he was third in the (Epsom) Derby, and got 1 1/4 miles very well," Hancock recounted for *The Blood-Horse* in 1971. (There is a pleasant footnote in that he was being interviewed for a three-part series by the late Charles Koch; in a total coincidence, Koch's son Gus later went to work for Claiborne and has served for many years as stallion manager.)

Hancock chased Nasrullah for several years:

"I got the British Bloodstock Agency to make a bid for him right out of training for $50,000, but the old Aga Khan had sold him just the week before to Joseph McGrath.[1] The year before I actually bought him, I almost got him for 100,000 pounds. Harry Guggenheim, Mr. Woodward, Eddie (E. P.) Taylor, and I tried to buy him. We dealt entirely in pounds. Eddie was going to pay for the horse and we were going to re-pay him, because he had pounds and wanted to get some dollars in exchange. Everything seemed in good order, but Eddie called me one night and said 'We're not going to get that horse for 100,000 pounds.' I asked him why, and he said 'the day after tomorrow they are going to devalue the pound. That man isn't going to let him go.' That's just what happened."

A year later, in 1950, Hancock was still thinking about Nasrullah, who was then ten. The horse by that time was a proven success, and one of his winners was the imported Noor, who would streak through a sensational season in which he defeated Citation four times in succession.

Hancock described to Koch the ultimate suc-

cess as coming after "a lot of negotiation." In the book *International Stallions and Studs*, Michael Seth-Smith quotes Hancock in some detail about one final hang-up: An agent who had contacted Hancock by phone some weeks before "phoned me (again) and told me that he had contacted Mr. McGrath at the Doncaster races on St. Leger day, and he signed an option for $320,000 on the back of an envelope…Part of the transaction was that I must pay some 'earnest' money by such and such a date, which was very early in the future. So, I cabled the money, and it got there on a bank holiday. The date was a bank holiday — I do not think anyone here knew that…I had a call from McGrath saying he did not feel I had an option. I told him I felt I did and had fulfilled everything and there was no bank holiday in America, that the money had been sent within the specified time, and that I felt I had an option and would have to turn it over to my attorney if I didn't. He said, 'Well, let's not do that — let's meet in New York with your attorney and mine and try to work something out.' I was afraid that it would be a disagreeable encounter but, in fact, Mr. McGrath and I liked each other immediately. We worked the thing out, whereby I gave him a service to the horse each year and paid him $340,000. He had, of course, a much bigger offer from California."

Hancock's widow, Waddell Hancock, recalls specifics of that deal of a half-century ago: "My daddy (Seth Walker) was a lawyer in Nashville (Tennessee). He was wild about Bull and just loved horses. He wanted Bull to have that horse, because he knew how much it meant to him. Bull asked him to help, and we all went up to New York — not that I had anything to do with it. Mr. McGrath had had an offer, we think from Neil McCarthy in California, and Bull thought he might be trying to get out of the deal. They all

		Phalaris, 1913	Polymelus Bromus
NEARCO, br, 1935	Pharos, 1920	Scapa Flow, 1914	Chaucer Anchora
	Nogara, 1928	Havresac II, 1915	Rabelais Hors Concours
		Catnip, 1910	Spearmint Sibola
NASRULLAH (GB), b h, March 2, 1940	Blenheim II, 1927	Blandford, 1919	Swynford Blanche
		Malva, 1919	Charles O'Malley Wild Arum
MUMTAZ BEGUM, b, 1932	Mumtaz Mahal, 1921	The Tetrarch, 1911	Roi Herode Vahren
		Lady Josephine, 1912	Sundridge Americus Girl

1st dam: Mumtaz Begum, b, 1932-1948. Bred by H.H. The Aga Khan (Fr). Raced 1 yr in Eng, 8 sts, 2 wins, $2,147. Dam of 10 named foals, 8 rnrs, 7 wnrs, 4 sw.

1937: Sun Princess, b f, by Solario. Unraced. Dam of 13 foals, 11 rnrs, 9 wnrs, including **TESSA GILLIAN** ($23,861), **ALASSIO, FLANEUR II, LUCKY BAG, ROYAL CHARGER, ROYAL JUSTICE, Madara**. Granddam of **TEST CASE, ITALIAN RIVIERA, GENTLE ART, TESSO, St Cyr, Palm Beach, Deep Plunge, Margaret Ann, Saul**.

1938: Mkata, b f, by Dastur. Unraced.

1939: Dodoma II, b f, by Dastur. Raced 2 yrs in Ire, 11 sts, 2 wins, $1,138. Dam of 14 foals, 12 rnrs, 7 wnrs, including **DARUBINI** ($71,492), **JAMBO, OMELIA II, DIABLERETTA** (champion 2yo filly in Eng), **Dandome** (in Fr), **Nanavati** (in Eng and Fr), **Trinidad** (in Eng). Granddam of **GINETTA, ALDIVONIE, Orientalist, Annie O., Princesse Retta, Satanella, Tabbas**. Sent to USA 1955.

1940: **NASRULLAH**, b c, by Nearco. Bred by H.H. The Aga Khan (Eng). Raced 2 yrs in Eng, 10 sts, 5 wins, $15,240. Champion 2yo colt in Eng. Won Champion S, Coventry S, Great Bradley S, Cavenham S; 2nd Middle Park S; 3rd New Derby S, Wilburton S. Sent to USA 1950. Sire of 425 foals, 98 sw, 5.16 AEI.

1941: Bibibeg, b f, by Bahram. Raced 1 yr in Ire, 5 sts, 1 win, $339. Dam of 12 foals, 10 rnrs, 8 wnrs, including **BIBI TOORI, HOUMYRA, Daoud Pasha** (in Eng and NA), **Kameran Khan** (in Brz and Eng). Granddam of **CARMEL, Father John, Finnastrida, Break Through**. Sent to USA 1954.

1942: **DARBHANGA**, b c, by Dastur. Raced 2 yrs in Eng, 13 sts, 6 wins, $8,018. Won Thurlow H, Chevington Nursery H, Balsham S. Sent to Swe 1945.

1943: **RIVAZ**, b f, by Nearco. Raced 1 yr in Eng, 4 sts, 2 wins. Won July S, Queen Mary S; 2nd Gimcrack S, Cheveley Park S. Dam of 11 foals, 11 rnrs, 10 wnrs, including **SPICY LIVING** ($251,204), **PALARIVA, TAYEH, Ozbeg** ($19,225, in Eng and NA), **Rive Doree** (in Ire). Granddam of **DRIN, ESQUIRAZA, ZAHEDAN, TOM OF LONDON, KHAIRUNISSA, Make It, Ribomar (GB), Gold Shalimar, Atrevida, Paraguana**. Sent to USA 1954. Died 1966.

1944: Barren.

1945: Eastward Bound, ch c, by Blue Peter. Raced 2 yrs in Eng, 5 sts, 0 wins, $137.

1946: **NIZAMI II**, b c, by Nearco. Raced 3 yrs in Eng, 17 sts, 2 wins, $5,883. Won Coombe S; 2nd Greenham S; 3rd Oxfordshire S. Sent to USA 1950. Sire. Died 1963.

1947: Malindi, b f, by Nearco. Raced 1 yr in Eng, 5 sts, 2 wins, $3,844. 2nd Berkshire S; 3rd Exeter S. Dam of 7 foals, 7 rnrs, 4 wnrs, including **PRINCE TAJ** ($14,222). Granddam of **Name and Fame**. Sent to USA 1958. Died 1962.

met." Mrs. Hancock does not remember her father's being involved in other horse deals on behalf of Claiborne, but he came through at a major moment: "As I recall, Nasrullah was due to arrive in Paris (Kentucky) on about Independence Day, and I said to Bull, 'It'll be Independence Day for us' — and it was."

The object of all these international longings

and dealings was a bay son of Nearco—Mumtaz Begum, by Blenheim II, bred by the Aga Khan and foaled in 1940. As is related in a chapter devoted to him, Nearco was an unbeaten product of the master breeder Federico Tesio and had been sent to stud in England. Nasrullah was in his first crop. The dam of Nasrullah, Mumtaz Begum, won a couple of sprint races at two. She was also the dam of Sun Princess, who later foaled a Nearco colt named Royal Charger. Nasrullah was Mumtaz Begum's fourth foal. Thus Mumtaz Begum was the dam of a multiple leading sire (Nasrullah) whose male line would produce the likes of Bold Ruler, Never Bend, Mill Reef, Nashua, Riverman, and Blushing Groom, and she was second dam of Royal Charger, whose sire line would produce Turn-to, Hail to Reason, Roberto, Halo, Sir Ivor, and Sunday Silence. Among modern mares, perhaps Special (whose dam, Thong, is a granddaughter of Nasrullah) — dam of Nureyev and granddam of Sadler's Wells — is on the way to approaching such lasting presence in the pedigrees of outstanding horses.

Mumtaz Begum's dam was Mumtaz Mahal. Apparently it was decreed by some omnipotent stewards of Turf jargon that Mumtaz Mahal would be known universally as the "flying filly," and this phrase tends to accompany her name in references even today. It was well earned, for this mottled gray daughter of The Tetrarch — a seminal "flyer" himself — won seven races at two and three and topped the English Free Handicap at two in 1923. Mumtaz Mahal was often spoken and written of in reverent phrases indicating a widespread opinion that she was the fastest filly ever seen in England.

In light of her subsequent produce record, it might be suspected that Mumtaz Mahal's stature as a racer has been embellished over the years.

To the contrary, at the end of her two-year-old form, she had already elicited adjectives reserved for the few. *The Bloodstock Breeders' Review* of 1923 remarked on the "phenomenal speed" shown in four of her first five races, and continued: "Off like a flash the moment the barrier was raised, she practically demoralized her opponents in the first furlong and was left to canter home at her leisure." Her trainer, Dick Dawson, was quoted that he had asked her to give twenty-eight pounds to a useful filly in his yard (Friar's Daughter) and, after Mumtaz Mahal beat her by half a furlong, "I was so astounded and excited that I nearly fell off my hack. Though I knew the grey to be an exceptionally good filly, I had no idea she was such a wonder."

Mumtaz Mahal descended from Americus, a product of Lucky Baldwin's expansive California breeding enterprise. Americus was sent to Ireland and sired Americus Girl, she, in turn, the dam of Lady Josephine. Lady Josephine produced the foundation mare Lady Juror in addition to Mumtaz Mahal. This was very much a family of mares that produced stallions: Lady Juror's eight stakes winners included Fair Trial, who led the English sire list and got the leading sire Court Martial as well as Petition (sire of the great filly Petite Etoile). In addition to her status in the ancestry of Nasrullah and Royal Charger, Mumtaz Mahal also foaled Mah Mahal, dam of leading sire Mahmoud and second dam of Migoli (sire of Gallant Man).

In Nasrullah, this extraordinary genetic package produced a well-grown, captivating bay colt, with an attitude. After winning the Coventry Stakes and another race and finishing second in the Middle Park Stakes from a total of four starts at two, Nasrullah was ranked best among colts and one pound below the Nearco filly Lady Sybil on

Nasrullah

the Free Handicap. Nasrullah, however, was the sort of individual whose impression is not limited to his actual accomplishments, or lack thereof, and he engendered divergent emotions. V. R. Orchard, charged with a detailed overview of the racing year for *The Bloodstock Breeders' Review*, stated frankly that, in his opinion, "his high place in the Free Handicap is hardly justified by his running." Orchard did not deny that Nasrullah was a special sort of customer: "Whatever else may be said of Nasrullah, it is clear that he is a colt of character. In appearance he is a rich bay of commanding proportions. His quarters are immensely powerful, and any good judge of a horse would put down this fine-looking colt as near perfect as possible if considering him apart from his racecourse performance."

As Abe Hewitt laconically described it, Nasrullah's "temperamental vagaries came into full flower" when the colt was three. Nasrullah won his seasonal debut, in the one-mile Chatteris Stakes, but only after slowing suddenly while in the lead. In the Two Thousand Guineas, he was equipped by trainer Frank Butters with blinkers, common in America but for years regarded as the "rogue's badge" in English racing. The blinkers did not induce Nasrullah to concentrate appreciably more, and after taking the lead, he pulled up enough to finish fourth despite the slashing efforts of the usually persuasive jockey Gordon Richards.

The Aga Khan's colt went onto the Derby, however, and again he went to the front, then lost interest and finished third behind Straight Deal and Umiddad. The quality seemed to be there, but not the racing professionalism. Butters continued along the classic trail, aiming Nasrullah for the St. Leger. In the one and a quarter-mile Cavensham Stakes, meant as an easy outing, Nasrullah won at 1-4, but in the same reluctant fashion of his first win of the year. In the St. Leger itself, he never made the lead and finished sixth as the fillies Herringbone and Ribbon ran one-two over Derby winner Straight Deal.

In the one and a quarter-mile Champion Stakes, over a straight course at Newmarket, jockey Richards contrived to get Nasrullah to win in spite of himself. He waited with such patience that by the time Nasrullah struck the lead and concluded the race was over — it was. He won by a length. On the handicap for three-year-olds, Nasrullah was rated but one pound below top colt Straight Deal. The two St. Leger fillies were ranked above both by scale.

Phil Bull, the articulate master of Timeform whose organization commented on all English-raced horses, continued to be enamored of Nasrullah while not blind to his faults. He commented in *Racehorses of 1943*: "Last year, I regarded Nasrullah as head and shoulders above the other colts of his age. I gave him a long and rather enthusiastic write up, and, in spite of his having failed in each of his classic ventures, in spite of his bad temper, his mulish antics, in spite of his exasperating unwillingness to do the job, etc., I fear that I am going to give him another write up. I know he doesn't deserve it, but I can't help it." Either Bull or his staff underscored such assessment by uncharacteristically judgmental captions under photos of Nasrullah, i.e., "Nasrullah pretending to be a gentleman"; "Nasrullah condescends to pass the post in front in the Chatteris Stakes"; "Nasrullah impersonating a mule."

The unusual colt had a two-year career of five wins from ten starts and earnings of $15,217 in wartime purses.

It was then that Hancock first tried to buy him, offering $50,000, but too late. Nasrullah first stood at Barton Stud, Suffolk, England, before being sent to Ireland.

Bull Lea

Bull Lea (above), a son of the imported Bull Dog, made Calumet Farm a powerhouse during the 1940s and '50s and led the sire list five times. His best offspring was 1948 Triple Crown winner Citation (left), who unfortunately did not emulate his sire in the breeding shed.

Bull Lea

Twilight Tear (above) was a member of Bull Lea's first crop and earned Horse of the Year honors in 1944. The 1967 Horse of the Year Damascus (left) descended from the Teddy line which also produced Bull Lea. As a sire, Damascus helped revitalize the Teddy line through such sons as Private Account, Time for a Change, and Timeless Moment.

Princequillo

Princequillo (top) was claimed for $2,500 then won the Jockey Club Gold Cup and other stakes. He sired sixty-five stakes winners, including Horse of the Year Round Table. Round Table, in turn, sired top runners on both sides of the Atlantic, including Apalachee (right). Meadowlake (above) is a great-grandson of Princequillo.

Rough'n Tumble

Rough'n Tumble (above) helped put the Florida breeding industry on the map. His best offspring was the brilliant Dr. Fager (left), who won four titles, including Horse of the Year, in a transcendent 1968 season. The Rough'n Tumble line remains strong four generations later in Holy Bull (below), the 1994 Horse of the Year and promising young sire.

Nearco

Federico Tesio's Nearco (top) was
unbeaten in fourteen starts, then
replicated his form in the breeding shed,
siring a skein of great stallions and
important racehorses. His son Nearctic
(right) sired the great Northern Dancer
while Amerigo (above) sired Fort Marcy
and other top U.S. racehorses.

Nasrullah

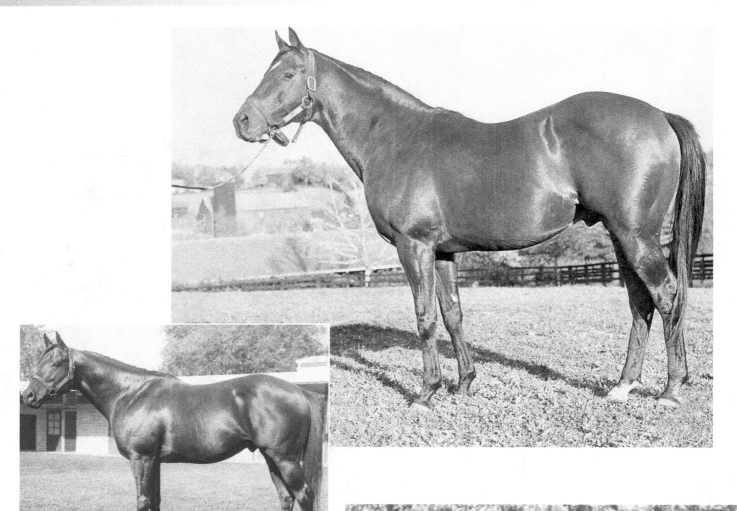

Nasrullah (top), from the first crop of Nearco, stood in England and Ireland before Claiborne Farm's A. B. Hancock Jr. managed to import him. Nasrullah led the American sire list five times. His best offspring included Horse of the Year Nashua (right), who displayed some of his sire's quirky traits, and Never Bend (above), sire of brilliant turf specialists Mill Reef and Riverman.

Hail to Reason

Hail to Reason (above) was brilliant at two before a life-threatening injury ended his racing career. At stud, he had immediate results, getting a Belmont Stakes winner in his first crop. Among his top sons at stud was Halo (left), who sired Sunday Silence (below), the 1989 Kentucky Derby winner and Japan's perennial leading sire.

Hail to Reason

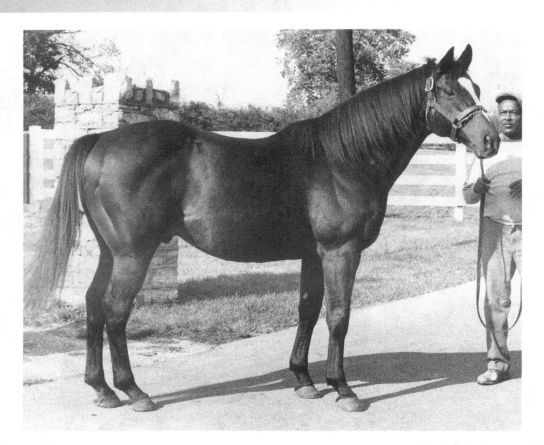

Hail to Reason also sired Roberto (above), who won the Epsom Derby for John W. Galbreath and who became a sire of sires in his own right. Among Hail to Reason's best female offspring was Straight Deal (right), the champion handicap mare of 1967.

By the time Nasrullah arrived at Claiborne (to be exalted in primitive Hancock family home movies), he was a proven commodity. By the end of 1951, Claiborne's new stallion had the added fillip of being the leading sire in England for that year. He also continued to be a rough customer. As explained by author Michael Seth-Smith,[2] Nasrullah had become all the more difficult because the war had sent so many young men away that young women had to be employed by trainer Butters. While time has proven female grooms and exercise riders a positive for the racing world, they had not been given much chance in those days, and Nasrullah apparently dominated them. Then, in his early years at stud, Seth-Smith recorded, the horse so much ruled the roost that it was obvious to McGrath's stud groom, Bill Milton, when he went to pick up the horse to take him to Brownstown Stud, that the previous staff was "terrified of Nasrullah."

Mrs. Hancock recalls that when Nasrullah got to Claiborne, Milton stayed on awhile:

"When he went out into the paddock, instead of taking hold of the halter, he would hold out a stick. Nasrullah would take hold of that stick and only then would the groom grab the halter. After awhile, Lawrence Robinson, who took care of him, came to Bull and said he'd have to be leaving. He said he knew how important that horse was, but holding a stick to him and out in the paddock just wasn't his way. Bull said, 'Lawrence, you're in charge. Just do it your way.' So he did."

Nasrullah had become so important in his own mind that, Mrs. Hancock recalls, he would throw a fit in his stall anytime he was not the first stallion led out. If he were first, he would then relent for other horses to be taken out to be shown.

In the spring of 1951, Nasrullah covered his first mares in this country, and his foal crop of 1952 began his parade of outstanding American-sired foals. He quickly became the first stallion to lead the sire list in both countries, topping the American list for the first time in 1955. (Northern Dancer later achieved this distinction, and, in an era of increasing internationalization, the *Thoroughbred Times'* method of purse inclusions shows Sadler's Wells as leading on both sides of the Atlantic, too.) Nasrullah followed up as leading American sire again in 1956, 1959, 1960, and 1962. He thus matched Bull Lea and Star Shoot among sires to have led the list as many as five times during the 20th Century. His own son Bold Ruler later eclipsed this mark, topping the list eight times.

Nasrullah's early crops included the One Thousand Guineas and Oaks winner Musidora, another One Thousand Guineas winner in Belle of All, Irish Derby winner Nathoo, North American champion Noor, and the first of his good sons for the stud, including Indian Hemp and Grey Sovereign. (All the same, his ascent to the top of the English list for 1951 was assisted by an administrative oddity. The King George VI and Queen Elizabeth Stakes winner of that year, Supreme Court, was from a mare who had been booked first to Persian Gulf and then covered later that same breeding season by Precipitation. Supreme Court's limbo status meant that, under the practice of the time, his purses were not attributed to either sire for purposes of compiling the earnings list. Adding his earnings to either Persian Gulf or Precipitation would have made either the year's leading sire.)

In addition to the many outstanding horses he conceived in this country, Nasrullah's 1954 Epsom Derby winner was conceived in England, but foaled here. This was Robert Sterling Clark's Never Say Die, a big, lengthy chestnut foaled at Jonabell Farm in Kentucky, but destined to race abroad for Clark. Never Say Die became the first

Nasrullah

American-bred to win the Epsom Derby since Iroquois in 1881, and he was the first winner of the event for the budding legend among riders, Lester Piggott. Never Say Die also added the St. Leger. Sent to the English National Stud, he was not overall a lasting success, but he did get another Derby winner in Raymond Guest's Larkspur, plus Howell Jackson's One Thousand Guineas-Oaks winner Never Too Late. Never Say Die led the English sire list of 1962.

The parade of shining princes and princesses that sprung from Nasrullah after he came to Kentucky creates a positive, visceral appreciation in the American Thoroughbred follower:

• *Nashua*, at times a reluctant champion but the all-time leading money earner at one time, the most expensive horse of his time, and Horse of the Year.

• *Bold Ruler*, a dark flying machine whose speed was flashed from two through four and who carried 134 pounds for ten furlongs.

• *Never Bend*, spectacular at two and classic-placed at three.

• *Jaipur*, another willful sort, but winner of two of the most stirring contests in memory, the 1962 Belmont Stakes and Travers.

• *Bald Eagle*, a reformed bad boy who won two Washington, D.C., Internationals on grass and also was a champion on dirt.

• *Nadir*, rakish winner of the Garden State Stakes when it was the richest race in the world.

There were star fillies as well:

• *Bug Brush*, who beat colts in world-record time.

• *Leallah*, champion at two.

• *Nasrina*, winner of the Gardenia.

• *Delta*, a consistent winner and a Broodmare of the Year.

These were among the very best, and there were many other good ones. The Nasrullahs came in profusion. When Bold Ruler lost for the first time, he was beaten by Nashville, son of Nasrullah; when Nashua was stunned in the Woodward Stakes late in his career, the winner was Mister Gus, son of Nasrullah.

All told, on both sides of the Atlantic, Nasrullah sired ninety-eight stakes winners, a sparkling twenty-three percent from foals. Nine were American champions.

He also got a brace of sons that excelled in the stud. Some of these came from among his best runners, while others were well below top rank as racers but got important winners and, inevitably, a few of the better racehorses faded in the breeding shed.

Nasrullah's best runners arguably were Nashua and Bold Ruler. Bold Ruler was an eight-time leading stallion, sire of Secretariat, and head of the present day sire line of Seattle Slew and A.P. Indy; Nashua, sired seventy-seven stakes winners (twelve percent), including two-time champion Shuvee, and was the broodmare sire of Mr. Prospector and Roberto.

Among the other highly ranked sons were the aforementioned Never Say Die, sire of Larkspur, and Noor, a moderate success. Jaipur was a disappointment, as was Mister Gus. Bald Eagle was not a prolonged success, but he got the speedy filly Too Bald (dam of Exceller and Capote) and a big, long-legged filly named San San, for whom everything came to together to win the 1972 Prix de l'Arc de Triomphe at three.

Indian Hemp, Grey Sovereign, and Red God were among Nasrullah's sons who made a high mark in the stud after less spectacular racing.

Indian Hemp sired the outstanding and versatile T. V. Lark, a California-bred who himself became America's leading sire in 1974.

Grey Sovereign's descent in the male line led to Caro, the sire of Cozzene, Madelia, With Approval, and Kentucky Derby winner Winning Colors; more recently, In Excess and his son Indian Charlie represent a branch of Caro's descent. Grey Sovereign also launched the branches of the Nasrullah legacy that include Zeddaan, Kalamoun, Kenmare, Tony Bin, Wolver Hollow, Humble Duty, and others.

Red God sired Blushing Groom, a champion in France and international sire of Nashwan, Sky Beauty, Mt. Livermore, and Rahy.

In Europe, another of the lingering, if lesser, influences, was through the Nasrullah colt Princely Gift, whose son Faberge sired the Arc de Triomphe winner Rheingold.

Yet another Nasrullah colt, Nasram, upset Santa Claus in the 1964 King George VI and Queen Elizabeth Stakes and, while perhaps not a prolific source of class, Nasram did get Naskra, sire of Star de Naskra and grandsire of Carr de Naskra.

In this country, another of Nasrullah's prominent sons was the high-class racehorse Fleet Nasrullah, whose early crops from California were so successful that he was recruited for Kentucky. Fleet Nasrullah's forty-six stakes winners included Convenience, Eastern Fleet, and Coursing. Another colt by Fleet Nasrullah was Gummo, who became something of a California institution, getting such exceptional horses as Flying Paster, Golden Act, and the millionaire Ancient Title.

The Nasrullah list seems to go on and on, literally: His son On-and-On was a Calumet Farm homebred who defeated Bald Eagle in the Brooklyn Handicap during the latter's handicap championship campaign of 1960. On-and-On generally was a disappointing stallion at a time Calumet needed a good one, but he did provide a major highlight as the sire of the farm's 1968 Kentucky Derby and Preakness winner, Forward Pass. (He also was the broodmare sire of Calumet's Alydar, who came along at a time when the farm needed a good racehorse.)

Nantallah was a Nasrullah colt who never won a stakes but was promising enough in a brief racing career that he wound up at Claiborne. Virtually wedded to the great mare Rough Shod II for a few years, he thus sired the champion filly Moccasin, the champion colt Ridan, and the high class Lt. Stevens. Yet another Nantallah—Rough Shod II foal was Thong, whose name appears in the bottom line of Nureyev and Sadler's Wells.

One of the interesting aspects of Nasrullah's career was the variety of bloodlines with which he mingled well:

Bold Ruler was out of a Discovery mare.

Nashua was out of a Johnstown mare.

Grey Sovereign was out of a Baytown mare.

Nadir was out of a Challenger II mare.

Bald Eagle was out of a Tiger mare.

Delta was out of a Stimulus mare.

Bug Brush was out of a Fighting Fox mare.

Leallah and On-and-On were out of Bull Lea mares.

Fleet Nasrullah was out of a Count Fleet mare.

Never Say Die was out of a War Admiral mare.

Red God was out of a Menow mare.

Noor was out of a Bahram mare.

Nasram was out of a Coaraze mare.

Never Bend was out of a Djeddah mare.

The greatest of the Nasrullah stallions, Bold Ruler, is subject of a separate chapter, as is one of the grandsons, Blushing Groom. For further elucidation on a couple of the other Nasrullah-line stallions, we have chosen to address Caro briefly, then more in depth on Nashua and Never Bend.

Caro

Caro, by Grey Sovereign, sired a total of seventy-eight stakes winners (thirteen percent), stand-

Nasrullah

ing first in France, then in Kentucky. His son Cozzene added another sire list leadership to the legend of Nasrullah's sire line when he topped the list in North America in 1996. That was the year his son Alphabet Soup defeated Cigar in the Breeders' Cup Classic. Cozzene, himself a Breeders' Cup Mile winner, also sired a Breeders' Cup Turf winner in Tikkanen, as well as Arlington Million winner Star of Cozzene, the millionairess Maxzene, and others. Cozzene stands at Gainesway Farm and has sired forty stakes winners (nine percent).

Also, In Excess and his son Indian Charlie represent a branch of Caro's descent through the son Siberian Express, winner of the French Two Thousand Guineas. Caro's sire, Grey Sovereign, also launched the branches of the Nasrullah legacy that include Zeddaan, Kalamoun, Kenmare, Mourtar, Tony Bin, Wolver Hollow, Humble Duty, and others.

Nashua

Nashua was bred by William Woodward Sr.'s Belair Stud and was out of Segula, a daughter of Belair's 1939 Kentucky Derby-Belmont winner Johnstown. Woodward had intended for Nashua to go to England, where the breeder had been sending a couple of horses a year since the 1920s, with the Epsom Derby his primary target. Woodward died when Nashua was a yearling, and the designated heir to his stable, William Jr., opted to keep the horse in this country.

Sent to Sunny Jim Fitzsimmons, Belair's trainer of long standing, Nashua won six of eight at two in 1954, including the Futurity and several other races against arch rival Summer Tan. He was voted the champion of his year. At three, Nashua showed some of the Nasrullah temperament. That winter, he was unbeaten in three races in Florida, including the Flamingo and Florida Derby, but he made jockey Eddie Arcaro's life chancy, propping once and almost letting a forlorn longshot catch him another time. In the Wood Memorial, he left his charge so late that Summer Tan seemed to have his number, before Nashua — son of Nasrullah — agreed to lunge to the wire in front.

In Kentucky, Nashua was thoroughly outrun by Swaps in the Derby. With Swaps sent home to California, Nashua set a record in the Preakness, won the Belmont and Dwyer handily, and then put in another just-barely win in holding off Traffic Judge in the Arlington Classic. A match race with Swaps was such a major event that national television carried it in midweek. Nashua raced to an early lead and never was headed, winning by six and a half lengths, but Swaps' soundness came into such question that the victory lacked the definitiveness that was sought. Nashua then took on older horses and was abruptly manhandled by older champion High Gun in the Sysonby before easily winning the Jockey Club Gold Cup at two miles. He had won ten of twelve at three, and his earnings of $752,550 for the year set a one-season record.

Nashua's quality, and quirks, had set him apart from most champions in the earlier days of televised racing. Then true sensationalism was thrust upon the entire stable when Woodward was fatally shot by his wife. The accident had reverberations for many years, including a fictional rendition known as *The Two Mrs. Grenvilles*. Meanwhile, Nashua was sold by the Woodward estate via sealed bid, to a syndicate headed by Leslie Combs II, for a record price of the time, $1,251,250.

Still in Fitzsimmons' care, Nashua won his comeback, in the Widener, to follow Citation as the second million-dollar earner. He later passed Citation to lead all earners. Although his record of six wins in ten starts at four was overshadowed by the 1956 record of Swaps — whom he never met again — Nashua was distinguished in winning the Widener, Grey Lag, Suburban, Camden, and Monmouth Handicaps, and set a record with a second Jockey Club Gold Cup win. He retired with twenty-two wins in thirty starts and earnings of $1,288,565.

Nashua was a tourist attraction for many years at Combs' Spendthrift Farm in Lexington. He lived to the age of thirty and sired seventy-seven stakes winners (twelve percent). Although none of his sons became champions or outstanding sires, he got a number of nice colts, such as Noble Nashua, Diplomat Way (broodmare sire of Skip Away), and Good Manners (a major sire in South America). Nashua's fillies seemed to be better than his colts, and several of them were major producers. Among them were three Coaching Club American Oaks winners: Marshua, Shuvee, and Bramalea. Shuvee like her sire won two Jockey Club Gold Cups, and Bramalea became the dam of the Epsom Derby winner and major sire Roberto. Another of Nashua's fillies was the nice stakes winner Gold Digger, who implanted the sire's (and Johnstown's) nonchalant ears and certain other qualities amid the genetic make-up of her son, the great stallion Mr. Prospector.

Never Bend

Captain Harry Guggenheim was the scion of a great American family of entrepreneurs. He developed various interests and served as a diplomat as well as publisher of *Newsday,* leaving a lasting mark in American journalism. Guggenheim was so aggressive a visionary in aerospace that Charles Lindbergh named him alongside Dr. Robert Goddard as the two prime movers in that area. Captain Harry — who flew in both world wars —

also developed an interest in the Turf, launching a stable in the 1930s. In time, this avocation took on administrative leadership, for he and Chris Chenery and John Hanes formed the committee appointed by Ogden Phipps of The Jockey Club to devise a plan to reorganize New York racing. It was in the early 1950s, and New York was losing its grasp on the qualities that made the phrase "big apple" apposite for years insofar as its place of prominence in racing. Guggenheim, Chenery, and Hanes thus laid out the plan that consolidated a number of the state's major tracks into the big three of Aqueduct, Belmont, and Saratoga under the banner of the New York Racing Association. (In fairness to this triumphant triumvirate, off-track betting and its political fissures were not a part of the New York scene at the time the NYRA was conceived.)

Guggenheim had had considerable success before hiring Woody Stephens as his private trainer in the 1950s. He had bred, but sold, the champion Crafty Admiral, and had not bred, but bought and raced, the Kentucky Derby winner Dark Star. During the 1960s, the author had the pleasure of compiling a private history of Guggenheim's Cain Hoy Stable at Captain Harry's behest. We had access to various correspondence from Guggenheim to Stephens. Given Woody's love of the action of the racetrack, we have often mused on a letter in which his boss reined him in, emphasizing that the aim was the classics, not winter racing: "So keep cool in Carolina."

Stephens was able to shake out of the winter quarters in South Carolina enough to win the Widener and Gulfstream Park Handicaps with Cain Hoy's budding champion Bald Eagle in 1960, and three years later he had convinced his boss to let him prep Never Bend at Hialeah.

After Bald Eagle's retirement, Guggenheim wrote to his contract jockey, Manuel Ycaza: "I told

Woody that one day I would give him a horse that all you have to do is put on the saddle and say 'go.' Such a horse was (Patrice Jacobs') Hail to Reason (champion two-year-old of 1960). He was easy to train and easy to ride."

In the spring of 1962, Guggenheim made good on that promise. He had sent to Woody Stephens the Cain Hoy homebred Never Bend, who was in the last crop by Nasrullah and was out of Cain Hoy's Kentucky Oaks winner Lalun. (Lalun was by Djeddah, who represented a sire line not included in this volume, but certainly important in the 20th Century, especially in Europe. This was the line of Tourbillon, whose American-based stallions included the leading sire Ambiorix. Djeddah's sire was Djebel, a son of Tourbillon. Djeddah, winner of England's Champion Stakes, sired Lalun, she the dam of Never Bend and Travers winners Bold Reason. Another daughter of Djeddah was Breath o' Morn, dam of 1967 Kentucky Derby winner Proud Clarion.)

Never Bend was out early in the spring of 1962 and was brilliant from the beginning. His generous use of his own speed perhaps contributed to his failing to stay in front in three of the top races of the year, the Sapling, Arlington-Washington Futurity, and Garden State Stakes. Nevertheless, he won the Futurity and Champagne by wide margins, also took the Cowdin, and had a record of seven wins in ten starts. He was the champion and Experimental Free Handicap topweight, and his earnings of $402,969 created a juvenile record at the time.

Guggenheim allowed Stephens to prepare Never Bend for the classics with a Florida winter campaign the next year, and Never Bend won the coveted Flamingo Stakes at Hialeah. Guggenheim did not shrink from a challenge, and, in addition to the American Triple Crown races, he nominated Never Bend for the Epsom Derby. A Kentucky-English Derby double appealed to his sporting nature, especially since it had never been achieved. Never Bend raced well at one and a quarter miles, but it proved not his best distance. He was second to Chateaugay in the Kentucky Derby, and third behind Candy Spots and Chateaugay in the Preakness. The Epsom trip would not have come off, anyway, but he came out of the Preakness the worse for wear and was put aside until late summer. Although his only later stakes triumph came in the Yankee Handicap, he gave a good account for his generation by finishing second to the older Mongo in the United Nations Handicap on grass and second to the great Kelso in the Woodward Stakes. Never Bend was retired with thirteen wins from twenty-three starts and earnings of $641,524.

He had been foaled at Claiborne Farm, where Guggenheim had had a long connection, but by the time he went to stud, the Cain Hoy stock had been sent over to Leslie Combs II's Spendthrift Farm, and there Never Bend went to stud.

Never Bend got a total of sixty-one stakes winners (seventeen percent). His most distinguished racers emerged in Europe. Paul Mellon, master of Rokeby Farm in Virginia, had an important string on both sides of the Atlantic, and he sent his 1968 Never Bend—Milan Mill, by Princequillo, colt to trainer Ian Balding in England. The racy colt was named Mill Reef, and he was a fine juvenile, after which he developed into one of the great horses of recent times. Galloping past any prejudice about stamina implied by Never Bend's record, Mill Reef won the Epsom Derby, Eclipse Stakes, King George VI and Queen Elizabeth Stakes, and then the climactic Prix de l'Arc de Triomphe at three in 1971. He was gravely injured the following year. After being saved by emergency surgery on a makeshift bed of hay bales at Balding's historic Kingsclere training yard, Mill Reef was kept in England by Mellon, who sportingly placed him at the English National Stud.

Another courier to Never Bend's worldwide influence was Riverman. One of those elite stallions who have sired more than 100 stakes winners, Riverman was bred by Guggenheim and was foaled in 1969. He was from the Prince John mare River Lady and was a weanling when Captain Guggenheim, late in his life, dispersed most of his breeding stock at Keeneland. Riverman was purchased for $41,000 by the great French horseman Alec Head on behalf of Mme. Pierre Wertheimer. The Wertheimer family had been important in French racing for many years, and the next generation, Jacques, passed the torch to his sons, who raced the 1993 North American Horse of the Year Kotashaan, representing the Mill Reef sire line as well.

Riverman won the French Two Thousand Guineas of 1972 along with three other French Stakes. At longer distances against the best competition, he was second to Brigadier Gerard in the Champion Stakes at one and a quarter miles and third behind the same champion in the King George VI and Queen Elizabeth Stakes at one and a half miles.

Riverman sired 128 stakes winners (thirteen percent). Among his distinctions was becoming the first sire in the history of the Prix de l'Arc de Triomphe to sire separate winners of consecutive runnings of the event. Both of his were fillies: Detroit (1980) and Gold River (1981). Detroit later foaled Arc winner Carnegie, thus becoming the only winner of the race to foal another Arc winner. In 1980, Riverman had been syndicated on an evaluation of $18 million and imported to Gainesway Farm in Kentucky. Riverman led the French sire lists in both of his Arc filly years, and

his international renown was particularly illustrated, too, by standings of 1987: He ranked second on the English sire list, fourth on the North American sire list, and fifth on the French list.

Riverman's other champions include the remarkable mare Triptych, a champion at various ages in Ireland, England, and France; the classic winner and outstanding international sire Irish River; plus Loup Sauvage, Rousillon, Bahri, and Lahib. Classic winners included Policeman, River Lady (same name as his dam), Houseproud, and Hailsham. In North America, his best runners include Rivlia, River Memories, River Special, and Virginia Rapids. As a successor, Irish River has sired seventy-five stakes winners (nine percent), including the Eclipse Award winners Paradise Creek and Hatoof, plus Brief Truce, River Bay, Leariva, and Exit to Nowhere.

Yet another of Never Bend's best runners was J. O. Tobin, an elegant homebred from Californian George Pope Jr.'s international operation. J. O. Tobin was the champion two-year-old of England in 1976, handed Seattle Slew his first loss the following year in the Swaps Stakes in California, and at four ran well enough at short and middle distances in this country to be named co-champion sprinter. Unlike Mill Reef and Riverman, however, J. O. Tobin was a perplexing disappointment at stud.

The present Aga Khan once told the author of his admiration of the Never Bend line, and His Highness certainly put it to good use. Among the Aga's homebred Mill Reef colts was the 1988 English Two Thousand Guineas winner Doyoun. Doyoun then sired the wonderful international star Daylami, champion grass horse in North America in 1999 off his Breeders' Cup Turf triumph. Daylami was bred by the Aga Khan and raced through much of his career for the Maktoum family's Godolphin stable.

Nasrullah

The Breeders' Cup Turf is a great example of the potency of the Mill Reef line. In addition to Daylami's victory, the first Breeders' Cup Turf was won by His Highness' Lashkari, a son of Mill Reef. Then, in 1993, the North American Horse of the Year, the Wertheimer family's Kotashaan, won the Breeders' Cup Turf to cement his Horse of the Year bid. Kotashaan was sired by the Aga Khan's French Derby winner Darshaan. The sire of Darshaan was Shirley Heights, who in 1978 had become the first son of Mill Reef to win the English Derby. Mill Reef led England's sire list in 1978 for the first of two times, and that year he was represented by the French Derby winner, Acamas, in addition to the English Derby winner. In turn, Shirley Heights sired Slip Anchor, the English Derby winner of 1985, while Mill Reef himself sired a later Epsom Derby winner in Reference Point in 1987.

Guggenheim may not have gotten Never Bend to Epsom, but the presence of that sire line has certainly vindicated his thinking that it might have been a good adventure.

More recently, Never Bend (who died in 1977) received a late honor when his aged daughter Anne Campbell was named Broodmare of the Year for 1999. Anne Campbell, twenty-seven in the year 2000, is the dam of 1999 Blue Grass and Haskell winner Menifee, earlier having foaled major winner and Kentucky Derby-Preakness runner-up Desert Wine. In addition to foaling those two millionaries, Anne Campbell is the second dam of Fasliyev, an outstanding juvenile in Europe in 1999.

Also, the much admired $3-million-earner Free House stems from a branch of Never Bend's line that had seemed to be destined for regional fame only, that through the son Never Tabled.

So, the proud and noble line which led to, and from, that mulish wartime character Nasrullah still can produce the sort of horse to make one nearly "fall off your hack." ❖

Bold Ruler

"Tenacious and indomitable in the face of superior fire power" read the Presidential Unit Citation. Alfred G. Vanderbilt may have been used to the comforts of wealth and privilege, but he proved a stout-hearted fellow when out on the ironically named Pacific as a World War II PT Boat commander. A grateful government could bestow honors, but there was nothing to be done about the fact that Miss Disco got away. Wartime reparations could hardly be so far reaching and elaborate as to figure out what compensation should be assigned a devoted Thoroughbred breeder and owner for having been prompted to sell the dam of Bold Ruler.

Vanderbilt had developed a love of Thoroughbreds as a child and, having risen to man's estate, immersed himself in buying, raising, and breeding an elite group for his Sagamore farm and stable. He was not in the business of breeding good horses for other owners to enjoy, but the war prompted him to sell some yearlings. In 1945, he caused a draft of his yearlings to be sent to the auction at Meadow Brook in New York, and among them was a filly by Vanderbilt's great champion Discovery and out of Outdone, by Pompey. Outdone had become one of the early stakes winners bred by Vanderbilt when, appropriately, she had won the Sagamore Handicap.

Outdone eventually foaled three stakes winners: the $232,920-earner Loser Weeper, the Oaklawn Handicap winner Thwarted, and Miss Disco herself. None of this was evident in 1945, however, when Sydney S. Schupper paid $2,100 for the Discovery—Outdone filly. Under the name Miss Disco, that filly became a stakes winner in 1947 when she won the Test Stakes. That afternoon, she came under the scrutiny of one George F. T. Ryall, a particularly articulate horse lover who for years wrote gracefully of the Turf for *New Yorker*. Years later, we knew Ryall as a wizened, but jovial little Canadian native who had been educated in England at Haileybury — a sturdy, stony enclave one might pass when motoring from London to Ascot. Ryall was a man of the world, and was not overly tentative in his opinions, but he was kindly enamored of the Thoroughbred, so it was not routine for him to watch a stakes race and decide to take a swipe in print at the winner. (He may have written for *New Yorker*, but he was not a movie reviewer, after all.) Ryall, then, enjoyed ever after the joke on himself that his 1947 report predicted airily that the Test Stakes would likely be the only moment of glory or distinction its winner would orchestrate for herself.

This evaluation was proving weak by the following year, when Miss Disco added more stakes

		Pharos, 1920	Phalaris Scapa Flow
	Nearco, 1935		
		Nogara, 1928	Havresac II Catnip
NASRULLAH, **b, 1940**			
		Blenheim II, 1927	Blandford Malva
	Mumtaz Begum, 1932		
		Mumtaz Mahal, 1921	The Tetrarch Lady Josephine
BOLD RULER, **dk b h,** **April 6, 1954**			
		Display, 1923	Fair Play Cicuta
	Discovery, 1931		
		Ariadne, 1926	Light Brigade Adrienne
MISS DISCO, **b, 1944**			
		Pompey, 1923	Sun Briar Cleopatra
	Outdone, 1936		
		Sweep Out, 1926	Sweep On Dugout

1st dam: MISS DISCO, b, 1944-1974. Bred by Alfred G. Vanderbilt (Ky). Raced 5 yrs, 54 sts, 10 wins, $80,250. Broodmare of the Year in 1958. Won New Rochelle H, Test S, Interborough H, American Legion H; 3rd Wilson S, Babylon H, Fashion S, Correction H. Dam of 11 named foals, 7 rnrs, 7 wnrs, 3 sw.

1951: Hill Rose, ch f, by Rosemont. Raced 3 yrs, 46 sts, 4 wins, $19,625. Dam of 12 foals, 12 rnrs, 9 wnrs, including **TRUE NORTH** ($308,073), **Geeare** ($47,213), **Bold Tim** ($8,535). Granddam of **GIVE ME A HINT**. Died 1975.

1952: **INDEPENDENCE**, b c, by Nasrullah. Raced 8 yrs, 74 sts, 12 wins, $132,088. Won Saratoga Stp H, Broad Hollow Stp H, Meadow Brook Stp H, Grand National Stp H; 2nd Brook Stp H (three times), Saratoga Stp H, Beverwyck Stp H, Georgetown Stp H, Harbor Hill Stp H, Indian River Stp H, Spring Maiden Stp S, International Stp H, Grand National Stp H, North American Stp H, Charles L. Appleton Memorial Stp H; 3rd Saratoga Stp H, Meadow Brook Stp H. Sire. Died 1977.

1953: Explorer, b f, by Nasrullah. Raced 1 yr, 19 sts, 6 wins, $21,430. Dam of 12 foals, 10 rnrs, 8 wnrs, including **ARMY COURT** ($39,227). Granddam of **Troja**. Sent to Eng 1967. Died 1977.

1954: **BOLD RULER**, dk b c, by Nasrullah. Bred by Wheatley Stable (Ky). Raced 3 yrs, 33 sts, 23 wins, $764,204. Horse of the Year, champion 3yo colt and sprinter. Won Preakness S, Futurity S, Flamingo S, Trenton H, Wood Memorial, Jerome H, Youthful S, Queens County H, Juvenile S, Benjamin Franklin H, Bahamas S, Vosburgh H, Monmouth H, Suburban H, Carter H, Toboggan H, Stymie H; 2nd Florida Derby, Metropolitan H, Everglades S; 3rd Belmont S, Woodward S. Sire of 356 foals, 82 sw, 7.73 AEI. Died 1971.

1955: **NASCO**, b c, by Nasrullah. Raced 3 yrs, 54 sts, 7 wins, $71,930. Won Saranac H; 2nd Dwyer H; 3rd Peter Pan H. Sire in Japan.

1956: Barren.

1957: Foolish One, b f, by Tom Fool. Unraced. Dam of 7 foals, 7 rnrs, 4 wnrs, including **MANDERA** ($16,259), **PROTANTO** ($322,085), **FUNNY FELLOW** ($301,215). Granddam of **AFRICAN DANCER, TOUCHING WOOD, FOOLS HOLME, KLAYTONE, AS SAKAB, SPECIFICITY,** Ridotto, **Demonstrative, Appealing One**.

1958: Eastern Princess, ch f, by Nasrullah. Raced 2 yrs, 21 sts, 5 wins, $33,005. 3rd Selima S, Colleen S, National Stallion S (Fillies). Dam of 12 foals, 10 rnrs, 8 wnrs, including **SHADY CHARACTER** ($164,235), **VANISHING ACT** ($10,995), **Dawn of Tomorrow** ($20,225). Died 1981.

1959: Barren.

1960: Highness, ch f, by Nasrullah. Raced 1 yr, 7 sts, 1 win, $3,400. Dam of 10 foals, 9 rnrs, 5 wnrs, including **Commoner** ($37,260). Granddam of **PRETTY DOES, MORGAN'S LEVEE, GROTON HIGH, CORRALERA, My Lady's Wim**. Died 1979.

1961: Barren.

1962: Success, ch f, by Turn-to. Unraced. Dam of 5 foals, 5 rnrs, 5 wnrs, including **Mambrino** ($43,751). Died 1985.

1963: Your Turn, b f, by Turn-to. Unraced. Dam of 6 foals, 5 rnrs, 5 wnrs. Died 1988.

1964: Barren.

1965: Great Adventure, ch c, by Nadir. Unraced. Died 1968.

1966: Barren.

victories in the Interborough, American Legion, and New Rochelle Handicaps. She raced for five years, eventually winning ten of fifty-four races and earning $80,250. The real glory was yet to come.

A. B. (Bull) Hancock Jr. was by then more or less in charge of his family's Claiborne Farm, owing to his father's poor health. Bull liked Miss Disco, but she got away from him, too. This time it was not wartime interruptions which affected Miss Disco's destiny, but loyalty to an important client, and just plain good sense.

"I had tried to buy Miss Disco myself several times," Hancock told Charles Koch in a 1971 interview for *The Blood-Horse*, "but never made it until one day the man who owned her called me and I was able to get her for twenty-seven five ($27,500)."

At the same time, a major Claiborne client, Mrs. Henry Carnegie Phipps, had wanted Hancock to buy something for her: "I missed on the mare I was trying to buy for Mrs. Phipps, so I told her I'd bought Miss Disco and that she could have her if she wanted her. 'What kind of a family is it?' she asked. 'It's pretty good,' I said. ' She was a nice race mare and I think she'd suit Nasrullah real well.' So, she sent me a check; we bred Miss Disco to Nasrullah. So Mrs. Phipps got Bold Ruler and I didn't."

Mrs. Phipps had founded Wheatley Stable with her brother in the 1920s and continued it on her own until her death in October of 1970. She was joined in her devotion to racing by her son, Ogden Phipps, and her daughter, Barbara Phipps Janney. The Phipps tradition has been among the constants and positives of American racing for some seventy-five years. Ogden Phipps' son, Ogden Mills (Dinny) Phipps, and daughter, Cynthia Phipps, have augmented the tradition by racing and breeding top-class horses, and Dinny Phipps' children and stepchildren have shown that they obviously represent a strong contingent for the future. Moreover, the breeding and racing operation of Barbara Janney and her husband, Stuart Janney Jr., produced the great Ruffian, plus Private Terms, and son Stuart Janney III bred and raced 1998 Travers Stakes winner Coronado's Quest.

Miss Disco produced three stakes-winning sons of Nasrullah: Independence scored all four of his major wins over jumps, and Nasco won only the Saranac Handicap, but the middle brother of the three was Bold Ruler.

As the foregoing chapter on Nasrullah outlines, that stallion was possessed of a somewhat bothersome streak of temperament. In Bold Ruler, the headstrong tendency came out in a deep prejudice toward the thought that if one were going to be a racehorse the thing to do was outrun all the others as soon as possible. This leaning was said to have been encouraged in part perhaps by his having suffered a tongue injury as a yearling and being sensitive to the bit thereafter. Sensitivity around the head also might have been aggravated further by his hitting his head on the gate in a race at two and coming back with a bloody mouth. At any rate, the fact that Bold Ruler did not always respond kindly to the pressure of the bit and reins to rate him cast a shadow over his reputation. The shadow lurked through his career and even affected the evaluation of his sons for many years, although vindication was spectacular.

Bold Ruler was a dark bay, a tall and lovely colt with a bit of white in his forehead, and ears that were just long enough that in some photographs they gave his head a deceptively common look. He was trained by Sunny Jim Fitzsimmons, who had handled the Wheatley and Ogden Phipps stables for many years, since before his career rose to glory with the Belair Stud horses of William

Bold Ruler

Woodward Sr. Those two lasting relationships overlapped for a quarter-century until the death of William Woodward Jr. in 1955. One of the most extraordinary concentrations of class in racing history was served to fans at Belmont Park on October 13, 1956. The day saw Nashua end his career by winning a second Jockey Club Gold Cup, while Bold Ruler put a stamp on his own developing brilliance by winning the Futurity Stakes. Fitzsimmons trained them both. (Nashua at that time raced for Leslie Combs II, but had been bred and raced by the Belair Woodwards at two and three.)

Prior to the Futurity, Bold Ruler had been one of those smart, early two-year-olds that begin to generate distant hopes in the spring of the year. While many a juvenile blossom withers quickly into obscurity, Bold Ruler was one of those whose early hint of potential was not exaggerated, but indeed understated. Fitzsimmons had him ready by April 9, when he won a maiden race at first asking. Next came victories in an allowance, the Youthful, another allowance, and the Juvenile. By June 6, he had made five starts in two months, and he had handled several colts that would prove exceptional at various stages of their careers — King Hairan, Clem, and Missile.

A back injury Bold Ruler suffered by slamming the gate at the start of the Juvenile, and then a hock problem, caused Fitzsimmons to wonder if he could get the colt back to the races at all that year. Bold Ruler missed the August meeting at Saratoga, just as he would at three and four, but he was back in time to prep for that autumn's Futurity. He was beaten for the first time on his return in allowance company at Belmont, and it was from this race that he came back bleeding from the mouth. Bold Ruler rebounded to win the Anticipation Purse, then was impressive in the Futurity on Belmont's impromptu Super Saturday. An opening quarter-mile in :21 4/5 had Bold Ruler in front in the Futurity, and jockey Eddie Arcaro let him stroll away to win handily from a nice field including Greek Game, Iron Liege, and Cohoes. That fall, Bold Ruler also had handled without trouble a quick Canadian colt named Nearctic. Thus, Belmont fans had seen on the track at the same time two colts for destiny: One a future eight-time leading sire that begot Secretariat and the other the father of the great stallion Northern Dancer!

Bold Ruler would probably have been voted the year's championship had he been put away after the Futurity. In the Garden State Stakes, however, laying off the pace worked against him and he ran up on the heels of the quickly-stopping early pacemaker. Bold Ruler fell far back as Calumet Farm's lightly raced Barbizon came on to defeat a sterling field. Bold Ruler seemed to sulk when things did not go his way in the Remsen and finished fourth, giving him consecutive year-ending losses despite a record for 1956 of seven wins in ten starts and earnings of $139,050. Barbizon won the championship balloting and also was assigned top weight of 126 pounds, one above Bold Ruler, on the Experimental Free Handicap.

The following winter, Bold Ruler at three returned his brilliant self, but there was an abundance of quality to come at him in relays. At Hialeah, he won the seven-furlong Bahamas, equaling the track record. Lurking behind him was a number from Calumet Farm which would make Barbizon look second-rate. This was Gen. Duke, and at a mile and one-eighth and getting twelve pounds from Bold Ruler, this late-developing colt held sway in the Everglades Stakes. At level weights in the Flamingo, Bold Ruler fought him off, again in track-record time. Then came Gen. Duke's surpassing victory in the Florida Derby, in which he ran past the other colt to win with authority and match the world record of 1:46 4/5 after Bold Ruler had led for a mile by shading 1:35.

Gen. Duke was sent to Kentucky, Bold Ruler to New York. In the Wood Memorial at a mile and an eighth, the Wheatley Stable colt encountered yet another developing three-year-old destined for stardom. This was Gallant Man, who tested him to the limit before Bold Ruler just got home in front by a nose, again in track-record time.

Gen. Duke came up lame only hours before the Kentucky Derby, and Bold Ruler was the post-time favorite. Two years before, Fitzsimmons and Arcaro had been beaten with the favorite when Nashua went under to Swaps. The standard line was that Arcaro had paid so much attention to Nashua's long-standing rival, Summer Tan, that he let Swaps steal away. The real story, though, probably was that Swaps just beat the stuffings out of both Nashua and Summer Tan that day. Over the years, Bold Ruler was associated with an excuse for his loss in the Derby, too, but, here again, the quality of what finished in front of him brings into question whether an excuse was appropriate.

"Like all people that are good in their profession, Fitzsimmons would say that the Derby was his fault," Ogden Phipps told us some years ago. "He told Arcaro to rate Bold Ruler. There was a horse called Federal Hill in there, and Fitz said not to go out with him, but to rate Bold Ruler. Arcaro said, 'I don't think I can rate him.' Fitzsimmons said, 'Well, the exercise riders can rate him. I don't know why you can't.'"

Arcaro was often quoted to the effect that, once again, regarding one horse (Gallant Man) the main opposition created a prevailing strategy:

" 'Take back off Federal Hill a little,' Mr. Fitz told me. 'Let him go out on the lead if he wants to.' That's what I was trying to do, but Bold Ruler went into the clubhouse turn like a wild horse. He was so full of run that he could have gone right on past Federal Hill and I should have let him do that, but it wasn't until then that I realized I was fighting him too hard…Then he was empty. I had discouraged and confused him by fighting him when he wanted to run." (Phil Bull, who had used the term "mulish" in assessing Nasrullah, might have given a knowing nod and wink at the thought of a son of that paradoxical colt turning sour on Arcaro.)

Bold Ruler finished fourth. This was the Derby in which the great rider Willie Shoemaker mistook the sixteenth pole for the finish line and rose in his irons for an instant. He and Gallant Man just failed to get to Gen. Duke's startling deputy, Iron Liege. Ralph Lowe, owner of Gallant Man, was said to have dreamt of something similar happening. He proved so loyal to Shoemaker in leaving him on Gallant Man that later a sportsmanship award was named for Lowe. (We have a memory from teenage fan days of *Sports Illustrated* — near the dawn of its bizarre "jinx" pattern — having given a unintended hint that something odd would happen. One of the little cartoon and poem couplings the magazine used to publish ran roughly: "He nears the wire with room to spare/ But watch his speed diminish/ He's taking time to comb his hair/ In case of photo finish.")

Allowed to roll along more freely, Bold Ruler dominated the Preakness. Iron Liege ran, but Gallant Man did not, and Gen. Duke never got back to competition. Bold Ruler had been given a mile and one-sixteenth prep over the Pimlico strip and had won that one easily, too.

The horse that had failed at one and a quarter miles would then be tested at one and a half miles

Bold Ruler

in the Belmont. Neither Fitz nor the Phippses were wont to pass up a challenge. John Nerud, the wily trainer of Gallant Man, figured Bold Ruler would insist on running freely again, the length of the Belmont not being something the horse would likely grasp before the fact. Nerud entered a colt named Bold Nero to be what later in this country would become known as a "rabbit." This pacemaker prompted Bold Ruler into such injudicious use of his prodigious speed that the time for one and a quarter miles was 2:01 2/5. This clocking had some fame at the time, for it was the time which had stood as the Kentucky Derby record since Whirlaway in 1941.

If Bold Ruler could have spoken to Arcaro in English, it was here that he probably would have said something like, "Oh, this is what you've been worrying about." There was still a quarter-mile left to run. Bold Ruler spoke instead via the language of wobbly, though noble, legs, and Shoemaker and Gallant Man sailed past. Shoe could have stood up that time without a problem, for Gallant Man won by eight lengths, setting a track and American record of 2:26 3/5. Bold Ruler faded to third, as Inside Tract also passed him.

Again, Bold Ruler got a summer's rest, prompted by fatigue, reaction to an encephalitis vaccine, and a nerve problem in a shoulder. He bounded back and had an unusually busy autumn for a colt of his class. He showed a superb combination of speed, middle distance stamina, weight-carrying ability, and indifference to track condition. To wit: He won the Jerome at a mile; carried 130 pounds and beat Roseben's fifty-one-year-old track record in the seven-furlong Vosburgh against older horses and peer Nearctic in the slop; carried 133 in winning the Queen's County Handicap; shipped to New Jersey and won the one and one-sixteenth-

mile Ben Franklin by a dozen lengths under 136 pounds.

Moreover, Bold Ruler participated in two showdowns of exceptional class. One he won; the other he did not. The Woodward brought together Gallant Man and Bold Ruler with two high-class older horses, Dedicate and Reneged. Dedicate won from Gallant Man. Bold Ruler was third. Later came the Trenton Handicap at Garden State Park for three-year-olds going one and a quarter miles. Joining Bold Ruler and Gallant Man was a colt called Round Table, who raced for Travis Kerr and had been unbeaten in his last eleven races. Round Table had been third in the Kentucky Derby. Bold Ruler and Round Table had been foaled at Claiborne Farm on the same night, April 6, 1954, and, along with Gallant Man and Gen. Duke, made a strong presentation on behalf of their group being as fine a bunch of three-year-olds as ever has been assembled in one year. (Bold Ruler and Round Table [refer to Princequillo chapter] were housed in stalls across the aisle from one another in Claiborne's stud barn as they both authored prolonged success at stud.)

For the Trenton, Arcaro and Fitzsimmons knew that Gallant Man and Round Table preferred to come from off the pace, and they recognized that this played into their hands, even though Bold Ruler had not yet won at one and a quarter miles. Furthermore, the off going compromised Round Table's chances. Bold Ruler set sail alone, opened an eight-length lead, and got home easily by two and a quarter lengths in 2:01 3/5.

Although he raced no more that year, Bold Ruler was nominated for both the one and one-sixteenth-mile Knickerbocker and one and three-sixteenths-mile Roamer Handicap. This subjected him to the uncompromising judgment of the knowledgeable racing secretary F. E. (Jimmy)

134

Kilroe. He was assigned 139 pounds for both. This weight was believed to be a record assignment for a three-year-old in this country and was a pound more than Man o' War had carried in winning the 1920 Potomac Handicap at three.

Bold Ruler had won eleven of sixteen races at three and earned $415,160. On the two major polls then extant, he was champion three-year-old in both and split Horse of the Year honors with Dedicate.

At four, Bold Ruler enhanced his reputation as a weight carrier and twice won demanding tests at one and a quarter miles. Since he was injured and retired before the two-mile Jockey Club Gold Cup, he never had another race at longer than one and a quarter miles.

Fitzsimmons brought him out at four for the six-furlong Toboggan, and Bold Ruler won under 133 pounds, giving sixteen to his old acquaintance Clem. At seven furlongs, and under 135 pounds, Bold Ruler then won the Carter Handicap. Next came his final meeting with Gallant Man, in the one-mile Metropolitan Handicap. Bold Ruler carried 135 pounds, Gallant Man 130. Bold Ruler was a natural miler, but the speedy pace of the Met put a premium on staying ability. This played into the style of Gallant Man, who came along and won by daylight. After eight meetings, the two stood even, each having finished ahead of the other four times. They would not meet again.

Bold Ruler then carried 133 pounds to win the one and one-eighth-mile Stymie Handicap. Next came the great Suburban Handicap. He was in under 134 for the one and a quarter-mile race which had been won under heavier burdens by only Whisk Broom II (139) and Grey Lag (135). Incredibly, Bold Ruler was giving twenty-five pounds to Clem, Adele Rand's consistently good campaigner. Clem made a ferocious run at Bold

Ruler, but the highweight courageously stood him off through the stretch to prevail by a nose. Clem's quality was underlined later in the year when Mrs. Rand's colt defeated champion Round Table in three consecutive meetings! (In forty-plus years since, only Forego has matched the feat of winning the Suburban under 134 pounds.)

Again carrying 134 pounds at the once-feared distance of one and a quarter miles, Bold Ruler won the Monmouth Handicap, giving twenty-one pounds to Sharpsburg. Still not ducking anything, the Bold Ruler camp headed for the Brooklyn Handicap, accepting 136 pounds. He finished next to last and came out of the race with a filled ankle. That was all for Bold Ruler. He was retired to Claiborne with twenty-three wins in thirty-three starts and earnings of $764,204.

The front-running style — which gives the impression at least of extra pressure in getting a distance — coupled with failure in the highest-visibility race, the Kentucky Derby, not to mention the Belmont debacle, created a lingering belief in Bold Ruler's middle-distance limitation. As a number of Bold Ruler's colts came up to the Derby as major contenders but failed, even Arcaro fell into the trap. The great rider was less comfortable with a microphone in his hand than a fist full of reins and mane, and perhaps nerves contributed to his remarking at least once years later as a racing commentator that Bold Ruler could not get one and a quarter miles. A viewer's immediate umbrage, of course, was wasted: "Don't you remember your own career, Eddie? You won with him in the Suburban and Monmouth under 134 pounds, yourself!"

A Bold Parade of Rulers

We have given considerable detail to the racing days of Bold Ruler in the thought that his reputa-

Bold Ruler

tion today is so much slanted toward his greatness at stud that some readers might be unaware of just what a splendid racehorse he had been. Nevertheless, we do not question that Bold Ruler was even better in the stud than on the track. The comfort in calling him a "Great" racehorse without qualification is reduced by the fact that, while he did get one and a quarter miles, that seemed his limit. Phipps remembers the subject with a true horseman's judgment tempering an owner's natural pride:

"Fitzsimmons said Bold Ruler was a faster horse and Nashua a better stayer. A mile was Bold Ruler's distance. Arcaro said he'd never been on a horse that broke faster...Like all good milers, if the race set up right, Bold Ruler could win at one and a quarter miles in good company."

Over the years, it has been enmeshed in racing lore that Fitzsimmons had to train Bold Ruler on Butazolidin to combat constant soreness, something he could not do on race day because of the era's medication policies. To whatever degree that is history as well as anecdote, it adds one more element to the trainer's expertise as well as the willingness of the horse to run his hardest.

Bold Ruler's first crop came to the races at two in 1962, and the pattern of early brilliance was quickly established with Speedwell and others. The next crop was better, featuring Chieftain, among others. In 1963, without the advantage of having any horses older than three, Bold Ruler led the sire list for the first time. He also topped the juvenile list that year. William Haggin Perry and Claiborne Farm's lovely filly Lamb Chop, from the first crop, won the Coaching Club American Oaks at one and a quarter miles en route to her three-year-old filly title of 1963. She was the first of Bold Ruler's ten American champions and eleven overall.

Bold Ruler remained on top for six more years

before Hail to Reason, Northern Dancer, and neighbor Round Table took turns leading the list. Bold Ruler returned to the top statistically in 1973, the year his ultimate son, Secretariat, won the Triple Crown and two years after the stallion's death. Bold Ruler led the juvenile sire list a total of six times.

Reigning as leading sire for seven consecutive years and a total of eight were both records for the 20th Century. The author has no argument with placing Northern Dancer eventually as a greater sire — certainly in terms of the impact of succeeding generations — but cannot recall any situation equal to the hold Bold Ruler seemed to have on racing during one phase. It might have something to do with one's impressionable age, of course, as well as Northern Dancer's impact being so geographically diffused in a more international age than Bold Ruler's. In any case, during the middle 1960s, a pattern emerged as each new crop came onto the scene: Not only would Bold Ruler have a star, but several of the best two-year-olds of the season would be his.

In 1964, Bold Ruler for the first time sired a Phipps family juvenile championship double: Wheatley Stable's Bold Lad was the champion juvenile colt and stablemate Queen Empress the champion two-year-old filly. Three years later, it was Ogden Phipps' turn: Vitriolic, by Bold Ruler, was champion two-year-old colt, and Queen of the Stage, by Bold Ruler, was champion two-year-old filly. In between, Wheatley had another champion Bold Ruler juvenile colt in Successor.

In 1964, in addition to Bold Lad's and Queen Empress' skein of major wins, Meadow Stable's Bold Experience won the Sorority and George D. Widener's Cornish Prince won the Sanford. In 1966, when Successor won the Garden State, Champagne, and Tremont as champion, Widener's

Bold Hour won the Futurity, Hopeful, and Flash, while the Phippses' Great Power won the Sapling and National Stallion Stakes. In 1967, when Ogden Phipps' Vitriolic and Queen of the Stage were champions, What a Pleasure won the Hopeful and National Stallion in the Wheatley Stable colors of Phipps' mother, and Meadow Stable's Syrian Sea won the Selima, Astarita, and Colleen.

In 1968, Top Knight, by Vertex, was the heretical juvenile champion, but among the Bold Rulers of that crop, King Emperor won the Pimlico-Laurel Futurity, Cowdin, and Sanford, and Reviewer won the Sapling and Saratoga Special. Not even Bold Ruler kept up the juvenile dominance year to year, but in 1972 came his son Secretariat, so spectacular at two that he won the Eclipse Award as Horse of the Year.

Eventually, the success of the privately owned Bold Ruler was such that the Phippses asked Bull Hancock to put in place an unusual management practice for him. Owners of distinguished mares would be invited to breed to the horse without paying a fee, provided they agreed to give one of every two of a mare's resulting foals to the Phippses.

"We thought of it one day and asked Bull to go to work on it the next," Ogden Phipps recalled for *The Blood-Horse* in 1989. "Our deal with most people was that, 'if the first foal is a colt you get it, and if it's a filly we get it.' We tried to make the arrangement only for champion runners or the dams of champions."

In those days, the era of large books was still in the distant future. Bold Ruler never sired more than thirty-five colts in any crop. The most famous arrangement was the breedings to Somethingroyal: Meadow Stable got a colt named Secretariat and Phipps got a filly named The Bride. From the Phippses' point of view, of course, the plan's long-term appeal was that it gave them ready access to outstanding bloodlines that augmented their own platinum broodmare families.

The bugaboo about Bold Ruler and distance was kept alive by results of the Kentucky Derby. Despite Lamb Chop's having won at one and a quarter miles at the highest levels two years before, Bold Lad's failure in the Kentucky Derby was marked down to a limitation because he was a Bold Ruler. Bold Lad had been so brilliant a two-year-old that he was weighted at 130 pounds to top the Experimental of 1964. The following year, he finished far back as favorite in the Derby, and the fact that he came out of the race with an injury that cancelled the rest of his three-year-old season did not seem to exonerate his pedigree totally. The next year, Stupendous finished fourth in the Derby, and then Successor was sixth in 1967. Perhaps equally as damning as the failures of Bold Rulers in the Derby was the large number of his bright two-year-olds which did not get to that race.

In the meantime, one and a quarter-mile race victories were recorded in other venues, but, as was the case of Bold Ruler as a runner himself — and as illustrated today by the one-day use of Dosage — getting one and a quarter miles in general and getting the distance as a three-year-old on the first Saturday in May tend to be seen as two distinct subjects. Among the best of the Bold Rulers to get one and a quarter miles was Bold Bidder, champion handicapper of 1966 in the colors of John R. Gaines after being purchased from Wheatley by an intermediary owner. Another was Bold Hour. Others, in addition to Lamb Chop, were the distaff champion Gamely and the multiple stakes winner Batteur, who both were also Bold Rulers in the partnership of Claiborne and William Haggin Perry. Also, Successor came back to win the one and five-eighths-mile Lawrence Realization later in his three-year-old season.

Bold Ruler

Triple Crown winner Secretariat, like Man o' War before him, was such a great horse that he fit no pattern. Perhaps such horses do not redound to the credit of their sires as much as more "conventional" champions. Still, Secretariat was a Bold Ruler that not only won the Derby in record time, but was even more astounding in setting a new record in the Belmont. Secretariat's 2:24 was a world record (and still an American record) for one and a half miles. Fractions faster than those that did in Bold Ruler merely set up Secretariat for a solitary, albeit hasty, parade through the stretch.

From Bold Ruler's last crop, born after his death, came one more exclamation point in Wajima, a superbly handsome colt that brought a record $600,000 as a yearling at Keeneland in 1973. (Relatively few Bold Rulers appeared on the market, and an earlier record had been set at $170,000 for One Bold Bid in 1964.) Wajima, racing for East-West Stable, whose ownership included dominant Japanese horseman Zenya Yoshida, developed too late for the classics of 1975. He then won the one and a quarter-mile Travers and defeated the great Forego in the one and a quarter-mile Marlboro Cup. Wajima had two victories over erstwhile three-year-old leader Foolish Pleasure and won the Eclipse Award in the division to become Bold Ruler's last champion.

Bold Ruler sired eighty-two stakes winners, for a remarkable twenty-three percent from foals. To reprise, his champions in this country were Lamb Chop, Bold Lad, Queen Empress, Bold Bidder, Gamely, Successor, Vitriolic, Queen of the Stage, Secretariat, and Wajima. Emblematic of his prowess was the naming of his remaining champion: Mrs. Henry Carnegie Phipps' twin sister, Beatrice Lady Granard, who lived in England, toasted Bold Lad by giving the same name to an Irish-bred Bold Ruler colt of her own. Naturally, that Bold Ruler was champion at two in England and Ireland.

Given the quality of broodmares sent him, it was not surprising that Bold Ruler was a successful broodmare sire, as well. His daughters foaled 119 stakes winners, including six champions.

A Decade of Derby Dominance

Beginning in 1970, sons of Bold Ruler created a pattern of siring Derby winners that was at odds with the reputation of the first generation. Perhaps it could be conjectured that Bold Ruler blood needed other influences to add stamina to the stallion's inheritable brilliance. On the other hand, a stallion could hardly ask for more classic influences than those already brought to the pedigrees of his offspring by the mares in the broodmare bands of the Phipps family, the Hancock family, and other patrons such as George D. Widener, Meadow Stable, the Brady family, and King Ranch.

Whatever the explanation, a series of Bold Ruler's sons, several from below his top rank as racehorses, began to get Derby winners. First was Bold Commander, a nice sort of horse but nothing to send home to Claiborne; he sired Dust Commander, winner of the Blue Grass and Kentucky Derby in 1970. In 1973 came Bold Ruler's own son, Secretariat. Then in 1974, handicap champion Bold Bidder, who stood at Gainesway Farm, sent out Cannonade to win the 100th running of the Derby. In 1975, the Derby was won by defending juvenile champion Foolish Pleasure, whose sire, What a Pleasure, was Wheatley Stable's former Hopeful winner that had been sent to Waldemar Farm in Florida.

What a Pleasure seemed poised to have a second consecutive Derby winner when Honest

Pleasure arrived at the race in 1976. Like Foolish Pleasure, he had been the dominant colt at two, earning the juvenile championship. In the Derby, however, the 2-5 Honest Pleasure never came to terms with the front-running Bold Forbes. The sire of the winner? Irish Castle, yet another non-championship son of Bold Ruler. Irish Castle had been a Phipps horse that, like What a Pleasure, won the Hopeful Stakes, and then he went to stud at The Stallion Station in Lexington. Irish Castle was out of the Tulyar mare Castle Forbes, Wheatley's champion two-year-old filly of 1963, and What a Pleasure was the ninth stakes winner from Wheatley's great mare Grey Flight, by Mahmoud.

In 1979, the brilliant colt Spectacular Bid became the second Derby winner by Bold Bidder and thus the fifth Derby winner of the seventies sired by a son of Bold Ruler. Of course, Bold Ruler himself had sired his own Derby winner of the decade in Secretariat, and, one of the two other Triple Crown winners of the 1970s also traced to him in the male line. This was the amazing Seattle Slew, whose sire, Bold Reasoning, was a son of the Bold Ruler horse Boldnesian.

The Florida-based Bold Ruler stallion What a Pleasure led the American sire list in consecutive years, 1975 and 1976. These were the great days of his sons the Pleasures — Foolish and Honest. John Greer's Foolish Pleasure was the unbeaten two-year-old champion of 1974 and won the Flamingo, Wood Memorial, and Kentucky Derby at three. Bert Firestone's Honest Pleasure was the two-year-old champion of 1975 and won the Flamingo, Florida Derby, Blue Grass Stakes, and Travers the next year. Honest Pleasure's full brother For the Moment came along in the next crop to win the Futurity and Blue Grass. What a Pleasure sired fifty stakes winners (ten percent).

In 1980, another son of Bold Ruler led the sire list. His name was Raja Baba, winner of three minor stakes, but out of the mare Missy Baba, who became the ancestress of classic winners Summer Squall and A.P. Indy, among others. Raja Baba stood at Hermitage Farm in Kentucky and was owned by William S. Farish and Warner L. Jones Jr. Raja Baba sired sixty-two stakes winners (eleven percent), including Well Decorated, Sweet Revenge, and El Baba.

Bold Ruler's best sons at the racetrack had mixed results in the stud. The great Secretariat, who stood his entire career at Claiborne, was counted by many a disappointment, but his special status lent a twist to that word. Expectations were probably unrealistic. At any rate, Secretariat sired fifty-seven stakes winners (nine percent), including 1986 Horse of the Year Lady's Secret and the smashing Preakness-Belmont winner and 1988 three-year-old champion Risen Star. Not surprisingly, Secretariat ascended then to the top of the broodmare sire list.

Another of Bold Ruler's best sons was the exceptional juvenile champion Bold Lad, who returned at four to win the Metropolitan Handicap. Bold Lad started out with the advantage of standing at Claiborne but later was located in France for a time and then Japan. He had limited success, but got the high-class European fillies Marble Arch and Bold Fascinator and the globetrotting handicap horse Sirlad.

Bold Bidder, the champion handicap horse of 1966, was a high-class sire, getting classic winners Spectacular Bid and Cannonade among fifty-three stakes winners (eleven percent). Spectacular Bid was ranked the tenth best American racehorse of the 20th Century for *The Blood-Horse* by a panel of seven historians and racing secretaries (nine places above Bold Ruler). Spectacular Bid was a champion all three years he ran and was unbeaten

Bold Ruler

in nine races as a well-tested handicap horse at four. Bold Bidder's other Derby winner, Cannonade, seemed to be making his way when he got the Belmont Stakes winner Caveat (in turn, sire of tough campaigner Awad). Again, however, the magic faded, although they have been useful sires.

Vitriolic, Successor, and Wajima were other champion sons by Bold Ruler, but all three had modest, or worse, stud records.

Raymond Guest's Chieftain, one of the first of the sharp Bold Rulers, won seven stakes and more than $400,000 and proved a significant sire. He got the New York Handicap Triple winner Fit to Fight (one of the better of the next generation at stud) as well as older distaff champion Cascapedia, Kentucky Oaks winner Lucky Lucky Lucky, and Silver Series, although his percentage (forty-three stakes winners, nine percent) was not exceptionally high.

Bold Hour was a classy Bold Ruler colt for George D. Widener and won eight important stakes from two through four, including the one and a quarter-mile Haskell Handicap over Damascus. He was moderately successful at stud, his twenty-seven stakes winners (five percent) including Travers winner Willow Hour and All Rainbows, dam of Kentucky Derby winner Winning Colors. Widener's Cornish Prince won the Sanford and Jim Dandy and statistically was quite a good stallion, getting fifty-two stakes winners (eleven percent). Several of his fillies — Wanda, Sparkalark, Patelin, Brenda Beauty — were near top class.

Another Bold Ruler of note was the classy Reviewer, who sired the great filly Ruffian and another champion filly in Revidere. Also, the Bold Ruler horse Bold and Brave sired Hall of Famer Bold'n Determined; Top Command sired the dominant three-year-old filly champion Mom's Command; the reliable Blade got fifty-one stakes winners (nine percent); Dewan got forty stakes winners (nine percent); and Jacinto got thirty-eight stakes winners (nine percent), including Peacefully, dam of Kentucky Derby winner Gato Del Sol. Other sons of Bold Ruler — Key to the Kingdom, Plum Bold, and Might — all had a few nice runners.

These and various others — some hardly successful as runners but more so at stud — contributed to a great dissemination of Bold Ruler blood through his sons.

In short, Bold Ruler was a great sire of runners, and strong sire of sires, for a number of his sons got an abundance of stakes winners in turn. What is surprising is how quickly the sire line faded, for the most part, in the next generations. By and large, even the sons of Bold Ruler that got good racehorses did not follow suit in consistently getting sons that took their own turns as outstanding sires. (Grandsons Bold Forbes, Dust Commander, and Fit to Fight are among those that have came close.) There undoubtedly are individuals prepared to give some explanation for this through a tedious explanation of patterns dealing with inbreedings, excessive refinement, anti-nicks, crosses, or outcrosses (maybe even left crosses). As in the case of Bull Lea and his feckless stallion sons, or the decline of Hyperion's sire line, we prefer to quote the character in *Amadeus*, who liked to look at a situation and simply conclude, "Well, there it is."

Slew to the Rescue

Just as European horsemen over the years feared for the once-dominant St. Simon line only to see it pop up again, we see little danger of the Bold Ruler branch of Nasrullah disappearing entirely. Consistent with the capricious nature of Thoroughbred genetics, it is not one of the best of the Bold Ruler colts that gives the strongest link to the present. Instead, the son that gave the line its biggest continuing boost was Boldnesian, sire of Bold Reasoning and grandsire of Seattle Slew.

Boldnesian was a Bold Ruler colt from Alanesian, she a brilliant filly acquired by the late William Haggin Perry some time before he began his enduring arrangement of sharing Claiborne-breds with the Hancock family. Boldnesian was the first of three stakes winners from the mare, followed by Princessnesian and Jackal. At three in 1966, Boldnesian came forward to win the Santa Anita Derby and seem a likely contender for greater glory, but he soon was stopped by a knee injury and sent to stud at Dr. William O. Reed's Mare Haven Farm in Florida. He got twenty-seven stakes winners (eleven percent), including the consistent Canadian champion sire Bold Ruckus, the filly Bold Bikini (dam of European classic winner Law Society), and Bold Reasoning.

Bold Reasoning combined two of the most potent of the branches of the Nearco sire line. Grandson of Bold Ruler on the top side, he was out of Reason to Earn, whose sire, Hail to Reason, was a leading sire who went back to Nearco in tail male via Turn-to and Royal Charger. Reason to Earn's dam, Sailing Home, was a half-sister to 1944 Belmont Stakes winner Bounding Home. If ever a pedigree seemed compatible with various glib, off-hand approaches this was it:

Like inbreeding to a great sire? The Nearco connection was there.

Have plenty of speed and need stamina influences? Bold Ruler sire line out of a mare whose granddam foaled a Belmont winner.

Prefer speed in the female family? Bounding

Home had two full siblings (Romping Home and Breezing Home) that won Saratoga stakes at two.

Like European influences in pedigrees mixed with stout "American" blood? Marching Home, second dam of Reason to Earn, was by John P. Grier and out of a Man o' War mare.

The Boldnesian—Reason to Earn colt was named Bold Reasoning. He was bred in Florida by Leon Savage and sold in 1970 at the two-year-old sale for $15,500. Racing for Kosgrove Stable, Bold Reasoning won eight of twelve races, including the Withers Stakes and Jersey Derby of 1971, and earned $189,564. In the Jersey Derby, he defeated Pass Catcher, who in his next start would win the Belmont Stakes. Bold Reasoning was accepted for duty at Claiborne Farm, and young Seth Hancock recommended him to a colorful Kentuckian named Ben Castleman, a horse breeder, state racing commissioner, and tavern owner. Castleman had some mares and a limited budget. On Hancock's advice, he sent to Bold Reasoning his Poker mare named My Charmer, who was from a good family of Maine Chance Farm — an across-the-pike neighbor of Castleman's little property just north of Lexington.

The result was a dark, husky sort of colt which brought $17,500 from the young partnership of Mickey and Karen Taylor and Dr. Jim and Sally Hill at the Fasig-Tipton Kentucky summer sale of 1975.

This colt was named Seattle Slew, and he soon took the Taylors and Hills — and American racing — on so theatrical an adventure that even now it seems too good to be true. It was this same fiery animal who has proved the key standard-bearer into the 21st Century for the sire line associated with his great-grandsire, Bold Ruler.

Seattle Slew dominated the Champagne Stakes in such brilliant fashion that he was voted champion two-year-old although it was the only stakes among his three races. The next year, the colt stepped up the dream world for the young owners and trainer Billy Turner Jr.: He went through the Triple Crown still undefeated in his career! No other horse ever had achieved that, nor has any since. The goddess named Perfection had at last danced into the light — and promptly saw her shadow. She then scuttled back to Reality: Seattle Slew lost his next race (the Swaps), did not run again at three, the owners and trainer split, the horse got sick and nearly died, his comeback was stop-and-go, and the jockey was replaced.

Having survived this neck-snapping sequence, Seattle Slew and the Hills and Taylors then had a sublime autumn in 1978. In the first meeting of Triple Crown winners in history, Seattle Slew dashed away from the younger Affirmed in the Marlboro Cup. He then added the Woodward over Exceller, went under to that rival by a scant margin in a marvelous bid for the Jockey Club Gold Cup, and ended his career with a win in the Stuyvesant under 134 pounds. Seattle Slew, champion at two, Horse of the Year at three, champion at four, had won fourteen of seventeen and earned $1,208,726. He stood first at Spendthrift Farm and then was moved to Three Chimneys Farm, both in Kentucky.

Seattle Slew is one of those great racehorses that have proven grand stallions, as well. His first crop included the two-time champion Slew o' Gold and the wonderful, unbeaten champion filly Landaluce. Soon followed the 1984 Kentucky Derby-Belmont winner Swale, juvenile champion Capote, and 1992 Horse of the Year A.P. Indy, winner of the Belmont Stakes and Breeders' Cup Classic. Seattle Slew's ninety-one stakes winners (eleven percent) also include Event of the Year,

Bold Ruler

Life at the Top, Adored, Slewpy, Seattle Song, Glowing Honor, Lakeway, and Seaside Attraction. Following his sire line's loftiest traditions, Seattle Slew led the American sire list in 1984.

Seattle Slew also has sired a slew of good stallions, although the highly promising Swale died before standing at stud. Capote is the sire of champion Boston Harbor; the California-based General Meeting is responsible for General Challenge and a host of other good runners; Slew o' Gold, Septieme Ciel, Slewpy, and Slew City Slew are among his other sons to have made a mark at stud.

A total of nine sons of Bold Ruler have male-line descendants listed in *The Blood-Horse Stallion Register* of 2000. Aside from the Seattle Slew connections, most are tenuous, but the What a Pleasure/Foolish Pleasure connection has the promising young horses Cobra King and Mecke, and Raja Baba's line has Yes It's True at the races and Notebook at stud.

Perhaps the brightest prospect for continuation, however, was the Lane's End Farm stallion A.P. Indy. As of early 2000, the Hall of Fame son of Hall of Famer Seattle Slew had already sired twenty-three stakes winners (nine percent), and they include the Blue Grass Stakes winner Pulpit, the flashy Old Trieste, Breeders' Cup-placed Golden Missile, and grade I fillies Tomisue's Delight and Runup the Colors — all from four crops. A. P. Indy eventually sired more than 150 black-type stakes winners. His son Pulpit's ongoing prowess as a stallion included begetting Tapit, which led the North American sire lists for four consecutive years (2014–2017).

The End of Long Ago

Nearly three decades have passed since the death of Bold Ruler.

142

In July of 1970, when he was sixteen years old, he showed signs of difficulty in breathing. Bleeding from the nostrils prompted a tracheotomy, and eventually a malignant mass near the brain was discovered by exploratory surgery. Mrs. Phipps and son Ogden were kept apprised, of course, and placed top priority on preventing the horse from suffering. Bold Ruler was sent for cobalt treatment to Auburn University, where veterinary scientists were aided and encouraged by consultation with specialists who had treated malignancy in humans. They were successful in a pioneering effort which put the cancer in remission.[1]

The horse was returned to Claiborne and, in what might be regarded as a bonus season, stood to virtually a full book in 1971. He thus begot a final crop that included the record-priced yearling and future champion Wajima as well as other stakes winners Singh, Alpine Lass, Our Hero, and Sugar Plum Time. Bold Ruler lived a normal life for a number of months, but by June of 1971 began to lose weight again. About a month later, a biopsy showed a return of the cancer and the horse was euthanized on July 12, 1971.

Mrs. Phipps had passed away the previous autumn, at about the time the horse was returned to Claiborne. The master of Claiborne, Bull Hancock, died of cancer the following year. If one goes around thinking about a legacy, the unbroken success of something his/her family already has represented for a half-century is about as good as can be imagined. Nasrullah, and Bold Ruler, had both had their input in making that transition a reality. ❖

Hail to Reason

The tale of Hail to Reason could be said to begin in Ireland, with his male ancestry. It came to fruition through a couple of New Yorkers that Damon Runyon might have invented — if they had not already been his pals. Hirsch Jacobs was one of America's and American racing's heartening success stories. Jacobs was a little fellow of nondescript financial background who through hard work, acumen, and the willingness to observe and learn, became a great horseman. His partner was Isidor Bieber, a Broadway figure who had some outstanding qualities himself, not the least of which were a goodly bankroll and the sense to collar Jacobs as his partner.

With Jacobs supplying the genius, Bieber-Jacobs rose from the former's career in training a claiming stable to the height of pedigree fashion. When Bieber-Jacobs held a reduction sale in 1966, the premier breeders and owners came to do battle for its stock. Until not long before his death in 1970, Hirsch Jacobs remained the trainer. He had been eleven times America's leading trainer in number of races won during the 1930s and 1940s and three times the leader in earnings (1946, 1960, and 1965). Bieber-Jacobs Stable later reigned as leading breeder in money earned for four consecutive years, 1964-67. The claiming and

subsequent championship campaigning of Stymie were instrumental in this leap from one peak to another, a transformation for Jacobs similar to those of hands-on horsemen Sam Hildreth, Guy Bedwell, and John E. Madden of earlier eras.

Hail to Reason was one of the runners which bore the mark of a Bieber theme in naming horses. Bieber used numerous horses to suggest his thought that, after two World Wars, it would not be a good idea for the world's nations to allow Germany to re-emerge as an armed power. The 1948 mare named Nothirdchance carried this message, as did her noble son, Hail to Reason. (As a summer member of the broodmare crew at Ocala Stud during college days, the author encountered another Bieber-named mare, Remember History; given the context of our personal universe at the time, we wondered if she had been named by a school teacher, college professor, or erstwhile poor student with a grudge.)

Horse names aside, Hirsch and Ethel Jacobs, of course, took to heart the naming of their actual children. When a daughter came along, they named her Patrice, in honor of pal Damon Runyon's wife. It was in Patrice Jacobs' colors that the partnership-bred and-owned Hail to Reason raced to championship honors in 1960.

The division of Nearco's legacy that led to, and

144

from, Hail to Reason dwelt for some years in an atmosphere of suspicion as to stamina. For once, this did not originate in America, which the world — and, to be frank, ourselves — often regard as a villainous land of sprint breeders. (Why struggle over a souffle, when a two-minute egg runs early and sells so well?) It was Nearco's own son, Royal Charger, who planted the seeds of doubt. Looking back, we might find this somewhat perplexing, for the line produces various winners of that enduring crucible of stamina, courage, and adaptability, to wit, the Epsom Derby. While Hail to Reason himself was unable to chip away at this prejudice as a racehorse, owing to an injury at two, his son Roberto was one of the figures instrumental in convincing the world that the Royal Charger line could be something more than sprinters and milers.

The gloriously named Royal Charger was the grandsire of Hail to Reason in tail male. Foaled in 1942, Royal Charger was sired by Nearco, and was out of Sun Princess, a half-sister to Nasrullah. When Royal Charger came to the races in the wartime season of 1944, Nasrullah was not yet known as a great sire, but as a brilliant, yet exasperating personality that had seemingly failed to live up to his physical potential.

Unlike most future sires of merit, Royal Charger failed to win at two. He made five starts, placing twice for trainer Jack Jarvis. At three, he won three of seven and an early-season victory encouraged his entry into the classic scene. He acquitted himself very well at a mile in the Two Thousand Guineas, finishing third to the fine pair of Court Martial and Dante. The Epsom Derby, at one and a half miles, was well beyond his scope, however, and he finished far behind Dante. At year's end, Royal Charger was ranked tenth on the three-year-old Free Handicap. At four, Royal Charger was kept to sprinting, aside from the

about one-mile Queen Anne Stakes, which was one of three races he won from nine starts in 1946. For his career, Royal Charger won six of twenty-one races and earned $20,386.

The colt was purchased by the Irish National Stud and, while a nice sort of colt with a wonderful pedigree, he was a long way from having the entire package as a sire prospect. He quickly proved that, like Phalaris and Nasrullah, he was better at siring racehorses than being one. In his early crops, he got the English One Thousand Guineas winner Happy Laughter and the Irish Two Thousand Guineas winner Sea Charger, as well as Royal Serenade, who began life as a crack sprinter but eventually won the one and a quarter-mile Hollywood Gold Cup.

As has been recounted in the chapter on Nasrullah, Mrs. A. B. Hancock Jr. recalls that it was believed the Californian Neil McCarthy was trying hard to buy that stallion when Claiborne Farm closed the deal for him in 1950. The following year, McCarthy did get Royal Charger, for a price reported at $300,000. The horse was imported and stood at Leslie Combs II's Spendthrift Farm in Kentucky. Royal Charger added considerably to his distinction. His American crops included Idun, who was a record-priced yearling filly when sold for $63,000 at Keeneland in 1956. Idun proceeded to be the unbeaten champion two-year-old filly of 1957 and repeat as three-year-old champion as well. Royal Charger also got a classic winner in this country in 1959 Preakness winner Royal Orbit, as well as the grass champion Mongo (also a major winner on dirt), and the additional distaff champion Royal Native. His lifetime total of fifty-eight stakes winners (sixteen percent) also included Seaneen, Finnegan, Irish Lancer, Royal Attack, Rainy Lake, and Royal Patrice. His producing daughters included Gay Hostess, dam of Kentucky Derby-Preakness winner Majestic Prince and English

		Nearco, 1935	**Pharos** / Nogara
	Royal Charger, 1942		
		Sun Princess, 1937	Solario / Mumtaz Begum
TURN-TO (GB), b, 1951			
		Admiral Drake, 1931	Craig an Eran / **Plucky Liege**
	Source Sucree, 1940		
		Lavendula, 1930	**Pharos** / Sweet Lavender
HAIL TO REASON, br h, April 18, 1958			
		Blue Larkspur, 1926	Black Servant / Blossom Time
	Blue Swords, 1940		
		Flaming Swords, 1933	Man o' War / Exalted
NOTHIRDCHANCE, b, 1948			
		Sir Gallahad III, 1920	Teddy / **Plucky Liege**
	Galla Colors, 1943		
		Rouge et Noir, 1934	St. Germans / Baton Rouge

1st dam: NOTHIRDCHANCE, b, 1948-1970. Bred by Bieber-Jacobs Stables (Ky). Raced 6 yrs, 93 sts, 11 wins, $112,660. Won Acorn S; 2nd Comely H, Ladies H; 3rd San Marcos H. Dam of 5 named foals, 5 rnrs, 4 wnrs, 2 sw.

1956: Remember History, ch f, by Palestinian. Raced 2 yrs, 19 sts, 2 wins, $6,575. Dam of 2 foals, 2 rnrs, 2 wnrs. Died 1972.

1957: Alas Thirdchance, ch g, by Count Turf. Raced 1 yr, 3 sts, 0 wins, $0. Died 1960.

1958: **HAIL TO REASON**, br c, by Turn-to. Bred by Bieber-Jacobs Stable (Ky). Raced 1 yr, 18 sts, 9 wins, $328,434. Champion 2yo colt. Won Hopeful S, Youthful S, Great American S, Sanford S, Sapling S, Tremont S, World's Playground S; 3rd Juvenile S. Sire of 308 foals, 43 sw, 4.48 AEI.

1959: Barren.

1960: Treachery, gr f, by Promised Land. Raced 5 yrs, 105 sts, 11 wins, $182,071. 2nd Delaware H, Santa Margarita H, Sheepshead Bay H (T), New Castle S, Distaff H; 3rd Sheepshead Bay H (T), Maskette H, Bed o' Roses H, Firenze H.

Dam of 10 foals, 8 rnrs, 4 wnrs. Granddam of **COLD COLONY**, **WILLIE'S FOLLY**, **REAL PRIZE**, **TURNING PLEASANT**, **Burn's Term**, **Classic Curves**, **Bold Pete**. Died 1982.

1961: Barren.

1962: Barren.

1963: **BE SUSPICIOUS**, b f, by Porterhouse. Raced 2 yrs, 35 sts, 3 wins, $41,657. Won Pasadena S; 2nd Santa Ynez S, La Centinela S. Dam of 12 foals, 8 rnrs, 6 wnrs, including **SECRET SCHEME** ($54,419), **HALF AN HOUR** ($30,923), **Blue Coast** ($48,581, in Fr and Ger). Granddam of **MEADOWLAKE, LEO CASTELLI, Shamrock McGroder, West Coast Native**. Died 1986.

1964: No report received.

1965: No report received.

1966: No report received.

1967: Not bred.

1968: Not bred.

1969: Barren.

juvenile champion Crowned Prince, and female-line ancestress of Derby winner Real Quiet and Epsom Derby winner Secreto.

Royal Charger also had sired Turn-to, before importation. Foaled in Ireland in 1951, Turn-to was bred by Major E. R. Miville and Mrs. G. L. Hastings. He was spotted by bloodstock agent Frank Moore O'Ferrall, whose farm in County Kildare was next to where the young colt was quartered. Moore O'Ferrall bought him on behalf of Claude Tanner when asked if he knew of a horse that might be a Kentucky Derby prospect. This was pretty astute, for the horse was barely a yearling.

Tanner died when the imported colt was still a yearling, and Mrs. Tanner asked Bull Hancock of

Claiborne Farm to sell him. Hancock liked the colt well enough to buy him at Keeneland for one of his clients, Captain Harry Guggenheim. Guggenheim's preference for names did not lean toward politics as directly as Bieber's, but he liked nautical names with or without an implied connection to warfare. The Royal Charger colt had already been named Source Royal, but Guggenheim changed it to Turn-to, sea talk for something like "get at it."

Turn-to got at it in a big way as a two-year-old in 1953. He won two of his first three races, including the Saratoga Special, which was gained via disqualification when the rider of Porterhouse inadvertently shivered his timbers with the whip. Turn-to bucked his shins when beaten by Artismo in the Hopeful Stakes and needed two months off, but was kept in training. Guggenheim and trainer Eddie Hayward had their eyes on the new late fall feature, the Garden State Stakes, which Eugene Mori had conceived and which overnight became the richest race in the world. At one and one-sixteenth miles, the New Jersey event played a role over two decades of two-year-old campaigns similar to that of the Breeders' Cup Juvenile today.

Turn-to was second to Goyamo in his prep for the big race and was 14-1 in the Garden State itself. He was with the leaders all the way, turned back several sharp challenges, and won by two lengths over Correlation. Goyamo was third. The race was worth $269,395. Porterhouse split the championship polls with Hasty Road, and Turn-to was ranked equal with Porterhouse atop the Experimental Free Handicap.

His claim to leadership of the division took on the force of persuasion early the next year, with his dashing victory in the Flamingo Stakes. He was the Kentucky Derby favorite when he got to Keeneland, but he was found in his stall one morning with a bowed tendon, and had to

be retired. He had won six of eight races and earned $280,032.

Turn-to was an immediate success, although he was always one of those horses with a reputation for getting quite a number of unsound offspring. When they were good, they were very, very good, and the first crop included the dominant two-year-old champion First Landing (later sire of Derby-Belmont winner Riva Ridge). Hail to Reason, the title horse of this chapter, came from Turn-to's third crop. Turn-to got twenty-five stakes winners, which was neither a high number nor high percentage — only seven percent. If "importance" could be expressed as a percentage, however, he would have had a soaring figure. His other best runners included Cyane, Captain's Gig, Flit-to, Reverse, Sally Ship, Waltz, Best Turn (sire of Davona Dale and Cox's Ridge), and Sir Gaylord.

Sir Gaylord was an imitator as well as a son — a star two-year-old, brilliant enough in Florida to become the Derby favorite, then injured and retired not long before the race. Sir Gaylord — along with Cyane and Best Turn — joined First Landing as an important sire among Turn-to's sons. It was Sir Gaylord who got Sir Ivor, the lovely colt who completed the Royal Charger line's redefinition by winning the Epsom Derby for Raymond Guest in 1968. The case might be made that the Royal Charger stallions got distance horses when the female aspects of the pedigree added some stoutness, and the time-honored cliche about "not staying, but winning on class" also greeted Sir Ivor. However, the colt's catapult in the final furlong to win the Derby, and his later victory at one and a half miles in the Washington, D.C., International, made the distinction between winning at one and a half miles and staying one and a half miles a tricky hair-split indeed. (Humphrey Finney, the sage seller and adviser, had been a paid consultant to Guggenheim for some years and, upon Sir Ivor's Epsom victory, sent a telegram congratulating the colt on behalf of "your Irish grandsire" — Turn-to.)

Sir Gaylord's sixty stakes winners (thirteen percent) also included the superb international sire Habitat, as well as Lord Gaylord, Gay Matelda, Gay Missile, and Bonnie and Gay. Sir Ivor himself continued his sire's importance at stud, with a reputation and record skewed toward fillies. His ninety-four stakes winners (twelve percent) included Arc de Triomphe winner Ivanjica, plus Optimistic Gal, Godetia, Cloonlara, and Sweet Alliance. He also did sire some good sons, such as Eclipse Award-winning handicapper Bates Motel.

Sir Ivor's legacy as a sire of fillies was countered later by the emergence of the astounding stallion Sir Tristram. This handsome colt was owned by Raymond Guest, the same sportsman who had purchased and raced Sir Ivor. Guest was game: He not only sent Sir Ivor over to win the Derby, but crossed the Atlantic — to great results on both sides — with his international jumping champion L'Escargot. Guest had less satisfactory results sending Tom Rolfe to France for the Prix de l'Arc de Triomphe or bringing Sir Tristram from France for the 1974 Kentucky Derby. Unable to win in top company in Europe or the United States, Sir Tristram found himself in the Antipodes, and he became a phenomenon, leading the Australian sire list five times, the Australian broodmare sire list three times, and siring 124 stakes winners. His son Zabeel succeeded him, turning out such as Octagonal, Might and Power, and others. The line once suspect at getting one and a half miles was now tacking on another half-mile and winning the Melbourne Cup at two miles!

Hail to Reason

The Classic Reason

Hail to Reason might have been Turn-to's most remarkable son. That this is even a question is testimony to the prowess of the line. Hail to Reason's juvenile campaign suggested a quality comparable to that of First Landing, and his record as a sire had stunning distinctions which could joust with any other of the Turn-to branch:

• Sire of an Epsom Derby winner.

• Sire of a different winner of each American Triple Crown race.

• Leading sire in America and sire of another to lead the list.

Hail to Reason was foaled from the Blue Swords mare Nothirdchance, who won a division of the Acorn Stakes in 1951 — eight years after her sire had become known as the frequent runner-up to the great Count Fleet. (Champion Kiss Me Kate won the other division of the 1951 Acorn.) Nothirdchance was a "very big, strong, strapping mare," as one of Hirsch Jacobs' sons, John, recalled for *The Blood-Horse* in 1976. "She wasn't what you would call a beautiful mare, but she was powerfully built. She was tough as they come — legs like iron. I believe Hail to Reason got a lot of his size from her." Surely, Nothirdchance was the sort of mare Hirsch Jacobs would love, for he believed in racing instead of training. In six seasons, she ran ninety-three times and won eleven races, earning $112,660.

Although the Jacobs family owned Stymie Manor in Maryland, many of their mares were boarded at Dr. Charles Hagyard's farm, signally named Hagyard Farm, just outside Lexington, Kentucky. Hail to Reason was foaled there on April 19, 1958. The big, growthy foal was so much a combatant in the fields that John Jacobs recalled how the youngster more or less commanded a group of about twenty other colts. Jacobs likened him to a prizefighter because of his "many nicks and bumps," but also recognized him as "like a kid standing six-foot at 15. He was all legs and no body."

While he was a tiger among his own kind, the young Hail to Reason was uneasy, and difficult, around people. The Jacobs' young daughter, Patrice, spent a great deal of time with the colt and was helpful in settling him into the sort of tractable animal whose demeanor would allow his prodigious physical abilities to be used correctly. There would come a time when this calmness, intelligence, and tractability would help save his life.

Most owners and trainers would have looked at this tall, deep, but lean colt and thought "wait, wait, wait." Hirsch Jacobs had spent too much time studying what actually happens when horses go into training and racing to subscribe to a stereotype.

"Racing is better for this colt than a lot of training," he said, and Hail to Reason made his debut on January 21 of his official two-year-old year, in a three-furlong dash at Santa Anita. He loped along, well-beaten, twice in that context, then, in New York, ran four times in five-furlong races within fifteen days — obviating the need for breezes — and he broke his maiden in the sixth race of his career. Soon, Hail to Reason graduated mentally and physically into an enormously efficient racehorse. By autumn, he had won nine of eighteen starts and was the overpowering champion of his division. His major wins came in a succession of the important juvenile stakes in New York and two in New Jersey: The Youthful, Great American, Tremont, Sapling, Sanford, Hopeful, and World's Playground. He hit a snag when he finished unplaced in the Saratoga Special. Jacobs diagnosed sore shins, treated them with white iodine, and sent him back ten days later to win the Hopeful by ten lengths in record time.

Even Hirsch Jacobs, masterful horseman that he was, could not bring Hail to Reason back after a later mishap, but he quite possibly saved the colt's life. On September 18, or eight days after the World's Playground, the big colt pulled up lame from a work at Aqueduct. He had "taken a bad step," in the lingo of observers of horse injuries, and fractured both sesamoids in the left foreleg. "Diabolical fate," the elder Jacobs was quoted as calling it sometime later. (It was reported that a lost shoe was found near where Hail to Reason broke down and was thought to have been the cause of the colt's "bad step.") At the moment, his son recalled, the father's quick action was pivotal. It was a Sunday morning and, in those days, as John Jacobs remembered, "There were no veterinarians round that early. I grabbed his leg. Father had me hold it up so he wouldn't step down on his ankle…We had no tranquilizers…When we got him back to the stall, Father rolled a plaster of Paris cast on the leg. I think the horse knew how seriously he was hurt, because he stood like a statue when we put that first cast on.

"It was life and death for a month, and it was a miracle Father pulled him through. The cast broke or cracked several times during the next month, but he was such a good patient. He protected himself. He'd never fight you or struggle with you…"

The next month, Hail to Reason was sent to his birthplace, Hagyard Farm, where the veterinarian owner also found him to be an ideal patient: "Hirsch Jacobs was a damn good horseman…(the horse) was still in a cast and couldn't put any weight on the injured hoof…I called in a blacksmith and elevated the shoe about an inch or an inch-and-a-half, and he immediately commenced bearing weight on it. He wasn't a sound horse by any means for a couple of years, but he had no real problem covering mares."

Hail to Reason was booked to only fifteen mares the first year, but settled them so quickly that a few extra seasons were added at $10,000 each. Later, shares in the horse would sell for as much as $162,000 at auction.

The first crop of Hail to Reason included five major winners. The Bieber-Jacobs Stable got the wonderful mare Straight Deal, who had the hardiness of Nothirdchance and considerably more class, earning $733,020 and reigning as champion handicap mare for 1967. Also in the first crop was Mr. and Mrs. Ben Cohen's Florida-bred colt foaled with such a deformed hind leg that the Ocala Stud staff were reduced to gradually straightening it by strapping a sweat scraper to it each day. Named Hail to All, this colt won the Belmont Stakes in 1965. Admiring, eventually sold for a then-world record $310,000 at a Bieber-Jacobs reduction sale in 1966, also came from that crop and was Hail to Reason's first stakes winner when she won the Arlington-Washington Lassie.

Among the breeders who used Hail to Reason to best advantage was John W. Galbreath of Darby Dan Farm. This was just, for Galbreath stood Ribot over many years and got only a few outstanding horses by that great sire who did so much for many other breeders. Galbreath's homebred Proud Clarion raced through the mist of Churchill Downs in 1967 to win the Kentucky Derby at 30-1. That gave Hail to Reason a Belmont winner and a Derby winner.

Three years later, in a moment of immeasurable sentiment for the Jacobs family, the Hail to Reason colt Personality won the Preakness Stakes to give the stallion a personal American Triple Crown. Personality was out of the Bieber-Jacobs' champion

Hail to Reason

homebred Affectionately. Hirsch Jacobs died early in 1970, and one of the last things he had suggested to John, his successor as trainer, was that the beloved colt would move up with blinkers. Personality wore them in the Preakness, and won enough other major races to share Horse of the Year honors that year.

Two years after completing his American triple, Hail to Reason was represented by Galbreath's sterling colt Roberto. A Darby Dan homebred named for baseball player Roberto Clemente — a star right fielder for the Pittsburgh Pirates (which Galbreath owned for many years) — Roberto was out of the Nashua filly Bramalea. The dam had defeated the champion Cicada in the 1962 Coaching Club American Oaks for Galbreath.

Galbreath received some criticism prior to the Epsom Derby in the spring of 1972, for he dictated to trainer Vincent O'Brien that rider Bill Williamson be replaced by the great champion rider Lester Piggott. Williamson had injured a shoulder in a spill in late May, but was approved to ride from a health standpoint. As he had been retained to ride in the Derby since finishing second on Roberto in the Two Thousand Guineas, the forty-nine-year-old Australian was the subject of a great deal of sympathy.

Piggott and Roberto got home by a short head over Rheingold in one of the epic struggles in the history of the race. There was some admission that Galbreath had been wise, for it did not take much in the way of mental calculation to suggest that, had Piggott been on the runner-up and Rheingold's rider, Ernie Johnson, on Roberto, the order might have been reversed.

Galbreath thus became the only individual to have both bred and owned winners of the Epsom Derby and Kentucky Derby. (He was joined in this company years later by Paul Mellon, breeder-owner of Epsom hero Mill Reef and 1993 Kentucky Derby winner Sea Hero.)

In the summer of 1972, Galbreath made more waves when he sent his American contract rider, Braulio Baeza, to ride Roberto in the Benson & Hedges, a recent addition to the top rung of English races (now known as the Juddmonte International.) This was no simple task, for the three-year-old Roberto would be facing one of the storied colts of modern English racing in Brigadier Gerard, a four-year-old unbeaten in fifteen races. Writing in *The Bloodstock Breeders' Review* of 1972, Tom Forrest admitted that he had judged in advance that the development created "a 10-pound disadvantage for Roberto. In fact, the Panamanian-born rider gave an exhibition of dashing, opportunist jockeyship which will never be forgotten."

Baeza gunned Roberto into a large lead early and even though Joe Mercer recognized danger and sent Brigadier Gerard after him, Roberto held a daylight margin at the end of the one and a quarter miles. Baeza had used a similar tactic as a tourist in France in 1967, when he rode the American grass champion Assagai in the Grand Prix de St. Cloud, but it did not work so well. Later in 1972, he set sail again on Roberto to lead early in the Prix de l'Arc de Triomphe; that time the Hail to Reason colt led to the 400-meter mark and then reeled and finished seventh.

Roberto was retired to Darby Dan with a record of seven wins in fourteen starts and earnings of $332,272.

To continue with the racing prowess of Hail to Reason's sons and daughters, the Jacobs family eventually bred nine of his stakes winners. These included the champion juvenile filly and important producer Regal Gleam as well as Priceless Gem, who would have been champion two-year-old filly of 1965 but for the unbeaten brilliance of Moccasin. Priceless Gem later brought a record price for a mare when sold at Keeneland for $395,000, and she was the dam of the popular French champion Allez France, a stunning filly who won the Arc de Triomphe in 1974.

Another of Hail to Reason's most important sons is Halo. A son of the grand producer Cosmah, Halo was bred by John R. Gaines and sold by him for $100,000 to Charles Engelhard — the dominant international yearling buyer of the day — at the 1970 Keeneland summer sale. Engelhard died the following year, and Mrs. Engelhard asked trainer Mack Miller to continue with the colt, who subsequently won the one and a half-mile Lawrence Realization and one other stakes. Mrs. Engelhard then agreed to sell the colt for $600,000 to Hollywood movie producer Irving Allen. When sent to Allen's Derisley Wood Stud in England, Halo was discovered to be a cribber. For reasons perhaps buried in the mists, or myths, of time, the English take this habit more seriously than do Americans, and it was seen as a legitimate reason for scuttling the deal.

Halo returned under ownership of the Windfields Farm of E. P. Taylor, for whom Miller sent the horse out to win the United Nations Handicap, his biggest victory. Halo went to stud at the Maryland division of Windfields and later was moved to Arthur Hancock III's Stone Farm in Kentucky after Texan Tom Tatham stepped up to purchase controlling interest in a move that proved as prescient as it was daring.

Hail to Reason died at eighteen in 1976. He had sired forty-three stakes winners (fourteen percent). In addition to those mentioned above, the many major ones included Travers winner Bold Reason, plus Stop the Music, Mr. Leader, Trillion, Silver True, Prince Thou Art, Hail to Patsy, Hail the Pirates, Hippodamia, Mrs. Warren, and Cum Laude Laurie.

Hail to Reason

A number of daughters became major producers. In addition to Priceless Gem, they included the aforementioned Admiring, from whom came the abundant brood of Glowing Tribute, Sea Hero, Roar, Wild Applause, Eastern Echo, and so on. The hardy mare Trillion, who was so consistent against top-class males that she won an American championship on grass in a season without a win, produced the multi-millionaire Triptych. In all, Hail to Reason became the broodmare sire of 114 stakes winners.

Sons in the Stud

As a sire of sires, Hail to Reason also excelled. Roberto would become so important that he often is identified as head of his own sire line — one more chapter in the ongoing saga of Phalaris and Nearco and Turn-to. Roberto was sent to stud at Darby Dan and sired eighty-six stakes winners (seventeen percent). They ran the gamut, geographically and in terms of speciality. As expected, he was a considerable influence of stamina, with such sons as grass champion Sunshine Forever, English St. Leger winner Touching Wood, and even Melbourne Cup winner At Talaq. There also were, however, a number of champions at two in Europe, among them Sookera and Critique, as well as Canadian champion two-year-old filly Legarto, Hopeful Stakes winner Capitol South, and the precocious juvenile (and outstanding sire) Red Ransom.

Not surprisingly, much of Roberto's mark as a sire of sires has come from his middle-distance horses. These include the following:

• *Brian's Time*, the Florida Derby winner who was exported to Japan and became a leading sire.

• *Silver Hawk*, the Craven Stakes winner who himself has become an important international stallion and landed the old sire line back in the winner's circle at Epsom when son Benny the Dip won the Derby of 1997.

• *Kris S.*, who had a solitary stakes win in the one and one-eighth-mile Bradbury but since has turned out an impressive brigade of sons and daughters such as champion fillies Hollywood Wildcat and Soaring Softly, other Breeders' Cup winners Prized and Brocco, plus You and I, Dr Fong, and Arch.

• *Lear Fan*, the French group I miler and English Guineas-placed sire of the Eclipse-winning filly Ryafan as well as Windsharp, Labeeb, Casual Lies, and Sikeston.

This list of Roberto's sons at stud is far from complete, for he also sired Darby Creek Road, Dynaformer, and Robellino.

Hail to Reason's son Halo was not as accomplished a racehorse as Roberto, but he, too, would become an exceptional sire and one of continuing influence. He was America's leading sire in 1983 and again in 1989, and he got sixty-one stakes winners (eight and a half percent). This is one and a half percent less than generally associated with top sires, but Halo (like grandsire Turn-to) made up in impact what he might have lacked in a few percentage points. Halo sired Sunday Silence, the superb colt who won the Kentucky Derby, Preakness, and Breeders' Cup Classic from archrival Easy Goer and was Horse of the Year in 1989. Sunday Silence was exported to Japan, where he has become a transcendent sire and even a public idol.

Sunday Silence was the second son of Halo to win the Kentucky Derby, having been preceded in 1983 by Sunny's Halo. Sunny's Halo was not so spectacular a sire, but got Dispersal, Irgun, Diane's Halo, and Race the Wild Wind among more than two dozen stakes winners.

Another son of Halo was Devil's Bag, who was regarded by Woody Stephens as the best young colt he ever trained as he toured through a majestic juvenile championship campaign of 1983. While Devil's Bag did not go on to be a classic winner, he has become a consistent sire, with three dozen stakes winners including crack handicappers Devil His Due and Twilight Agenda and Japanese champion Taiki Shuttle.

Several of Halo's sons that were not quite at the top in terms of his runners have come on to be significant sires as of 2000, this echelon including Saint Ballado, the sire of Captain Bodgit; the repatriated Southern Halo, a top sire in South America and now the sire of More Than Ready; Lively One, sire of juvenile champion Answer Lively; and Jolie's Halo, sire of Hal's Hope. The classic-placed Strodes Creek is among the youngest of Halo's sons at stud.

Halo's daughters also are a distinguished group. They include Canadian and North American champion Glorious Song (dam of Rahy and Singspiel); Coaching Club American and Kentucky Oaks winner Goodbye Halo; plus Rainbow Connection, Misty Gallore, and Tilt My Halo.

Whereas siring Roberto and Halo would have assured Hail to Reason a lasting presence in the tail male of pedigrees, they were hardly his only good sons at stud. His son Mr. Leader was a remarkable old fellow who lived to be thirty-plus. Mr. Leader was the working horseman's and careful yearling buyer's faithful friend, siring eighty-three stakes winners but never being especially fashionable. His colts include two Santa Anita Handicap winners, Ruhlmann and Martial Law; a Travers winner, Wise Times; and a Suburban Handicap winner, Quiet Little Table.

Hail the Pirates was another son of Hail to Reason. He won stakes on both sides of the Atlantic from three through six. Standing in Kentucky, Hail the Pirates sired the three-year-old filly champion Wayward Lass and two Spinster Stakes winners, Try Something New and Hail a Cab.

Even the house of Hail could not escape ironies, however. Among the sons that made little mark at stud were Proud Clarion, Personality, and Hail to All — his three American classic winners, although Proud Clarion did get Marlboro Cup winner Proud Birdie.

This was hardly damaging, though, for many others rushed in to fill the void.

As noted, Sunday Silence was a transcendent horse for Japan. He was sent to stud there after North American breeders failed to show enough enthusiasm for Arthur Hancock III to turn down the multimillion offer to export him. Sunday Silence (Halo–Wishing Well, by Understanding) had been bred by Oak Cliff Thoroughbreds and raised at Hancock's Stone Farm in Kentucky. He raced for an owners' partnership of Hancock, Dr. Ernest Gaillard, and Charlie Whittingham (who trained him). Sunday Silence won the Kentucky Derby, Preakness, and Breeders' Cup Classic in 1989, when he was Horse of the Year.

Eventually, the thirteen-time leading sire of Japan (and sire of 172 stakes winners), along with his sons, engendered international interest from fashionable breeders around the world. An archetypal example was when the internationally renowned Coolmore operation bred the champion Galileo filly Rhododendron to Deep Impact, a two-time Japanese Horse of the Year by Sunday Silence.

The Deep Impact–Rhododendron cross-produced Auguste Rodin, which in 2023 won the Epsom Derby and Irish Derby and then capped his year by winning the Breeders' Cup Turf. Thirty-four years after Sunday Silence won the Breeders' Cup Classic, a globe-trotting grandson put his own stamp on the climactic North American series. ❖

Blushing Groom

A variety of racing proclivities was embodied in the pedigree of Blushing Groom. He was by a Nasrullah colt that was a sprinter-miler, and he was out of the daughter of a one-time steeplechase champion. While such a combination might most often produce a genetic hodgepodge resulting in an animal not particularly good at anything, in Blushing Groom it was a recipe for enduring richness.

Blushing Groom himself was a sort of French version of Nasrullah, without the worrisome temperament. He was brilliant at two, then a crack miler that failed to stay successfully in the Epsom Derby, in which he finished third. In the stud, Blushing Groom could sire most any kind of top-level horse:

• The grand *Nashwan*, winner of the Guineas and Derby and sire of the hardy Swain.

• The incredible *Arazi*, dashing on turf and sensational on dirt.

• *Rainbow Quest*, winner of the Prix de l' Arc de Triomphe and sire of Epsom Derby winner Quest for Fame.

• The middle-distance horse *Sillery*, sire of Breeders' Cup Mile winner Silic.

• Travers winner *Runaway Groom*, sire of sprint champion Cherokee Run.

• *Blushing John*, a classic winner on grass at a mile in France and a champion on dirt going one and a quarter miles in this country.

• The champion American distaffer *Sky Beauty*, plus such other good fillies for dirt racing as Blush With Pride, Too Chic (dam of champion Queena), and You'd Be Surprised.

• The official Epsom Oaks winner *Snow Bride*, dam of unbeaten Lammtarra.

• The speedy *Rahy*, sire of champion Serena's Song.

• Sprinter *Mt. Livermore*, sire of two-time champion sprinter Housebuster and juvenile filly champion Eliza; plus stallions in the stud as farflung as Argentina (Shy Tom sired a Triple Crown winner) and Australia (Nassipour got Melbourne Cup one-two finishers).

Red God, sire of Blushing Groom, was a home-bred from Captain Harry F. Guggenheim's Cain Hoy Stable. Guggenheim had been part of one group which Bull Hancock put together and almost bought Nasrullah, and after the horse eventually was purchased, Guggenheim made good use of him. Among the high-class Nasrullah runners bred and raced by Guggenheim were American handicap champion Bald Eagle and his full brother One-Eyed King, along with Flying Fury and Victory Morn. The ace in the Guggenheim-Nasrullah set was Never Bend, champion at two in this country and the influential sire of Mill Reef, among others.

Red God was not of the standard of Never Bend or Bald Eagle, but was a useful racehorse and over the years a sire of merit. He was foaled in 1954 and was out of the Menow mare Spring Run, also dam of Cain Hoy's Blue Grass Stakes winner Racing Fool. In 1955, Guggenheim wrote to Cecil Boyd-Rochfort, who trained his English runners: "I think I have a colt that is a good prospect for you. In fact, when I saw him last at Claiborne, my trainer was with me and his eye had a gleam of satisfaction when he saw the colt. I promptly informed him that there was no occasion to rejoice, because I had about made up my mind to send the colt to you in England."

Red God was a strong, short-backed sort, and Boyd-Rochfort liked him, too. Since Red God was the only two-year-old by former English leading sire Nasrullah trained in that country that year, the British had heightened interest in him. The colt was well backed for his debut in the Coventry Stakes, but finished eighth. Given some time, he reappeared at Goodwood, where he won the Richmond Stakes handily in a miserable rain storm. Red God then failed in the Champagne and Middle Park and was tied for fourth among colts on the 1956 English Free Handicap. Trainer and owner were uncertain whether his failings had indicated a lack of will or insufficient recovery from a setback that had caused him to miss the Gimcrack Stakes. Whatever his evaluation, Guggenheim decided to take him home.

Red God won his first start at three in the United States, but injured a hock and was out for the year. At four, he defeated Cohoes by four lengths while getting four pounds, in the seven-furlong Roseben Handicap at Belmont Park. He had a career total of five wins in fourteen starts and

was sent back across the Atlantic to stud. Red God eventually sired fifty-eight stakes winners (twelve percent). While he did not generally dwell in the upper marks of fashion, his offspring did include a number of champions in the shorter distance categories. Blushing Groom was his brilliant best, but the others included champions Folle Rousse and Ruby Laser, and stakes winners Bayraan, Yellow God, and Ela Marita. The year Blushing Groom emerged as the best two-year-old in France, Red God was also represented by one of the classic three-year-olds, Jacques Wertheimer's French Two Thousand Guineas winner Red Lord.

Runaway Bride, dam of Blushing Groom, was cleverly named, being by Wild Risk. Although foaled in France, Wild Risk was bred by American Joseph E. Widener. During the German occupation of France, Wild Risk was cared for at Haras du Mesnil, then sold cheaply. Wild Risk had a club foot, but became one of the all-time champion steeplechasers in France. He was in a country and at a time that being consigned to jumps was not a death knell insofar as a breeding opportunity on the flat, but it was not a high recommendation, either. After getting few foals early on, Wild Risk emerged as the sire of King George VI and Queen Elizabeth Stakes winner Vimy, Prix Vermeille winner Wild Miss, and Washington, D.C., International winner Worden II. By 1961, when his son Balto won the Grand Prix de Paris, Wild Risk had climbed to the top, leading the French sire list. Three years later came his fine son Le Fabuleux, winner of the French Derby, and Wild Risk led the list again. Le Fabuleux, son of a former club-footed jumper, had enough international appeal that he was imported to Claiborne Farm. He sired forty-one stakes winners and proved a useful source of stamina.

Runaway Bride, dam of Blushing Groom, went back three generations in the bottom line to

		Nearco, 1935	Pharos / Nogara
	Nasrullah, 1940		
RED GOD, ch, 1954		Mumtaz Begum, 1932	Blenheim II / Mumtaz Mahal
		Menow, 1935	Pharamond II / Alcibiades
	Spring Run, 1948		
BLUSHING GROOM (Fr), ch h, 1974		Boola Brook, 1937	Bull Dog / Brookdale
		Rialto, 1923	Rabelais / La Grelee
	Wild Risk, 1940		
		Wild Violet, 1935	Blandford / Wood Violet
RUNAWAY BRIDE (GB), b, 1962		Tudor Minstrel, 1944	Owen Tudor / Sansonnet
	Aimee, 1957		
		Emali, 1945	Umidwar / Eclair

1st dam: Runaway Bride (GB), b, 1962-1984. Bred by H.H. The Aga Khan (Eng). Raced 2 yrs in Eng, Fr, and Ire, 11 sts, 0 wins, $364. Dam of 14 named foals, 11 rnrs, 8 wnrs, 3 sw. Sent to USA 1978.

1968: Well Done, b g, by Immortality. Raced 5 yrs in Eng and Ire, 18 sts, 3 wins, $2,270.

1969: Hot Shoes, b f, by Red God. Unraced.

1970: Robinie (GB), gr f, by Fortino II. Unraced. Dam of 8 foals, 5 rnrs, 3 wnrs. Granddam of **Bird Hunter**. Sent to USA 1984.

1971: **BAYRAAN**, b c, by Red God. Raced 3 yrs in Fr, 16 sts, 5 wins, $17,365. Won Prix des Chenes (Fr-III), Prix de Seine-et-Oise (Fr-III); 2nd Prix de la Foret (Fr-I), Prix du Gros-Chene (Fr-III). Sent to Japan 1975.

1972: Elope, b f, by Jimmy Reppin. Raced 2 yrs in Eng, 8 sts, 0 wins, $0. Dam of 6 foals, 4 rnrs, 2 wnrs. Granddam of **Allthruthenight**.

1973: **CHATEAU GAILLARD**, gr g, by Silver Shark. Raced 8 yrs in Fr, 37 sts, 10 wins, $58,452. Won Prix Alain de Goulaine, Prix de la Croix Dauphine Hurdle; 2nd Prix Juigne Hurdle, Prix Leopold d'Orsetti Hurdle.

1974: **BLUSHING GROOM**, ch c, by Red God. Bred by J. McNamee Sullivan (Fr). Raced 2 yrs in Eng and Fr, 10 sts, 7 wins, $407,153. Champion 2yo colt in Fr. Won Poule d'Essai des Poulains (Fr-I), Grand Criterium (Fr-I), Prix Morny (Fr-I), Prix de la Salamandre (Fr-I), Prix Robert Papin (Fr-I), Prix de Fontainebleau (Fr-III); 2nd Prix Jacques Le Marois (Fr-I); 3rd Epsom Derby (Eng-I). Sire of 523 foals, 144 sw, 4.01 AEI. Sent to USA 1977. Died 1992.

1975: Zivato, gr c, by Zeddaan. Raced 2 yrs in Fr, 7 sts, 1 win, $12,621. Sent to NZ 1979.

1976: Dead foal.

1977: Not bred.

1978: Bold Escape, b f, by Bold Forbes. Raced 1 yr, 5 sts, 0 wins, $2,200. Dam of 12 foals, 11 rnrs, 7 wnrs, including **CANAVERAL** ($258,061), **RIDGE ESCAPE** ($137,324). Granddam of **AYRTON SYMBOLI**, **Dance Nice**. Died 1996.

1979: Bridal Notion, dkb/br f, by Bold Forbes. Unraced. Died 1983.

1980: **Allicance**, b f, by Alleged. Raced 2 yrs in Fr, 12 sts, 1 win, $50,736. 2nd Prix de Flore (Fr-III), Prix des Tuileries; 3rd Prix de Royaumont (Fr-III), Prix de la Porte de Passy. Dam of 12 foals, 10 rnrs, 8 wnrs, including **ROYAL KINGDOM (Ire)** ($147,985, Eng-II), **MATADOR** ($115,322), **BEAUTE DANGEREUSE** ($26,497), **Jezebel Monroe** ($12,376 in Eng). Granddam of **ENTICE**, **LEROS**. ($1,000,000 keejul yrlg).

1981: Chilly Frolic, gr f, by Icecapade. Raced 1 yr, 2 sts, 0 wins, $210. Died 1984. ($450,000 keejul yrlg).

1982: Side Chapel, b c, by Raja Baba. Raced 1 yr in Ire, 3 sts, 1 win, $3,397. Sire in Japan. ($2,600,000 keejul yrlg).

1983: No report received.

1984: **Nearlywed**, b f, by Alleged. Raced 3 yrs in Eng and NA, 17 sts, 3 wins, $63,494. 2nd Queen Charlotte H (gr. IIIT). Dam of 4 foals, 4 rnrs, 3 wnrs. Sent to Japan 1992. ($1,050,000 keejul yrlg).

Eclair, dam of Khaled. This also is the family of Mill Reef. (A quick glance at the name of the third dam might briefly imply a remarkable prescience on someone's part; the name, on closer look, however, is not "e-mail," but Emali.) Runaway Bride came from a family owned for some generations by the Aga Khan's ancestry, but the Aga culled her after her failure on the race course. Emergence of her stakes-winning son Bayraan encouraged His Highness to consider her weanling colt of 1974. The Red God—Runaway Bride foal was bred by John McNamee-Sullivan, but, coincidentally, was foaled in France at Haras de Marly-la-Ville, where the mare had been sent to be covered by one of the Aga Khan's stallions, Zeddaan.

With Keith Freeman acting on his behalf, the Aga Khan purchased Blushing Groom for 16,500 guineas at the 1974 Newmarket December sales. The Aga Khan had discarded an unsatisfactory oyster, but rescued the pearl.

Quests and Beauties

Blushing Groom was trained by François Mathet, one of the masters of the French Turf. Madame Mathet made her late husband's meticulously recorded logs available to John Sparkman, who in 1989 authored an article in *The Blood-Horse* about Blushing Groom. The log contains details of trials, which Mathet — in the tradition of European trainers over the years — had devised in order to evaluate his charges and prepare them for the most appropriate tests for each. Comments about the two-year-old Blushing Groom include "brilliant," "came from behind, won easily," and "best at the end," prior to the colt's debut. "Inexplicable defeat" was Mathet's entry for Blushing Groom's first race. He had no cause to use the "d" word again for a long time.

Blushing Groom reeled off a high-quality string of victories which made him the clear-cut champion two-year-old of France. Since he also thrashed J. O. Tobin, the English juvenile champion, Blushing Groom had pride of place among all European-raced juveniles of that year.

The Aga Khan's colt raced through victories in the Prix Robert Papin, Prix Salamandre, Prix Morny, and the climactic Grand Criterium. This constitutes the four most important two-year-old races for French-trained runners. In the last-named, at a mile, J. O. Tobin was third, about four lengths behind.

A precocious two-year-old is always suspect to get a classic distance until he proves he can, and Mathet recognized that Blushing Groom was not guaranteed to stay at three. The Aga Khan since then has had three Epsom Derby winners, well on the way to matching his grandfather's total of five. In 1977, however, as Mathet addressed Blushing Groom, His Highness had never won the Epsom classic himself, but it was obvious and understandable that the Derby was chief among his ambitions on the Turf. Blushing Groom was given the best regimen Mathet could devise to allow him his optimum chance to achieve the owner's ambition.

One of the most fascinating races never run — officially — in French history took place as a training event under Mathet's masterful direction on March 17, 1977. Going a mile on heavy ground at Chantilly, Blushing Groom finished first in this training move, a length ahead of Crystal Palace. General was third. By year's end, Blushing Groom had proven a classic winner at a mile, and Crystal Palace had won the French Derby for Mathet and his owner, Baron Guy de Rothschild. Third-placed General, a son of Brigadier Gerard, was a group III winner in France and later was sent to Argentina, where he sired the Santa Anita Handicap winner and influential stallion Lord At War.

Blushing Groom

"He had an extraordinary action and seemed not to touch the ground," Mathet would say of Blushing Groom. In the spring of his three-year-old season, the Red God colt won the Prix de Fontainbleau and then the French Two Thousand Guineas equivalent at a mile. There could be no more delay. The time had come to test him going one and a half miles, and he was favored for the Epsom Derby, despite the questions of his stamina. In the running, he was well-placed, came on to challenge a quarter-mile from home, but could offer only courage, not competitiveness, with the top pair through the final demanding furlongs. He was third, beaten five lengths by winner The Minstrel, who edged Hot Grove in a raging duel.

Blushing Groom raced but once more. The one-mile Prix Jacques le Marois was run at such a dawdling pace early that its results were hardly conclusive. Blushing Groom finished a closing second to the filly Flying Water.

John R. Gaines, then master of Gainesway Farm in Kentucky and a leader among international syndicators of stallions in the 1970s through the early '90s, had contracted some months before that Blushing Groom would come to Kentucky at the end of his racing career. "He had all the things anyone could possibly want in a sire prospect," Gaines later said, "but the thing that impressed me the most was his way of going. He had a beautiful, swinging, rhythmical action. It was marvelous to see."

As the spring-summer of 1977 unfolded, any thoughts of further racing the colt took a backseat to the pure logistics of getting the horse across the Atlantic. An outbreak of a disease in stallions known as contagious equine metritis spread from England and clearly would cause a ban on international shipment. Rather than pursue further racing targets, those in charge of such stallion prospects as The Minstrel and Caro, as well as Blushing Groom, moved quickly. The horses were dashed to Kentucky before the ban was put into place. The feared outbreak occurred.

Blushing Groom had been syndicated on the basis of total valuation of $6 million, and he was a bargain. He stood at Gainesway his entire career, even though Gaines sold the farm to Graham Beck a number of years later. In 1988, the stallion underwent surgery to remove a cancerous testicle. He recovered and got thirty-five mares in foal in 1989. With a reduced book, he got thirteen mares in foal in 1990, but none in 1991, after which he was pensioned. Blushing Groom's condition deteriorated, and he was euthanized in 1992.

Blushing Groom sired ninety-two stakes winners (eighteen percent) and sixty of them won graded or group races. He was the leading sire in England in 1989 and leading broodmare sire there in 1995.

The author recalls first seeing Blushing Groom early in his time at Gainesway. There was a hint of what it must have been like to see a young Hyperion, for Blushing Groom was a fine chestnut with style and tidiness that could almost camouflage his power. Helen Alexander of King Ranch had tutored us on the thought that a horse that could stay well enough to be third in the Epsom Derby would certainly have enough stamina to be a fine sire over here. She proved correct, and her family did very well with Blushing Groom offspring. Too Chic, for instance, bred and raced in the name of one of Alexander's sisters, Emory Hamilton, was a grade I winner and foaled the champion distaffer Queena.

Because of his success in France, and given the clout of international buyers during Blushing

Groom's stud career, a number of his best prospects where gobbled up at sales by European-based stables. There was plenty of quality to go around.

The first crop included Albert Coppola's Runaway Groom, who, despite his stylish sire, was seen as something of a maverick when he won the Travers Stakes of 1982; this image was prompted by the fact that he was defeating all the season's American classic winners — Conquistador Cielo, Aloma's Ruler, and Gato Del Sol.

Among the first of Blushing Groom's stars abroad was Prince Khalid Abdullah's Rainbow Quest, who was a second-ranked juvenile and champion three-year-old in England, then a champion older horse in that country and France. Rainbow Quest won the Coronation Cup, then took the Prix de l'Arc de Triomphe on the disqualification of Sagace in 1985.

Allen Paulson's Blushing John won the French Two Thousand Guineas equivalent in 1988. Returned to this country, he became the champion older horse of 1989 when he won the grade I Hollywood Gold Cup and Pimlico Special as well as two grade II stakes. Blushing John was a competitive third behind Sunday Silence and Easy Goer in a storied Breeders' Cup Classic.

Few horses have ever enjoyed as spectacular a moment as Blushing Groom's Arazi created in the 1991 Breeders' Cup Juvenile. The dominant two-year-old champion of France, Arazi had matched his sire's quartet of top class races: the Robert Papin, Salamandre, Morny, and Grand Criterium. Trainer François Boutin was induced by Paulson's ever-ready sportsmanship to bring the slim little chestnut to this country for the Breeders' Cup Juvenile. Parked on the outside of a fourteen-horse field in his first ever start off the turf, Arazi may have gotten a face full of dirt, but he gave racing an eyeful of brilliance. He dashed up to the high-class Bertrando

and before anyone could savor a battle shaping up, Arazi was free and clear. He toured in isolation through the stretch, winning by five lengths.

Huzzahs were immediately followed by reminiscences of Secretariat. Arazi underwent knee surgery, had a win in his only start the next spring, and was returned for the Kentucky Derby. In many a year of watching star Derby contenders from the vantage point of Churchill Downs' backstretch, we recall only one that drew such a frontside crowd that cheers could be heard across the track as he rushed down the stretch in a morning workout. This was little Arazi. Sadly, the bubble burst, and he was unplaced on Derby Day, but he came back eventually to win the group II Prix du Rond Point in France on Arc de Triomphe Weekend.

The late Georgia Hofmann's Sky Beauty was another of Blushing Groom's best. Trained by Hall of Famer Allen Jerkens, Sky Beauty contended for best of her age for three consecutive years, but late defeats blunted her campaigns at two and three. She won, for example, the New York Filly Triple Crown consisting of the Acorn, Mother Goose, and Coaching Club American Oaks, but joined Shuvee as a winner of those races that was not voted champion of her year. At four in 1994, however, there was no blocking Sky Beauty from an Eclipse Award although, again, she had a dismal run in the Breeders' Cup. She had won all her earlier five races that year, including the grade I Shuvee, Hempstead, Ruffian, and Go for Wand, carrying up to 130 pounds successfully. All told, Sky Beauty won fifteen of twenty-one races and earned $1,336,000.

If we are taking into account speed, stamina, and class, Nashwan perhaps was the best of the Blushing Grooms. Sheikh Mohammed, from the ruling Maktoum family of Dubai, paid a big ticket

Blushing Groom

to be partner with Paulson in ownership of Arazi. One of his brothers, in a family dominant at sales and racetracks for the last two decades, is Sheikh Hamdan, who bred Nashwan at his Shadwell Stud in Kentucky. Nashwan was a lengthy, chestnut colt out of Height of Fashion. The mare was a high-class stakes winner from one of the classic-producing families of Her Majesty Queen Elizabeth II. Sheikh Hamdan purchased Height of Fashion (eventually dam of five stakes winners) for a price reported from 1.4 million to 1.8 million pounds. The Queen was said to be willing to part with the mare because she wanted to purchase the West Ilsley training yard where Major Dick Hern had been established for many years on a lease arrangement. The Queen apparently takes the attitude that it would create public discomfort were she to use anything but personal wealth — as opposed to the Crown's resources — to finance her passion for Thoroughbreds.

Thus, the Queen, who has won all the English classics save the Derby, sold a homebred mare that was destined to produce a winner of that elusive, lifelong goal. Added to the irony was that Hern's large stable, in addition to some of her horses, was to include the Blushing Groom—Height of Fashion colt. Nashwan won both his starts at two and came to hand at three for Hern in time to win the Two Thousand Guineas over Exbourne, Danehill, and Markofdistinction, a high-quality field indeed.

At Epsom in 1989, we could not help hoping for success for another American-bred, Cacoethes: A son of Alydar bred by the accomplished Hollywood producer Ray Stark would create a very appealing saga. The pre-race sight of Nashwan galloping past the stands, his strides consuming prodigious space through no discernible effort, put a pronounced droop in the American flag of our hopes.

We soon contented ourselves with boasting of the homegrown connection of the favorite, as Nashwan swooped through the historic stretch a clear winner over Cacoethes. Sheikh Hamdan and the wheelchair-bound Hern made so touching, and right, a scene in the winner's circle that, by the time the champagne was a distant memory so was our enthusiasm for any other result in the Derby.

Nashwan dropped back to ten furlongs and won the Coral-Eclipse Stakes handily over two other high-class runners, Opening Verse and Indian Skimmer. He had a close call with Cacoethes in the King George VI and Queen Elizabeth Stakes, but prevailed. Still unbeaten, he was prepping for the Arc when stunningly beaten into third in Golden Pheasant's Prix Niel. He continued for a time on course for the Arc, then was taken out of the race and a later intent toward the Champion Stakes was ended in an announcement that he had a fever. Nashwan's career thus ended with six wins in seven races and earnings of $1,447,003. He was sent to stud at the English division of Shadwell. Sheikh Hamdan could hardly go around changing the name of a property every time he has an outstanding horse, but this horse was so special to him that he named the stallion operation of the Kentucky Shadwell division after Nashwan.

While various quarters struggle to make the word "champion" specific and more meaningful than throwing the term at any "really good horse," the difference in International procedures undermines use of the term with simplicity and consistency. How many champions did Blushing Groom sire? Let us count the ways of deciding. In the United States, the blessed Eclipse Awards are the one and only legitimate measure: He got three — Sky Beauty, Arazi, and Blushing John. In Canada, the Sovereign Awards carry the same status: He got two, Runaway Groom and the filly Blushing Katy. In Europe, there are the Cartier Awards, but championships more often are equated with topping a country's handicap in any of a plethora of distance/gender divisions, while topping a division on the International Classifications would also seem to constitute a strong claim to being a champion. We count eleven handicap highweights among Blushing Groom's get, at various distances in individual European countries or the International Classifications: Al Bahathri, Arazi, Baillamont, Classic Tale, Crystal Glitters, Fire the Groom, Groom Dancer, Heart of Groom, Kefaah, Nashwan, and Rainbow Quest.

An irony in Blushing Groom's career was his filly Snow Bride. In 1989, Snow Bride finished second to the Aga Khan's Aliysa, who after a prolonged lab and court battle was disqualified for carrying metabolites of a banned substance. The Aga Khan's dismay at this development was hardly assuaged by his old warrior Blushing Groom getting credit as sire of another classic winner — the first to sire the Derby and Oaks winner in the same year since Solario got the 1937 winners, Mid-Day Sun and Exhibitionist. Prior to 1937, the double had not occurred since 1900, when the great St. Simon was represented by Diamond Jubilee and La Roche. Snow Bride later was bred to 1970 Derby winner Nijinsky II and foaled the unbeaten 1995 Derby-King George-Arc winner Lammtarra. Thus, again technically, she was part of the only instance of a Derby and Oaks winner producing a Derby winner. (The Aga Khan had won the Epsom Derby the year before the Aliysa affair with Kahyasi, son of the Blushing Groom mare Kadissya.)

A Groom of Grooms

A striking number of Blushing Groom's best sons also have become successful sires. The exceptions include Arazi and Blushing John, and while statistically Blushing John disappointed, he did sire the sensational filly Blushing K.D., winner of the Kentucky Oaks.

Nashwan is the sire of Swain, a remarkable campaigner who won two runnings of the group I King George and Queen Elizabeth Stakes among a total of eight major wins from ages three through six. In 1998, Swain lost the Dubai World Cup by a nose to Silver Charm. In his last start, he veered nearly to the outside rail at Churchill Downs but still got third behind Awesome Again in a superb Breeders' Cup Classic field. In addition to Swain, Nashwan has sired twenty stakes winners, also including the American grass distaff champion Wandesta and English-Irish division topweights One So Wonderful and Myself.

Blushing Groom's Arc winner, Rainbow Quest, also standing in England, got his sixtieth stakes winner in 1999. Among his stakes winners is the Epsom Derby winner, Quest for Fame, who also won the Hollywood Turf Handicap in this country. Rainbow Quest, like Nashwan, has an Eclipse Award-winning grass filly, Fiji. In addition, he has an Arc de Triomphe winner in Saumarez, and his other European champions include Sought Out, Raintrap, Sunshack, Splash of Colour, and Nedawi — ranging from two-year-old stars to stayers. Other sons of Rainbow Quest include Urgent Request, who won the Santa Anita Handicap, and Sakura Laurel, who was Horse of the Year and champion older mare in Japan.

Runaway Groom, while in a sense obscure on Travers Day of 1982, has tugged an indifferent female family far up the fashion scale. At twenty-two, he is the sire of more than forty stakes win-

Blushing Groom

ners, including the sprint champion and Preakness runner-up Cherokee Run; the latter topped the freshman sire list in 1999 when his first crop included the brilliant juvenile filly champion Chilukki. The versatility of the Blushing Grooms showed up, also, in Runaway Groom's son Wekiva Springs, who won sprint stakes but also the one-and-a-quarter-mile grade I Gulfstream and Suburban Handicaps and the one and one-eighth-mile Brooklyn. Runaway Groom also sired the Champagne Stakes winner The Groom is Red.

Blushing Groom's son Mt. Livermore was a crack sprinter, winning the Carter, Fall Highweight, Boojum, and Jaipur and earning more than $600,000 in the mid-1980s. He is the sire of forty-four stakes winners, and, here again, the versatility is repeated. They include two-time Eclipse Award winning sprinter Housebuster, the Breeders' Cup Juvenile Fillies winner and champion Eliza, and the Canadian Horses of the Year Peaks and Valleys and Mt. Sassafras. Peaks and Valleys' Molson Export Million and grade I Meadowlands Cup wins came at one and one-eighth miles. Mt. Sassafras also won the Gulfstream Park Handicap at one and a quarter miles, in addition to his Canadian performances. (Mt. Sassafras was virtually lapped on top three finishers Alphabet Soup, Louis Quatorze, and Cigar at the wire in the 1996 Breeders' Cup Classic.) Pyramid Peak, another Mt. Livermore, won the Flamingo and was second in the Travers. All these were major winners on dirt, whereas another Mt. Livermore, Subordination, won the grade I Hollywood Derby and Eddie Read Handicaps on grass, as well as the Brooklyn Handicap on dirt.

The Blushing Groom colt Rahy had an oft-interrupted campaign. His ten-length victory in the one-mile Bel Air Handicap at four, however, seemed to ratify the suggestion of quality made in placing in the Middle Park Stakes in England at two. Rahy was an immediate factor at stud and has more than thirty stakes winners. His best is the hickory filly Serena's Song, champion three-year-old filly of 1995, winner over colts in top company, and the leading-earning female with $3,283,388. While Serena's Song starred on dirt, Rahy's resolute miler Hawksley Hill has won primarily on grass. Others by Rahy include Exotic Wood, Mariah's Storm, and Tokio Perfect.

Among the Blushing Groom stallions to have had major success abroad, Candy Stripes, age eighteen, has been returned to Kentucky from Argentina, where he sired the American grade I winner Different among more than twenty stakes winners.

As matters stand, more than twenty years after he entered stud, the name of Blushing Groom sits proudly atop one of the most vibrant and flourishing branches of the noble line of Nasrullah. ❖

Ribot

ypsying home from the Jersey Shore racetracks one summer, we delivered our van companion, the antsy filly Tobette, to her new Kentucky home and waved adieu to the van driver. A layover in Lexington while en route to Florida presented a long-awaited opportunity to gaze upon Ribot. Possessed of neither local connections nor sufficient age to rent a car, we could think of no choice but to walk out from Broadway & Main to Darby Dan Farm, a distance of about six miles over good going, town and country.

Luckily, farm manager Olin Gentry was showing the stallions to a gaggle of visitors — a softish group that took a car to get there — and we hovered nearby to benefit from the timing. We had expected to be moved by Ribot and were ready to gasp at his outward magnificence. After all, Eddie Arcaro had been impressed by the way this animal flew past Career Boy, whom Arcaro was riding in the Arc, so surely we would find reason to be awestruck. Truth to tell, Ribot was fine to look at, but nothing spectacular. He was a nice bay, with black points, but one step from plain. The guilt and bewilderment this impression brought on at age nineteen were eventually assuaged by others' evaluations. Kent Hollingsworth wrote in

The Blood-Horse on Ribot's passing ten years later, in 1972, that, "As an individual, Ribot was ordinary in appearance, regal in manner." Abram S. Hewitt in *Sire Lines* concurred: "Physically, Ribot was not a very impressive horse. We were told he stood 16 hands high at maturity, but there was nothing flashy or eye-catching about him," although the "strong development of the thighs and gaskins" meant that "his driving power was unmistakable."

Federico Tesio, Ribot's iconoclastic Italian breeder-owner-trainer, was said to have mused as he watched the little colt in action that "I don't know. I don't know; there is something about him."

Tesio died several months before Ribot got to the races, so we are left to conjecture whether, after the horse's unbeaten career, Tesio would have regarded Ribot as the best he ever bred. Tesio already had other unbeaten horses to choose from — Cavaliere d'Arpino and Nearco — as well as Donatello II. Tesio was quoted as putting Cavaliere d'Arpino at the top of his list. Ribot, however, was so impressive that many observers then and since have found themselves torn between him and Sea-Bird when trying to identify Europe's greatest of the 20th Century.

Ribot came from the male line of Cavaliere d'Arpino, his great-grandsire. Cavaliere d'Arpino

		Cavaliere d'Arpino, 1926	Havresac II / Chuette
	Bellini, 1937		
TENERANI, b, 1944		Bella Minna, 1923	Bachelor's Double / Santa Minna
		Apelle, 1923	Sardanapale / Angelina
	Tofanella, 1931		
RIBOT (GB), b h, February 27, 1952		Try Try Again, 1922	Cylgad / Perseverance
		Pharos, 1920	Phalaris / Scapa Flow
	El Greco, 1934		
		Gay Gamp, 1923	Gay Crusader / Parasol
ROMANELLA, ch, 1943		Papyrus, 1920	Tracery / Miss Matty
	Barbara Burrini, 1937		
		Bucolic, 1926	Buchan / Volcanic

1st dam: ROMANELLA, ch, 1943-1969. Bred by Razza Dormello-Olgiata (Italy). Raced 1 yr in Italy, 7 sts, 5 wins. Champion 2yo filly in Italy. Won Premio Eupili, Premio Primi Passi, Triennale Italiano, Criterium Nazionale. Dam of 14 named foals, 11 rnrs, 10 wnrs, 5 sw.

1947: **Rovezzana**, b f, by Niccolo Dell'Arca. Raced 1 yr in Italy, 9 sts, 3 wins. 3rd Premio Sedraiano. Dam of 9 foals, 2 rnrs, 1 wnr. Granddam of **FINNEY, Nile Queen**. Died 1968.

1948: **ROSALBA BERNINI**, b f, by Niccolo Dell'Arca. Raced 2 yrs in Italy, 7 sts, 3 wins, $2,264. Won Premio Dormello; 2nd Premio Bimbi, Premio Pallanza. Dam of 7 foals, 2 rnrs, 2 wnrs, including **RUBINA, Raoul Millais** (in Italy). Granddam of **ROI REGENT**.

1950: **Rabirio**, ch c, by Airborne. Raced 3 yrs in Italy, 30 sts, 1 win, $504. Sire.

1951: **RADOWSKA**, ro f, by Airborne. Raced 3 yrs in Italy, 36 sts, 12 wins, $5,706. Won Premio Jockey Club, Premio U.N.I.R.E., Premio Delle Cascine, Premio Sesto, Premio Costa Alta, Premio Vitellia; 2nd Premio Seregno, Premio Ettore Bocconi; 3rd Premio Del Jockey Club, Premio Adda.

1952: **RIBOT**, b c, by Tenerani. Bred by Razza Dormello-Olgiata (Eng). Raced 3 yrs in Italy, Fr, and Eng, 16 sts, 16 wins, $286,151. Champion 2yo colt in Italy. Won Prix de l'Arc de Triomphe (twice), King George VI and Queen Elizabeth S, Gran Criterium, Criterium Nazionale, Premio Pisa, Premio Besana, Premio del Jockey Club, Premio Emanuele Filiberto, Premio Miazzale, Gran Premio de Milano. Sent to USA 1960. Sire of 423 foals, 67 sw, 4.09 AEI. Died 1972.

1953: Raffaellina, b f, by Tenerani. Unraced.

1954: Roderiga, b f, by My Love. Unraced. Dam of 3 foals, 3 rnrs, 3 wnrs, including **ROMANINO, Romiti** (in Italy). Sent to USA 1966.

1956: Rodin, ch c, by Supreme Court. Raced 1 yr in Italy, 3 sts, 0 wins, $387. Sire.

1957: **ROSSELLINA**, b f, by Tenerani. Raced 2 yrs in Italy, 6 sts, 3 wins, $5,086. Won Premio Saccaroa, Premio Elena. Dam of 11 foals, 9 rnrs, 6 wnrs, including **REALGAR** ($8,625), **RUYSDAEL II** ($7,256, champion in Italy). Granddam of **TIPPERARY FIXER, Rennequin, Tina's Express**.

1958: Rousseau II, ch c, by Owen Tudor. Raced 1 yr in Eng, 4 sts, 1 win, $1,388. Sire. Sent to USA 1974. Died 1981.

1961: Romagnola, ch f, by Tenerani. Unraced. Dam of 6 foals, 3 rnrs, 2 wnrs. Granddam of **My Robert**.

1962: **Romney II**, b c, by Shantung. Raced 2 yrs in Italy, 7 sts, 3 wins, $2,672. 3rd Premio Volta, Premio Botticelli.

1964: **RAEBURN II**, b c, by Botticelli. Raced 3 yrs in Italy, 5 sts, 3 wins, $36,112. Won Premio Parioli-Coppa d'Oro del Jockey Club Italiano; 2nd Derby Italiano; 3rd Premio d'Aprile. Sire.

1966: Remondina, ch f, by Antelami. Raced 1 yr in Italy, 1 st, 0 wins, $128. Dam of 9 foals, 5 rnrs, 1 wnr. Granddam of **SEVEN CARD DRAW**. Sent to USA 1975. Died 1985.

was a son of the eleven-time leading Italian sire Havresac II, a St. Simon-line horse by Rabelais (also sire of Rialto, who, in turn, sired Blushing Groom's broodmare sire, Wild Risk). Joe Estes, like Hollingsworth a former editor of *The Blood-Horse*, wrote that:

> The pedigree of Ribot illustrates, at several points, Federico Tesio's unrivaled capacity for discovering excellence where other horsemen found mediocrity. For many years, Tesio made a practice of going to England to obtain recruits for the Dormello-Olgiata broodmare band. At the Newmarket December sale of 1932, Tesio got Tofanella, then a yearling, for 140 guineas; Tofanella won the Brown Band, Germany's leading international race prior to World War II, and in addition to Tenerani, she produced Italian St. Leger winner Trevisana and the dam of Toulouse Lautrec. For 1,200 guineas, Tesio bought Bella Mina, dam of Bellini, which sired Tenerani. Barbara Burrini, Ribot's grand-dam, he bought for 350 guineas at the December sale of 1937, when she was a weanling. Barbara Burrini won six races at distances from seven furlongs to 1 1/2 miles. Among her several good winners, the best was Romanella, Ribot's dam, whose victories included the Triennale and Criterium Nazionale.

Ribot was sired by Tenerani, one of the numerous Italian stars which Tesio sent out of his locale to prove international ability. Tenerani, whose home scores included the Italian Derby, won the Goodwood Cup and the Queen Elizabeth Stakes in England. Tenerani was by Bellini, who had a short and unlucky stud career. Bellini got only thirteen foals in three years before Tesio was induced to trade him to the German forces in return for fodder the farm was unable to obtain otherwise.

Romanella, the dam of Ribot, also produced two Italian classic winners, Raeburn and Rossellina. Romanella was said to have soured of racing by the time she was three, the decision to retire her also encouraged by the development of ringbone. No inherited temperament which compromised being a racehorse hampered Ribot, but, as we shall see, idiosyncrasies certainly played a part in his stud career.

Hewitt pointed out a difference between the progression toward Ribot and the other masterful building-in-pedigree architecture of Tesio. This was in the lack of a top-class race mare in the ancestry of the original purchase in the female family. From the vantage point of the middle 1970s, Hewitt commented further that, "Some of the best students the author (Hewitt) knows report that they have studied Ribot's pedigree in an effort to explain his brilliance, on the Turf and at stud. They have arrived nowhere, and the author, too, is at the same spot. Explainable or not, though, Ribot was in all probability the most remarkable Thoroughbred of modern times."

Tesio, whose partner was Marchese Mario Incisa della Rochetta, has been portrayed so often as a genius that his image may be misleading. It is easy to see him as the secluded little geneticist, puttering around in his garden and gazing into the inner qualities of his crop — his garden being paddocks and his crop being Thoroughbreds. According to one who knew him, such a picture omits a vital quality, i.e., Tesio's fierce competitiveness and jealousy of his own position. Lieutenant Colonel Adrian Scrope, long the stud manager for Lord Derby, told of arranging for the French breeder Elizabeth Couturie to visit the Tesio farm, Dormello, in Northern Italy. "I warned

Ribot

her in advance that any advice given to her by Tesio would probably be the opposite of what she ought to do," Scrope said. He sensed that Mme. Couturie thought he was being unfair about Tesio, but she got the point after Tesio had advised her never to use artificial fertilizer on her paddocks. She and Scrope later were "fossicking about [a masterful British phrase] one of the stud yards" to pass the time, opened a barn door, and found bags of the stuff stacked almost to the ceiling!

"Tesio just didn't want anyone to beat him at his own game," Scrope continued. "He was a great competitor, and, really, the book (on breeding) that he wrote reveals absolutely nothing."

When Ribot came out for his debut at two in 1954 it was on the Fourth of July, but this was not of much moment since he was racing in Italy. (He technically was an English-bred, for he was foaled at the National Stud, Newmarket, since Tenerani was standing there and the dam was returned to him in 1952.) Ribot had only one close call among his three races at two, this being when the brazen Gail pushed him to a head margin in the most important juvenile race of Italy, the seven and a half-furlong Gran Criterium. (A ten-length margin the next spring was a more accurate measure of their developing merits.) Ribot earlier had won the five-furlong Premio Tramuschio and six-furlong Criterium Nazionale.

The quote attributed to Tesio about the hint of Ribot's special nature is somewhat at odds with the fact that the colt was not nominated for the Italian Derby. Perhaps the diminutive nature of the compact bay early on had prompted the omission. At any rate, Ribot by strict definition did not become a classic winner — that definition following the time-honored fact that, in England, only the One Thousand Guineas, Two Thousand

Guineas, Derby, Oaks, and St. Leger are classics, notwithstanding the importance of other races. Ribot won none of the races which are generally reported as being the Italian equivalents of these races, although he did win the ten-furlong Premio Emanuele Filiberto; this race is sometimes called a "classic" in that rather loose use of the word which obfuscates the issue.

Ribot defeated Gail by ten lengths in the Filiberto, so thoughts of an ongoing rivalry in a competitive sense were rendered moot. Ribot at three won three other races in Italy with names scarcely familiar to American readers, but blessed with some of the same lyric quality as Ribot's pedigree — Premio Pisa, Premio Brembo, Premio Besana. It was time for the Marchese, trainer Ugo Penco, and jockey Enrico Camici (speaking of lyrical names!) to test Ribot in an international crucible. The Prix de l'Arc de Triomphe at Longchamp did not yet have the status worldwide that it would soon develop, but it was certainly seen as a climactic test for Europeans. Ribot dashed a good field, winning by three lengths over Beau Prince II. Twenty-one other doubters slunk into the dappling shadows of a Parisian autumn as converts.

There was more for Ribot as a three-year-old, for he was entered for another one and a half-mile race, the Premio del Jockey Club in Milan in late October. Writing in *The Bloodstock Breeders' Review* of 1955, Franco Varola gave a dosage of testimony to the sporting and nationalistic feelings harbored by the Marchese and Tesio's widow: "To risk a winner of the Arc, who was, moreover, unbeaten, in a race which, even if he won, would not enhance his already high reputation, was considered hazardous..." Ribot, however, had won one of the greatest races in Europe "and it was only right that if Italian fans could be offered the same kind of entertainment, they should have it."

The kind of entertainment Ribot's national fans, and worshippers, received that day moved Varola further: "With three furlongs to go, Camici decided it was time to let Ribot free; from then on it was a solo for Ribot. We had seen horses like Apelle and Nearco win by more than 15 lengths, but they usually started accumulating their advantage right at the start. It was perhaps the first time that a horse at San Siro put 15 lengths in the space of three furlongs between himself and horses of proven international class."

Ribot was put up for the winter, and Varola conjectured that only the Ascot Gold Cup or the King George VI and Queen Elizabeth Stakes in England "would add to his reputation next year." As matters transpired, Ribot won one of those and added even more to his reputation by a repeat win in the Arc itself.

At four in 1956, Ribot warmed up for the big dances by winning the Premio Guilio Venino, Premio Vittuane, and Premio Garbagnae, alternating between ten and twelve furlongs, between May 12 and June 6. Eleven days later, he went out for his first major race at four and won the one and seven-eighths-mile Gran Premio di Milano by eight lengths. The next month found him at Ascot, England, for one of the tests Varola had named — the one and a half-mile King George VI and Queen Elizabeth Stakes. This race was only five years old, but, in a country where racing traditions already were in the two-century realm, it was obvious the event was reshaping the pattern of England's top races. It was satisfactorily placed, it seemed then, to give the best three-year-olds a run at older horses and then still have time to retool to complete the classic schedule in the St. Leger. Along the way, the King George also chopped at the ten-furlong Eclipse Stakes' status for providing that sort of weight-for-age midsum-mer test. The emergence of the King George recognized — and accelerated — the decline of the two-mile-plus Ascot Gold Cup as a viable target for the best class of runners.

Ribot's King George Day was a dismal thing, and it had the overtones of disaster. Timidity, realism, and the inevitable conditioning woes of some of the better contenders, combined to preclude any single top-class challenger from lining up to face Ribot. Aside from the hefty purse, he had nothing much to win, and a great deal of aura to lose, and this decision was to be thrashed out in exceptionally deep footing. Camici spoke later of how "Ribot resented the very heavy going, and I had the feeling that he wanted to ask me why I was humiliating him by asking him to run in the dreadful mud. However, as soon as he reached firmer ground, and while the other horses were more or less in distress, he went into his usual stride and beat them by several lengths." Defeating High Veldt by five lengths did not necessarily speak to the souls of the aficionados who had hoped that greatness on swift wings would excite them to ecstasies. Still, it was a thoroughly good job, and kept the unbeaten status intact.

About six weeks later, back home, Ribot won the nine-furlong Premio del Piazzale by eight lengths. There was but one challenge left, and that was a repeat performance in the Arc de Triomphe. According to the scrupulously researched book *The Arc*, by Arthur Fitzgerald (Genesis Publications Ltd., London, 1997), the Marchese revealed (after the race) that he had been very doubtful of the wisdom of running Ribot at all: "The previous Friday, the champion blew so hard after a mile and a half gallop that it was feared he was not fit. Donna Lydia Tesio, however, had overruled the Marchese's suggestion that Ribot be withdrawn, insisting on the same audacious policy always adopted by her late husband."

Ribot

That running of the Arc represented an important step up in terms of its prestige in North America. In each of the last two previous years, owners of American champions had toyed with the idea of sending their heroes to the event. While Alfred Vanderbilt, owner of Native Dancer, and Robert Kleberg, owner of High Gun, had the fortitude for adventure, neither of the horses was free of problems at the key moment. In 1956, C. V. Whitney stepped up. He did not have a proven champion at his disposal at the moment, but Career Boy and Fisherman were a high-class pair. He sent both, the older Fisherman as pacemaker and three-year-old Career Boy as the designated stretch flyer.

In the intervening forty-four years, a few other intrepid American owners have sent home-trained runners to make this challenge, but Career Boy's fourth-place finish of that 1956 running remains the best result for an American invader. (Various horses bred in America have won the Arc, but they all had been based in European training yards and trained and raced in a European manner.)

Jockey Eddie Arcaro said he thought at one moment that he and Career Boy were going to win, but "then a horse went by me so fast I couldn't recognize him. Come to find out — that was Ribot!"

Evan Shipman, Ernest Hemingway's old drinking pal from 1920s Paris, had long since settled down to a career of Thoroughbred coverage for *Daily Racing Form*, and he still had at the ready an apt turn of phrase. After re-visiting Paris and watching Ribot's 1956 Arc, Shipman concluded succinctly that Ribot was one of those rare Thoroughbreds who "gives his name to an epoch."

The great Ribot thus had won his sixteen races, in three countries, at two, three, and four, and retired unbeaten with the equivalent of $294,414 in earnings.

He had weathered many a circumstance with some acquiescence to the tenets of gentlemanly behavior, but he had his limits. When paraded before an adoring Italian audience, in one of those ceremonies by which mankind pays homage to his best racehorses, Ribot tossed Camici and ran off. Parades, he apparently felt, were preludes to combat — a serious matter — and not peacock strolls in the park.

Ribot entered stud in England, at Lord Derby's Woodland Stud, then for three seasons stood at his owner's Italian stud. Tesio had written that he tried to avoid standing stallions himself, lest convenience dictate mating decisions otherwise to be avoided. He apparently did not hold to this as a strict rule, and neither did the Marchese.

John W. Galbreath of Ohio was turning his Darby Dan Farm Kentucky division into one of the major bulwarks of American breeding and racing, and he leased Ribot for five years for $1,350,000. To put this in context of the times, it had been only five years since Nashua was purchased by sealed bid for $1,251,250, a record for a Thoroughbred. Galbreath was contracting for perhaps one-third of Ribot's life as a stallion, for an extraordinary price. Ribot arrived in America in June of 1960 and, whether he liked the idea or not, was displayed to the crowd at Belmont Park. He then was sent to Kentucky. By the end of the next year, his first crop had produced his first Arc de Triomphe successor in the form of Molvedo. In 1964, Ribot got his other Arc winner in Prince Royal II.

Another outstanding runner from his early crops was Ragusa, who made American Harry Guggenheim the leading breeder of England and Ireland and Ribot the leading sire in 1963. Ragusa, who had been sold to James R. Mullion, dashed through victories in the Irish Sweeps Derby, King George VI and Queen Elizabeth, and the English St. Leger. On the Free Handicap,

Bold Ruler

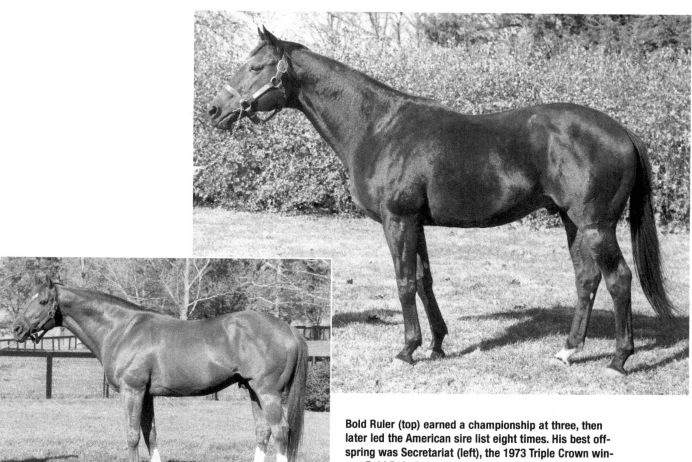

Bold Ruler (top) earned a championship at three, then later led the American sire list eight times. His best offspring was Secretariat (left), the 1973 Triple Crown winner. Bold Ruler's line lives on in Seattle Slew (below), the 1977 Triple Crown winner who has earned his own reputation as a sire of sires.

Blushing Groom

Blushing Groom (top) was France's top two-year-old, then one of Europe's best milers at three. At stud, he sired ninety-two stakes winners, including Rainbow Quest (right), a champion in England at three and now an important sire, and Rahy (above), sire of all-time leading female money earner Serena's Song.

Blushing Groom's daughter Sky Beauty (left) won the
New York Filly Triple Crown at three, then the older
female championship. Blushing Groom is the grandsire
of American sprint champion and promising young sire
Cherokee Run (top) and Swain (below), a hardknocking
campaigner who won two runnings of the King George
VI and Queen Elizabeth Diamond Stakes.

Ribot

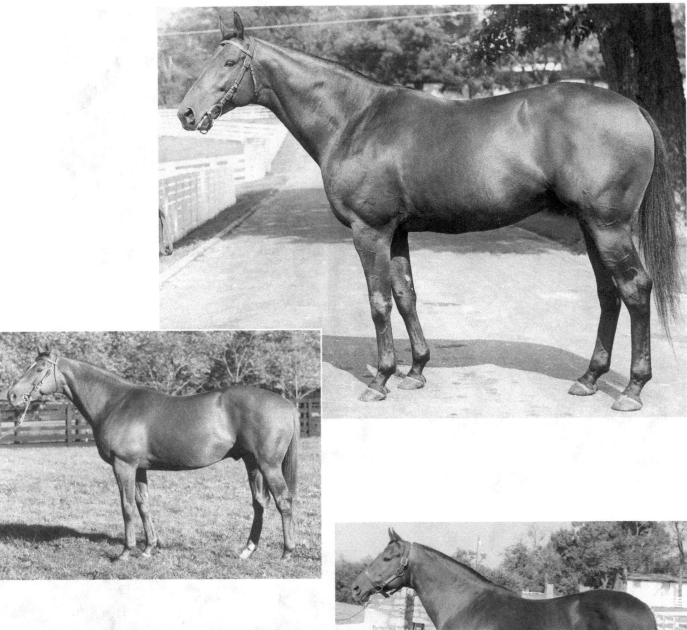

Ribot (top) won two runnings of the Prix de l'Arc de Triomphe in an unbeaten career. He eventually stood in the United States, where he sired Belmont Stakes winner Arts and Letters (above) and the brilliant two-year-old champion and influential sire Graustark (right).

Native Dancer

Native Dancer (top) won twenty-one of twenty-two races and the imagination of early television audiences who thrilled to the spectacle of the "Gray Ghost." At stud, he had a profound influence on both sides of the Atlantic. His daughter Natalma (above) produced the immortal Northern Dancer. A grandson, Darn That Alarm (right), is the sire of multiple grade I stakes winner Turnback the Alarm.

Native Dancer

Native Dancer's son Sea-Bird (above) is considered by some to be the greatest European racehorse of the 20th Century. Sea-Bird's son Arctic Tern (below) is shown winning the 1977 Prix Ganay. A great-grandson, Diesis (left), stands in the United States but has sired a number of European champions and classic winners.

Mr. Prospector

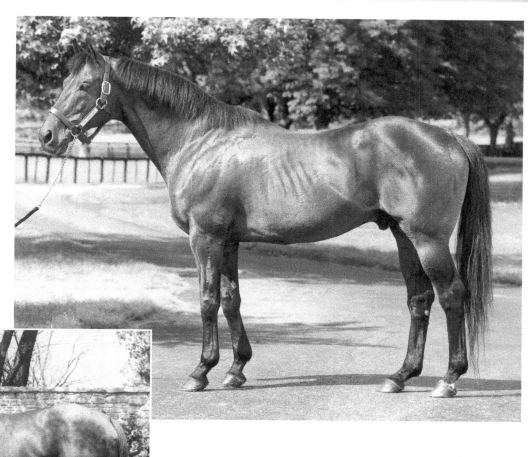

Mr. Prospector is the all-time leading sire of stakes winners with more than 160. As a sire of sires, he has gotten Woodman (left), and U.S. sprint champion Gulch (below).

Mr. Prospector

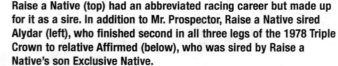

Raise a Native (top) had an abbreviated racing career but made up for it as a sire. In addition to Mr. Prospector, Raise a Native sired Alydar (left), who finished second in all three legs of the 1978 Triple Crown to relative Affirmed (below), who was sired by Raise a Native's son Exclusive Native.

though, he was ranked a pound below Relko, who had beaten him in the English Derby.

Hollingsworth's obituary article of Ribot commented that he was "acknowledged as the world's greatest sire of classic winners." Ribot quickly began turning them out on this side of the Atlantic to follow up on Ragusa, and others. His first American-sired crop included Raymond Guest's appealing little Tom Rolfe, who defeated another Ribot colt, Dapper Dan, in the 1965 Preakness. Dapper Dan had been second for Ogden Phipps in the Kentucky Derby. Tom Rolfe was the champion three-year-old of 1965. Guest sent him to try for his own Arc, and he ran rather well to be fifth behind the great and dominant Sea-Bird.

The emphasis on speed in this country might have made Ribot seem something less than a perfect match over here, but the horse furnished enough precocity that he was not totally out of his realm. Moreover, there were plenty of buyers and breeders by that time who recognized the value of sending American-breds abroad. The dominant buyer of the time — something of a one-man Maktoum family — was Charles W. Engelhard, an American who dealt in platinum in the business world and in platinum pedigrees in the horse world. He made six-figure yearling prices, if not commonplace, at least an annual expectation.

The author was having an impromptu audience with Engelhard in the old bar adjacent to the Keeneland sales pavilion one night during the late 1960s, when Engelhard mentioned that that afternoon he had seen Ribot for the first time. He said he found it interesting that so many of the better runners from that brace of Ribots he had bought at auction turned out to be so similar to the horse. The best of these were the remarkable pair of full brothers, Ribocco and Ribero. In Engelhard's colors, these two scored consecutive classic doubles in 1967 and 1968, each winning both the Irish Sweeps Derby and the English St. Leger. Another among many good Engelhard purchases was Ribofilio, who had a different career, coming to hand quickly enough to reign as England's top two-year-old of 1968.

Engelhard's success with Ribots of a certain stripe notwithstanding, the stallion got good horses in other colors, sizes, and shapes, as well. Perhaps his most spectacular son was Graustark, a massive, deep chestnut who worked so well before his first start that he was looked upon as a star before even racing. Graustark did not disappoint in any way he could help, but after thrilling crowds with seven consecutive wins, including two stakes, he fractured a coffin bone during the running (apparently) of the 1966 Blue Grass Stakes. The unbeaten wonder was edged by Abe's Hope in a photo. Graustark was so precocious that the theory circulated for years in Lexington that he must actually have been by Swaps, who also stood at Darby Dan. The theory focused on Swaps being a chestnut, too, but Graustark's dam, Flower Bowl, was by the chestnut Alibhai, son of Hyperion. The thought that Graustark was more precocious than any other Ribot colts was made less relevant by the fact that he was more precocious than any other Swaps colt, too!

Graustark's full brother, the more conventional bay, His Majesty, was not as brilliant a colt, but he lasted longer. His Majesty won the Everglades Stakes at three and came back to place at four in the Widener and Seminole Handicaps.

In 1969, Paul Mellon's light chestnut Ribot colt Arts and Letters joined the sire's line-up of classic winners. After failing to catch unbeaten Majestic Prince in torrid stretch duels in the Kentucky Derby and Preakness, Arts and Letters soared to the top of his crop. He left the battered Majestic Prince far behind in the Belmont Stakes, then toured through the Travers, Woodward, and Jockey Club Gold Cup. Trainer Elliott Burch won the Belmont three times and used the one-mile Metropolitan Handicap as a prep for the Belmont in all three cases. Arts and Letters won this handicap against older horses, demonstrating that he possessed miler speed as well as stamina. He was voted Horse of the Year for 1969.

Among the other top echelon of American breeders to use Ribot to good advantage were the Phippses. Ogden Phipps' homebred Ribot colt Boucher was sent to England and won the St. Leger. James Cox Brady likewise sent his Ribot filly Long Look to trainer Vincent O'Brien, in Ireland, and the filly won the Epsom Oaks for Brady. (It was a Ribot colt that O'Brien thought of as his main interest when he first visited Windfields Farm in Canada in 1968. There his attention was diverted to a Northern Dancer colt, later known as Nijinsky II, whom O'Brien trained to win the English Triple Crown to help launch a new direction in international bloodstock.)

Another Ribot filly to win a classic was Regal Exception, who won the 1972 Irish Oaks for Robin Scully, while the Ribot filly Alice Frey won the Italian Oaks. Thus, Ribot had sired twelve classic winners on both sides of the Atlantic among his total of sixty-seven stakes winners (sixteen percent). With his offspring spread through several countries, he led the English-Irish sire list three times (1963, '67, '68), ranked as high as second in Italy and third in France, and was twice in the top ten in North America at the time of his death from a twisted intestine in 1972. Among his good stakes winners not mentioned heretofore were Destro, Romulus, Riboccare, Blood Royal, Andrea Mantegna, Early to Rise, Maribeau, Sette Bello, Riot Act II, and Sir Ribot.

Ribot

That Ribot remained in this country to the end of his life was a function of his personality. There was enough fear for his safety — and perhaps that of his handlers — were he to be flown back to Italy, that his owners were prevailed upon to extend the lease. Certainly Ribot became a difficult customer. He disliked the sight of other horses when outdoors, although for a time he developed a strange affection for fellow stallion Decathlon's nearby presence. Ribot attacked a tree in his paddock and spent part of his time in his stall on his hind legs, gnawing and pawing a wooden plank near the ceiling. It was said that he once spotted a camera hidden up there to monitor his safety, and sulked until it was removed.

Farm manager Olin Gentry told us he suspected that, at some time along the way, Ribot had reared up so violently that he fell over backwards and "scrambled what brains he had."

Succeeding Generations

Of Ribot's sons, Tom Rolfe, Graustark, and His Majesty had major success at stud and they and their sons remain extant in pedigrees today both as sires of sires and broodmare sires. There is no overwhelming assurance, however, that Ribot descent as a sire line will continue consistently strong.

Arts and Letters was a good stallion, too, but not at the level of the others named above. Among Ribot's best stayers in Europe, only Ragusa made much of a mark at stud. He sired the Epsom Derby winner Morston as well as Ballymore, who won the Irish Two Thousand Guineas in the first start of his career. The Arc winners Molvedo and Prince Royal II were disappointments, although the latter did sire one high-class colt in Unconscious. Likewise, the sterling brothers Ribocco and Ribero slipped quickly into obscurity. Latin Lover (Australia) and Con Brio II (South

America) were among sons of Ribot that carried the blood successfully to other outposts.

Ironically, two full brothers who neither won as much as $100,000 at the racetrack were two of his best sons at stud. These were Graustark and His Majesty. Graustark sired fifty-two stakes winners (eight percent), including Paul Mellon's three-year-old champion Key to the Mint; the Belmont Stakes winner Avatar; Breeders' Cup Classic winner Proud Truth; French Derby winner Caracolero; the American classic-placed Jim French; the Woodward and Jockey Club Gold Cup winner Prove Out, and the champion three-year-old filly of 1978, Tempest Queen. Graustark mares have foaled 136 stakes winners, and the seven stakes winners from his daughter Glowing Tribute include the Kentucky Derby winner Sea Hero.

Key to the Mint followed suit as a successful stallion, getting forty-seven stakes winners (seven percent). His son Java Gold, regarded by Mack Miller as the best horse he trained, won the Travers, Whitney, and Marlboro Cup, among others. Another son, Plugged Nickle, was voted champion sprinter, but was more versatile then that title suggests. The Key to the Mint horse Sauce Boat was a high-class colt and sired more than thirty stakes winners. Key to the Mint also sired the mares Wings of Grace, Sugar and Spice, Gold and Ivory, and the wonderful producer Kamar.

It seems probable that, like the Graustark influence in general, the Key to the Mint presence will remain stronger as sires of broodmares. Key to the Mint himself is the broodmare sire of 100 stakes winners, including Swain. Also, Sauce Boat is broodmare sire of forty-eight stakes winners, including the Preakness and Belmont Stakes winner Tabasco Cat.

The influence of Graustark's brother, His Majesty, however, is a strong link in the ongoing importance of Ribot as a sire of sires. His Majesty is the sire and paternal grandsire of two Kentucky Derby winners. He led the American sire list in 1982 and was the sire of fifty-seven stakes winners (nine percent). The His Majesty colt Pleasant Colony was the champion three-year-old of 1981 when he won the Kentucky Derby, Preakness, Woodward, and Wood Memorial. As a tall, leggy sort that stayed so well, Pleasant Colony was not universally looked upon as a top prospect for this country, but he has proven to be a tremendous stallion. He is the sire of sixty-five stakes winners (thirteen percent). He has gotten his share of stayers — such as the magnificent Irish Derby and King George VI and Queen Elizabeth Stakes winner St. Jovite, the Belmont Stakes winner Colonial Affair, and the multi-millionaire Behrens. On the other hand, Pleasant Colony also sired the two-year-old filly champion Pleasant Stage. Typifying the combination of speed and staying power was the Pleasant Colony colt Pleasant Tap, whose career ranged from placing in the Kentucky Derby and Breeders' Cup Sprint to winning the Jockey Club Gold Cup as champion handicap horse of 1992.

His Majesty also sired Jersey Derby winner Cormorant, sire, in turn, of the 1994 Kentucky Derby winner Go for Gin. Cormorant's forty-five stakes winners also include the champion filly Saratoga Dew.

Other sons of His Majesty to make some mark at stud included Battonier (whose son Cavonnier came within a nose of giving the line a third Kentucky Derby winner). The His Majesty stallion Valiant Nature, as well as St. Jovite and Go for Gin, represent future prospects.

His Majesty is also the broodmare sire of seventy-five stakes winners.

Ribot's first American-sired champion, Tom Rolfe, was another significant sire and one who

Ribot

was a major step in keeping the sire line healthy for some years. Tom Rolfe sired forty-nine stakes winners (eight percent). He got a number of horses with stamina as well as high class, on dirt and grass, among them the American grass champion Run the Gantlet (in turn, the sire of grass champion April Run, plus Commanche Run, Providential, and Ardross). Others of this ilk by Tom Rolfe were Droll Role and London Company.

However, Tom Rolfe was best known perhaps as the sire of Hoist the Flag. This sensational colt was unbeaten aside from a disqualification and was the Kentucky Derby favorite in the spring of 1971 until suffering a leg injury that required state-of-the-art surgery to save his life. Hoist the Flag survived to sire fifty-one stakes winners (an impressive twenty-one percent), including the juvenile filly champion Sensational, as well as Linkage, Stalwart, Strike the Colors, Up the Flagpole, True Colors, Flying Partner, and May Day Eighty.

Hoist the Flag's major contribution to the legacy of his sire line though, is his son Alleged, who duplicated Ribot's feat of winning the Arc in consecutive years, scoring in 1977-78. Alleged sired an exceptional total of stakes winners, ninety-seven (ten percent). They included the grass course champion Miss Alleged, the Irish Derby winner Law Society, and other champions in European divisions such as Mutarram, Strategic Choice, Legal Case, and Always Earnest. Despite this abundance, however, Alleged is not a strong presence as a sire of sires in North America.

All these have been prominent broodmare sires, of course. The 102 stakes winners from Tom Rolfe mares include the champion and international sire Forty Niner; Hoist the Flag's daughters produced eighty-two stakes winners; and Alleged mares had accounted for eighty-five stakes winners through 1999.

Arguably the most accomplished racing son of Ribot was Arts and Letters, who stood at Greentree Stud as did Graustark's son Key to the Mint. (The farm became part of Gainesway after it was purchased by Graham Beck.) Arts and Letters did his bit to extend the classic traditions of the sire line when he begot 1980 Preakness winner Codex (in turn, the sire of the high-class winners Lost Code and Badger Land).

Arts and Letters' thirty stakes winners represented only six percent of his foals. His fifty-six stakes winners as a broodmare sire include the 1996 Breeders' Cup Classic winner, Alphabet Soup.

A lesson taught by history over and over is that the most exceptional of horses almost certainly will not sire a racehorse as good as themselves. This becomes something of a matter of rhetoric and a statement of the obvious. Such horses set the bar too high. Ribot certainly did. ❖

SPEED
RULES

Native Dancer

Thoroughbred racing's rebuff of television in the medium's early years remains an often repeated refrain of regret. This may be heartfelt and more or less universally accepted, but it is about as accurate as recalling that the Model T was blue. There may have been pockets of resistance, but racing accepted considerable airing early on, although television did not do for that sport what the cameras did for some others. *The Blood-Horse* ran an announcement in 1958 that CBS had committed to telecast a Saturday stakes every week for twenty-five weeks, beginning the week after the telecast of the Kentucky Derby. The race of the week in those days might be subject to being overrun by a long baseball game, but the introduction of video replay in sports, with the 1958 Preakness, alleviated that problem to some extent. At any rate, it is interesting that a national network had racing so heavily on its mind early in the same year as the Baltimore Colts' overtime win over the New York Giants — often seen as pivotal in the mushrooming popularity of the National Football League.

Nearly a decade before, a particularly visionary racetrack executive, Alfred G. Vanderbilt (a friend of CBS head Bill Paley), already was intrigued by television's potential. As a board member of Westchester Racing Association, which then owned Belmont Park, Vanderbilt was willing to bet on television. He even put his mouth where his money was, so to speak, appearing on camera a few times to explain the build up and call the race. He then arranged for former jockey Sammy Renick to take over.

By a fortuitous coincidence, Vanderbilt a few years later made an extraordinary contribution by providing early television its first Thoroughbred star. This was his large, powerful gray colt, Native Dancer, who became beloved as the "Gray Ghost." In a time of flickery, black-and-white sets, it helped that the stretch runner's coat color stood out as he charged across the screen.

Native Dancer, like Man o' War, lost only once. The Gray Ghost's timing was dreadful, for the loss came in the Kentucky Derby.

Native Dancer was a son of 1945 Preakness winner Polynesian and out of Geisha. The dam was by Discovery, whom Vanderbilt had purchased in the 1930s and campaigned as his first top horse. Geisha was not much of a race mare, but did win a maiden race. Geisha's dam, Miyako, was by John P. Grier and was a full sister to the 1938 champion two-year-old, El Chico. The next dam, La Chica, also foaled Planetoid, she, in turn, the dam of the great broodmare Grey Flight. Native Dancer represented the sort of mingling of old American lines with European stock which abetted our country's rise to the point that Europeans began seeking top stock over here.

Vanderbilt owned Sagamore Farm in the lovely Worthington Valley of Maryland, but Geisha was boarded at Dan Scott Farm near Lexington, Kentucky, where she foaled Native Dancer on March 27, 1950. The colt was sent to Vanderbilt's trainer at the time, Bill Winfrey, who sent him out in mid-April of 1952. He won, then scored by six lengths in the Youthful Stakes, bucking his shins. Put up until Saratoga, Native Dancer re-asserted his status by winning the Flash, Saratoga Special, and Grand Union Hotel Stakes, and was 1-4 when he won the Hopeful Stakes. The latter marked the first time he was pressed, but he beat Tiger Skin by two lengths.

Moving back to Belmont, he continued the standard campaign for a top New York juvenile, tuning up for the Futurity by winning the Anticipation Purse. Anticipation in the Futurity was replaced briefly by concern, for Native Dancer was blocked early in the running and had to show some bulldog tenacity as well as his proven speed. Native Dancer shouldered through a small opening to win by two and a quarter lengths over another Polynesian colt, Tahitian King. His time was a world record for six and a half furlongs on a straight course, the Futurity at that time being run on the Widener Chute across the Belmont infield. He got the distance in 1:14 2/5.

Winfrey selected the East View Stakes for Native Dancer's lone race at two of more than sprint distances. The gray colt obliged by winning the one and one-sixteenth-mile event in rather lackadaisical fashion. He not only was the consensus two-year-old champion, but was voted Horse of the Year in one poll, a rare honor for a two-year-old. Native Dancer was ranked at 130 pounds to top the Experimental Free Handicap.

Native Dancer was sent to California, but did not race at Santa Anita over the winter. Instead, he was fired for osselets (arthritis of the fetlock joint) and trained toward a return in the spring. He came back to win the one and one-sixteenth-mile Gotham and one and one-eighth-mile Wood Memorial. Winfrey sent along another Vanderbilt horse, Social Outcast, for the Kentucky Derby of 1953, Native Dancer's first race outside New York. The Vanderbilt pair was made the 7-10 favorite.

Native Dancer was fouled in the first turn by Money Broker, an incident which was serious, but perhaps has been exaggerated over the years. Vanderbilt told us many years later that he felt jockey Eric Guerin overreacted to the problem, but that he had never criticized the ride while Guerin was alive. "After all, you're on Native Dancer," Vanderbilt mused, questioning whether ducking to the rail to save ground in the final turn made sense. Dark Star, Captain Harry Guggenheim's 25-1 shot, had taken the track early and still had the lead in the upper stretch. Guerin, having sent Native Dancer to the rail, then had to steer him out again. The gray seemed to have a clear shot for some time before he began closing rapidly, and Dark Star ran a game race. Native Dancer came charging at the end, but was a head short. *Daily Racing Form*'s official chart saluted the winner while recognizing the brilliance of the runner-up: "Dark Star...responded readily when set down in the drive and lasted to withstand Native Dancer, but won with little left...Native Dancer...finished strongly, but could not overtake the winner, although probably best."

As had been true after Man o' War's only loss, Native Dancer's unscathed status was underlined by the short odds of his next race. In Native Dancer's case, this was the one-mile Withers Stakes, which he won two weeks later at 1-20. In

		Sickle, 1924	Phalaris / Selene
	Unbreakable, 1935		
POLYNESIAN, br, 1942		Blue Glass, 1917	Prince Palatine / Hour Glass
		Polymelian, 1914	Polymelus / Pasquita
	Black Polly, 1936		
NATIVE DANCER, gr h, March 27, 1950		Black Queen, 1930	Pompey / Black Maria
		Display, 1923	Fair Play / Cicuta
	Discovery, 1931		
GEISHA, ro, 1943		Ariadne, 1926	Light Brigade / Adrienne
		John P. Grier, 1917	Whisk Broom II / Wonder
	Miyako, 1935		
		La Chica, 1930	Sweep / La Grisette

1st dam: Geisha, ro, 1943-1959. Bred by Alfred G. Vanderbilt (Md). Raced 2 yrs, 11 sts, 1 win, $4,120. Dam of 8 named foals, 6 rnrs, 4 wnrs, 1 sw.

1948: Orientation, ch f, by Questionnaire. Raced 3 yrs, 22 sts, 3 wins, $5,985. Dam of 14 foals, 12 rnrs, 10 wnrs, including **INITIATE** ($78,311), **UNDULATION** ($52,714), **HAPPY HULL** ($38,817), **CITIZENSHIP** ($17,980). Granddam of **GREEN GLADE, MORRIS DANCER, BOLUSKA, Tiercel, Oxford Court, Kew Gardens, Chi Go Gary.**

1950: NATIVE DANCER, gr c, by Polynesian. Bred by Alfred G. Vanderbilt (Ky). Raced 3 yrs, 22 sts, 21 wins, $785,240. Horse of the Year (twice), champion 2 and 3yo colt, and champion older male. Won Preakness S, Belmont S, Futurity S (EWR, Bel, 6 1/2 furlongs in 1:14.40), Hopeful S, Arlington Classic, Metropolitan H, Youthful S, Withers S, Travers S, Wood Memorial, Dwyer S, American Derby, Gotham S, East View S, Saratoga Special S, Grand Union Hotel S, Flash S; 2nd Kentucky Derby. Sire of 304 foals, 44 sw, 3.15 AEI.

1951: Performance, ro c, by Amphitheatre. Raced 5 yrs, 70 sts, 9 wins, $32,110. Sire.

1953: Teahouse, ch f, by Polynesian. Unraced. Dam of 8 foals, 6 rnrs, 6 wnrs, including **AUGUST SUN** ($82,807), **RUM** ($54,139), **CUP OF TEA** ($44,529). Granddam of **SPLITTING HEADACHE, CHIPPER, Stiff Upper Lip.** Died 1971.

1954: Almond Eyes, gr f, by Polynesian. Unraced. Dam of 4 foals, 3 rnrs, 1 wnr, **Hail to East** ($28,800), **Kimono II** ($1,929, in Eng). Granddam of **Cheaters East.** Died 1966.

1955: Mysterious East, gr f, by Polynesian. Raced 1 yr, 8 sts, 0 wins, $200. Dam of 10 foals, 7 rnrs, 4 wnrs. Granddam of **Zulu Prophecy, Castinette, Forward Dancer.** Died 1984.

1956: Barren.

1957: Noble Savage, gr g, by Polynesian. Raced 2 yrs, 12 sts, 0 wins, $940.

1958: Barren.

1959: Face East, ch c, by Polynesian. Raced 3 yrs, 28 sts, 2 wins, $11,625. Sire.

---

the Preakness, Native Dancer was 1-5, although Dark Star was there to try to prove the Derby had been no fluke. Dark Star, however, bowed a tendon, so there was no opportunity for a repeat. Native Dancer surged to the front earlier than was his custom, and an outsider named Jamie K. got to within a neck of the favorite at the finish.

The suggestion that Native Dancer would be

vulnerable to a stretch challenge when the distance increased to one and a half miles for the Belmont was not dramatically reflected in the odds. He was 2-5. Again, the gray held off Jamie K. by only a neck, but the runner-up's rider, Eddie Arcaro, famously assessed that "If we go around again, Native Dancer's still not gonna let me get past him."

Native Dancer's next races stair-stepped down

two furlongs at a time, again underscoring his versatility as well as Winfrey's training touch. He won the mile and a quarter Dwyer and, in Chicago, rolled to a nine-length victory in the Arlington Classic at a mile. After a gallop at his frequent price of 1-20 in the Travers, he was returned to Chicago for the American Derby. Guerin was serving a suspension, so for the only time in his career Native Dancer had another rider. Arcaro filled in admirably, but got a scare before Native Dancer kicked into his stretch run. *Daily Racing Form*'s Charlie Hatton captured the moment: "Coming to the head of the stretch, he was some six lengths out of it. One wondered if he could be third, and apparently so did Arcaro, for he was shaken out of his usual poise and pumping hard on The Dancer, who was loafing. Once in the stretch, however, the champion decided to let them have it. There was a gray blur for perhaps a sixteenth of a mile, and there he was, jauntily winning with his ears pricked and looking over the fence interestedly at photographers at the finish." Arcaro was impressed: "He's everything they've said about him. Sheer power is the only way to describe him."

The 1953 season was one of unusual quality, for the handicap division was being dominated by Greentree Stable's Tom Fool. The powerful four-year-old was unbeaten in ten starts that year. Vanderbilt was never one to back down from a sporting challenge, and it would have been likely that the two wonderful colts would have met in the autumn, but Native Dancer turned up with a bruise in the left fore. The bruise had to be cut out following the American Derby. He was through for the year. Native Dancer reigned as obvious three-year-old champion, but the older, weight-carrying Tom Fool prevailed as Horse of the Year. Tom Fool was retired thereafter, so they never met.

At four, Native Dancer had but three races as Winfrey dealt with recurrent soundness problems. Even without Tom Fool in action, Greentree almost lowered Native Dancer's colors. Following a six-furlong win under 126 pounds, Native Dancer took up 130 pounds in the first big handicap of the New York spring, the one-mile Metropolitan. Greentree's Straight Face was in with 117. This was the race before which Greentree co-owner John Hay Whitney found himself in such admiration of the gray that he mused, "It's strange, but I hope The Dancer wins."

Whitney was almost disappointed by winning it himself, for Straight Face was seven lengths ahead of the favorite with a quarter-mile to run. The gray finally swooped down, picking up the remaining four of those lengths in the final furlong to win by a neck in 1:35 1/5. Winfrey could not get Native Dancer over his ills enough to run again until the Saratoga meeting, at which he won a seven-furlong race, the Oneonta, by nine lengths under a steadying 137. Soreness in the right foreleg persuaded owner and trainer that it was no longer wise to persevere, and Native Dancer was retired. Vanderbilt had been willing to test the champion further, even sending Winfrey to France to scout the situation relative to running in the Prix de l'Arc de Triomphe.

Native Dancer was retired to Sagamore with twenty-one wins in twenty-two starts and earnings of $785,240. He was again voted Horse of the Year on one poll despite the brevity of his four-year-old campaign, and, of course, was handicap champion as well. A quick maturing two-year-old, a classic winner, and a weight carrier, Native Dancer arguably was inherently capable of the most nearly perfect campaign in history. He clearly had the quality to have won a Triple Crown, although it is unfair to Dark Star to presume that this should have happened, and Native Dancer

Native Dancer

had an owner willing to let him be tested in the finest tradition of American handicap racing. (Vanderbilt accepted more than 140 pounds for the great Discovery.) Native Dancer, alas, lacked the soundness, or the luck which staying sound entails, to achieve all he seemed capable of achieving. Even so, he was one of the most memorable of American racing heroes.

At stud, Native Dancer was highly successful, and the importance of his blood has been spread further by various descendants. The gray died young, at seventeen, after surgery attempting to relieve an intestinal blockage. He sired forty-four stakes winners (fourteen percent), and they were all over the map, both literally and figuratively, as to style and distance. He got an official Kentucky Derby winner, Kauai King, and the only disqualified Derby winner in history, Dancer's Image. He also got the brilliant juvenile Raise a Native, whose career was limited to four races, the Flamingo Stakes-Florida Derby winner Native Charger, Kentucky Oaks winner Native Street, Vanderbilt's Spinaway Stakes winner Good Move, and such good-class stakes winners as Protanto, Rattle Dancer, Gala Performance, and Jig Time.

In Europe, Native Dancer's stakes winners included Hula Dancer, champion juvenile filly of France in 1962 and winner of the English One Thousand Guineas and Champion Stakes at three; another filly, Secret Step, hailed as the leading sprinter in England in 1962 and 1963; and Dan Cupid, runner-up to Herbager in the 1959 French Derby and afterward the sire of Sea-Bird.

The Brothers from England

Before reviewing further the ongoing influence of Native Dancer in international breeding and racing, we shall backtrack to look at the male line that produced him. Sitting atop is the ubiquitous presence of Phalaris, the English sprinter who occupies a similar place on the line associated with Nearco [refer to separate chapter]. Sons of Phalaris included the full brothers Sickle and Pharamond II. They were out of Selene, who would stamp her name deeper in history by foaling the champion racer and international sire Hyperion [refer to separate chapter]. Hyperion had not emerged at the time Sickle and Pharamond II were imported to this country, however, so those two horses' acquisitions may be counted as instances of considerable cleverness and timing on the part of a pair of Americans. Sickle was leased to stand in Kentucky by Joseph E. Widener, who subsequently exercised his option to purchase, and Pharamond II was purchased to stand in Kentucky by Hal Price Headley.

Both founded important sire lines: To Sickle traced Native Dancer and all that he accomplished, while to Pharamond II traced Native Dancer's contemporary Tom Fool, sire of Buckpasser.

Middle Park Stakes winner Pharamond II got for Headley (a Kentucky breeder-owner-salesman-track operator) the champion Menow. In turn, Menow sired Tom Fool, the Greentree Stable purchase who won all ten races in his four-year-old season and carried up to 136 pounds in becoming the second horse ever to sweep the New York Handicap Triple (Metropolitan, Suburban, Brooklyn). Tom Fool had the Bluegrass snickering behind its collective hand when he launched his stallion career with such timidity that he was said to have backed into a water trough when confronted with one mare. (The layout of breeding sheds on professional farms makes this difficult to fathom, but illustrates the reputation as a shy breeder which Tom Fool initially engendered.)

Tom Fool learned his lessons and proved a high-quality sire, getting thirty-six stakes winners. They included Kentucky Derby-Preakness winner Tim Tam, plus Jester (sire of Tri Jet and grandsire of Copelan), Tompion, Weatherwise, Dunce, Dunce Cap II, Cyrano, Funloving, and Silly Season. His greatest was Ogden Phipps' Buckpasser, a champion at two, three, and four and himself sire of thirty-five stakes winners, including Silver Buck, Buckaroo, L'Enjoleur, La Prevoyante, Numbered Account, Buckfinder, State Dinner, and Relaxing. While Buckpasser's status as a broodmare sire is defining his ongoing influence more than his place in this sire line, he certainly was no failure as a sire of sires. His son Buckaroo led the sire list and got Derby winner Spend a Buck; his son Norcliffe got At the Threshold, in turn sire of Derby winner Lil E. Tee; and his son Silver Buck got the Derby-Preakness winner Silver Charm, standing his first season at stud in 2000. Lite the Fuse, Montbrook, and Groovy are other current stallions tracing in tail male to Buckpasser, but, again, Buckpasser's towering status is as the broodmare sire of 142 stakes winners already.

To return to the parallel line that produced Native Dancer, his Phalaris—Selene tail-male ancestor was Sickle. Perhaps a slightly higher class racehorse than Pharamond II, Sickle won only three of ten races for Lord Derby, but was classic-placed, finishing third when beaten a half-length in the 1927 Two Thousand Guineas. He led the American sire list in 1936 and again in 1938, and his some forty-three stakes winners (fourteen percent) included Star Pilot, Stagehand, Cravat, Brevity, Concordian, Misty Isle, Reaping Reward, Jabot, and Brownian — a very high-class group. It was, however, the Sickle colt Unbreakable who linked in the sire line to Native Dancer.

Unbreakable was bred by Joseph E. Widener

and was foaled from Blue Glass, a daughter of the St. Simon-line stallion Prince Palatine (also in the sire line which produced Princequillo). Widener sent him to Captain Cecil Boyd-Rochfort in England, and Unbreakable won five of fourteen races over three years. He won three of six at two, placed in top company, and was ranked within five pounds of the top on the English Free Handicap. The next year he ran in both the Two Thousand Guineas and Epsom Derby, but was a long shot and did little more than allow Widener to say he had a horse in the English classics. Unbreakable was pushed down to sixteen pounds below the best on the three-year-old Free Handicap. He had two races at four, winning the Victoria Cup, whose distance of seven furlongs was perhaps his natural best. Unbreakable was returned to America to stand at Widener's Elmendorf Farm. He was at least as good a sire as his racing record would foretell. Unbreakable's thirteen stakes winners represented only six percent of his foals, but one of them was a classic winner, Polynesian, who insured that Unbreakable's would be the least-renowned name in more than a half-century of champions' pedigrees.

Polynesian's pedigree on the bottom side had more of the sprint/stamina combination created by Phalaris and Prince Palatine. He was out of Black Polly, who won only one race but was a granddaughter of the good race mare Black Maria. Black Polly was by the speedy Polymelian, whose sire, Polymelus, was also the sire of the great Phalaris. Thus, Polynesian was inbred to Polymelus.

Black Polly died of colic a few weeks after foaling Polynesian, who, thereupon, was raised on cow's milk fed from a bucket. Her colt grew impressively enough, however, that he was chosen by trainer Morris Dixon as best of the lot when Widener's son, P. A. B. Widener II, wanted to pre-

Native Dancer

sent one of his father's Elmendorf crop as an anniversary present to his wife. Thus, Polynesian raced in the name of Mrs. P. A. B. Widener II (who mined well from the succeeding bloodline, breeding and racing the aforementioned Hula Dancer and Dan Cupid).

Polynesian, a brown colt of medium size, won five of his ten races at two. Early in the year, he suffered from tying-up and, while being rested was attacked by hornets in his turn-out paddock. He became wildly upset and was drenched with perspiration, after which he seemed to have worked himself out of the tying-up. (Polynesian's subsequent importance notwithstanding, unleashing a swarm of petulant hornets on a patient never caught on as a treatment for tying-up.) Toward the end of his two-year-old season, Polynesian won four consecutive races, including the Sagamore Stakes, and was rated seven pounds below topweights Pavot and Free For All on the Experimental Free Handicap. The following spring, Polynesian did not run well enough early to encourage a try in the Kentucky Derby, but he enhanced his standing considerably by defeating the 1-5 Pavot in the one-mile Withers Stakes. Polynesian then won the Preakness Stakes, in which Derby winner Hoop, Jr. bowed a tendon and Pavot was unplaced. The Widener colt did not contest the Belmont, in which Pavot rebounded, and Polynesian in general failed to live up to the status as a classic winner through the rest of his three-year-old season.

Polynesian had active campaigns of twenty races at four and fourteen races at five. He seemed to act as if, before every race, somebody shouted "Watch out for the hornets," for he had a tendency to squander his speed early. This won many a day for him, as when he blazed six furlongs in 1:08 4/5 to win the Roseben Handicap on the Widener Chute; carried 130 pounds to win the six-furlong Rumson; or carried 126 to match Clang's world record for six furlongs in 1:09 1/5 in the Pageant Handicap. Throughout his four-year-old season, he also would turn in admirable, but losing efforts against the best at middle distances. Then, at five, he went on a streak of winning eight races from nine starts midway during the season. His wins included several sprint stakes under as much as 134 pounds, but also the one and one-sixteenth-mile Long Branch and one and one-eighth-mile Omnibus Handicaps against second-level competition.

Dixon accomplished the rare feat of putting one over on Ben A. Jones of Calumet that autumn. When Polynesian was weighted at 140 pounds for the Fall Highweight Handicap, the world more or less assumed that was his target. Dixon, however, slipped him into a six-furlong allowance race on the same day, and the horse wound up beating Calumet Farm's Armed, whom Jones was prepping for his match race against Assault.

Polynesian had won twenty-seven of fifty-eight races and placed twenty other times to earn a total of $310,410. The horse had shown great speed as well as middle-distance ability, and his sons and daughters reflected both. His thirty-seven stakes winners (twelve percent) were topped, of course, by Native Dancer, who could do all things. Others ranged from a late-closing juvenile with a one-stakes championship (Garden State Stakes) in Barbizon to such brilliant speed merchants as Alanesian (foundation mare), Poly Hi, Polly's Jet, Mommy Dear, and world-record sprinter Imbros. A lesser stakes winner by Polynesian was Banquet Bell, dam of champions Primonetta and Chateaugay. (Banquet Bell also became the second dam of the inbred Preakness-Belmont winner

Little Current, whose sire, Sea-Bird, went back to Polynesian on the top line through Dan Cupid to Native Dancer.)

Dancers Across the Seas

The impression that Sea-Bird was a lovely colt, but rather narrow in front, provided little comfort the day he charged us. We were standing in his paddock at Haras du Petit Tellier with the farm owner, Paul Chedeville. It was 1972, and John Galbreath's lease to stand the great horse at Darby Dan Farm in Kentucky had expired. Something less than the great sire Galbreath hoped for, Sea-Bird had been returned to his homeland, France. As the charging stallion came closer, the image of litheness became obscured by the powerful chest of an aggrieved rhino. For protection, Chedeville seemed willing to depend upon a spindly buggy whip he held in the air. Of the two of us, he alone harbored any confidence in this object. In the author's mind, it came down to a preference between announcements: "(Visiting Turf Writer) Killed By Champion Race Horse" or "Fractures Ankle In Cowardly Dash." We blinked and awaited the collision. Sea-Bird, fortunately, agreed with our companion that the buggy whip was something to take seriously. He skittered to a stop that would have thrilled Arc runner-up Reliance seven years earlier, and we were soon petting and commenting upon one of the great horses of the 20th Century — with what we hoped was sufficient aplomb to distract attention from a visibly throbbing chest cavity.

Sea-Bird was one of various symbols of the great expanse of Native Dancer's influence. As the sire of Raise a Native and broodmare sire of Northern Dancer, Native Dancer would, of course, be assured immortalization via hundreds of important pedigrees. [Refer to chapters on Northern Dancer and Mr. Prospector, son of Raise

a Native.] Incredibly, however, there are several other male-line connections from Native Dancer to important horses, in addition to those linked to Raise a Native.

Native Dancer's son Dan Cupid represented one of them. The classic-placed Dan Cupid was the sire of Sea-Bird. Whenever European observers and/or horsemen address their greatest horses of the 20th Century, the top place seems to lie between Ribot and Sea-Bird, the latter a winner with great authority and panache in the 1965 Epsom Derby and Prix de l'Arc de Triomphe. Sadly, Jean Ternynck's homebred Sea-Bird died of an intestinal blockage the year after our harrowing visit. Sea-Bird got an exceptional nineteen percent stakes winners (thirty-three), but without ever seeming to have established himself as a great stallion. In a few instances, he did get exceptional quality: The filly Allez France was a beloved heroine of the French whose many top-class wins included the 1974 Arc de Triomphe; Sea-Bird's nice American colt Arctic Tern sired Bering, winner of the French Derby and runner-up to the great Dancing Brave in one of the best runnings of the Arc. The Sea-Bird colt Gyr was so impressive that the sire's trainer, Etienne Pollet, put off his own retirement; Gyr may not have lived up to his sire, but he was second in Nijinsky II's Epsom Derby and won the Grand Prix de Saint-Cloud. In America, where he stood for most of his career, Sea-Bird got Galbreath's three-year-old champion of 1974 in Preakness-Belmont winner Little Current, as well as the high-class filly and mare Kittiwake.

Also in Europe, the Native Dancer line has flourished in the descent from an unlikely source, Atan. A Native Dancer colt foaled in 1961, Atan won his only race and got only four stakes winners from 212 foals, a below-average two percent. One

Native Dancer

of those, however, was the remarkable Sharpen Up, winner of the 1971 Middle Park Stakes in England and two other stakes. Sharpen Up followed the sire line's penchant for getting horses of differing proclivities. Sharpen Up's superb record of eighty-three stakes winners (thirteen percent) included the Breeders' Cup Turf and One Thousand Guineas winner Pebbles; the Prix de l'Arc de Triomphe winner Trempolino; the champion milers Kris and Selkirk; champion sprinter Sharpo; champion English two-year-old Diesis; and a smattering of American-raced horses, including Monmouth Oaks winner Dream Deal.

Several of Sharpen Up's sons continued the line of Native Dancer, by then three generations removed. Among the Sharpen Up horses at stud has been Kris, who lost only twice in sixteen starts. Kris' seventy-one stakes winners include Oh So Sharp, who in 1985 became the first filly to win three English classics since Meld in 1955. Raced by Sheikh Mohammed bin Rashid al Maktoum, Oh So Sharp won the One Thousand Guineas and Oaks against her own gender and added the St. Leger against colts — becoming a sort of poster girl for the repeating distance versatility of this entire sire line. Another Kris filly, Unite, also won the English Oaks.

Today, the Atan branch of the Native Dancer sire list is frequently in the news through the exploits of Diesis, son of Sharpen Up. Also a Middle Park Stakes winner, Diesis added the Dewhurst to reign as England's top two-year-old of 1982. The full brother to Kris stands at Alice Chandler's Mill Ridge Farm in Kentucky. (It was Mrs. Chandler's father, Hal Price Headley, who imported Pharamond II, brother of Diesis' distant ancestor Sickle.) Many of Diesis' sixty-three stakes winners to date (eleven percent), have been raced abroad, and, like his brother, he has sired two Epsom Oaks winners, Diminuendo (1988) and Ramruma (1999). Both of those fillies also added the Irish Oaks, and Ramruma finished second against males in the St. Leger. (A third brother to Diesis and Kris is Keen, exported to stud in Australia.)

Sons of Diesis include the English champion Halling, Irish champion Elmaamul, Rothmans International winner Husband, and Hollywood Turf Handicap winner Storm Trooper. Halling was twice winner of both the Eclipse Stakes and Juddmonte International, a pair of the best races in England. True to the heritage of versatility that has prevailed in the sire line since Polynesian, Diesis, that sire of Oaks winners, also sired Keen Hunter, who took one of Europe's best sprint stakes, the Prix de l'Abbaye de Longchamp.

Yet another son of Sharpen Up is Selkirk, a twelve-year-old safely launched at stud with Matriarch Handicap winner Squeak, English One Thousand Guineas winner Wince, and Epsom Derby-placed Border Arrow in his early crops.

Other sons of Native Dancer were successful sires in North America, and some of them still have representation today. The gray Native Dancer colt Native Charger chased two-year-old champion Bold Lad in 1964, then won both the Flamingo and Florida Derby at three. He got the champion filly Forward Gal and a son, High Echelon, who was (what else?) versatile enough to win both the Futurity Stakes and Belmont Stakes.

The Native Dancer colt Restless Native was out of Vanderbilt's champion Next Move and was kept for stud although he was not a stakes winner himself. Restless Native had some success, getting the hardy Maryland mare Twixt and the Belmont Stakes runner-up Jolly Johu.

Rattle Dancer was atypical of the Native Dancers

in that he made his mark in California. The C. V. Whitney homebred won the Hollywood Juvenile Championship at two in 1961. He then sired twenty-two stakes winners (nine percent).

Another example was the Native Dancer colt, Jig Time, a gray like the sire, whose twenty-three stakes winners included the Fountain of Youth Stakes winner Darn That Alarm. The latter, a Florida stallion, sired a fine filly in Turnback the Alarm, winner of the Coaching Club American Oaks, Mother Goose Stakes, Go for Wand, Shuvee, and Hempstead, all grade I races. The gray stallion Pistols and Roses, winner of the Blue Grass, Flamingo, and two Donn Handicaps, is a son of Darn That Alarm.

The most prolific sire line tracing to Native Dancer, at least by American standards, is that of his brilliant son Raise a Native. That numerous branch is reviewed in the chapter named for Raise a Native's son Mr. Prospector.

The dueling Affirmed and Alydar wound up with similar records in terms of black-type stakes winners sired. Affirmed had a slight edge, eighty-one to seventy-seven. Affirmed's sire, Exclusive Native, wound up with sixty-nine black-type stakes winners.

Of those who have carried the line in the decades of the 21st Century, the prolific sire line of Mr. Prospector is of particular importance. Mr. Prospector sired a total of 182 black-type stakes winners by the time of his death in 1999 (the year before publication of *Dynasties*). Selected recent highlights in the descent of the Native Dancer sire line through Mr. Prospector follow:

• *Fappiano* (son of Mr. Prospector) had a total of only forty-seven black-type winners, but his line of descent has been rich. It includes his 1990

Kentucky Derby winner Unbridled, himself the sire of internationalist Empire Maker. Unbridled's branch of the sire line led three generations later to 2015 Triple Crown winner, Horse of the Year, and Hall of Famer American Pharoah. Also, Unbridled's array of important sons included Unbridled's Song, whose own coterie of major offspring included Arrogate, the spectacular albeit short-lived Hall of Famer and earner of more than $17 million. Four generations down the sire line descent of Fappiano came Run Runner, the 2017 Horse of the Year, Hall of Famer, and rising young stallion.

• *Machiavellian* (son of Mr. Prospector) sired Street Cry, whose daughter Zenyatta earned 21st Century immortality with her record of nineteen wins in succession before her only defeat. Zenyatta won four Eclipse Awards, including Horse of the Year of 2010, and was elected to the Hall of Fame.

• *Smart Strike* (son of Mr. Prospector) was a high-class stakes winner bred in Canada and became the sire of 136 black-type stakes winners. Smart Strike was North America's leading sire in 2007, 2008, and 2009. As of 2024, his standout son in terms of contemporary visibility was Curlin, which was Horse of the Year in two of his sire's leading years, 2007 and 2008. Curlin has gone on to his own distinctions at stud, including being the leading sire of Breeders' Cup winners (eight individual horses). The Hall of Famer's Breeders' Cup winners include Vino Rosso, Stellar Wind, and Good Magic.

Nearly a century ago, the name of Native Dancer was introduced to the Turf and soon became synonymous with brilliance, courage, and class. It still is. ❖

Mr. Prospector

atrice Jacobs was not totally comfortable with her father's being quoted to the effect that Raise a Native was the most brilliant two-year-old he had ever seen. After all, her father was the great trainer Hirsch Jacobs, who just three years before had won a two-year-old championship with the family's and partner's homebred Hail to Reason. Did it count for nothing that Hail to Reason had slain his division with uncompromising speed in the colors of Jacobs' own young daughter — Patrice herself?

Such was the impression created by the brief career of Raise a Native — a Native Dancer colt who became a great stallion and sired other great ones, including Mr. Prospector. As life rocked along, Miss Jacobs would later marry Raise a Native's owner, Lou Wolfson. One presumes that, over the last few decades, she has had occasion to remind herself to be tactful when the subject of Raise a Native and Hail to Reason might come up at family dinners — her husband with his own set of memories, her mother with hers. The fact that one of Raise a Native's sons, Exclusive Native, sired the Wolfsons' great Triple Crown winner Affirmed perhaps gives an easy out for any such discussion.

Raise a Native was bred by Mr. and Mrs. Cortright Wetherill, owners of Happy Hill Farm in Pennsylvania, and was foaled at R. A. Alexander's Bosque Bonita Farm, in Versailles, Kentucky, where the Wetherill mares were boarded. He was a bright chestnut in the sixth crop of the great Native Dancer and was out of Raise You, a daughter of the good-class Teddy stallion Case Ace. Raise You had won the Colleen, Polly Drummond, and New Jersey Futurity at two in 1948 and was already the dam of Kingmaker, winner of the Whitney and five other important stakes. Raise You was foaled from Lady Glory, a daughter of American Flag, one of Man o' War's best sons.

The Native Dancer—Raise You colt was sold for $22,000 to Mrs. E. H. Augustus at the 1961 Keeneland fall mixed sale. Such were the finances of the weanling market at the time that the price constituted an all-time American auction record for a weanling. The following summer, Mrs. Augustus included the colt in her Keswick Stables consignment to the Saratoga yearling sale. He was still a marketable number and was purchased for $39,000 by one Louis E. Wolfson. This was a long way from another record, however. The $100,000 barrier had already been broached, and breached, at American yearling auctions, and the top price at Saratoga that August was $83,000 (another from the Keswick Stable consignment).

Wolfson was a Jacksonville, Florida-based entrepreneur, sportsman, and political activist who was bent on building his new Harbor View Farm and Stable into a leadership position. He was darned efficient, and quick, about it. In addition to such astute early purchases as Francis S., Roman Brother, Roving Minstrel, and Garwol — besides Raise a Native — Wolfson coaxed out of retirement the trainer Burley Parke, who had handled Occupy, Occupation, Free For All, and others, in the 1940s and the champion Noor in 1950.

The Native Dancer—Raise You colt was named Raise a Native, and he came to hand quickly enough for an old master of training two-year-olds that Parke sent him down Hialeah's stretch for a three-furlong dash as early as February 28, 1963. Two years earlier, Hialeah fans had seen Ridan scoot down that stretch in a similar two-year-old debut, and he went right on through the season undefeated. They, perhaps, were not easily impressed by precocity, but Raise a Native's ability to put six lengths between himself and his runner-up in a matter of 33 2/5 seconds was compelling nonetheless. Parke apparently knew he had something worth coming out of retirement for, so he waited to run Raise a Native again for more than two months. At Aqueduct, the Harbor View colt won a five-furlong allowance race by eight lengths, then less than a month later took the Juvenile Stakes by two and a half, and after seven more weeks added the Great American by two over Mr. Brick and Chieftain. These races came at five and five and a half furlongs, and in each he matched or lowered the track record. (Not to quibble, but it should be remembered that the new Aqueduct had opened only four years earlier.) No wonder even Hirsch Jacobs was impressed!

The Sapling Stakes in early August was the next target. Then, however, on August 2, a day before the event, Raise a Native bowed a tendon while blowing out. Whether Zodiacal entities danced, mourned, battled, or won poker games from one another, we know not; however, the record shows that August 2, 1963, the day Raise a Native was finished, was also the day of the racing debut of a relative far away — a little colt named Northern Dancer.

Raise a Native had won all four of his races, and his earnings of $45,955 were a pale measure of his status. By year's end, Hurry to Market came along to win the Garden State Stakes and the juvenile championship, but Tommy Trotter harked back to Raise a Native's dominance to place him on top of the Experimental Free Handicap at 126 pounds. Raise a Native went to stud at Leslie Combs II's Spendthrift Farm near Lexington, Kentucky.

A colt from his second crop followed in his own tradition of auction records. The incredibly handsome Raise a Native colt to be named Majestic Prince brought a world-record bid of $250,000 at Keeneland in the summer of 1967. Majestic Prince was consigned by Spendthrift and was owned by Combs in partnership with Frank McMahon, who entered the top bid to take full ownership. Majestic Prince confounded the prevailing tradition of the time of top-priced yearlings being disappointments. Turned over to former jockey great John Longden for training, Majestic Prince went unbeaten through his first nine races, including the 1969 Kentucky Derby and Preakness!

The suspicion that Raise a Native's get might not like classic distances was thus alleviated. That question, of course, had been engendered by Raise a Native's own career being restricted to the business of a precocious juvenile. Ironically, it also had been encouraged to some extent by Wolfson's colt from the sire's first crop. This was Exclusive Native, who won the Sanford Stakes at two and the Arlington Classic (one mile) at three. Such worries were rendered inoperative, of course, when Exclusive Native sired the Triple Crown winner Affirmed.

		Unbreakable, 1935	Sickle Blue Glass
	Polynesian, 1942		
		Black Polly, 1936	Polymelian Black Queen
NATIVE DANCER, gr, 1950			
		Discovery, 1931	Display Ariadne
	Geisha, 1943		
RAISE A NATIVE, ch h, April 18, 1961		Miyako, 1935	John P. Grier La Chica
		Teddy, 1913	Ajax Rondeau
	Case Ace, 1934		
		Sweetheart, 1920	Ultimus Humanity
RAISE YOU, ch, 1946			
		American Flag, 1922	Man o' War Lady Comfey
	Lady Glory, 1934		
		Beloved, 1927	Whisk Broom II Bill and Coo

1st dam: RAISE YOU, ch, 1946. Bred by Country Life Farm (Md). Raced 3 yrs, 24 sts, 5 wins, $37,220. Won Colleen S, Polly Drummond S, New Jersey Futurity. Dam of 14 named foals, 12 rnrs, 11 wnrs, 2 sw.

1952: Double Dealer, b g, by Double Jay. Raced 7 yrs, 73 sts, 12 wins, $37,965.

1953: **KINGMAKER**, ch g, by Princequillo. Raced 5 yrs, 47 sts, 13 wins, $243,205. Won New Orleans H, Grey Lag H (NTR, Jam, 9 furlongs in 1:48.20), Whitney S, Kent S, Royal Palm H, Excelsior H; 2nd Jersey S, Yankee H, Chesapeake S, Paumonok H; 3rd Governor's Gold Cup, Edgemere H.

1954: Jujitsu, b g, by Polynesian. Raced 3 yrs, 26 sts, 8 wins, $20,970. 2nd Dade County H. Died 1959.

1955: Queens Full, b f, by Princequillo. Raced 2 yrs, 9 sts, 1 win, $4,135. Dam of 8 foals, 7 rnrs, 6 wnrs. Granddam of **She's a Holdup**.

1956: Barren.

1957: **National Gallery**, ch g, by Daumier. Raced 6 yrs, 65 sts, 12 wins, $45,657. 3rd Atlantic City H, Philadelphia Turf H. Died 1965.

1958: **My Sister Kate**, ch f, by Native Dancer. Raced 2 yrs, 25 sts, 5 wins, $24,765. 2nd Falls City H. Dam of 8 foals, 7 rnrs, 4 wnrs, including **Mr. Quillo** ($23,043), **Inkosana** ($9,970). Granddam of **PRINCESS POLONIA, SIR BORDEAUX, RAISE A KING, ROSCIUS, SHARP HOOFER, JOJO'S SPIRIT, IVORINA, Ordavoss**. Died 1979.

1959: Plenty Papaya, b f, by Polynesian. Raced 1 yr, 2 sts, 0 wins, $0. Dam of 2 foals, 2 rnrs, 2 wnrs. Died 1968.

1960: Aces Swinging, ro f, by Native Dancer. Raced 2 yrs, 23 sts, 4 wins, $17,435. Dam of 13 foals, 11 rnrs, 8 wnrs, including

ONE ON THE AISLE ($239,278, gr. I), **KAPALUA BUTTERFLY** ($177,929), **Brokopondo** ($13,935, in Eng), **Tigresse d'Amour** ($10,665, in Fr). Granddam of **WHO'S TO PAY, LT. PINKERTON, LIGHTS AND MUSIC, POLISH HOLIDAY, AQUAKISS (Fr), Boss Shannon, Tiger Flower (Ire)**. Died 1982.

1961: **RAISE A NATIVE**, ch c, by Native Dancer. Bred by Happy Hill Farm (Ky). Raced 1 yr, 4 sts, 4 wins, $45,955. Champion 2yo colt. Won Juvenile S (ETR, Aqu, 5 furlongs in :57.80), Great American S (NTR, Aqu, 5 1/2 furlongs in 1:02.60). Sire of 838 foals, 78 sw, 2.36 AEI.

1962: Spit'n the Ocean, ch f, by Sailor. Raced 2 yrs, 10 sts, 1 win, $4,080. Dam of 11 foals, 9 rnrs, 5 wnrs, including **Harbor Pilot** ($146,521). Granddam of **Cecis Lil Bandit, Turning Home**.

1963: Big Stakes, b f, by Swoon's Son. Unraced. Dam of 2 foals, 2 rnrs, 2 wnrs. Granddam of **RAISIN THUNDER, Storm Scope**. Died 1970.

1964: Barren.

1965: Toast of the Town, dkb/br f, by Native Dancer. Unraced. Dam of 7 foals, 5 rnrs, 4 wnrs, including **The Absentee** ($26,188), **Eastman (GB)** ($2,983, in Eng, Nor, and Swe).

1966: Grand Old Flag, gr f, by Native Dancer. Raced 3 yrs, 30 sts, 3 wins, $10,815.

1967: Show Stopper, ro f, by Native Dancer. Raced 1 yr, 8 sts, 1 win, $11,205. 2nd Politely S. Dam of 13 foals, 9 rnrs, 3 wnrs. Granddam of **RUSSELLITO, Shadowfay, Pro Show, Premier Run**. Died 1989.

1968: Not bred.

Raise a Native never led the American sire list, but three of his sons did, and he became one of the most prominent stallions of the 20th Century, a distinguished sire of runners, great sire of sires, and broodmare sire of 171 stakes winners.

At the races, Raise a Native got seventy-eight stakes winners (nine percent) before his death on July 28, 1988. He was among the many with a reputation for getting unsoundness, but the breeders of his best sons and daughters could live with it. In addition to Majestic Prince, Raise a Native's best racehorses included Alydar, the extraordinary Calumet Farm colt who won eleven major stakes and ran second to Affirmed in all three Triple Crown events of 1978. Others by Raise a Native, here and in Europe, included Crowned Prince, Laomedonte, Clear Choice, Highland Park, Native Royalty, Where You Lead, Son Ange, Raise a Cup, and, the title horse of this chapter, Mr. Prospector.

Several sons of Raise a Native proved extraordinary sires. The three who topped the sire list were Exclusive Native (1978-79), Mr. Prospector (1987-88), and Alydar (1990).

In Affirmed, Exclusive Native got a horse in the Native Dancer tradition. An early two-year-old stakes winner who went on through the year to be the season's champion, Wolfson's Affirmed then swept the Triple Crown and proved a notable weight carrier at four while repeating as Horse of the Year. He was sound, game, professional, and exemplary in both speed and stamina. Unlike Native Dancer, Affirmed never missed an intended race because of lameness, and he won twenty-two of twenty-nine races and earned $2,393,818. Age twenty-five in 2000 and standing at Jonabell Farm in Kentucky, Affirmed is the sire of seventy-four stakes winners (eleven percent) in North America and Europe, including two-time Eclipse Award winner Flawlessly, plus Peteski,

Zoman, Trusted Partner, Mossflower, Affirmed Success, Charlie Barley, and Bint Pasha.

Exclusive Native got a total of sixty-six stakes winners (thirteen percent). Besides Affirmed, they included the champion Genuine Risk, who gave him his second Kentucky Derby winner in three years — and horse racing its second female Derby winner ever. Others by Exclusive Native were champion Outstandingly, plus Our Native, My Darling One, Valdez, Commemorate, Life's Hope, and Premiership.

Although Alydar was forced screaming into the backseat as a racehorse by Affirmed, he was always seen as a better prospect for top-rung success as a fashionable sire. So it proved. The son of the On-and-On mare Sweet Tooth had a shortened, but illustrious career, at Calumet Farm. He died in 1990 and, chillingly, there apparently remains in the minds of at least one prosecutor the thought that his death might have been arranged in connection with the financial collapse of the proud old farm.

The first crop of Alydar came out running, for it included the champion filly Althea as well as one of the other contenders for filly honors, Miss Oceana (later a record-priced broodmare at seven million dollars when sold by Newstead Farm at Fasig-Tipton Kentucky).

Alydar got outstanding colts as well:

• *Alysheba*, winner of the Kentucky Derby and Preakness in 1987, of the Breeders' Cup Classic as Horse of the Year in 1988, and earner of $6,679,242.

• *Criminal Type*, Horse of the Year for 1990.

• *Easy Goer*, champion at two and winner of the 1990 Belmont Stakes and other top stakes.

• *Strike the Gold*, winner of the 1991 Kentucky Derby and 1992 Pimlico Special.

• *Turkoman*, champion older horse of 1986; plus a high-class international brigade embracing Cacoethes, Dare and Go, Saratoga Six, Stella Madrid, Endear, Alydaress, Clabber Girl, and Talinum.

		Polynesian, 1942	Unbreakable / Black Polly
	Native Dancer, 1950	Geisha, 1943	Discovery / Miyako
RAISE A NATIVE, ch, 1961		Case Ace, 1934	Teddy / Sweetheart
	Raise You, 1946	Lady Glory, 1934	American Flag / Beloved
MR. PROSPECTOR, b h, January 28, 1970		Nasrullah, 1940	Nearco / Mumtaz Begum
	Nashua, 1952	Segula, 1942	Johnstown / Sekhmet
GOLD DIGGER, b, 1962		Count Fleet, 1940	Reigh Count / Quickly
	Sequence, 1946	Miss Dogwood, 1939	Bull Dog / Myrtlewood

1st dam: GOLD DIGGER, b, 1962-1990. Bred by Brownell and Leslie Combs II (Ky). Raced 3 yrs, 35 sts, 10 wins, $127,255. Won Gallorette S (twice), Columbiana H, Yo Tambien H, Marigold S; 2nd Kentucky Oaks; 3rd Matron S. Dam of 12 named foals, 7 rnrs, 7 wnrs, 3 sw.

1969: **Search for Gold**, b c, by Raise a Native. Raced 1 yr, 5 sts, 1 win, $16,020. 2nd National Stallion S. Sire of 594 foals, 17 sw, AEI 1.02. Died 1992.

1970: **MR. PROSPECTOR**, b c, by Raise a Native. Bred by Leslie Combs II (Ky). Raced 2 yrs, 14 sts, 7 wins, $112,171. Won Gravesend H, Whirlaway H (NTR, GS, 6 furlongs in 1:08.60); 2nd Carter H (gr. II), Firecracker H (gr. III), Royal Poinciana H, Derby Trial; 3rd Paumonok H (gr. III). NTR, GP, 6 furlongs in 1:07.80. Sire of 1,156 foals, 168 sw, 4.13 AEI. Died 1999.

1971: **GOLD STANDARD**, b c, by Sea-Bird. Raced 9 yrs, 80 sts, 7 wins, $163,542. Won Cortez H (T), Los Feliz S; 2nd South Bay H (T); 3rd Arcadia H (gr. III).

1972: Myrtlewood Lass, b f, by Ribot. Raced 2 yrs, 14 sts, 2 wins, $19,722. Dam of 8 foals, 7 rnrs, 5 wnrs, including **Rathman** ($54,567), **Timber Way** ($45,462), **Amelia Bearhart** ($24,211, Broodmare of the Year in Can in 1996). Granddam of **CHIEF BEARHART**, **EXPLOSIVE RED**, **RUBY RANSOM**, **Memorized**, **Silver Joy**, **Sundown Serenade**. Died 1994.

1973: Kentucky Gold, b c, by Raise a Native. Raced 1 yr, 7 sts, 1 win, $5,950. Sire of 234 foals, AEI 0.62.

1974: Certain Class, ch f, by Raise a Native. Unraced. Died 1976.

1975: No report received.

1976: Red Ryder, ch c, by Raise a Native. Unraced. Sire in SAf.

1977: **LILLIAN RUSSELL**, ch f, by Prince John. Raced 2 yrs, 16 sts, 7 wins, $144,567. Won Cleopatra H, Mint Julep H; 2nd Rampart H, Busher H, Susan's Girl H (T), Kentucky Cardinal H. Dam of 10 foals, 3 rnrs, 3 wnrs. Granddam of **IGOTRHYTHM**, **SLEW GIN FIZZ**, **LIL'S BOY**, **Majestic Madge**, **Yubraalee**, **The First Lady**.

1978: Barren.

1979: Yukon, b c, by Northern Dancer. Unraced. Sire of 372 foals, 16 sw, AEI 1.23. ($1,400,000 keejul yrlg).

1980: No report received.

1981: Gold Mine, b f, by Raise a Native. Unraced. Dam of 7 foals, 5 rnrs, 2 wnrs, including **ETIQUETTE** ($139,857). Granddam of **AMERICAN CHAMP**, **QUEEN TUTTA**, **Short Engagement**. Died 1995.

1982: Twenty Four Karat, b c, by Exclusive Native. Raced 2 yrs, 5 sts, 1 win, $21,380. Sent to NZ 1992.

1983: Barren.

1984: Vaal Reef, ch c, by Raise a Native. Unraced. Sire in India.

A prejudice against Alydar's sons as sires of sires cropped up early and, to a large extent, has been justified, although Easy Goer might well have broken through but for his early death at age eight due to anaphylactic shock. (Autopsy results also revealed that Easy Goer was suffering from cancer, but that the cancer was most likely not related to the stallion's death, although it would eventually have been fatal.)

The aforementioned Raise a Native classic

winner Majestic Prince was less of a sire than many might have expected, but he did get thirty-three stakes winners (nine percent), including the important and enduring international stallion Majestic Light (sixty-nine stakes winners, nine percent). Recent horses tracing to Majestic Prince in tail male include the international turf star Val's Prince and the American juvenile champion Maria's Mon.

Various other sons of Raise a Native did their part to flesh out the sire line further, in several cases succeeding in the stud beyond their racing status. These include Raise a Cup (sire of champion filly Before Dawn), Native Royalty, Marshua's Dancer, Raise a Bid, and Son Ange.

A Prospector Like No Other

We come now, at last, to Raise a Native's signature son at stud, Mr. Prospector. Bred by Leslie Combs II, master of Spendthrift Farm, Mr. Prospector was produced from the stakes-winning Nashua filly Gold Digger. Gold Digger traced to Spendthrift foundation mare Myrtlewood, a family from which also came another outstanding modern stallion in Seattle Slew.

In 1971, when Mr. Prospector was one of the anticipated headliners for the perennial leading consignor at the Keeneland summer sale, the trainer Jimmy Croll had been asked to look for a colt that might make a sire prospect after his racing career. This assignment came from A. I. (Butch) Savin, a Northeastern businessman who had established Aisco Farm in Ocala, Florida. Savin was savvy enough to have picked up on the fact that the only way for a Florida farm to stand a top stallion was for the farm owner to have raced the horse and be willing to turn down offers from Kentucky if the colt were good enough to elicit them.

Had Savin assigned Hercules himself to the task, he could not have been flushed with better results. Croll loved the Raise a Native—Gold Digger colt and, although his own experience was such that he could not look up once bidding got into six figures, his patron, Savin, went to a sale-topping $220,000 to buy the colt.

We recall Mr. Prospector at three as a classy and stylish, medium-sized bay, although as he grew older he often was described as having a plain sort of head. This perhaps was due in part to the casual ears which he got from Nashua, courtesy of the latter's grandsire, Johnstown.

Our confidence in the personal memory of Mr. Prospector's attractiveness is buoyed, of course, by the thought that "plain" sorts rarely top the Keeneland summer sale!

Once Savin had made his big move, Croll had to deal with the animal. This proved part pleasure, and part pressure. Named Mr. Prospector, the colt was possessed of startling speed. Had it not been for Croll's intuitive horsemanship, though, Mr. Prospector might well have passed into history as a lovely prospect who broke down early. His opportunity at stud would have been seriously diminished. At the time he was deemed ready for his debut, at Saratoga, the exercise rider told Croll that the colt had taken a couple of bad steps. X rays showed nothing, but Croll was not convinced. He called for additional X rays, from different angles, and at last a tiny flaw was spotted. Thus, Mr. Prospector was put aside rather than be entered in a maiden race that week — an eventuality that might have brought on a more serious problem.

The other aspect of that development, however, was that Croll had so unseasoned a prospect on his hands that he knew it defied experience to push the colt to the Kentucky Derby. When Mr. Prospector flashed an incredible 1:07 4/5 for six furlongs early in his three-year-old season, though,

Mr. Prospector

Savin was stricken with Derby Fever. The victory of his own Royal and Regal in the Florida Derby was not so intoxicating as the allowance race victory of Mr. Prospector. Urged to carry on — or else — Croll sent Mr. Prospector to Kentucky, where he dropped back after leading early during an allowance race of one and one-sixteenth miles. Then, in the Derby Trial, with his Kentucky Derby status probably still up in the air, Mr. Prospector came through the stretch, tiring and failing, with his tongue lolling out the side of his mouth. X rays revealed a chipped bone in the right front ankle. Croll, who knew that pushing the colt toward the Derby was the wrong thing, had the most ironic of all choices to explain to the understandably enthusiastic owner: "I'm glad to say we can't do the thing you wanted most," or, "I'm sorry to say we must now do the thing I knew we should."

Croll years later told the author that he regretted that he could never get Mr. Prospector to the races at two and that the horse was never completely sound as an older campaigner. It could hardly have made him a better sire, but, of course, a lifelong horseman would wonder just what sort of beast did he have at his command. Croll arguably had saved Mr. Prospector as a pivotal stallion by his acumen when the horse was two, and he gently steered him through a later campaign, during which the horse won two sprint stakes, the Gravesend and Whirlaway Handicaps. Mr. Prospector once saw greatness from an angle other than what he might prefer, i.e., when Forego roared past him to win the seven-furlong Carter Handicap by two and a quarter lengths. All told, Mr. Prospector, the erstwhile Derby candidate, won seven of fourteen races and earned $112,171 — barely half his purchase price.

Savin had what he had wanted, a sire prospect for his farm in Florida.

Mr. Prospector's first crop began to implant the reality that sentiment is one thing, a really first-rate stallion is another. That first crop included It's in the Air, whom Wolfson purchased for $300,000 the day before she won the Arlington-Washington Lassie Stakes. It's in the Air shared juvenile filly championship honors with Candy Eclair in 1978.

It's in the Air and other nice stakes winners attracted the notice of knowledgeable horseman and sportsman Peter Brant. Mr. Prospector, Brant suggested to Seth Hancock of the prestigious Claiborne Farm in Kentucky, was a horse worth considering. The Florida connection could hardly turn its back on such an opportunity. Mr. Prospector was acquired as a new Claiborne stallion for 1981. He remained an honored member of the Claiborne stallion roster until his death in 1999.

There was, for a time, an understandable stigma against Mr. Prospector getting stayers. Hancock himself remarked to the author in the paddock prior to the 1982 Belmont Stakes that he had his doubts about a Mr. Prospector getting a mile and a half. A few minutes later, Henryk de Kwiatkowski's Conquistador Cielo, son of Mr. Prospector, won his Belmont Stakes by fourteen lengths. Winner of the one-mile Metropolitan earlier that week, Conquistador Cielo wound up as Horse of the Year and became a lastingly successful Claiborne stallion. (He was syndicated on an evaluation of more than $36 million during an early-1980s boom in the bloodstock market.)

The parameters of Mr. Prospector had thus been set: A quickly developing juvenile filly champion was within his scope, and so was a colt asked to get the greatest distance required of a classic contender in America. For more than two decades now, the name Mr. Prospector has been affixed to the best, and, in the true tradition of the great

Native Dancer, they come in various shapes, sizes, and specialities, and the star sons at the race track have followed up as important stallions.

Before his death at twenty-nine, Mr. Prospector had scaled the heights to supplant Northern Dancer and Nijinsky II as the all-time leader in number of stakes winners. By the end of 1999, Mr. Prospector was the sire of 168 stakes winners (sixteen percent). Incorporating those already mentioned, Mr. Prospector's most accomplished runners include the following:

• *Conquistador Cielo*, 1982 Belmont winner and Horse of the Year.

• *It's in the Air*, 1978 co-champion juvenile filly.

• *Forty Niner*, 1987 juvenile champion and winner of the Travers, etc., at three.

• *Ravinella*, Guineas winner in England and France and champion in both countries.

• *Gulch*, 1988 sprint champion but placed as well in the Belmont.

• *Rhythm*, 1989 American juvenile champion.

• *Queena*, 1991 American older distaff champion.

• *Golden Attraction*, 1995 juvenile filly champion.

• *Gold Beauty*, 1982 sprint champion (dam of Dayjur and Maplejinsky, and granddam of Sky Beauty).

• *Eillo*, 1984 sprint champion.

• *Tank's Prospect*, Preakness winner.

• *Mogambo*, Champagne Stakes winner.

• *Gone West*, Dwyer, Gotham, Withers Stakes winner.

• *Afleet*, Canadian Horse of the Year.

• *Seeking the Gold*, $2-million earner.

• *Fappiano*, Metropolitan Handicap winner.

• Other European champions and/or classic winners Kingmambo, Woodman, Machiavellian, Coup de Genie, Tersa, Distant View, and Ta Rib.

Mr. Prospector is the broodmare sire of 179 stakes winners, through 1999. Unlike many old fellows with impressive figures on that side, however, he has such standing as a sire of sires that his daughters cannot overwhelm his sons in producing excellence.

Again, to summarize, the distinction of Mr. Prospector's sons at stud is illustrated (but not circumscribed) by the following highlights:

• *Woodman*, sire of sixty-two stakes winners (seven percent), including Preakness-Belmont winner and champion Hansel, Preakness winner and champion Timber Country, English classic winner and champion Bosra Sham, French classic winner and champion Hector Protector, Japanese sprinter-miler champion Hishi Akebono, and others.

• *Fappiano*, sire of forty-eight stakes winners (twelve percent), including Kentucky Derby-Breeders' Cup Classic winner Unbridled, sprint champion Rubiano, juvenile champion Tasso, Florida Derby winner Cryptoclearance, and NYRA Mile winner Quiet American.

• *Forty Niner*, sire of thirty-nine stakes winners (eleven percent), including Belmont winner Editor's Note, Travers winner Coronado's Quest, plus Roar, End Sweep, Ecton Park, Gold Fever, and Marley Vale.

• *Gulch*, sire of thirty stakes winners (eight percent), including Kentucky Derby-Belmont winner and champion Thunder Gulch, Super Derby winner Wallenda, and English One Thousand Guineas winner Harayir.

• *Seeking the Gold*, sire of thirty-six stakes winners (eleven percent), including Eclipse Award winning fillies Flanders and Heavenly Prize, Dubai World Cup winner Dubai Millennium, French-Japanese group I winner Seeking the Pearl, and Florida Derby winner Cape Town.

• *Miswaki*, sire of seventy-six stakes winners (nine percent), including American Horse of the Year Black Tie Affair, Prix de l'Arc de Triomphe winner Urban Sea, and Prix de l'Abbaye winner Kistena.

Mr. Prospector

• **Gone West**, sire of forty-six stakes winners (ten percent), including two-time Breeders' Cup Mile winner Da Hoss, English Two Thousand Guineas winner Zafonic, mile world-record setter Elusive Quality, plus West by West, Grand Slam, Lassigny, Pembroke, and Mr. Greeley.

• **Kingmambo**, young sire of Belmont Stakes-Travers-Futurity winner Lemon Drop Kid and Japan Cup winner El Condor Pasa, plus the 2000 English Two Thousand Guineas winner Kings Best.

• **Conquistador Cielo**, sire of fifty-nine stakes winners (nine percent), including $2.8-million-earner Marquetry (sire of champion Artax) and Jockey Club Gold Cup winner Wagon Limit.

• **Crafty Prospector**, sire of sixty-nine stakes winners (eleven percent), including Crafty Friend, Miss Golden Circle, and Robyn Dancer.

• **Machiavellian**, sire of twenty-seven stakes winners (eleven percent), including Dubai World Cup winner Almutawakel and French Two Thousand Guineas winner Vettori.

• **Afleet**, sire of forty-five stakes winners (ten percent), including grade I winners Twist Afleet and Flat Fleet Feet.

There are various other sons of Mr. Prospector in that generation who have made notable marks at stud nationally or regionally, among them Jade Hunter, Allen's Prospect, Carson City, Distinctive Pro, Northern Prospect, and Two Punch (sire of Smoke Glacken and Punch Line). The returns will continue to pour in, for *The Blood-Horse Stallion Register* of 2000 lists 110 sons of Mr. Prospector at stud.

The next generation has been active for some years already and promises a strong future. Sons of Fappiano particularly have charged into the classic/championship scene of late: Unbridled has already sired Kentucky Derby winner Grindstone, champion Banshee Breeze, and Breeders' Cup Juvenile winners Unbridled's Song and Anees; Cryptoclearance is the sire of Belmont Stakes winner and older male champion Victory Gallop; and Quiet American is the sire of Derby-Preakness winner and champion Real Quiet and distaff champion Hidden Lake.

Then, too, the record of the Mr. Prospectors at the races was still being compiled as the 21st Century began. As these chapters were written, early in the year 2000, the Mr. Prospector colt Fusaichi Pegasus — a $4-million Keeneland yearling — had emerged as the Kentucky Derby winner and was perhaps headed for the Triple Crown. At the same time, the stallion career of the next generation's Kingmambo was gaining even more momentum. Mr. Prospector's son Fusaichi Pegasus won the Kentucky Derby the same day another son, Kingmambo, a French classic winner, had been toasted as the sire of the English Two Thousand Guineas winner, Kings Best.

Fusaichi Pegasus was bred by Arthur Hancock III, owner of Stone Farm, and Robert McNair, owner of Stonerside Farm. The two breeding operations are neighbors of each other and are also neighbors of Claiborne Farm in Paris, Kentucky. Hancock sold a portion of his farm to McNair, a figure looming large in American sports, not only for his superb and growing collection of bloodstock but for his bold acquisition of a franchise to replace the Oilers of the National Football League in his adopted city of Houston, Texas.

Fusaichi Pegasus was foaled from Angel Fever, a Danzig mare which McNair and Hancock had acquired from the Loblolly Stable dispersal at Keeneland for $525,000.

The Mr. Prospector colt was coveted by the leading buyers at the Keeneland July select yearling sale of 1998, so much so that the Coolmore team joined with newcomer Satish Sanan to avoid bidding against each other. Stunningly, this confident combine was outbid by the iconoclastic Japanese entrepreneur Fusao Sekiguchi, who bid $4-million dollars and afterward was not timid about suggesting this was at least $1 million below his limit. Sekiguchi likes to name horses by using the first syllable of his own name with "ichi", which in Japanese means best or No. 1. Combining that with some flying imagery gives him a personally gratifying name. As an earlier example, his Fusaichi Concorde won the Japanese Derby in 1996.

Fusaichi Pegasus was selected with the help of the buyer's Kentucky adviser, trainer John Ward, then sent to the renowned Neil Drysdale, a Hall of Fame trainer whose record included a superb campaign with the injury-prone champion A.P. Indy — also Japanese-owned. By the time the exceedingly handsome Fusaichi Pegasus arrived at Kentucky Derby Day in the spring of 2000, he had created almost as many headlines for such antics as rearing up and sitting down on the backstretch as for facile victories, including his romp in the Wood Memorial. He was soon seen, however, to have been transformed from an exuberant youth into a powerfully efficient racing machine, and his gallop through and around traffic to win the one and a quarter-mile Kentucky Derby was more than an exclamation point to the career of Mr. Prospector. It was an emphatic reminder that, twenty-seven years after his own failure in the Derby Trial, the spirit of the stallion was not about to abandon the cherished Downs.

So, the Native Dancer-Raise a Native-Mr. Prospector branch still thrives, nearing a century since the career of the line's nominal founder, Phalaris. ❖

WORLDWIDE
INFLUENCES

Northern Dancer

 he Japan-based international publication *Futurity* in early 2000 published its annual resume of the world's top racehorses. Of 146 champions and other grade/group I winners of 1999 highlighted, sixty-five represented the Northern Dancer sire line and 114 had Northern Dancer somewhere in their pedigrees. The survey embraced North America, England, Ireland, France, Italy, Germany, Japan, Australia, Hong Kong, and Dubai.

Thus, nearly four decades after he was foaled in what then was regarded a secondary breeding land, Canadian-bred Northern Dancer appeared in the pedigrees of seventy-eight percent of a contemporary group of distinguished runners around the world. Forty-five percent traced to him in tail male.

How a chunky little Canadian bay with splashy white markings came to have such status is perhaps the signature tale of international racing and breeding in the last semester of the 20th Century. As would be expected, great horses, great horsemen, and that essential ingredient of luck had their roles to play.

The author, while still not quite an official adult, was privileged to introduce Northern Dancer to readers of *The Blood-Horse* magazine. This came via a standard report in a section of the weekly magazine then styled "Stakes & Horses" in

the summer of 1963. Northern Dancer had won the $10,000-added Summer Stakes at a mile at Fort Erie, following Pierlou as the second stakes winner in the first crop by Nearctic. Looking at this report today, we note the omission of such phrases as "future classic winner," or "great stallion prospect." Space, we can only conclude, must have been exceedingly tight in that issue.

The young stallion Nearctic resulted from an impressive rise in fortunes, both in business and the Turf, for a native son of Ottawa, Ontario, one Edward Plunkett Taylor. Son of a military man, E. P. Taylor was born in 1901 and was of a time, place, and acumen to launch into a burgeoning career after World War I. He noted that the Ontario brewing industry was fragmented, so he began borrowing to buy up small companies and consolidate them. Profitability followed. Some years later, he caused the same pattern to unfold in Ontario racing, with the result that one of the top racetracks in North America, Woodbine, was born in the 1950s. Again, where many little businesses had struggled, a few large ones would flourish.

Taylor's liking of horse racing, accompanied by sufficient wherewithal, led to the formation of Cosgrave Stable in 1936. He later bought a farm that was known as National Stud, although it was privately owned, and in time he changed the name to Windfields Farm. In Taylor's mind, and heart, was conceived the personal conviction that high-class international Thoroughbreds could be raised there. As this notion grew, so did his efforts to prove it correct. The signature image of Canada — shined by Hollywood — was of a frozen climate with Mounties on horseback. Well, the horseback part was all right with Taylor, and no question the winters are formidable, but horses are highly adaptable, and, anyway, the summers are warm and the autumns lovely in and around Toronto.

By 1952, Taylor was playing in the top levels of breeding and racing. He had been one of a small group that joined with Bull Hancock to try to purchase Nasrullah for Kentucky. Purse levels in Canada did not justify any bloodstock of that ilk, but Taylor — with such lieutenants as Gil Darlington and later Peter Poole and Joe Thomas — had an extraordinary knack for taking inexpensive animals and breeding upward from them. In 1952, though, he was not dealing only in inexpensive stock. He told friend and bloodstock agent George Blackwell to purchase him the best mare in the Newmarket December sale. Blackwell, who came to admire Taylor as "the most dynamic man I ever knew," made a career of spotting bargains at sales. Turn him loose with top dollar, though, and he would get results, too. The 1952 Newmarket sale was held in an atmosphere of massive international raiding. The gross for the sale dropped to the lowest since the war year of 1943, and the English and Irish breeders seemed uneasy, or unable, to purchase to replenish individual broodmare bands. The British Bloodstock Agency accounted for more than one-fifth of the aggregate prices, largely for exports. The leading buyer was Frenchman Maurice de Rothschild, and groups from as far afield as Peru and Australia were active buyers. It fell, though, to the Canadian Taylor to pay top dollar, 10,500 guineas, to Martin Benson's Beech House Stud for Lady Angela. The mare was a daughter of the great Hyperion and was in foal to Beech House's grand stallion Nearco.

Taylor left the mare in England to foal, since he was determined that she be returned to Nearco (sire of Nasrullah). Benson said a season would be available, but only if dollars were sent to pay for it, to which Taylor replied to Blackwell: "That's all right. I'm not breaking any law. Perhaps he is {Canadian}, but I'm not."

Taylor's first Nearco—Lady Angela foal was the English-bred Empire Day, and the colt would not have encouraged the thought that he would one day be connected to this ultra-masculine business of widespread sire lines. He was a light-boned, weak chestnut, and although he later got a nice Canadian stakes winner named E. Day, Empire Day had to be counted a disappointment.

Not so the next Nearco—Lady Angela colt, the Canadian-bred named Nearctic. Taylor sent him to New York at two, where he defeated a nice field including Clem and Amarullah in the Saratoga Special of 1956. Nearctic was no match for the likes of Bold Ruler and King Hairan later that summer and fall, but he was spotted carefully for the next two years and was a nice stakes winner on both sides of the border. Nearctic was Horse of the Year at four in Canada.

At one point, the Argentine-born trainer Horatio Luro [refer to Princequillo chapter] was asked to try to solve Nearctic's speed-crazy tendencies. Luro turned to the French jockey Rae Johnstone, who was visiting America between European racing seasons that winter. Luro was prescribing long, slow gallops, but his exercise rider was unable to impose this regimen on

		Pharos, 1920	Phalaris Scapa Flow
	Nearco, 1935		
		Nogara, 1928	Havresac II Catnip
NEARCTIC, br, 1954			
		Hyperion, 1930	Gainsborough Selene
	Lady Angela, 1944		
		Sister Sarah, 1930	Abbots Trace Sarita
NORTHERN DANCER, b h, May 27, 1961			
		Polynesian, 1942	Unbreakable Black Polly
	Native Dancer, 1950		
		Geisha, 1943	Discovery Miyako
NATALMA, b, 1957			
		Mahmoud, 1933	Blenheim II Mah Mahal
	Almahmoud, 1947		
		Arbitrator, 1937	Peace Chance Mother Goose

1st dam: Natalma, b, 1957-1985. Bred by Mrs. E.H. Augustus and Daniel G. Van Clief (Va). Raced 2 yrs, 7 sts, 3 wins, $16,015. 3rd Spinaway S. Dam of 14 named foals, 12 rnrs, 10 wnrs, 4 sw.

1961: NORTHERN DANCER, b c, by Nearctic. Bred by E.P. Taylor (Can). Raced 2 yrs, 18 sts, 14 wins, $580,647. Horse of the Year and champion 2yo colt in Can, champion 3yo colt. Won Kentucky Derby, Preakness S, Blue Grass S, Florida Derby, Flamingo S, Queen's Plate, Carlton S, Coronation Futurity, Remsen S, Summer S; 2nd Cup and Saucer S, Vandal S; 3rd Belmont S. Sire of 645 foals, 146 sw, 4.11 AEI. Died 1990.

1962: NATIVE VICTOR, dk b g, by Victoria Park. Raced 8 yrs, 105 sts, 18 wins, $71,711. Won Kingarvie S, Fairbank H, Canadian H; 2nd Greenwood H, Valedictory H, Kingarvie S, R. James Speers Memorial H; 3rd Durham Cup H, Autumn H, Horometer S.

1963: Arctic Dancer, b f, by Nearctic. Raced 1 yr, 2 sts, 0 wins, $2,500. 2nd My Dear S. Dam of 8 foals, 6 rnrs, 5 wnrs, including **LA PREVOYANTE** ($572,417, Horse of the Year and champion older female in Can, champion 2yo filly in USA and Can). Granddam of **DRAPEAU TRICOLORE, DAMPIERRE, DANSEUR DE CORDE, DANSEUR ETOILE, L'Anse Au Griffon**. Died 1976.

1964: REGAL DANCER, gr g, by Grey Monarch. Raced 6 yrs, 49 sts, 13 wins, $51,570. Won Jacques Cartier S.

1965: Dk b/br f, by Nearctic. Died 1966.

1966: Northern Native, dkb/br c, by Nearctic. Raced 2 yrs, 13 sts, 4 wins, $19,150. 2nd Plate Trial; 3rd Toronto Cup H (T). Sent to Eng 1978. Sire of 180 foals, 7 sw, AEI 1.26.

1967: Barren.

1968: Northern Ace, b c, by Nearctic. Raced 3 yrs, 22 sts, 5 wins, $15,960. Sent to Swe 1972. Died 1979.

1969: Native Era, dkb/br f, by Victorian Era. Unraced. Dam of 9 foals, 7 rnrs, 6 wnrs, including **Northern Sister** ($140,952).

Granddam of **MARATHON, GRAY NOT BAY, BARZANA DANA, Dancing Success, Sky Trist**.

1970: No report received.

1971: Nostrum, b c, by Dr. Fager. Raced 2 yrs, 13 sts, 4 wins, $52,226. 2nd Sport Page H, Keystone Inaugural H. Sire of 304 foals, 16 sw, AEI 1.47.

1972: Transalantic, ch c, by Nearctic. Raced 2 yrs in Fr, 3 sts, 1 win, $9,833. Sire in Japan.

1973: No report received.

1974: Spring Adieu, b f, by Buckpasser. Raced 1 yr, 7 sts, 3 wins, $13,757. Dam of 12 foals, 9 rnrs, 2 wnrs. Granddam of **DANEHILL, EAGLE EYED, HARPIA, EUPHONIC, YOUTHFUL LEGS, PASSING TRICK, Needham Star, Anziyan, Chayim, Lady's Delight**. Died 1994.

1975: No report received.

1976: Tai, dkb/br c, by Buckpasser. Raced 1 yr, 5 sts, 1 win, $11,615. 3rd Plate Trial (R). Sire of 104 foals, AEI 0.73.

1977: Barren.

1978: Raise the Standard, b f, by Hoist the Flag. Unraced. Dam of 11 foals, 6 rnrs, 3 wnrs, including **COUP DE FOLIE** ($67,570). Granddam of **COUP DE GENIE, MACHIAVELLIAN, ORPEN, EXIT TO NOWHERE, JULES, HYDRO CALIDO, ETTERBY PARK, OCEAN OF WISDOM**.

1979: Polar Sky, b c, by Snow Knight. Raced 1 yr in Ire, 1 st, 0 wins, $0. Died 1982. ($550,000 keejul yrlg).

1980: Barren.

1981: BORN A LADY, b f, by Tentam. Raced 1 yr, 12 sts, 4 wins, $57,544. Won Pearl Necklace S (R); 2nd Drop Me A Note S (R). Dam of 10 foals, 7 rnrs, 6 wnrs, including **ARROWTOWN** ($330,765), **Lady Bonanza** ($870,008, in Japan). ($725,000 keejul yrlg).

1982: Barren.

Nearctic. Johnstone did. Improvement came with finesse, for the rider known as Le Crocodil was willing to spend as much as an hour in the morning hacking Nearctic at Santa Anita to settle him. It was not the last time the Luro touch would be a positive influence upon the House of Nearctic.

Nearctic carried up to 130 pounds successfully and stretched out to win as important a race as the Michigan Mile, and he went to stud at Windfields with twenty-one wins in forty-seven starts and earnings of $152,384. His first book of mares included the classy Natalma, a daughter of the great Native Dancer. Taylor had purchased Natalma for $35,000 at the Saratoga yearling sale of 1958. Natalma was bred by Daniel G. Van Clief and Mrs. E. H. Augustus and was out of Almahmoud (also dam of Cosmah and thus grand-dam of the distinguished sire Halo). She was the second-priciest filly sold at Saratoga that August.

Luro trained Natalma, who needed some of the same morning gentling treatment that her future mate, Nearctic, had required. The filly also had to be sent to the University of Pennsylvania for surgical removal of a knee chip. Before all that, however, she had proven a high-class filly, finishing first ahead of Irish Jay in the Spinaway Stakes, although disqualified after ducking from the whip in the stretch.

The Kentucky Oaks was on the masterful Luro's schedule for Natalma the next spring, but the blaze-faced bay filly came back lame from a splendid work. It was determined that a calcium deposit in the knee which had undergone surgery was causing pain. She was retired with three official wins from seven starts and earnings of $16,015. Thus, she was available for the first book of the strongly built brown colt Nearctic.

Her first foal was born at Windfields late the following spring, on May 27, 1961. Call him a late foal, call him small, but call him Northern Dancer.

It is worth noting that Nearctic was far from a one-star sire. In Canada, he turned out a parade of national champions, some sleek and bright and chestnut, others a bit plainer and brown or bay, but few chunky little fellows splashed with white. Nearctic's influence broadened after he and Northern Dancer were moved to the new Maryland division of Windfields. Nearctic sired forty-nine stakes winners (fifteen percent), including the English Two Thousand Guineas winner Nonoalco, the Belmont Stakes runner-up Cool Reception, and Matron Stakes winner Cold Comfort. Among Nearctic's other sons at stud were Explodent (whose sixty-five stakes winners included Explosive Red, Country Queen, Mi Selecto, and English Two Thousand Guineas runner-up Exbourne); and Icecapade (whose seventy-three stakes winners include Clever Trick [sire of Phone Trick, who, in turn, sired Horse of the Year Favorite Trick] and Breeders' Cup Classic winner Wild Again — themselves each sire of more than fifty stakes winners and also vehicles of continuing sire-line branches as of the year 2000).

In his efforts to boost Ontario breeding and racing, Taylor had by far the largest breeding and racing operation, but he knew it would take other stables to make a healthy circuit. He had hit on an idea that enabled him to market some horses to defray expenses, help fill cards and stakes schedules at Ontario tracks, and still leave his own racing stable with plenty of incoming prospects. The formula was a pre-priced yearling sale at Windfields (earlier National Stud), a longish drive out of Toronto in the town of Oshawa. Potential buyers, many of them Montreal and Toronto businessmen, were invited to have cocktails and inspect the entire crop of yearlings, each of which had an announced, set price. Once the buyers had collectively signed up to purchase half of the crop,

Northern Dancer

the sale was ended. No one could say Taylor was selling only culls, no one could say they were being "bid up" by a monopolist, but still Taylor did not ravage his own resources.

Despite a physical stature that could almost invite the word "runt," Northern Dancer was impressive enough in his muscling, powerful quarters, and manner, that he was very highly priced for a Canadian-bred yearling at the time. Clearly, at $25,000, he was a colt Taylor was not willing to part with unless someone were willing to pay top dollar in the context of the time and place. No one did.

Luro, and Blackwell, recalled trying to interest Morris Fleming in Northern Dancer, both of them appreciating the colt's conformation despite his lack of height. Luro, having a healthy respect for both the sire and dam, both of whom he had trained, was particularly tough to dissuade by size. Fleming, however, thought that if one were going to spend a lot of money on one yearling, it would be good to have salvage value if things went poorly. Thus, he opted for a filly, who, named Muskoka, began chasing Northern Dancer futilely in their early races the following summer.

Taylor sold a great many major stakes winners — and future bulwarks in Canadian breeding — but he got by with offering but not selling Northern Dancer, just as he had with Nearctic.

Northern Dancer was trained at two by T. P. (Peaches) Fleming, who is often recalled as an assistant to Luro but who had a division of Windfields horses in his own name. The muscular, blocky Northern Dancer came out on August 2, 1963, and won a five and a half-furlong maiden race at Fort Erie. At that time, Fort Erie, along with Woodbine and Greenwood, was owned by the Taylor-led Ontario Jockey Club, and was sort of a Saratoga of Canada — an August track near the resort town of Niagara Falls and appreciated for its brightly floral infield. Northern Dancer then was second in the Vandal Stakes before stretching to a mile to win the Summer Stakes on grass. This gave him three races in a month, all at Fort Erie.

As Luro recounted the story for author Joe Hirsch in *The Grand Senor*, he cut short his annual French visit during the hay-fever season to return to Canada, with Northern Dancer the main reason. Whether this version unduly stresses the Senor's prescience or not, Northern Dancer had a month off. At Woodbine, however, he was beaten by 90-1 shot Grand Garcon in the one and one-sixteenth-mile Cup and Saucer Stakes. (Peaches Fleming might have grumbled to himself, "I didn't need El Grand One to figure out how to get this horse beat!") The Ontario circuit tended to test two-year-olds a bit more quickly for distance than the top United States juvenile races. Northern Dancer then won an allowance race at one mile and seventy yards, and took the Coronation Futurity by six and a quarter lengths at one and one-eighth miles. It was still only October 12, the same day Roman Brother won New York's one-mile Champagne Stakes in his first start at more than seven furlongs.

Northern Dancer, who had been ridden in four of his first six races by the young Ron Turcotte, was guided by an Ontario regular named James Fitzsimmons when he dropped back to seven furlong three weeks later to win the Carleton Stakes at Greenwood. It was later recalled by Luro that, after that race in the mud, he discerned the beginnings of a quarter crack on the right hind hoof. Nevertheless, this obvious Canadian juvenile champion was sent to New York for two more races in mid- and late November, fitted with a bar shoe. At a mile, he came from off the pace to defeat Futurity winner Bupers by eight lengths in an allowance race, and then led from the start to win the Remsen, which then was run at a mile, on November 27. The great rider Manuel Ycaza rode him in both his New York races.

Tommy Trotter was then assigning weights for The Jockey Club's Experimental Free Handicap. It was a disruptive year, with Raise a Native having been brilliant early, but retired before running as much as six furlongs, while Hurry to Market came on late to win the Garden State Stakes at one and one-sixteenth miles. Trotter put top weight of 126 on Raise a Native and a pound less on Hurry to Market. Northern Dancer was hardly ignored, being assigned 123 pounds, as sixth-ranking colt.

In hindsight, it is difficult to reconcile the decision to carry on with the New York races once Northern Dancer had begun to have problems with a hoof. One possibility that seems heretical from this distance is that Taylor and Luro harbored such doubts about the colt's ultimate potential that maximizing what he could accomplish at two became the overriding strategy. There is also the possibility, of course, that Taylor was not aware of the quarter crack (a split in the hoof wall, indicating pressure from within), that Luro had been dealing with it successfully, and regarded it as part of his job.

By the end of the campaign, though, a decision had to be made. Joe Thomas, Taylor's sort of all-around breeding and racing manager, was conservative, and Luro had no ready response to the suggestion that time, and only time, was the solution for a quarter crack. A van was ordered. Northern Dancer would go back to Toronto, and, one presumes, the summer jewel of Toronto, the Queen's Plate, would be the target for a colt who otherwise might have had Kentucky Derby potential.

Even at the time Nearctic suffered from a quar-ter crack problem, Luro had heard vague stories about the condition being treated with vulcanized patches. At the time, however, he went with the time-honored solution of giving the hoof time to grow out, like a fingernail. About the time Northern Dancer was scheduled to begin the trip back to Toronto in 1963, Luro read of blacksmith Bill Bane's success in treating the quarter crack of a trotter named Adios Jr., who subsequently won several races. As retold by Hirsch, Luro called a friend, trainer Laz Barrera, got encouraging details, and put the proposition to Taylor. The van back home was cancelled, Bane was flown to New York and, with an acetylene torch, placed on Northern Dancer the vulcanized rubber patch which would become known as the "Bane Patch."

Bane assured Luro that he could begin training the colt normally after a week of walking and that the hoof would grow out and the patch would get to the point of being sloughed off without special maintenance.

Given the later career of Northern Dancer, and the status of Canadian racing at the time, it is irresistible to contemplate the role of the Bane Patch, and Luro's cutting-edge determination, on breeding history. Without the treatment, Northern Dancer might well have rampaged through his division at home the next summer. He also might have been good enough for Taylor to send him back to New York, where in the best autumn races he would have faced older horses Gun Bow and Kelso. The questions are fairly put: Would he have won any race so glamorous as to have a spate of yearlings accepted for the select summer sales in his first crop? Would his prestige have been such as to prompt Taylor to alter his Windfields marketing program and enter a consignment in the Woodbine sale at announced reserves? Without that change, would Vincent O'Brien have traveled to Toronto in

Northern Dancer

the summer of 1968, where he spotted a Northern Dancer colt to be named Nijinsky II? Without Nijinsky II how might the worldwide reputation of Northern Dancer have been altered?

Well, the Bane treatment was applied, and Northern Dancer did have the opportunity to run in the most glamorous of races.

Luro was a master at setting a target and training a horse up to it in the European fashion, rather than racing a horse to peak fitness. Nevertheless, this heavy-eating, chunky little colt seemed likely to need a tightener before the one and one-eighth-mile Flamingo that winter in Florida, so he was given a sprint prep. Chieftain won, and Luro's instructions to jockey Bobby Ussery not to use the whip were forgotten. Northern Dancer suddenly needed his own version of what his sire and dam had needed: He was so soured that he refused to go to the track, so Luro had several mornings of just leading him back and forth in the tree-lined path near the Hialeah racecourse, along with a bit of tranquilizer.

Northern Dancer won the Flamingo, the Florida Derby, and a sprint race in between. The great rider Bill Shoemaker rode him in the two big races, but he was also the regular rider on the West Coast of the impressive Hill Rise. The short-legged, chunky Northern Dancer just could not strike Shoemaker as a better Kentucky Derby mount than the tall, longer-legged Hill Rise. So, Luro selected Bill Hartack to ride Northern Dancer. At Keeneland that spring, the author encountered Luro on a number of occasions, grazing Northern Dancer in the abundant grass patches among barns. Always the Senor expressed satisfaction at the little colt's progress as he blossomed in the verdant spring. (Hill Rise was also on the scene, and his trainer, Bill Finnegan, was equally content.) Northern Dancer was what Hirsch would recall as a "big little horse" by that time, and he and Hartack finessed a handy victory over a moderate field in the one and one-eighth-mile Blue Grass Stakes.

Finally, the Kentucky Derby was at hand. Hill Rise was favored, but the little Northern Dancer proved more nimble, darted to the lead after a mile, and turned back the big strides of the Californian to win by a neck. Canada had a Derby winner — and in record time! The clocking was an even two minutes. Ironically, it reduced the record set by Decidedly, whom Luro had trained two years before for George Pope Jr. — owner of Hill Rise!

Taylor's son, Charles, later succeeded his father and had an impressive run of success as head of Windfields before his death, less than a decade after the death of his father. In 1964, however, Taylor was pursuing stages of his other distinguished career, as an international war correspondent, political journalist, and author. He was amused in recalling that, in Asia, a cable about something called Northern Dancer winning the Derby in two minutes, roses, etc., was viewed suspiciously as some nefarious code. (It probably did not help matters that a colt named The Scoundrel finished third.)

Two weeks later, Hill Rise was favored again for the shorter Preakness, but Northern Dancer brushed him back in the upper stretch and won by two and a quarter lengths. The Scoundrel got up for second.

Now, Canada had not just a Derby winner, but a live candidate for the American Triple Crown. The Belmont was the remaining obstacle, and what a challenge it was. Not since Citation in 1948 had any horse won all three races, though such good ones as Native Dancer, Nashua, Needles, Tim Tam, Carry Back, and Chateaugay had won two-thirds of the series in between. Luro would have preferred to concede. Northern Dancer was, after all, a short-striding little fellow. Getting one and a quarter miles was really something that had shown his wonderful courage, as opposed to his natural proclivity, and now the Belmont loomed at one and a half miles. Taylor was too much the sportsman to turn his back and deny racing the chance to see its new star tested in the most visible, traditional way.

So, Northern Dancer was sent out for the Triple Crown. Hartack apparently felt he was in a no-win situation. Sharing Luro's thought that the distance was beyond the colt in top company, he tried to conserve his speed early. When Northern Dancer flattened out in the stretch, it was easy for non-participants to conjecture that he had become discouraged from being choked down early — as Bold Ruler had under Eddie Arcaro in the Kentucky Derby in 1957. At any rate, Quadrangle gloried in the distance and won by a couple of lengths, and Roman Brother also passed the tired Northern Dancer to be second.

For what it is worth, the author has often repeated — sometimes in heated and losing discussions with Canadians — that believing Northern Dancer "should" have won the Belmont means failing to give him credit for the courage and indomitable spirit he showed in winning the Derby, already at a distance beyond his preference.

Northern Dancer had but one more race. He glided home easily by seven lengths in the Queen's Plate, giving his homeland a glorious and dignified occasion to embrace him. At Belmont Park, Northern Dancer strained a tendon in preparation for a trip to Chicago for the American Derby, with the Travers Stakes a later summer goal. Luro was cautious, of course, but could not get the colt back to 100 percent. Taylor, Luro, and Windfields exec-

utive Thomas concluded the horse should be retired. He went back home to Windfields, Oshawa, Ontario, with full honors, winner of fourteen races from eighteen starts and earnings of $580,647. He was Horse of the Year in Canada and was voted champion three-year-old in this country. Today, a Canadian-bred being so honored would be a matter of pride — without wonderment — at home, but in Northern Dancer's day there was no precedent for a horse bred in Canada being a champion in any division in this country.

A Little Horse, Enduring Greatness

Some of the clay flooring in a section of the Windfields breeding shed was rearranged to help Northern Dancer cover larger mares in the spring of 1965. (He was sometimes described as standing 15.1 hands, although the mark of 15.2 was claimed for him in *The Blood-Horse Stallion Register* by the mid-1980s.) By the summer of 1968, the little stallion was already the sire of his first star, Windfields' flashy chestnut Viceregal, unbeaten at two and Canadian Horse of the Year. The following April, Viceregal was injured in a race at Keeneland, knocking him out of a classic spring that would have seen him facing Majestic Prince and Arts and Letters. Standing in the infield, with frustration still prevalent on Preakness Day, Taylor remarked to us that he regarded Viceregal as the best horse he had ever bred.

Well, a case might be made that this marvelous colt would have been destined to be even better than Northern Dancer. Even so, his tenure as Taylor's best almost certainly would have been short, for waiting in the wings was another Windfields-bred by Northern Dancer, a huge, leggy, powerful reality named Nijinsky II.

So had begun the unfinished symphony. Galloping melodies flowed, one into another, and a crescendo of impressive force for one moment

Northern Dancer

could seem almost meek the next. As has been recognized often, the song of a sire line in Thoroughbred breeding often is the work of a soloist — preserving, surviving. In the glorious work of Northern Dancer, though, it was a repeating and competing crash, and clash, of many cymbals. It was not a question of whether there would be great sons at stud, but how many, and which might emerge as the greatest of all.

We have devoted short individual chapters, found elsewhere, to four of Northern Dancer's sons. Their short-hand credentials are as follows:

• *Nijinsky II*, only English Triple Crown winner of the last sixty-five years; sire of 155 stakes winners, including three Epsom Derby winners and North American Horse of the Year Ferdinand; leading sire in England; leading broodmare sire in North America.

• *Danzig*, three-time leading North American sire, sire of 152 stakes winners, including Dance Smartly, Chief's Crown, Dayjur, Danehill, and Lure.

• *Nureyev*, sire of 111 stakes winners, including American champions Theatrical, Miesque, and others; Prix de l'Arc de Triomphe winner Peintre Celebre; leading sire in France.

• *Sadler's Wells*, Irish classic winner; eight-time leading sire in England/Ireland; sire of 145 stakes winners including Arc winners Montjeu and Carnegie, plus Salsabil, Old Vic, Dream Well, Barathea, In the Wings, and Northern Spur.

(A grandson, Storm Cat, also is featured in an individual chapter.)

That, of course, is but a sampling, for Northern Dancer himself sired 146 stakes winners, a virtuoso twenty-three percent. Twenty-six individuals were regarded as champions in major countries, according to the various criteria for championship designation. Northern Dancer was a remarkable sire of sires, and his sons were also sires of sires. (He was, of course, also a great sire of broodmares, his daughters having produced 219 stakes winners.)

Northern Dancer stood initially in Canada, where the $10,000 stud fee strained prevailing industry economics for even the most admiring of his countrymen. In 1968, Taylor established another division of Windfields, in the gentle, horse-conducive country of Maryland's Eastern Shore. Northern Dancer and Nearctic were moved to that location. In the 1970s, Northern Dancer was syndicated on a valuation of $2,400,000. In time, his success was such that, when he was twenty years old, an offer of $40 million ($1 million per share) was suggested. Windfields and the syndicate turned it down.

Taylor suffered a stroke in 1980 and lapsed into such poor health that he could not participate in any decisions. He eventually became the breeder of record of well over 300 stakes winners, far outstripping any previous breeders' mark. His son, Charles, accepted the challenge and kept Windfields healthy as it became a dominant consignor at Keeneland and other sales, as well as still racing homebreds. Noreen Taylor has chosen to continue Windfields after the death of her husband, Charles Taylor.

Windfields' Maryland farm was sold during the 1980s, but a section was maintained so that Northern Dancer could remain in familiar surroundings. He was retired from breeding at the age of twenty-six in 1987. Three years later, he suffered an attack of colic. At twenty-nine, surgery was not a consideration, and the old patriarch was gently euthanized.

Northern Dancer led the North American sire list in 1971, muscling in amid years led by Bold

Ruler, Round Table, and Hail to Reason. To underscore the ongoing force of Northern Dancer, we find that sons Lyphard and Danzig have led the North American list a total of four times, and grandsons Palace Music, Deputy Minister, and Storm Cat an additional four times, so far. Thus, in the last twenty-nine years of the 1900s, Northern Dancer and his descending sire line produced the North American leading sire a total of nine times.

Truth be told, however, in some ways Northern Dancer was less prominent on his own continent than he would be elsewhere. Even now, those *Futurity* figures cited above are skewed by foreign statistics. While, of all the horses considered in the *Futurity* reprise of 1999, there were seventy-eight percent with Northern Dancer blood and forty-five percent from the sire line, in North America specifically, only twenty-three percent represented the sire line while fifty-seven percent had Northern Dancer somewhere in the pedigrees. (His contemporary Raise a Native accounted for the sire line of thirty-one percent of those American horses and was somewhere in the pedigrees of forty-seven percent.)

The late George Blackwell, the bloodstock agent who had purchased the granddam, observed with inescapable pride over the years as the presence of Northern Dancer seeped more deeply into the make-up of the Turf and of the image of a racehorse: "He changed what good horses could look like. You could look at a horse and know he had Northern Dancer blood in him."

Terence Collier of Fasig-Tipton Company has seen various carriers of that blood — in several generations now — and he also worked with the late John Finney, who was in the stand when Nijinsky II sold. Collier said that "initially it is easy to say that the small size is the legacy of Northern Dancer, but that is not correct. From the start,

they came in all shapes and sizes. The little ones also got horses in all shapes and sizes. From the first, the Northern Joves (sire of Candy Eclair) and the One for Alls (Bring Out the Band, The Very One) got large and small horses."

Collier noted that "what horsemen had to forgive more than anything with the Northern Dancers was the hind leg. That seemed to breed through, regardless of size. There is no question that a knowledgeable European buyer and a knowledgeable American buyer will want a different hind leg. The Americans are more afraid of what they would call a sickle hock. The Europeans would not say they like a sickle hock, but they are more forgiving. They say 'his hocks are a bit behind him.' "

Collier agreed that this characteristic might well have something to do with the heavy European slant toward the great success of the line. It is, presumably, a case of image following function. European horsemen no doubt are more forgiving because they have seen more horses succeed with hocks somewhat "behind them." The fact that horses in Europe race on grass and undulating surfaces perhaps has a role.

Joss Collins of the British Bloodstock Agency did not concur with the generalization about hocks, but agreed that some physical aspects, including flat feet, might have steered Northern Dancer's success toward Europe. Also, "I think Vincent O'Brien found that they were horses you could train for a target, but they were not horses you could just get fit and run them every few weeks." Collins noted that there also was often a reason to be careful "because of wind." He explained that the angle at which the head and neck joined frequently had the potential to restrict airflow, although as one of the team that bought Nureyev and had seen Northern Dancer, he was certainly careful not to overstate any such obser-

Northern Dancer

vation! While in agreement that the good Northern Dancers came large and small, long and short, Collins said the precedent set by Lyphard and other smallish Northern Dancers undoubtedly lent encouragement to buyers and breeders when they did encounter one of the "ponified" ones.

Alec Head, the great French horseman who purchased and trained one of the best Northern Dancers, Lyphard, recalled of the early impression of Northern Dancer: "He was a small horse, but he was all there — everywhere. And it is interesting how inbreeding to him is now working. Marcel Boussac tried that with his Tourbillon blood, but those were fine horses and they got finer and finer and weaker and weaker." Clearly no such regression has impeded the progress of the Northern Dancer blood.

The European connection began early, with Nijinsky II from the second crop. Nijinsky II was followed by two other Epsom Derby winners by Northern Dancer in The Minstrel and Secreto, and Northern Dancer topped the English sire list four times: 1970, 1977, 1983, 1984. In France, Northern Dancer stood as high as second on the sire list. He has been among the top five broodmare sires in North America, England, Japan, and the United Arab Emirates.

The closely inbred Northern Taste reigned for some time as Japan's dominant sire. (He was by Northern Dancer and out of Lady Victoria, a half-sister to Nearctic.)

Of the stallions listed above for special chapter treatment, three of them — Nijinsky II, Nureyev, and Sadler's Wells — did their racing abroad, and Sadler's Wells stands in Ireland. There were many other successes in Europe for the Northern Dancers, although the swings in international economics meant that a number of those sons stood in North America but sent a great many sons and daughters back overseas.

Lyphard was one of the more remarkable sons from Northern Dancer's early crops. While Nijinsky II was a large and impressive colt with a great deal of scope, Lyphard took the diminutive stature of the sire almost to heart. A stylish, white-faced little Hackney of a colt, he was purchased by one of the world's sage horsemen. Alec Head harvested the little colt as a yearling for Mme. Pierre Wertheimer for 15,000 guineas ($37,800) at Newmarket. Lyphard had been bred in Pennsylvania by Mrs. J. O. Burgwin and had been purchased previously as a weanling, for $35,000, by Captain A. D. D. Rogers at Keeneland. He was out of the good staying American-raced mare Goofed, by Court Martial. He was named for the ballet dancer Serge Lifar, but Head took the precaution of altering the name; he had once been sued by the Talleyrand descendants for giving a horse that name! Lyphard was a high-class colt. His stakes wins included the group I Prix Jacques le Marois at a mile, and he also won at a mile and a quarter, but he had embarrassment as well as size to overcome in winning the respect of European breeders. Head had won the Epsom Derby as trainer of Lavandin in the 1950s, and Lyphard also was sent for the great race, in 1972. He was one of the top three choices. Lyphard was close at Tattenham Corner, but took a wild swing almost to the outside rail before getting himself straightened out in the stretch. The loss in ground was estimated at a dozen lengths in the press, but was probably more. Head knew that Lyphard was a ridgling, and the undescended testicle created pain when he was required to turn to the left at speed. (Still, to use the English expression, he certainly "made a balls of it" in his Derby bid.) "We did not want to do surgery. We thought the undescended one eventually would descend, and it did when he got to stud," Head recalled.

At stud, Lyphard began in Europe and later was acquired for Gainesway Farm in Kentucky. He was among the small Northern Dancers who proved able to get horses of various shapes and sizes. In addition to leading the American sire list in 1986, he led the French list twice and the French broodmare sire list twice, and he has been as high as second on the broodmare sire list here. His best of many champions was Dancing Brave, who evoked some thoughts of Sea-Bird when he crushed an extraordinary field to win the 1986 Prix de l'Arc de Triomphe. Dancing Brave also won the English Two Thousand Guineas and, while he negotiated Tattenham Corner better than his sire had, he was edged by Shahrastani in the Derby. (The winner was by Nijinsky II.) Dancing Brave finally put things right at Epsom for his branch of the sire line when he sired the 1993 Derby winner Commander in Chief. Dancing Brave was a fine sire of good horses and was sent to Japan.

The Lyphard filly Three Troikas gave the Head family one of its great days when she, too, won an Arc de Triomphe, in 1979 — carrying the colors of Alec Head's wife, Ghislaine, trained by their daughter Christiane (Criquette), and ridden by their son Freddy!

Manila was a star among Lyphard's American-raced foals. He came to hand late at three and won nine major turf stakes over two seasons, and he was the Eclipse Award winner in the grass division following his 1986 Breeders' Cup Turf victory. Manila was generally disappointing as a sire, but got a very good turf horse in Bien Bien. Manila now stands in Turkey.

Lyphard sired a total of 115 stakes winners (fourteen percent), and others among the best also included Al Nasr, Jolypha, Reine de Saba, Dancing Maid, Ski Paradise, Sabin, Sangue, Queens Court Queen,

Durtal, Chain Bracelet, and Rainbows for Life. Lyphard's Wish, Lypheor, Pharly, Alzao, and Al Nasr have been among those who extended Lyphard's branch of the sire line. Another is the leading French sire Linamix (son of Mendez, by Bellypha, by Lyphard). Linamix is the sire of Sagamix, who gave the sire line another bright moment in the Arc when he won the race in 1998.

The Boys of Epsom

Nijinsky II was Northern Dancer's first Epsom Derby winner, and he was followed by The Minstrel (1977) and Secreto (1984).

The Derby is ancient enough to have had its 200th running in 1979, but to date only four stallions have sired four winners apiece, while ten others have sired three apiece. Northern Dancer is of that second echelon, and so is his son Nijinsky II.

The Minstrel was another Windfields-bred and was among the brigade of Northern Dancers purchased by the visionary English horseman Robert Sangster. In addition to the Epsom Derby of 1977, The Minstrel won the Irish Derby and the King George VI and Queen Elizabeth Stakes. The blaze-faced chestnut was out of Fleur, a half-sister to Nijinsky II. The Minstrel sired fifty-eight stakes winners (eleven percent), and they numbered the Breeders' Cup Mile winner Opening Verse, more than a half-dozen European division champions, and outstanding middle distance horse Palace Music.

It was Palace Music who ascended to the top of the North American sire list in 1995. Various plans had been developed to get Palace Music to other parts of the world, seasonally or permanently, but before he left he happened to sire a colt to be named Cigar — the world's leading money-earner with nearly $10 million, author of a sixteen-race winning streak that tied Citation's modern record for major

Northern Dancer

races here, and two-time Horse of the Year. Cigar was among the few handicappers of the last couple of decades to carry as much as 130 pounds, and he also was sent on a daring trip to the first Dubai World Cup, which he duly won. Cigar, a large and lengthy great-grandson of little Northern Dancer, was a grand racehorse, but proved to be sterile. He is greeted by horse lovers as a hero at the Kentucky Horse Park north of Lexington.

Northern Dancer's third Epsom Derby winner was Secreto, who just got home in a photo in 1984 from El Gran Senor. (The runner-up, named in honor of trainer Luro, was also a son of Northern Dancer.) Secreto was one of the rare top-class sons of Northern Dancer who was seen as a disappointment as a sire, but he dwelt in a stern context. One sire's disappointing son is another's lifeline for posterity. Secreto got more than thirty stakes winners, including the English Two Thousand Guineas winner Mystiko and two champions in Italy.

The prowess of the little patriarch Northern Dancer was illustrated further by the success of the second-place finisher in the 1984 Epsom Derby. El Gran Senor started his career with seriously low in-foal figures, and, still, he became a very important stallion! The offspring of El Gran Senor include forty-eight stakes winners (thirteen percent), and among them are Breeders' Cup Sprint winner Lit de Justice, English and Irish Two Thousand Guineas winner Rodrigo de Triano, Strub Stakes winner Helmsman, King George VI and Queen Elizabeth winner Belmez, Super Derby winner Senor Thomas, and the near-champion grass filly Toussaud.

In Northern Dancer's legacy, horses of a quality that would make them heroes to other sire lines are almost too far down the list to mention, much less extol. An example is Be My Guest (seventy-two stakes winners), sire of the French-Irish Derby winner Assert, 1990 Belmont Stakes winner Go and Go, champion Most Welcome, and others. There is also Try My Best, sire of Breeders' Cup Mile winner Last Tycoon. The American-bred sprinter Topsider, by Northern Dancer, developed quite an international impact on his own, his sixty-one stakes winners including American champion North Sider and champion French miler Salse. (In a striking commentary on versatility, Salse sired an English St. Leger winner in Classic Cliche and a sprint star in Lemon Souffle.)

Yet another example of Northern Dancer's extending influence to classic connections by skipping a generation is the offspring of the son Night Shift. Winner of a single race, Night Shift is from one of those old Windfields families that raised themselves to international status. His dam, Ciboulette, is by Chop Chop and out of a daughter of the sire named Windfields, by Bunty Lawless. Ciboulette foaled the high-class Northern Dancer filly Fanfreluche, as well as Night Shift. The latter has sired fifty-two stakes winners including European division champions such as In the Groove and Lochangel; in 1999, Night Shift was represented by the Aga Khan's French Oaks winner Daryaba.

Others in the Northern Dancer brigade that distinguished themselves abroad include Ajdal, Broadway Dancer, Danzatore, Lomond, Northern Trick, Shareef Dancer, Tate Gallery, Minsky, Unfuwain, and Wajd. That some of these were champions and/or classic winners in top racing countries, and perhaps have additional impact on the breed, and yet receive only courtesy naming in a chapter on Northern Dancer, is, we hope, an illustration of what a pervasive animal we are addressing.

Vice Regent and the Accidental Deputy

The pattern which produced the two-time leading sire Deputy Minister, grandson of Northern Dancer, was a sort of reprise of Windfields Farm's history. Taylor had laid a foundation by melding secondary racing sons of top European bloodlines with hardy home mares. This pattern was mirrored in the pedigree of Deputy Minister, who is inbred to a local Toronto hero of the 1930s-40s in Bunty Lawless. It was Bunty Lawless who sired the horse Taylor and his wife named Windfields, and Windfields was the sire of the unraced mare Victoriana; in turn, Victoriana produced a breakthrough international horse, Victoria Park, who won the Queen's Plate and also placed in the Kentucky Derby and Preakness Stakes for Taylor. Inbreeding to top individuals is common, but it is not exactly anticipated that today a leading sire would be inbred to Bunty Lawless. Deputy Minister is, however, for his dam, the claiming filly Mint Copy, is by Bunty's Flight, a 1953 son by the old Canadian. (Deputy Minister is also inbred to Polynesian, sire of Native Dancer.)

Mint Copy was bred to Northern Dancer's son, Vice Regent, who at first had to be reckoned one of the lesser Northern Dancers. Vice Regent was in the stallion's second crop and was a full brother to the first hero, Viceregal. Vice Regent flashed some brilliance, but had his career interrupted and limited to five races. At the time he went to stud, his sire had been moved from Canada and the great Nijinsky II clearly was headed for Kentucky. Windfields' standing Vice Regent could be read as a move on behalf of the Canadian breeding sector that had no access to the top levels. Had it not been for such horses, many Canadian breeders would have been shut out of the early Northern Dancer phenomenon. Ironically, while Viceregal initially disappointed (later sent to France, but eventually important in

Japan), Vice Regent became one of the better of the Northern Dancers. He got 103 stakes winners (fifteen percent), including Regal Classic, Ruling Angel, Bessarabian, Regal Intention, as well as the aforementioned Deputy Minister.

Mint Copy, dam of Deputy Minister, had been claimed for $6,250 in 1975 and later improved to be stakes-placed. She was owned by the little Centurion Stable of Morton and Marjoh Levy. Mrs. Levy's father, John Agro, had been involved with a Canadian stable. "I was even named like a horse," Mrs. Levy told *The Blood-Horse* in 1981: "Mar for Mary, my mother; Joh, for John, my father."

The Levys also had another filly at the time, and both apparently were through with racing. Breeding would be an alternative to the modest buying at yearling sales they had done. They decided to sell one of the fillies, though, and on advice of trainer Bill Marko, held on to Mint Copy. She was sent to Vice Regent, who by then had been successful enough to be standing for $3,500. As co-breeder of a horse that would achieve the pinnacles many major breeders strive and contrive toward, Marjoh Levy made no claims to pattern or prescience: "It was an accident that caused Deputy Minister."

If named like his co-owner, Deputy Minister would have come out under the name Vice Mint. Instead, he quickly put into the headlines the name destined to lead the sire list and turn out a brigade of grade I winners. Deputy Minister was brilliant early at two in Ontario, went to New York to win the Youthful, and had the Levy phone ringing with such questions as "Who are you?" and "What do you want for that horse?" The Willmots of Kinghaven Farm already knew them, but were interested in the second answer. A half-interest was sold, and the colt was transferred from Marko to John Tammaro. Deputy Minister earned Horse of the Year honors in Canada at two in 1981 and also was voted the Eclipse Award as champion juvenile of all North America. To his early sprint stakes he added victories in the Laurel Futurity and Young America Stakes. Deputy Minister did not make it to the classics at three. At four, however, he came back to win the Gulfstream Sprint Championship, Donn Handicap, and Tom Fool Stakes. Robert Brennan's Due Process Stable had bought into the horse by then.

Deputy Minister stands at Fred Seitz' Brookdale Farm in Kentucky and is managed in part by Ric Waldman, who has had a longstanding affiliation with Windfields as well as with William T. Young's Overbrook Farm. Overbrook is the home of the most recent leading sire, Storm Cat.

For Brookdale Farm to stand a leading sire has precedent, at least in name. Seitz grew up in New Jersey and revered the old property known as Brookdale, in Red Bank, for which he named his Kentucky farm. Early in the 20th Century, the Brookdale in Red Bank had been leased by Harry Payne Whitney before he bought a farm in Kentucky. Broomstick launched his three years as leading sire from the New Jersey Brookdale.

Deputy Minister sired back-to-back, two-time champion fillies in his first three crops: Open Mind won the Breeders' Cup Juvenile Fillies in 1988 and swept the New York Filly Triple Crown and Alabama Stakes the next year; Go for Wand had a similar campaign, winning the Breeders' Cup Juvenile Fillies in 1989 and winning the Alabama and selected other top races at three. Go for Wand was fatally injured in a haunting mishap in the Breeders' Cup Distaff later in 1990.

Due Process Stable's spectacular stretch-runner Dehere was champion juvenile colt of 1993 for Deputy Minister and was a favorite for the classics

Northern Dancer

before an injury in early 1994. Then, in 1997, Deputy Minister's Touch Gold won a classic, the Belmont Stakes, as well as the Haskell, and in 1998, the sire's Queen's Plate winner Awesome Again capped an unbeaten four-year-old season by defeating a stellar field in the Breeders' Cup Classic. Also among Deputy Minister's sixty-four stakes winners (ten percent) are horses ranging from the Hopeful Stakes winner Salt Lake to the mile and a half grass specialist Flag Down. Deputy Minister also got the Kentucky Oaks and Spinster winner Keeper Hill, the Travers winner Deputy Commander, the Santa Anita Handicap winner Mr Purple, another Spinster winner in Clear Mandate, Jerome Handicap winner French Deputy, and the Strub and Dwyer winner Victory Speech. His Mane Minister was third in the Kentucky Derby, Preakness, and Belmont.

In the line's tradition, Deputy Minister is also the sire of Silver Deputy, another Brookdale stallion who got the streaking two-time Eclipse Award-winning filly Silverbulletday. Silver Deputy's three dozen stakes winners also include the Queen's Plate winner Archers Bay and several other champions in Canada, where the tale began.

Dancing With the Band

Another branch that produced classic victories came through the Northern Dancer colt Sovereign Dancer. He was from Phipps family breeding, and his second dam was the great mare Grey Flight. Lightly raced, Sovereign Dancer sired 1984 Preakness winner Gate Dancer while standing in Florida. He was later moved to Kentucky and got a second Preakness winner, Louis Quatorze, who won the classic in 1996 and is in the early stages of his own stud career. Sovereign Dancer's fifty-four stakes winners (nine percent) also included the American grass champion Itsallgreektome, the champion French miler Priolo (sire of 1999 French Two Thousand Guineas winner Sendawar), as well as Leo Castelli, Conte di Savoya, Wall Street Dancer, and others.

Another son of Northern Dancer whose career has been concentrated in America is Dixieland Band. Something of a senior citizen himself by now, Dixieland Band, age twenty, stands at William Farish's Lane's End Farm in Kentucky. He raced for Mrs. Farish's parents, Mr. and Mrs. Bayard Sharp. Dixieland Band was a solid grade II stakes winner, and he has sired eighty-two stakes winners (twelve percent). They include the similarly named graded stakes winners Dixie Brass and Dixieland Brass, as well as Chimes Band, Jambalaya Jazz, and Drum Taps. Dixie Brass scored his biggest win at a mile, in the grade I Metropolitan Handicap; Drum Taps added one and a half miles to that distance and won England's historic Ascot Gold Cup. (A similar range was authored by another Kentucky-based Northern Dancer horse, the Stone Farm stallion Northern Baby, now twenty-four. Northern Baby sired a Sapling-Hopeful winner in Deposit Ticket, a champion French miler in Bairn, and an English St. Leger winner in Michelozzo.)

Obviously, addressing the subject of Northern Dancer is an exercise in cruel pruning. As is true of branches with European leanings, there are a number of other sons who are ill-used by being ignored or merely enumerated. We can but wince apologetically at the thought of horses as important as the following being relegated by the realities of space to the "also sireds": One for All, Alma North, Dance Act, Dance Number, Far North, Fanfreluche, Giboulee, Glow, Herat, Larida, Nice Dancer, Northernette, Northfields, Spit Curl, True North, White Star Line, Wild Applause.

Then, too, there also have been such successful regional stallions as Maryland's Carnivalay and Mari's Book and New York's Compliance, not to mention a list of Canadian stallions.

Sixty years after Northern Dancer won the Kentucky, the importance of his sire line around the world is still strong and continuing. Following are a few of the highlights:

In North America, the key members who carried on the sire line include Storm Bird and his son Storm Cat. Their recent male line descendants include Triple Crown winner and Hall of Famer Justify, plus Giant's Causeway, Not This Time, and Harlan's Holiday. The last named, Harlan's Holiday, enhanced his branch of the sire line by siring Into Mischief, which in 2023 became the first horse to lead the American sire list five years in succession since Bold Ruler.

Others by Northern Dancer include Danzig, whose own son Danehill once held the world record for number of Graded/Group 1 winners with eighty-four. Danzig's major sons also include the current sire War Front. (The sire line of Northern Dancer's son Vice Regent produced American Horse of the Year Awesome Again, among others.)

In Europe, Northern Dancer's son Sadler's Wells achieved a Great Britain/Ireland record by leading the sire list fourteen years in succession. Furthermore, Sadler's Wells sired Galileo, himself a twelve-time leading sire in Great Britain/Ireland and the all-time leading sire of Epsom Derby winners with five. It was Galileo who broke Danehill's record of Graded/Group 1 winners. In 2024, one of Galileo's champion sons, Frankel, reached the milestone of 100 group/graded winners more quickly than any earlier stallion.

The Dancer is gone, but the Dance goes on. ❖

Nijinsky II

By 1968, E. P. Taylor had proven his point that top stock could be raised in his home province of Ontario. Northern Dancer had shown that clearly, winning the Kentucky Derby and Preakness, and now the little colt was off to a fine start at stud. With his yearling crop of 1968, Taylor made another of his many contributions to the Canadian industry. By consigning to the Canadian Thoroughbred Horse Society's yearling sale at Woodbine, he could help boost that auction into the big time. Earlier, he had held private, pre-priced sales at his Windfields Farm, and he clung to a sort of pre-pricing by entering his top prospects with announced reserves. Buyers were welcome to meet the price and then bid upward; otherwise, Taylor was perfectly content to keep them to race.

Ribot was a bigger name in those days than Northern Dancer, and it was a Ribot colt that was priced highest, at $100,000. The great trainer Vincent O'Brien had traveled from Ballydoyle in Ireland to inspect the Ribot colt, but he was struck more by a powerful, large bay by Northern Dancer. At that time, Northern Dancer was an unknown entity in Europe, but this fellow was too compelling to let pedigree skepticism stand in O'Brien's way. Windfields still had a division in the rapidly growing Toronto suburb of Willowdale, so

the yearling who would become Nijinsky II could be seen galloping in a paddock, with high rises visible in the distance.

Nijinsky II was out of a very good race filly, Flaming Page, who had won the Queen's Plate for Taylor. Flaming Page, however, was by the sire Bull Page, one of the lesser sons of the great Bull Lea. Bull Page had been relegated to Western Canada and, with a total of nineteen stakes winners to his credit, hardly constituted any additional appeal to O'Brien, or other international buyers who visited the Woodbine sale for the first time.

The Northern Dancer—Flaming Page colt was pre-priced at $60,000, but the bidding went to a Canadian record, $84,000. A fellow named George Scott had the honor of bidding and signing for the colt on behalf of his boss, the platinum magnate Charles W. Engelhard. O'Brien would train the horse for Engelhard, who had already won several classic races in England, but not the Derby. The colt was named in England for the great ballet dancer Nijinsky, whose widow was amused by following the colt's subsequent career. (When returned to North America to stud, the horse had to be known as Nijinsky II, since there was already a horse named Nijinsky in this country.)

Nijinsky II whipped through an unbeaten two-year-old season as champion in England, prepped well at three, and won the Two Thousand Guineas. Each step along the way was a milestone for Canadian breeding, and collectively helped peel away doubts about Northern Dancer.

In the Derby, Nijinsky II and Lester Piggott came dashing along late to pull away from the magnificent Sea-Bird colt Gyr and others in a notably strong field. Then came a victory in the Irish Sweeps Derby, followed by a deft handling of the previous year's Epsom Derby winner, Blakeney, in the King George VI and Queen Elizabeth Stakes.

No horse had won England's Triple Crown since Bahram in 1935. Engelhard was game to try, and Nijinsky II after a rest obliged, taking the St. Leger comfortably, if not spectacularly. (Piggott was thrown from his mount in the previous race that afternoon at Doncaster, but was not injured.)

O'Brien had had to treat a skin irritation on Nijinsky II, but there were no worrisome signs of the horse's tailing off as he sought to conclude his career unbeaten in the Prix de l'Arc de Triomphe. He was an enormous hero, and the firestorm of flashbulbs that swirled around him in the Longchamp paddock hardly helped the composure of a colt already known to get keyed up before a race. Still, Nijinsky II seemed to have the race won as he and Piggott came abreast of Sassafras in the final furlong. It was not going to be as easy as his other victories, but he seemed all right. Bull Hancock Jr., who would stand him at Claiborne Farm, was observed apparently to breathe a sigh of relief. Then, the picture changed. Piggott's whip stroked Nijinsky II on the right, and the colt veered to his left. At the post, too far away for visiting Americans to feel familiar with the angle, it was Yves Saint-Martin on Sassafras who waved a fist in the air.

Nijinsky II has been defeated!

Engelhard applied to the situation that tendency racing people have to feel a responsibility on behalf of the horse. It was the people around him who had let Nijinsky II down, Engelhard told *The Blood-Horse*, not the other way around. Now having been a party to depriving Nijinsky II the honor of retiring undefeated, Engelhard yearned at least to let him retire off a victory. A run in the Champion Stakes was added to the schedule, but if the St. Leger was eventually seen to have taken more out of the colt than realized, it was more sentiment than sense to presume that he would jump back to full sap after the Arc. Nijinsky II lost again, to Lorenzaccio.

With eleven wins from thirteen starts, Nijinsky II had earned $677,117. That summer, his syndication had been arranged, for a record $5,440,000. He spent his entire career at Claiborne, where meticulous care extended his service for many years after serious development of laminitis in 1984. Nijinsky II died in 1992, at the age of twenty-five.

For a time, in the early 1990s, Nijinsky II was jousting with Mr. Prospector for the mathematical title as all-time leader in stakes winners. The big Northern Dancer horse eventually reached 155 (eighteen percent), but Mr. Prospector went on to 169. As a sire of outstanding classic winners, and as a sire of sires, Nijinsky II certainly qualified among the best of his era. He matched his own sire's distinction of siring three Epsom Derby winners (Golden Fleece, Shahrastani, and Lammtarra), and another Nijinsky II horse, Ile de Bourbon, got a Derby winner in Kahyasi. To date, the Derby winners have not been the most powerful in the continuing sire line. Golden Fleece died young, and Shahrastani's record has been spotty on both sides of the Atlantic.

Lammtarra, who had a unique unbeaten career and also won the King George VI and Queen Elizabeth plus the Arc, was sold to Japan for a reported $30 million. His first foals are only three in 2000.

		Nearco, 1935	Pharos / Nogara
	Nearctic, 1954		
		Lady Angela, 1944	Hyperion / Sister Sarah
NORTHERN DANCER, b, 1961			
		Native Dancer, 1950	Polynesian / Geisha
	Natalma, 1957		
		Almahmoud, 1947	Mahmoud / Arbitrator
NIJINSKY II, b h, February 21, 1967			
		Bull Lea, 1935	Bull Dog / Rose Leaves
	Bull Page, 1947		
		Our Page, 1940	Blue Larkspur / Occult
FLAMING PAGE, b, 1959			
		Menow, 1935	Pharamond II / Alcibiades
	Flaring Top, 1947		
		Flaming Top, 1941	Omaha / Firetop

1st dam: FLAMING PAGE, b, 1959-1984. Bred by E.P. Taylor (Can). Raced 2 yrs, 16 sts, 4 wins, $108,836. Champion 3yo filly in Can. Won Shady Well S, Canadian Oaks, Queen's Plate; 2nd Kentucky Oaks, Princess Elizabeth S; 3rd Coronation Futurity S. Dam of 3 named foals, 3 rnrs, 3 wnrs, 2 sw.
1964: Fleur, b f, by Victoria Park. Raced 2 yrs, 22 sts, 3 wins, $9,235. 3rd Summer S (T). Dam of 9 foals, 7 rnrs, 5 wnrs, including **THE MINSTREL** ($581,266, Horse of the Year in Eng, Eng-I, Ire-I), **FAR NORTH** ($45,283), **PILGRIM** ($24,239), **FLOWER PRINCESS** ($21,792). Granddam of **DANCE FLOWER, Dancing Halo**. Died 1981.
1965: Slipped twins.
1966: Dead foal.
1967: NIJINSKY II, b c, by Northern Dancer. Bred by E.P. Taylor (Can). Raced 2 yrs in Eng, Ire, and Fr, 13 sts, 11 wins, $667,220. Champion 2 and 3yo colt in Eng and Ire. Won Epsom Derby, Irish Sweeps Derby, St. Leger, Two Thousand Guineas, Gladness S, King George VI and Queen Elizabeth S,

Anglesey S, Beresford S, Railway S, Dewhurst S; 2nd Prix de l'Arc de Triomphe, Champion S. Sire of 862 foals, 155 sw, 4.50 AEI. Died 1992.
1968: MINSKY, ch c, by Northern Dancer. Raced 3 yrs in Eng, Ire, and NA, 28 sts, 8 wins, $83,014. Champion 2yo colt in Ire, champion 3yo colt in Can. Won Durham Cup H (twice), Tetrarch, Railway S, Beresord S, Gladness S; 2nd Discovery H, Observer Gold Cup; 3rd Niagara H (T). Sent to Japan 1973.
1969: Dead foal.
1970: No report received.
1971: Barren.
1972: Barren.
1973: No report received.
1974: No report received.
1975: No report received.
1976: No report received.
1977: Not bred.

Nijinsky II's son Caerleon was a classic winner and an exceptional sire. The Claiborne Farm-bred export won the 1983 French Derby and England's Benson & Hedges Gold Cup and proceeded to sire 101 stakes winners (eleven percent), the best ones including the 1991 Epsom Derby and Irish Derby winner Generous. Caerleon's runners in this country included the powerful older distaffer Kostroma.

From Nijinsky II's first crop had come Green Dancer, winner of the Observer Gold Cup (then perhaps the top two-year-old race in England). The following year, Green Dancer won the French Two Thousand Guineas equivalent. Standing at Gainesway Farm in Kentucky, Green Dancer has sired eighty-two stakes winners (nine percent) and led the French sire list in 1991. His wonderful son Suave Dancer tracked Generous in the Irish Derby of 1991, but swooped down far ahead of him in winning the Arc de Triomphe that autumn. Green Dancer's prowess has been heavily European oriented, but his son Greinton won the Santa Anita Handicap and Hollywood Gold Cup.

Nijinsky II's son Royal Academy provided a touching moment when he carried Lester Piggott to a resounding victory in the 1990 Breeders' Cup Mile, at the twilight of the great English jockey's prolonged career. Royal Academy, now at Ashford Stud in Kentucky, has been turning out stakes winners at a good clip, eleven percent for a total of forty-six, including English One Thousand Guineas winner Sleepytime. Kings Lake, by Nijinsky II, won Ireland's Two Thousand Guineas, and another son, Shadeed, won the English version; Shadeed, standing in Kentucky at Gainsborough Farm, got the Queen's Plate winner and Preakness runner-up Alydeed, as well as such European champions as Sayyedati and Shadayid.

Other sons and daughters of Nijinsky II primarily associated with Europe include Solford, Princess Lida, Gorytus, Niniski, Vision, Caucasus, and Cherry Hinton.

On this side of the Atlantic, Nijinsky II's signature horse was probably Elizabeth Keck's Ferdinand. Just as Royal Academy gave Lester Piggott a late-career highlight, the big Ferdinand was nimble enough to drop over to the rail for Bill Shoemaker and give the fifty-four-year-old rider his fourth career win in the Kentucky Derby. Following that 1986 classic success, Ferdinand came back at four to be Horse of the Year, his and Shoe's campaign climaxed by an epic duel in which he edged Kentucky Derby winner Alysheba in the 1987 Breeders' Cup Classic. Ferdinand was the first Derby winner for legendary trainer Charlie Whittingham.

In a sire line primarily populated with bays and browns, Shahrastani and Ferdinand were among distinguished racing sons of Nijinsky II who were chestnut. There was some sense of prejudice against a chestnut Nijinsky II, and, probably coincidentally, neither horse has been highly successful to date. Ferdinand was exported to Japan, where his influence is yet to be measured. Another good chestnut son of Nijinsky II was the remarkably versatile Dancing Spree, who won the 1989 Breeders' Cup Sprint and also the one and a quarter-mile Suburban Handicap.

Other good racing sons of Nijinsky II who did not excel at stud were the Withers Stakes winner Czaravich, the handy grass specialist Dance of Life, plus Hostage, Dancing Champ, Fred Astaire, and Upper Nile.

Other American-based horses have matched, or exceeded expectations, or at least have had promising starts. Sky Classic is another chestnut, a large, handsome sort who was seen as a potential star from the time of his debut for Ernie Samuel's powerful Sam-Son Farm of Canada. Sky Classic was Canada's champion two-year-old in 1989. At four, he won the Rothmans International and at five toured through an exemplary series of the East's and Midwest's best races for grass-course stayers. He took five major stakes in four states: the Turf Classic and Early Times Manhattan in New York, the Caesars International in New Jersey, the Early Times Dixie in Maryland, and the Arlington Handicap in Illinois. A narrow loss to Fraise in the Breeders' Cup Turf did not preclude Sky Classic from winning the Eclipse Award for the male grass division for 1992. At stud at Pin Oak Stud in Kentucky, Sky Classic, as anticipated, has turned out to be the late-developing sort and has seventeen stakes winners, including Thornfield and Idle Rich.

Nijinsky II

The Nijinsky II colt Baldski, out of the major producer Too Bald, was a moderate stakes winner, but became a prominent stallion in Florida. He sired forty-nine stakes winners (nine percent), including Chaposa Springs, Once Wild, and Appealing Skier. Another Nijinsky II stallion to make a high mark in Florida is Sword Dance, a moderate winner in Ireland, but winner of the Del Mar Handicap in California. Sword Dance has sired the Arlington Million and San Juan Capistrano winner Marlin and the high-class Blazing Swords among a dozen stakes winners (six percent).

Several Nijinsky II stallions have gotten the occasional, major star: Sportin' Life demonstrated the stamina in the strain by siring the Belmont Stakes winner Bet Twice, while Texas-based Manzotti sired the Coaching Club American Oaks winner Two Altazano. On the other hand, the Nijinsky II stallion Moscow Ballet, standing in California, got the brilliant sprinting filly Soviet Problem, who tested champion Cherokee Run in the Breeders' Cup Sprint.

The aforementioned Fraise, who defeated Nijinsky II's Sky Classic in the Breeders' Cup Turf, is a third-generation descendant of the sire. Nijinsky II's son Whiskey Road was sent to Australia, where his offspring included the remarkable Strawberry Road, a major winner on three continents. Strawberry Road stood in Kentucky, and his early death was a major blow insofar as a staying line of sound horses was concerned. In addition to Fraise, Strawberry Road's thirty-seven stakes winners (ten percent) include the Eclipse Award-winning fillies Escena and Ajina, Santa Anita Derby winner Dinard, Spinster and Hollywood Oaks winner Fowda, and Flamingo Stakes winner Chilito.

The intent of this volume is to review sires in terms of their prowess in getting racehorses and subsequent breeding stock. The sales segment is another matter, but we cannot leave the subject of Nijinsky II's sons without mention of Seattle Dancer. A half-brother to Triple Crown winner Seattle Slew and English classic winner Lomond, Seattle Dancer was sold at Keeneland for $13.1 million, an astounding price even for the inflated spiral of prices in the middle 1980s. He could have become the leading money earner, holding the record even today, and still have fallen several million dollars short of recouping his purchase price. Clearly, of course, he was purchased as a stallion prospect, not to mention an ego massage of the highest order. Seattle Dancer was no champion, but neither was he a failure on the racecourse, for he won at the group II level, Ireland's Gallinule Stakes, and subsequently became a modestly successful sire, his daughters including Kentucky Oaks winner Pike Place Dancer.

Nijinsky II also got a number of outstanding fillies that raced in this country. Pride of place among them goes to De La Rose, the champion filly on grass in 1981. Other good Nijinsky II fillies include Alabama Stakes winner Maplejinsky, plus Number, Nijana, Folk Art, Jeanne Jones, Bemissed, Bound, Summer Fling, Summertime Promise, Terpsichorist, and Love You by Heart. Nijinsky II so far is the broodmare sire of 194 stakes winners.

Thirty years ago, we were lucky enough to be in attendance at Epsom when the big colt we had seen sell at Woodbine came rumbling and rambling up the demanding hill of the Derby. Nijinsky II would go on to win the English Triple Crown, something achieved only fourteen times before and never again since. There was champagne aplenty that day at Epsom for any in the camp of Nijinsky II — and the fizz proved unending. ❖

Northern Dancer

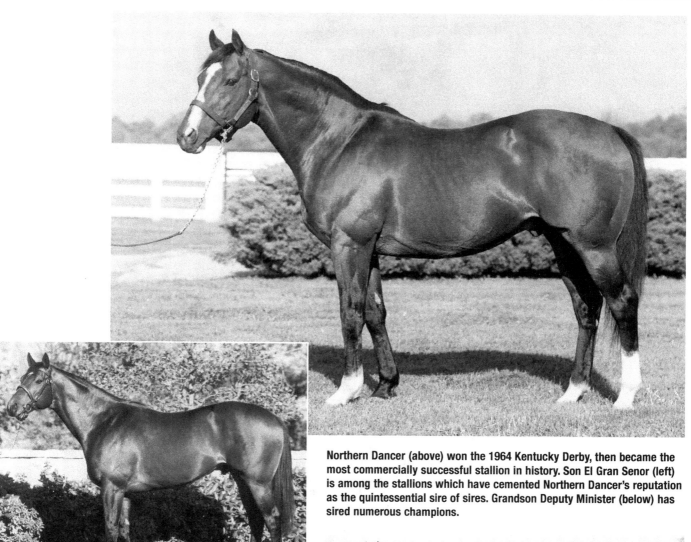

Northern Dancer (above) won the 1964 Kentucky Derby, then became the most commercially successful stallion in history. Son El Gran Senor (left) is among the stallions which have cemented Northern Dancer's reputation as the quintessential sire of sires. Grandson Deputy Minister (below) has sired numerous champions.

Northern Dancer

Lyphard (above), who bore a striking resemblance to Northern Dancer, sired 115 stakes winners, many of which raced in Europe. The offspring of Dixieland Band (right) have excelled in the United States. Storm Bird (below) has sired classic winners in both Europe and America.

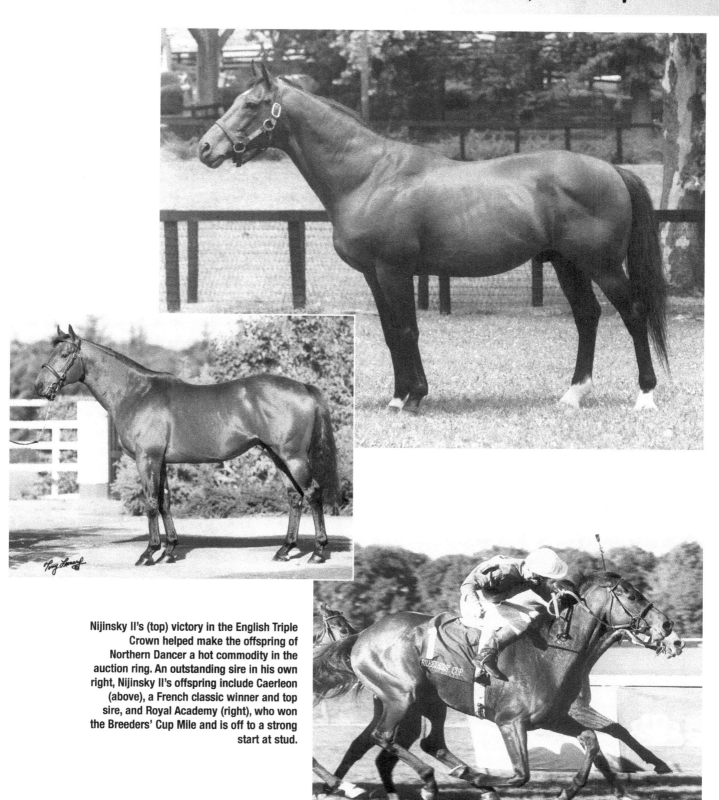

Nijinsky II's (top) victory in the English Triple Crown helped make the offspring of Northern Dancer a hot commodity in the auction ring. An outstanding sire in his own right, Nijinsky II's offspring include Caerleon (above), a French classic winner and top sire, and Royal Academy (right), who won the Breeders' Cup Mile and is off to a strong start at stud.

Nureyev

Northern Dancer's son Nureyev (top) had a
brief racing career, but his impact at stud
continues. Among his best offspring are
Miesque (above), two-time winner of the
Breeders' Cup Mile, and Theatrical (right),
winner of the Breeders' Cup Turf and a
source of top grass horses.

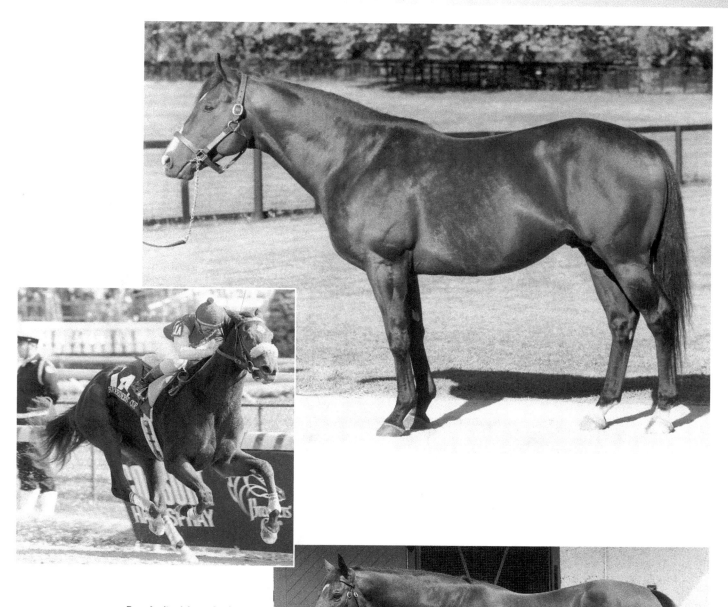

Danzig

Danzig (top) has sired top-class horses of every ilk, from Canadian Horse of the Year Dance Smartly (above) to Danehill (right), a group I winner in Europe who has led the Australian sire list three times.

Sadler's Wells

Sadler's Wells (top) has reigned as Europe's leading sire in recent years, getting such outstanding offspring as the filly Salsabil (above), who defeated males in the Irish Derby, and Montjeu (right), dual classic winner and Prix de l'Arc de Triomphe victor.

Sons of Sadler's Wells are having an impact at stud. Irish juvenile champion El Prado (above) stands in Kentucky and has had early promising results. In the Wings (below) won the Breeders' Cup Turf and has made an early mark at stud in siring the resilient globe-trotter Singspiel (left), winner of the Dubai World Cup, Japan Cup, Canadian International, and England's Coronation Cup and Juddmonte International.

Storm Cat

Storm Cat (top), a son of Storm Bird, has been wildly successful at stud. Some of his best sons and daughters include juvenile star and promising young sire Hennessy (right) and Sharp Cat (above), a multiple grade I winner. Storm Cat also has sired the Preakness/Belmont winner Tabasco Cat and Breeders' Cup Classic winner Cat Thief.

Nureyev

 he late Stavros Niarchos' name in Thoroughbred publications almost invariably was preceded, or followed, by the phrase "Greek shipping magnate." There was good reason. Turf writers were not familiar with the nomenclature of Niarchos' professional career, and "Greek shipping magnate" got across a sense of what he was about: He was a gentleman of Greece, was in the business of transportation via ocean, and was very good at it. (Why tamper: Tanker tycoon? Agent of the Aegean?)

So, having said "Greek shipping magnate," the racing writer could speed along to more important stuff, like his horses. Niarchos proved very successful as a breeder and an owner, but he also had to prove very game. In 1956, Niarchos paid a record price for a broodmare when he went to $126,000 to acquire Segula at Keeneland. Segula had produced the Horse of the Year Nashua, but never had any success approaching that for Niarchos. In the 1970s, however, Niarchos came back at the top levels of American sales. In 1978, his representatives hooked those of Robert Sangster. Niarchos and the most prominent international buyer of the moment were both circling one of the archetypal jewels of the era — a tidy little Northern Dancer with a superb female family. Niarchos

won the bidding duel, going to $1.3 million, then the second-highest price ever spent on a yearling.

Joss Collins, of the British Bloodstock Agency, recalls discussions as part of the team of advisers to Niarchos. "There was a lot of concern about buying such a small and backward horse for a man who had been out of the business and was getting back in," he admitted. "But Nureyev just had such a presence about him." Later that summer, Collins, Sir Phillip Payne-Gallwey, and others were looking for another Northern Dancer at Saratoga on Niarchos' behalf. One they liked "was lame. It wasn't just splints. He was lame. So, we did not buy Danzig."

The first of the Northern Dancers raced in Europe had been named for the historic ballet dancer, Nijinsky. Niarchos' colt was named for a contemporary ballet classicist, Nureyev. Few namesakes of horses have been so lucky as those two fellows.

Niarchos also bought the old Marcel Boussac stud farm in France. This was, and remains, as pleasant a spot as the earth has conjured up — at least to anyone responding to horses, staunch old stables, manorial houses, flower gardens, and peaceful patrols of swans gliding across Monet ponds. From the viewpoint of someone non-competitive against the French language, about the

		Nearco, 1935	Pharos Nogara
	Nearctic, 1954		
		Lady Angela, 1944	**Hyperion** Sister Sarah
NORTHERN DANCER, b, 1961			
		Native Dancer, 1950	Polynesian Geisha
	Natalma, 1957		
		Almahmoud, 1947	Mahmoud Arbitrator
NUREYEV, b h, May 2, 1977			
		Aristophanes, 1948	**Hyperion** Commotion
	Forli, 1963		
		Trevisa, 1951	Advocate Veneta
SPECIAL, b, 1969			
		Nantallah, 1953	Nasrullah Shimmer
	Thong, 1964		
		Rough Shod II, 1944	Gold Bridge Dalmary

1st dam: Special, b, 1969-1999. Bred by Claiborne Farm (Ky). Raced 1 yr, 1 st, 0 wins, $0. Dam of 9 named foals, 6 rnrs, 6 wnrs, 3 sw.

1973: Not bred.

1974: Kilavea, b f, by Hawaii (SAf). Raced 1 yr in Eng, 1 st, 1 win, $2,067. Dam of 10 foals, 10 rnrs, 6 wnrs, including **KILINISKI (Ire)** ($60,433), **Le Patineur** ($129,040, in Fr). Granddam of **BIENAMADO, NINOTCHKA, Anti Parasite, Exhilaration.**

1975: Fairy Bridge, b f, by Bold Reason. Raced 1 yr in Ire, 2 sts, 2 wins, $4,781. Dam of 9 foals, 7 rnrs, 6 wnrs, including **SADLER'S WELLS** ($713,690, champion miler in Fr, Eng-I, Ire-I), **TATE GALLERY** ($68,586, Ire-I), **FAIRY GOLD** ($107,934), **PUPPET DANCE** ($67,465), **Fairy Dancer** ($3,972, in Ire). Granddam of **Monsajem.** Died 1991.

1976: Barren.

1977: **NUREYEV**, b c, by Northern Dancer. Bred by Claiborne Farm, Lessee (Ky). Raced 2 yrs in Eng and Fr, 3 sts, 2 wins, $42,522. Champion miler in Fr. Won Prix Thomas Bryon (Fr-III), Prix Djebel. Sire of 750 foals, 111 sw, 3.86 AEI.

1978: Wield, dkb/br f, by Judger. Unraced. Dam of 8 foals, 2 rnrs, 1 wnr. Sent to India 1990.

1979: **NUMBER**, b f, by Nijinsky II. Raced 2 yrs, 26 sts, 8 wins, $301,793. Won Hempstead H (gr. II), Firenze H (gr. II), First Flight H (gr. III); 2nd Shuvee H (gr. II), Gazelle H (gr. II), Ballerina S (gr. III); 3rd Test S (gr. II), Bewitch S (gr. III). Dam of 11 foals, 10 rnrs, 9 wnrs, including **JADE ROBBERY**

($246,845, Fr-I), **NUMEROUS** ($255,348), **CHEQUER** ($180,545), **Add** ($84,762). Granddam of **INFLATE.** Died 1997.

1980: Barren.

1981: Barren.

1982: Barren.

1983: Sort, ch c, by Nijinsky II. Unraced. Sire in PR of 119 foals, AEI 0.58.

1984: **BOUND**, b f, by Nijinsky II. Raced 3 yrs, 23 sts, 4 wins, $339,744. Won Churchill Downs Budweiser Breeders' Cup H; 2nd Alcibiades S (gr. II), Louisville Budweiser Breeders' Cup H (gr. III), Thoroughbred Club of America S (gr. III), Beaumont S; 3rd Acorn S (gr. I), Rampart H (gr. II), Shirley Jones H (gr. III). Dam of 7 foals, 5 rnrs, 5 wnrs, including **LIMIT** ($84,483), **Liable** ($235,071). Granddam of **Barrier.**

1985: Durrah, b f, by Nijinsky II. Raced 2 yrs in Fr, 7 sts, 1 win, $15,712. Dam of 6 foals, 6 rnrs, 6 wnrs. ($1,400,000 keejul yrlg).

1986: Barren.

1987: Slipped.

1988: Statement, dkb/br c, by Private Account. Unraced. Sent to Chile 1991.

1989: Barren.

1990: B c, by Devil's Bag. Died 1991. ($10,000 keesep yrlg).

1991: Barren.

1992: Barren.

1993: Not bred.

only tweaking this scene could stand would be tidying up the name, Haras de Fresnay-le-Buffard. We were awed by this place when visiting in 1972,

and it was no less enthralling the last time we were there, which provided a look at a Mr. Prospector—Miesque colt later known as Kingmambo.

Niarchos' daughter Maria is carrying on the place, which is managed by Tim Richardson.

Nureyev was bred by Seth Hancock at Claiborne Farm. Like his father and grandfather before him, Hancock had an impressive stallion roster of his own to choose from, but also like his antecedents, he acknowledged a good horse in another farm's stud barn. Special, whom he bred to Northern Dancer in 1976 — in the fourth year on his own after the death of his father, A. B. (Bull) Hancock Jr. — was by the Argentine-bred Claiborne stallion Forli. Special's dam was Thong, a full sister to that stunning triumvirate of Moccasin, Ridan, and Lt. Stevens. These were all by the Claiborne stallion Nantallah and out of one of Bull Hancock's best bits of mining, the mare Rough Shod II.

Nureyev was one in that set of Northern Dancers that took strongly after the sire in his diminutive size but sturdy shape. He was trained first in England, but then was turned over to French trainer François Boutin, who got him ready for group company without a prep race. In his debut, Nureyev won the group III Prix Thomas Bryon at Saint-Cloud. This debut had not come until November, so he ran no more at two, but the one performance was enough to place him below only one colt on the Free Handicap for French two-year-olds. When Nureyev reappeared the following April to win the Prix Djebel by six lengths, he was immediately made favorite for the English Two Thousand Guineas. Boutin had won the English classic with Nonoalco six years before, and in the spring of 1980 was aiming at another attempt, on Niarchos' behalf. Remarked the Timeform publication *Racehorses of 1980*: "We came away from Maisons-Laffitte convinced that Nureyev would win the Guineas. We hadn't seen a more impressive classic trial for many a long year."

Jockey Philippe Paquet was criticized in that publication for his subsequent ride in the Guineas at Newmarket. By that account, his confidence in the horse crossed the border into disdain for his rivals. He was so far back early that when he was making his big rush to the front and was confronted by a wall of horses, he had insufficient time to pull up and go around. He fouled Posse (eventually third) in the process of breaking through, and, with Nureyev showing a fine turn of foot, wore down the very good colt Known Fact.

While the little colt may have gotten full marks for acceleration, bravery, and determination, it was the stewards who had the ultimate determination in their hands. No Guineas winner had ever been disqualified since the race's establishment in 1809. The stewards debated for forty-five minutes before placing Nureyev last.

The colt lost no caste and was, in fact, favored for the Epsom Derby, but he soon was affected by a viral bout. He did not start again. Nureyev had never been beaten to the wire, but had an official record of two wins in three starts and earnings of only the equivalent of $42,522.

While the disqualification was galling to Niarchos and Boutin, no doubt, the result insofar as breeding apparently did not hamper the future. In fact, it might have been a boost for one while no knock on the other. It is difficult to imagine that Nureyev would have accomplished more in the stud with the "all right" sign hovering above his Guineas performance. On the other hand, the status of classic winner might have turned a few heads more in favor of Known Fact, who proved a very successful sire in his own right.

Large or Small, Sprint or Stay

A Kentucky breeder was telling us one day that a youngish stallion he still had hopes for could "get

Nureyev

you any kind of horse." It was tempting to say, "No, *Nureyev* can get you any kind of horse." The versatility that has been remarked upon often in his and other sire lines is incarnate in the record of the little horse. Looking only at the last three years, 1997-99, a few selected examples of Nureyevs are the following:

• *Peintre Celebre*, not only winner of the 1997 Prix de l'Arc de Triomphe at one and a half miles, but hailed as one of the most brilliant of recent Arc victors. ("It is difficult to find the appropriate words that do justice to Peintre Celebre's tremendous achievement of utterly demolishing such a high-class field..." remarked Arthur Fitzgerald in his history of the race.)

• *Stravinsky*, England's top sprinter of 1999.

• *Spinning World*, classic winner and champion at a mile in Europe and winner of the 1997 Breeders' Cup Mile.

•*Fasliyev*, highweight two-year-old in England, France, and Ireland in 1999.

• *Reams of Verse*, winner of the Epsom Oaks and highweight two-year-old filly in England.

• *Atticus*, winner of the grade I Oaklawn Handicap on dirt a few weeks after setting the world record of 1:31 4/5 for a mile on grass.

Nureyev has sired 111 stakes winners (fifteen percent). He has led the French sire list twice, a decade apart (1987 and 1997), and has ranked as high as third three times in England and as high as fifth in North America. He is also the broodmare sire of eighty-two stakes winners. (In a superb 1997 in Europe, when Nureyev had the Arc winner and the champion miler Spinning World, he was also the broodmare sire of Desert King, winner of the Irish Derby and Irish Two Thousand Guineas.)

In addition to the above recent winners, Nureyev has produced older sons who might prove him one of his sire line's better sire of sires. A key example is the Nureyev horse Theatrical. Antithesis physically of the little stallion, Theatrical is a tall, lengthy horse who gets similar animals. As a racehorse, Theatrical was always classy, and he got better with age. He placed in the Irish Derby at three and the Breeders' Cup Turf at four. He came to full flower at five, when his six grade I grass wins were climaxed by defeating Arc winner Trempolino in the Breeders' Cup Turf. Theatrical was voted the Eclipse Award for the division over the powerful Lyphard colt Manila. He won ten of twenty-two races and earned just under three million dollars.

At stud, Theatrical has sired horses of stamina like himself. His forty-six stakes winners (seven percent) include the North American and English grade/group I winner Royal Anthem; grade I winner on dirt Geri; Irish Derby winner Zagreb; three-time Japanese distaff champion Hishi Amazon; and French One Thousand Guineas winner Madeleine's Dream. His grade I winners also include Auntie Mame, Vaudeville, Duda, Broadway Flyer, and (Australian) Victoria Derby winner Portland Player.

Other sons of Nureyev at stud include Zilzal, the once-beaten English Horse of the Year in 1989 and sire of French One Thousand Guineas winner Always Loyal and several other group I winners. Another Nureyev is the speedy English and French champion Soviet Star, whose twenty-four stakes winners include the durable Soviet Line. Other grade/group I winning sons of Nureyev include Stately Don, Polar Falcon, Wolfhound, Alwuhush, Joyeux Danseur, and Kitwood.

The many high-class fillies by Nureyev are led by the American Hall of Famer Miesque, whose two Breeders' Cup Mile wins in two North American starts earned her a pair of Eclipse

Awards. Miesque also won the English and French One Thousand Guineas and was a multiple champion in Europe. (She already has produced two European classic winners among four stakes winners, including Kingmambo, who, in turn, has sired Belmont Stakes winner Lemon Drop Kid and Japan Cup winner El Condor Pasa.)

The other top Nureyev racing fillies include Irish Guineas and Sussex Stakes winner and French champion Sonic Lady, Irish Guineas winner and champion Mehthaaf, and other European division champions Gayane and Flagbird.

A Sling in Time

The inner will that led Nureyev to knock Posse off stride in the Two Thousand Guineas twenty years ago might have been a good thing in ways not recognized at the time. In 1987, Nureyev had been at stud at Kentucky's Walmac International for six years, after initially standing a season at Fresnay-le-Buffard. On the morning of May 5, he serviced a mare and was turned out in his paddock in routine fashion. A few minutes later, he had contrived, as horses will, to put himself in serious trouble. He somehow had fractured the right hind leg just below the hock. Dr. J. D. Howard, resident veterinarian at J. T. L. Jones' Walmac, later told *The Blood-Horse* that the leg right under the hock "was just like on a swivel. It just flopped. I thought, 'There's no way.'"

Thinking the worst did not mean *accepting* the worst. Howard bandaged the leg to immobilize it, and the horse was taken to the Lexington veterinary firm of Hagyard-Davidson-McGee. A top team consisting of veterinarians Paul Thorpe, Michael Spirito, Craig Franks, and John D. Wheat performed surgery. Wheat happened to be in town on a trip from his post at the University of California-Davis — where a major unit is now named for him. With that specific combination of

horse lover and realist that is balanced in the make-up of driven veterinarians, this team of pros did its best, then sat back to figure the odds were ten percent that the patient would survive. Four screws were inserted to stabilize the injury, and a cast was placed from foot to stifle. Nureyev was supported by a sling, but he grew so fatigued after a few days that it seemed he was about to give up the fight. The veterinarians and other handlers by then in attendance could only rouse him by slapping him around to make him mad.

Nureyev was once again faced with an antagonistic posse, and once again he came at it. This time, there were no stewards to second-guess him.

An extraordinary series of provisions were made for an extraordinary horse. A separate stall with a hydraulic hoist was assembled on the Hagyard-Davidson-McGee property, and a race track ambulance was called in all the way from Louisiana to take the patient the short distance from one building on the property to the new one. Under round-the-clock observation, Nureyev somehow learned to live on three legs with the additional support of a sling that was highly mobile because it was affixed on overhead rails.

Crisis followed crisis: Breaking off some of the screws in the leg, discomfort after a replaced cast, a respiratory infection, fears of colitis (countered by intravenous fluids), and so on. Weeks passed. Finally, Howard made an intuitive decision. The sling had been a life saver, but Nureyev seemed finally to be failing, the inner strength tapped and tapped again to its end. Howard had the crew bring in a large, thick mat, and they lowered the sling and lay the horse down — to rest, perchance to die.

Nureyev was off his feet for the first time in fifty-nine days, and he accepted the lowering and raising to be a regular routine. The cast eventually could be replaced by a special brace, and a regimen of electro-stimulus was introduced to combat atrophy of the muscles. Nureyev gradually was getting stronger.

So, owing to the knowledge, devotion, and imagination of a considerable number of humans, the horse lived and thrived. He returned to stud service in time for the following breeding season. The numbers of his foal crops conceal reality: thirty-four foals conceived in his shortened 1987 season before the accident, thir-

Nureyev

ty-seven in the foal crop conceived in the year following! His crops, never large by current standards, rose to as many as sixty-five. Of his 111 stakes winners to date, forty-eight were conceived in the years after the injury. Peintre Celebre, Reams of Verse, Spinning World, Atticus, Stravinksy, and Fasliyev have more than a sire in common. They are spiritually all by Nureyev—Bonus Years, by Dedicated Pros. ❖

Danzig

 comfortable, defensive image in predicting sire success is to require a top-class racehorse with good breeding, including a strong female family. Fitting Danzig into this mold takes a bit of mental gymnastics: Top-class racehorse? Well, true, he never actually won a stakes, but he looked like he could have if he had only run in one. Good female family? Well, one can trip lightly past the $4,700 purchase price of the dam when she was a yearling, emphasizing that she did after all become a stakes winner; omitting the part about her own sire having gotten only eight stakes winners in a dismal stud career, one can leap back to the third dam, Epsom Oaks winner Steady Aim! So, there it is: Danzig, obviously a (potential) top-class racehorse out of a good family — a classic family even.

On the top side, no shenanigans are necessary. Danzig is, after all, by Northern Dancer, and by the time he came along the racing world had observed the precedent for small, close-coupled little colts by that sire slipping in among the better ones.

Far back in the ancestry of Danzig was the mare Hammerkop, who was so versatile that she won five good sprint stakes at two, the Yorkshire Oaks at three, and two runnings of the two and three-quarter-mile Alexandra Plate. The Danzigs perhaps have not proven quite as adaptable to different circumstances as Hammerkop, but excellence over a variety of distances and surfaces has been a hallmark of his offspring. Consider:

• *Pine Bluff*, a lengthy, powerful classic type who won the Preakness on American dirt.

• *Dayjur*, a powerful little chunk who was one of the top modern sprinters on European grass and then came within two jumps of winning a Breeders' Cup Sprint on dirt.

• *Chief's Crown*, champion at two and classic-placed over here, and sire of an English Derby winner (Erhaab).

• *Dance Smartly*, Triple Crown winner against males on dirt and grass up to one and a half miles in Canada, winner of the Breeders' Cup Distaff, former all-time leading female earner.

• *Danehill*, group I sprinter in England and an exceptional sire in both hemispheres.

• *Lure*, twice winner of the Breeders' Cup Mile.

• *Danzig Connection*, winner of the Belmont Stakes.

• *Polish Precedent*, a champion miler in Europe, but sire of Breeders' Cup Turf winner Pilsudski.

Danzig was bred in partnership by William S. Farish and Marshall Jenney. They acquired the mare, Pas de Nom, after she had won the Inferno Stakes for Beverly Roma in Canada. The quick filly had won her debut for trainer Frank Merrill

		Nearco, 1935	Pharos Nogara
	Nearctic, 1954		
		Lady Angela, 1944	Hyperion Sister Sarah
NORTHERN DANCER, b, 1961			
		Native Dancer, 1950	Polynesian Geisha
	Natalma, 1957		
		Almahmoud, 1947	Mahmoud Arbitrator
DANZIG, b h, February 12, 1977			
		Crafty Admiral, 1948	Fighting Fox Admiral's Lady
	Admiral's Voyage, 1959		
		Olympia Lou, 1952	Olympia Louisiana Lou
PAS DE NOM, dkb/br, 1968			
		Petition, 1944	Fair Trial Art Paper
	Petitioner, 1952		
		Steady Aim, 1943	Felstead Quick Arrow

1st dam: PAS DE NOM, dkb/br, 1968-1993. Bred by Decourcy W. Graham (Ky). Raced 4 yrs, 42 sts, 9 wins, $121,741. Won Virginia Belle S, Jasmine S, Seashore S, Inferno S; 2nd Barbara Fritchie H (gr. III), Miss Woodford S, Yo Tambien H; 3rd Mimosa S, Boniface S, Pan Zareta H. Dam of 11 named foals, 8 rnrs, 4 wnrs, 0 sw. ($110,000, 1987 keenov, The Minstrel).

1975: Dame Margot, b f, by Northern Dancer. Unraced. Dam of 13 foals, 9 rnrs, 4 wnrs, including **LORD OF THE NIGHT** ($414,176). Sent to Eng 1987. Died 1998.

1976: Not bred.

1977: Danzig, b c, by Northern Dancer. Bred by Derry Meeting Farm and William S. Farish III (Ky). Raced 2 yrs, 3 sts, 3 wins, $32,400. Sire of 907 foals, 150 sw, 4.74 AEI.

1978: Barren.

1979: Ibtihaj, b f, by Raja Baba. Raced 2 yrs in Eng, 9 sts, 1 win, $8,324. Dam of 10 foals, 9 rnrs, 3 wnrs. Granddam of **MUBHIJ, Tabheej**. Died 1999. ($330,000 ftsaug yrlg).

1980: Accused, dkb/br c, by Alleged. Raced 2 yrs in Eng and NA, 8 sts, 0 wins, $6,529. Sire of 153 foals, AEI 0.85. ($125,000 ftsaug yrlg).

1981: Foal died.

1982: Barren.

1983: Pas de Power, dkb/br c, by Lines of Power. Unraced. Died 1985. ($6,500 ftksep yrlg; $50,000 ftkmay 2yo).

1984: Religiously, dkb/br c, by Alleged. Unraced. Sire in Ire.

1985: Bro, dkb/br c, by Full Out. Raced 1 yr in Eng, 2 sts, 0 wins, $0. Died 1988.

1986: Barren.

1987: Slipped.

1988: Nom d'Amour, dkb/br f, by The Minstrel. Raced 2 yrs, 9 sts, 0 wins, $10,000. Dam of 5 foals, 4 rnrs, 3 wnrs. Sent to Japan 1997. ($105,000 ftsaug yrlg).

1989: Pasta, dkb/br f, by Robellino. Raced 1 yr, 9 sts, 2 wins, $35,401. Sent to India 1994.

1990: Barren.

1991: Barren.

1992: Binary Star, b c, by Waquoit. Raced 1 yr in Fr, 1 st, 0 wins, $0. Sire in Eng ($55,000 ftsaug yrlg).

1993: Open Pass, dkb/br g, by Opening Verse. Raced 3 yrs, 26 sts, 1 win, $6,796. ($170,000 ftsaug yrlg; $250,000 keeapr 2yo).

at Gulfstream. For Farish and Jenney, Pas de Nom won the Virginia Belle Stakes and divisions of the Jasmine Stakes and Seashore Stakes. She was clearly a high-class filly with good speed, and she won nine of forty-two races and earned $121,741. Her first two foals were by Northern Dancer. The first was Dame Margot (who foaled stakes winner Lord of the Night), and her second was Danzig. Pas de Nom herself never foaled a stakes winner, but she did not have to in order to place a secure stamp on breeding history.

Pas de Nom's sire, Admiral's Voyage, was a fine stakes winner for Fred W. Hooper, and by the good sire Crafty Admiral, who was also the broodmare sire of Triple Crown winner Affirmed. Admiral's Voyage came across admirably in some of the sternest races of his three-year-old season of 1962. He fought to the finish of the Wood Memorial in a dead heat with Sunrise County and got the decision via disqualification. In the Belmont Stakes, Admiral's Voyage tested the eventual champion, Jaipur, right to the wire, losing in a photo after one and a half miles. Admiral's Voyage was given a good chance at stud, but sired only eight stakes winners. Some of them had aggressive names — King's N' Things and Zeus — but the eight represented only three percent of his foals.

Farish, co-breeder of Danzig, owns Lane's End Farm in Kentucky. He has a Texas background, his family founded the old Standard Oil, and since early in life he has been a horseman (polo in addition to racing) as well as a businessman with divergent interests. *The Blood-Horse* fell into the pattern of referring to him as a "Texas oilman" when he got into racing in the late 1960s with the likes of Kaskaskia and later Bee Bee Bee. Some years later, having developed a farm of several thousand acres and installed one of the top stallion operations in the Thoroughbred world, Farish modestly asked if maybe he qualified to be a "Kentucky breeder." Done.

Farish is a low-key sort of fellow personally, but the trappings of prominence are unavoidable. His friendship and business connections to former President Bush were well publicized, as have been visits to Lane's End by Queen Elizabeth II. Farish is also chairman of Churchill Downs, chairman of the executive committee of the Breeders' Cup, chairman of the American Horse Council, and vice chairman of The Jockey Club. He has bred and/or raced 220 stakes winners, many in partnerships with Warner L. Jones Jr., W. S. Kilroy, Stephen Hilbert, and his aunt, Martha Gerry.

Jenney, his partner in breeding leading sire Danzig, operates Derry Meeting Farm in Pennsylvania, where the colt was foaled. Derry Meeting is perennially a prominent consignor to the Saratoga yearling sale in August. Other distinguished Derry Meeting-breds include Mrs. Penny, winner of the Cheveley Park Stakes, French Oaks, and Prix Vermeille.

Danzig was sent as a yearling to Saratoga in the summer of 1978. Terence Collier, who has been a mainstay in Fasig-Tipton Company since 1976, recalls that it was Lynn de Kwiatkowski, then the wife of Henryk de Kwiatkowski, who was enthralled by the little colt and spent considerable time studying him. De Kwiatkowski was the buyer, at $310,000 — almost exactly a million dollars less than was paid at Keeneland that summer for another little Northern Dancer destined for lasting fame, Nureyev.

Henryk de Kwiatkowski, who named his Kennelot Stable after a beloved filly and mare, has subsequently become known as the man who stepped in to purchase Calumet Farm from a bankruptcy auction and preserve the signature beauty of the great Lexington institution. He also purchased and raced to championships and/or classic victories such as Conquistador Cielo, Danzig Connection, and De La Rose.

When de Kwiatkowski sent Danzig to Woody Stephens, he was apparently turning over to the great trainer one of the more brilliant pupils Stephens ever had. Danzig had speed in the extreme, and he won his debut at two by eight and a half lengths. Thereafter, however, Stephens had to stop on him to have chips removed from a knee. The trainer brought the colt back and at three he seemed poised to be one of those challengers that join the fray after the classic colts have sorted themselves out. Danzig won additional overnight races by seven and a half lengths and five and three-quarter lengths. Apparently headed for a stakes-class test, however, he was again stopped by knee trouble. He would race no more, having won three of three to earn slightly more than one-tenth his purchase price, or $32,400.

Seth Hancock, head of Claiborne Farm, inherited, and has enhanced, a tradition of proven stakes winners and/or already proven sires distinguishing his stallion barn. He is also mindful, however, of precedent for accepting the potential over the proven. After all, his father, Bull Hancock, stood the speedy non-stakes winner Nantallah, who was destined to sire the marvelous homebred Moccasin as well as some major winners for farm clients. Seth accepted Danzig and, given the go-go economics of the time, syndicated the horse at a per share cost ($80,000) more than double Danzig's career earnings.

Danzig's first crop produced a champion in time to distinguish himself as the first winner of a Breeders' Cup race. Chief's Crown won the Breeders' Cup Juvenile in 1984 to climax his two-year-old championship season. At three, he placed in all three Triple Crown races; in two of them, he was third and another Danzig colt, Stephan's Odyssey, was second. Chief's Crown also won the Marlboro Cup and Travers Stakes. At stud, he got off to a promising start, but for a time was one of the stallions that prompted some premature speculation that the Danzigs — however good they were at the races — were not going to be good sires themselves. The swooping move from seeming defeat by the Chief's Crown colt Erhaab to win the 1994 Epsom Derby was but one of many shakes blown from that flimsy roof of conjecture. Chief's Crown, who died in 1997, sired forty-one stakes winners (eight percent), not a great figure,

Danzig

but in addition to an Epsom Derby winner, they included Breeders' Cup Turf winner and champion Chief Bearhart, English juvenile champion Grand Lodge; Chief Honcho, Concerto, and others.

In 1991, Danzig led the American sire list for the first time, and he stayed on top for two more years. He thus became the first horse since Bold Ruler to lead the list more than two years. Danzig through 1999 had sired 150 stakes winners (eighteen percent) to pose a threat to become the all-time leader. Other strong elements to the Danzig branch have emerged, in addition to Chief's Crown and son Erhaab, to help continue the Northern Dancer line. Danehill was one of the dual-hemisphere stallions that gave a good name to that club. Having stood both at Coolmore in Ireland and in Australia, Danehill is already the sire of 114 stakes winners, including the Irish Derby winner Desert King. In Australia, Danehill has led the sire list three times, and his brigade of top Australian runners include the Cox Plate winner Dane Ripper, Rosehill Guineas winner Danewin, and Golden Slipper winners Merlene and Catbird.

Another classic winner sired by a son of Danzig was Sea Hero. He is a son of Polish Navy, a Phipps Stable Danzig homebred who won the Woodward and Champagne. Polish Navy is the sire of only a dozen stakes winners, but in Paul Mellon's Sea Hero, he got an intriguing customer. Sea Hero won three of the top races for the best echelon of Eastern horses in America. At two, he won the Champagne. The following spring, trainer Mack Miller brought him along in time to peak on the first Saturday in May, when he won the Kentucky Derby. That summer, when Sea Hero won the Travers, he became the first to win both those historic three-year-old races since Shut Out in 1942. He was an in-and-out sort of runner, but he picked his spots to be "in." His likeness now adorns the paddock at Saratoga, statuary courtesy of the late Mr. Mellon. Sea Hero's sire, Polish Navy, is also the sire of grade I Secretariat Stakes winner Ghazi.

A European-based Danzig stallion with success at stud is Green Desert, now seventeen, a group I sprinter in England and runner-up in the Two Thousand Guineas. Green Desert's forty-seven stakes winners (ten percent) include the Irish Two Thousand Guineas and Moulin de Longchamp winner Desert Prince, the Breeders' Cup Sprint winner Sheikh Albadou, English two-year-old champions Owington and (filly) Bint Allayl, French juvenile filly champion Absurde, group I Lockinge Stakes winner Cape Cross, plus Tamarisk, Desert Style, and others.

Belong to Me is a Danzig stallion who earned his way quickly from New York to Kentucky. Farish, co-breeder of the sire, stands Belong to Me at Lane's End. Belong to Me's early crops included the Acorn, Mother Goose, and Test Stakes winner Jersey Girl, Spinaway Stakes winner Circle of Life, and Hopeful Stakes winner Lucky Roberto.

Honor Grades is a stakes-placed Danzig who is a half-brother to classic winners A.P. Indy and Summer Squall. Honor Grades is the sire of the millionaire Honor Glide, a major one and a quarter-mile horse on grass in this country.

Another moderate winner among the Danzigs, Deerhound, sired Breeders' Cup Juvenile Fillies winner and Eclipse Award winner Countess Diana. Ascot Knight, by Danzig, won the Scottish Derby and placed in group I company in England before entering stud in Canada. He is the sire of twenty-three stakes winners from eight crops, including the Man o' War Stakes and Caesars International winner Influent and Italian Derby winner Bahamian Knight. The Danzig horse

Polish Numbers, out of champion Numbered Account, did not win a stakes but has become a leading regional sire in Maryland, his early crops including the grade I turf filly Tenski among nearly two dozen stakes winners.

Of the Danzigs highlighted earlier, several others merit more detail. The superb miler Lure came up virtually sterile when first sent to stud and, while he has since gotten some foals, his impact cannot be predicted. Pine Bluff, the Danzig colt who won the 1992 Preakness, sired an outstanding classic prospect in Lil's Lad, but that colt was injured prior to the 1998 Kentucky Derby and after a brief return to the races in the fall of 1998 and spring of 1999, he was retired. Dayjur, handy winner of such races as the Prix de l'Abbaye, Keeneland Nunthorpe, and Ladbroke Sprint, was named Horse of the Year in England in 1990. He endeared himself to Americans in a reverse and perverse way, when he seemingly fumbled away victory in the Breeders' Cup Sprint by taking prodigious leaps over shadows in the final sixteenth. Dayjur has been an enigma as a sire. His figures are modest, sixteen stakes winners (seven percent), but they include Irish Juvenile filly champion Asfurah, Middle Park Stakes winner Hayil, and the stellar American turf sprinter Danjur.

More than seventy-five sons of Danzig are known to be at stud. In addition to those named, some of the more accomplished racehorses, many now in the early stages of their stud careers, include Langfuhr, Furiously, Boundary, Bianconi, Dumaani, Dove Hunt, Military, Partner's Hero, Anabaa, Strolling Along, Shaadi, Mujahid, Maroof, Elnadim, Adjudicating, Zieten, Slavic, Nicholas, and Mull of Kintyre.

The Danzig fillies have been a distinguished lot as well, and he is broodmare sire of sixty-five stakes winners. In addition to Dance Smartly,

Danzig

Danzig's best racing daughters include Alabama winner Versailles Treaty, Kentucky Oaks and Spinster winner Dispute, French juvenile filly champion Pas de Reponse, English juvenile filly champion Blue Duster, additional Prix de l'Abbaye winners Agnes World and Polonia, Japanese juvenile filly champion Yamanin Paradise, plus Tribulation, Lotka, Yashmak, and Easy Now.

The only non-stakes winner of modern times to become the leading American sire is well positioned to join many others in the Northern Dancer sire line whose names drive on well into the 21st Century. ❖

Sadler's Wells

erhaps destined to prove the most remarkable of all the Northern Dancer stallions is Sadler's Wells, now nineteen. Sheer numbers are not the best way to project comparisons, but his total of 145 stakes winners from foals as of early 2000 is eye-catching. That figure needs be tempered, of course, by noting that Sadler's Wells has spent most of his career in a time of stallion books of 100 or more. In trying to put him in perspective with other great sires of the 20th Century, a more relevant fact is that he led the English/Irish sire list eight consecutive years and nine times in the last decade of the century. Hyperion was the only earlier stallion to lead the list as many as six times in that century. Hyperion had a total of 527 foals, whereas Sadler's Wells already is far above that figure and covered 156 mares in 1999 alone. Percentages favor Hyperion at the moment, twenty-two percent stakes winners to sixteen percent for Sadler's Wells.

There is a vague feeling of heresy in suggesting that an English stallion may be approaching the greatness of Hyperion, but that undoubtedly has to do with one's age and the number of years the earlier horse has resided in the mental pantheon of Thoroughbred heroes. Perhaps older types in the 1950s bristled at the first suggestion that Hyperion was nearing the St. Simon class.

Ultimate comparisons are premature, for Sadler's Wells has not had the opportunity to stand the test of time insofar as how many of his sons become important stallions — one of the keys to Hyperion's lasting renown. If judged by the quality of his best runners, however — and the size of the cavalry unit they could populate — Sadler's Wells certainly stands up to an exalted standard.

In 1999, the Sadler's Wells contingent was led by the three-year-old Montjeu, whose courageous rally caught El Condor Pasa in time to become the sire's second Prix de l'Arc de Triomphe winner (following Carnegie). Earlier, Montjeu had won both the French and Irish Derbys, in the latter race leading a one-two-three brigade of Sadler's Wells foals.

Saffron Walden, the Irish Two Thousand Guineas winner, was also among the twenty-two stakes winners for Sadler's Wells in 1999, as were E. P. Taylor Stakes winner Insight, Irish St. Leger winner Kayf Tara, and Racing Post Trophy winner Aristotle. Sadler's Wells had been a major force for a decade prior to that, or since Steve Cauthen partnered with the colt Old Vic from the stallion's first crop. Also winner of both the Irish and French Derbys, Old Vic was even rated ahead of Nashwan among European three-year-olds of 1989.

		Nearco, 1935	Pharos Nogara
	Nearctic, 1954		
		Lady Angela, 1944	Hyperion Sister Sarah
NORTHERN DANCER, b, 1961			
		Native Dancer, 1950	Polynesian Geisha
	Natalma, 1957		
SADLER'S WELLS, b h, April 11, 1981		Almahmoud, 1947	Mahmoud Arbitrator
		Hail to Reason, 1958	Turn-to Nothirdchance
	Bold Reason, 1968		
		Lalun, 1952	Djeddah Be Faithful
FAIRY BRIDGE, b, 1975			
		Forli, 1963	Aristophanes Trevisa
	Special, 1969		
		Thong, 1964	Nantallah Rough Shod II

1st dam: Fairy Bridge, b, 1975-1991. Bred by Claiborne Farm (Ky). Raced 1 yr in Ire, 2 sts, 2 wins, $4,781. Champion 2yo filly in Ire. Dam of 9 named foals, 7 rnrs, 6 wnrs, 4 sw.
1980: B f, by Vaguely Noble.
1981: **SADLER'S WELLS**, b c, by Northern Dancer. Bred by Swettenham Stud and Partners (Ky). Raced 2 yrs in Eng, Ire, and Fr, 11 sts, 6 wins, $713,690. Champion miler in Fr. Won Airlie Coolmore Irish Two Thousand Guineas (Ire-I), Coral-Eclipse S (Eng-I), Phoenix Champion S (Ire-I), Derrinstown Stud Derby Trial S (Ire-II), Panasonic Beresford S (Ire-II); 2nd Prix du Jockey Club (Fr-I), King George VI and Queen Elizabeth S, Gladness S. Sire in Ire of 1,193 foals, 144 sw, 4.01 AEI.
1982: Fairy King, b c, by Northern Dancer. Raced 1 yr in Ire, 1 st, 0 wins, $0. Sire in Ire of 655 foals, AEI 2.32. Died 1999.
1983: **TATE GALLERY**, b c, by Northern Dancer. Raced 2 yrs in Eng and Ire, 5 sts, 2 wins, $68,586. Won B.B.A. Goffs National S (Ire-I); 3rd Michael Smurfit Gladness S. Sire in Ire of 223 foals, 13 sw, 1.37 AEI.

1984: **Fairy Dancer**, b f, by Nijinsky II. Raced 2 yrs in Ire, 2 sts, 1 win, $3,972. 3rd Pegasus Stud One Thousand Guineas Trial. Dam of 9 foals, 8 rnrs, 8 wnrs, including **Monsajem** ($135,017, in Eng).
1985: **FAIRY GOLD**, b f, by Northern Dancer. Raced 1 yr in Ire, 5 sts, 2 wins, $107,934. Won Oldtown Stud Debutante S (Ire-III); 2nd Moyglare Stud S (Ire-I), Ballygowan Railway S (Ire-III); 3rd Heinz 57 Phoenix S (Ire-I). Died 1990.
1986: **PUPPET DANCE**, ch f, by Northern Dancer. Raced 2 yrs in Fr, 11 sts, 2 wins, $67,465. Won Prix Soya; 3rd Prix Eclipse (Fr-III), Prix Imprudence. Dam of 7 foals, 5 rnrs, 2 wnrs.
1987: Classic Music, b c, by Northern Dancer. Unraced. Sire in Ire of 111 foals, 2 sw, 0.67 AEI.
1988: Hermitage, b c, by Storm Bird. Unraced. Sire in SAf.
1989: B c, by Storm Bird. Sent to Ire 1989.
1990: Barren.
1991: Perugino, dkb/br c, by Danzig. Raced 1 yr in Ire, 1 st, 1 win, $7,767. Sire in Ire of 155 foals, 5 sw, AEI 1.02.

Other of Sadler's Wells top runners to date include the following:

• Breeders' Cup winners **Northern Spur**, **Barathea**, **In the Wings**; Northern Spur won the 1995 Turf, Barathea the 1994 Mile, and In the Wings the 1990 Turf.

• **Salsabil**, a magnificent filly who defeated colts in the Irish Derby and also won the English Oaks and One Thousand Guineas and the Prix Marcel Boussac and Prix Vermeille in France.

• Additional English Oaks winners **Intrepidity** and **Moonshell**.

• **Opera House**, winner of a superb English triple of the King George VI and Queen Elizabeth, Eclipse Stakes, and Coronation Cup.

• **Dream Well**, like Old Vic and Montjeu,

another winner of both the French and Irish Derbys.

• *King's Theatre*, another King George VI and Queen Elizabeth winner.

• *King of Kings*, winner of the English Two Thousand Guineas after winning three stakes at two.

Other champions, classic winners, and group I winners in Europe to represent Sadler's Wells include Entrepreneur, El Prado, Saddlers' Hall, Stagecraft, Ebadiyla, Luna Wells, In Command, Leggera, and Balalaika.

In this country, the aforementioned Northern Spur was the Eclipse Award winner in the grass division in 1995; and, something of a footnote for such a sire, Corregio was a champion steeplechaser.

In the Wings made an early mark at stud in siring the astoundingly resilient globe-trotter Singspiel, winner of the Dubai World Cup, Japan Cup, Canadian International, and England's Coronation Cup and Juddmonte International. In the Wings also is the sire of Irish Derby winner Winged Love and the Italian champion Central Park.

Opera House's major winners in Japan include 1999 champion three-year-old colt T. M. Opera O as well as Nihon Pillow Jupiter. In North America, the Sadler's Wells stallion El Prado, a champion in Ireland at two, is having promising early results. In South Africa, the Sadler's Wells stallion Fort Wood (Grand Prix de Paris winner from the great mare Fall Aspen) sired the country's Triple Crown winner in Horse Chestnut. Winner of his only North American race, the Broward Handicap, Horse Chestnut has since been retired to stud at Claiborne Farm.

Special in Name and Gifts

In addition to being by the legendary Canadian-bred Northern Dancer, Sadler's Wells is out of an American-bred mare. The dam, Fairy Bridge, rep-resents one of the more astute purchases of recent times, and was a giveback by the American industry to the Anglo-Irish. Fairy Bridge was out of Special, and Special was from Thong, a full sister to Moccasin, Ridan, and Lt. Stevens. This trio were stars among the produce of Rough Shod II, an English mare imported to Claiborne Farm in this country in the early 1950s. Rough Shod II had been a moderate runner, winning once from seven starts. The descent to Special and Fairy Bridge was but one of many contributions from Rough Shod II, whose descendants also included Drumtop, Topsider, Gamely, and Cellini.

Special was unplaced in her only start. She then commenced an exceptional producing record: In addition to being the second dam of Sadler's Wells (and his distinguished brother Fairy King), Special was the first dam of the great stallion Nureyev [refer to separate chapter]. Special, who died at age thirty late in 1999, thus ranks with the likes of Plucky Liege and Selene as a maternal wellspring of successful stallions of the 20th Century. Moreover, Special foaled the stakes winners and important producers Number and Bound.

In 1976, when Fairy Bridge appeared as a year-ling in the Keeneland sale ring, many of the modern aspects of this heritage were unknown. Nureyev was *in utero*, for instance. Nevertheless, in the context of that time, Special was already known to be a full sister to top sprinter-miler Thatch and to Coronation Stakes winner Lisadell, and a half-sister to the group II winner King Pellinore. The specific British Bloodstock Agency buying team representing the Robert Sangster organization scooped up Special's 1976 Keeneland yearling filly for only $40,000. She was by Bold Reason, and while from the vantage point of history it might be assumed that this fact kept her price low, at the time Bold Reason was a

231

Sadler's Wells

young Travers Stakes winner out of the dam of Never Bend, so the gloss was not yet off. (By the end of 1976, the repatriated King Pellinore had proven a major winner in California.)

Fairy Bridge won her only two races at two and was put to stud. Her 1981 foal was a Northern Dancer with a bit of the white splashes so familiar in the line. The longish pasterns might have caused some concern, but not the white socks behind. Sadler's Wells was named for an historic London dance, opera, and lyric theatre stage and he has become rather historic himself. Although he won both of his races at two, he was something of a second-stringer in trainer Vincent O'Brien's yard. O'Brien's menu of Northern Dancers that year also included El Gran Senor. El Gran Senor defeated Sadler's Wells in the Gladness Stakes in April of their three-year-old season, then won the Two Thousand Guineas and was prepared for the Epsom Derby. At Epsom, El Gran Senor was edged by another Northern Dancer, Secreto (trained by O'Brien's son David), but then won the Irish Sweeps Derby, proving that the assigned pecking order had some foundation.

Sadler's Wells, however, also became a classic winner. After the Gladness, he won the Irish Two Thousand Guineas, but even then, he was not the stable's obvious hope; jockey Pat Eddery had chosen to ride another O'Brien candidate. Caerleon had become the first O'Brien horse to win a French classic when he scored in the French Derby, and Sadler's Wells was sent to emulate that effort. He failed to hold off another future pedigree influence, Darshaan. In light of his subsequent career, it is interesting to note that the French Derby alleviated a lurking thought in his stable that he might be deficient in stamina up to a mile and a half.

So, instead of retreating to mile races, O'Brien entered Sadler's Wells against older horses for the Eclipse Stakes at one and a quarter miles. Sadler's Wells was game in defeating Time Charter and Morcon. With the distance stepped up to one and a half miles, Sadler's Wells finished second to Teenoso in the King George VI and Queen Elizabeth, but with Darshaan and Time Charter trailing. Sadler's Wells was soundly beaten in the Benson & Hedges, but bounced back to win the new Phoenix Champion Stakes against a weak field. He was sent on to the Prix de l'Arc de Triomphe. The result of the Arc could be read as reason to denigrate him as a one and a half-mile horse, for he finished eighth. If we look a bit closer, and take into account how often horses are thrashed in the testing final furlongs of the Arc, his race is no disgrace. He was pushed along enough to be with the leading element turning for home. Dropping to eighth meant he still finished well up in a field of twenty-two, with Time Charter, Oaks winner Sun Princess, Estrapade, and the next year's Arc winner, Rainbow Quest, behind him. Sadler's Wells had won six of eleven races and earned $665,990.

He was clearly a top-class sire prospect, for, by then, the $40,000 yearling who became his dam was seen as a half-sister to the brilliant Nureyev. The high-headed Sadler's Wells, who raced in the Sangster colors, was sent to stud at Airlie-Coolmore in Ireland, in which Sangster was a visible partner, a role since taken by John Magnier. Coolmore has become a pioneer in the once-bizarre practice of shuttling stallions to the Southern Hemisphere to serve a second season after standing a breeding session on Northern Hemisphere time.

Underscoring the sire quality of this family is Sadler's Wells' full brother, Fairy King, who was second to him on the English/Irish sire list last year. Fairy King was the luckless brother. He fractured a sesamoid in his only start at three, but trainer Vincent O'Brien reportedly thought enough of him that he recommended him to son-in-law Philip Myerscough as a stallion at his stud farm. Fairy King later was moved to Coolmore. Although he died at seventeen, he had vindicated O'Brien's confidence. In addition to ranking second to his brother in 1999, Fairy King got two exceptional animals in 1996 Prix de l'Arc de Triomphe winner Helissio and 1999 Epsom Derby winner Oath. Fairy King's other runners included the English and French champion Revoque and Sangster's Gimcrack Stakes and Irish Two Thousand Guineas winner Turtle Island. Turtle Island, in turn, sired the 1999 English Two Thousand Guineas winner Island Sands.

As the current century develops, Sadler's Wells will be a challenging standard to look back upon for comparisons. ❖

Storm Cat

In a private moment, two of the most professional of modern Thoroughbred leaders might cast sentimental eyes to the heavens, raise a glass, and say in awe: "Destiny, thy name is Terlingua."

D. Wayne Lukas was enthralled by Terlingua before he even saw her; W. T. Young wound up owning her outright without original intent. Young bred and raced her sterling son Storm Cat; Lukas has trained a brace of Storm Cat's enormously talented offspring on Young's behalf.

Terlingua, then, has been pivotal to the success of a Hall of Fame trainer and a breeder-owner of distinguished status.

Turning first to Young: An eighty-two-year-old Lexington, Kentucky, native, Young crafted a successful business career on various fronts. He developed Big Top peanut butter, then sold it to Procter & Gamble, which re-named it Jif. Young went on to success in various other businesses, including storage and transport and was chairman of Royal Crown Cola. Young became a philanthropist of the highest order, and his $5-million gift to the University of Kentucky launched its W. T. Young Library.

Lukas is a native of a small Wisconsin town and, as a highly driven young man, taught school and coached basketball while racing horses on the side. He left the teaching profession to become a leading Quarter Horse trainer. Later, at a time he was gradually shifting to Thoroughbreds, Lukas trained the brilliant filly Terlingua. Elected to the National Museum of Racing Hall of Fame in 1999, he has conditioned a series of major horses by Terlingua's son Storm Cat, among them classic winner Tabasco Cat and 1999 Breeders' Cup Classic winner Cat Thief.

Terlingua had "star" in her stars from the beginning. She was in the second crop of the Triple Crown winner and public hero Secretariat. Her dam was the speedy Crimson Saint, who had been trained by Lukas' former father-in-law, Rod Kaufman. The flamboyant Kentucky breeder Tom Gentry bought Crimson Saint for $295,000 when she was carrying Terlingua and sold the filly as a yearling at Keeneland. Lukas was a newcomer at the Keeneland summer sale in 1977, but, as he said the next year, "I thought about her so many times before going to Keeneland that I knew exactly what she looked like. I could see the cross of that large horse on that mare, with all that conformation for speed, and I had a picture of her in my mind. When I went up to the Gentry barn, no one had to say, 'this is the filly' — I knew exactly the one I had come to see without anyone pointing her out."

Lukas warned his patron, L. R. French, that Gentry's salesmanship was directing a great deal of attention on the flashy filly. He said she might bring a half-million. Successful Texans don't like the implication, even unintended, that Kentucky might be over their heads; French said "bring her home." When Lukas called back later to say he had purchased the filly for $275,000, she seemed like a bargain. French later sold a half-interest to his friend Barry Beal. Both being residents of Midland, Texas, they named her for a Texas town known for its chili-cooking championship.

The self-confident young Lukas started Terlingua for the first time in a stakes, the Nursery, at Hollywood Park. She won that, then took the Hollywood Lassie. Further emboldened, Lukas ran her against colts in the Hollywood Juvenile Championship, and she won that, too. Although she seemed to train less impressively at Del Mar, Terlingua won the one-mile Debutante there by nine lengths. Lukas sent her East. The Del Mar experience gave him confidence when she again seemed not to train so well at Belmont Park. She was scuttled in the Frizette and later lost again in the Alcibiades.

The successful handling of Terlingua was a lesson Lukas would tuck away for future reference. He spent a good deal of time with her, settling her, and her physical type he never has had reason to shun: Strong quarters, powerful, reminiscent of the days when he had both breeds in his stable and would not tell his exercise riders whether they were on Thoroughbred or Quarter Horse prospects in early training. ("I believe Terlingua could have been as good a 400-yard horse as there is in America," Lukas said in 1978.)

That Lukas would some day train Terlingua's grandson to win the Belmont at one and a half miles followed some wide angles and long dis-

tances in the connect-the-dots of life. W. T. Young began buying property for his eventual Overbrook Farm in Lexington in the early 1970s. By the end of the decade, he was ready to make some major investments in horses. He turned for advice to some Lexingtonians he had known in other circles or had heard about: John A. Bell III, owner of Jonabell Farm; veteran bloodstock agent and farm manager Vic Heerman; and the noted veterinarian Robert Copelan. Ironically, it was a connection that eventually encountered some financial setbacks that brought Terlingua to Young. In the early 1980s, Dr. Bill Lockridge, who was operating Ashford Stud in partnership with Robert Hefner, developed a package of three attractive stakes mares — the Prix de l'Arc de Triomphe winner Three Troikas, Terlingua, and Cinegita — through various connections. They were to be bred to the young Ashford horse Storm Bird, among the most visible, though least proven, of the young Northern Dancer stallions of the day.

Young bought in. Three Troikas disappointed, but Cinegita foaled a pair of stakes winners and became the second dam of Overbrook champion Flanders — she, in turn, the dam of Surfside. Terlingua in 1983 foaled the dark bay or brown colt to be named Storm Cat.

"It really has to be considered pure luck," Young told *The Blood-Horse* in 2000. "First of all, Bill Lockridge is responsible for the mating that produced Storm Cat. He talked me into buying Terlingua. Ashford owned half and I owned half. I later bought them out when they got into financial trouble. Storm Cat was entered in the 1984 Keeneland summer yearling sale, but Keeneland asked us to take him out and sell him instead in September because he tested positive (for equine viral arteritis). I couldn't understand that, so I decided to race him."

		Nearctic, 1954	Nearco Lady Angela
	Northern Dancer, 1961		
STORM BIRD, b, 1978		Natalma, 1957	Native Dancer Almahmoud
		New Providence, 1956	Bull Page Fair Colleen
	South Ocean, 1967		
STORM CAT, **dkb/br h,** **February 27, 1983**		Shining Sun, 1962	Chop Chop Solar Display
		Bold Ruler, 1954	Nasrullah Miss Disco
	Secretariat, 1970		
		Somethingroyal, 1952	Princequillo Imperatrice
TERLINGUA, ch, 1976		Crimson Satan, 1959	Spy Song Papila
	Crimson Saint, 1969		
		Bolero Rose, 1958	Bolero First Rose

1st dam: TERLINGUA, ch, 1976. Bred by Tom Gentry (Ky). Raced 3 yrs, 17 sts, 7 wins, $423,896. Won Hollywood Juvenile Championship S (gr. II), Del Mar Debutante S (gr. II), Hollywood Lassie S (gr. II), Santa Ynez S (gr. III), Las Flores H, La Brea S, Nursery S; 2nd Santa Susana S (gr. I), Alcibiades S (gr. II), Sierra Madre H, Starlet S; 3rd Frizette S (gr. I). Dam of 9 named foals, 8 rnrs, 6 wnrs, 2 sw.

1982: Lyphard's Dancer, ch f, by Lyphard. Unraced. Dam of 5 foals, 5 rnrs, 5 wnrs, including **C'MON LETS DANCE** ($106,125). Died 1992. ($825,000 keejul yrlg).

1983: STORM CAT, dkb/br c, by Storm Bird. Bred by W.T. Young Storage (Pa). Raced 2 yrs, 8 sts, 4 wins, $570,610. Won Young America S (gr. I); 2nd Breeders' Cup Juvenile (gr. I), World Appeal S. Sire of 718 foals, 79 sw, 3.89 AEI.

1984: CHAPEL OF DREAMS, ch f, by Northern Dancer. Raced 4 yrs, 24 sts, 7 wins, $643,912. Won Palomar H (gr. IIT), Wilshire H (gr. IIT), Golden Poppy H (gr. IIIT), Calder Budweiser Breeders' Cup H (T), First National Bank of Maryland Ladies H (RT); 2nd Ramona H (gr. IT), Gamely H (gr. IT), Del Mar Oaks (gr. IIT), All Along S (T), San Clemente S (RT); 3rd Beverly Hills H (gr. IT), Suwannee River H (gr. IIIT), First National Bank of Maryland Ladies S (RT). Dam of 7 foals, 7 rnrs, 6 wnrs, including **Seeking the Dream** ($131,819, in Fr and NA). ($850,000 keejul yrlg).

1985: Barren.

1986: Tiajuana, b c, by Slew o' Gold. Raced 3 yrs, 24 sts, 3 wins, $66,679. Sent to Eng 1991.

1987: Dead foal.

1988: Barren.

1989: Provo, ch c, by Alydar. Raced 3 yrs, 24 sts, 2 wins, $40,992. Sent to Cyp 1994.

1990: Wheaton, ch c, by Alydar. Raced 2 yrs, 11 sts, 1 win, $6,503. Sire of 85 foals, 1.49 AEI.

1991: Barren.

1992: Pueblo, ch f, by Mr. Prospector. Raced 1 yr, 4 sts, 0 wins, $7,488.

1993: Pioneering, ch c, by Mr. Prospector. Raced 1 yr, 6 sts, 2 wins, $39,426.

1994: Barren.

1995: Barren.

1996: Namesake, ch c, by Storm Bird. Raced 2 yrs, 4 sts, 0 wins, $6,940.

1997: Slipped.

1998: Ch f, by Carson City.

1999: Slipped.

Storm Bird, sire of Storm Cat, was well named, in an allegorical sense. He came along in that storm of high-flying auction prices in the 1980s. He was a Windfields Farm product, by Northern Dancer and out of South Ocean, by New Providence. The mare had won the 1969 Yearling Sales Stakes and 1970 Canadian Oaks as the first stakes winner raced in the name of Charles Taylor, son of Windfields founder E. P. Taylor (and for some years later the head of the great breeding-racing-sale operation). South Ocean later became a prominent mare, producing the grade I winner Northernette as well as Storm Bird and two other stakes winners. This was the family of the 1950 American juvenile champion, Battlefield. At the 1979 Keeneland summer sale Robert Sangster and his team bought Storm Bird for $1,000,000. The following year, he won all his five races, including the Dewhurst Stakes (over To-Agori-Mou and Miswaki) and three other stakes. He was the top-rated two-year-old of 1980 in both England and Ireland.

Dame Misfortune, who previously had left Storm Bird to his own devices, settled in over his stall at Vincent O'Brien's pristine yard in Ireland. One night, an ex-employee broke into his stall and hacked at his mane and tail — maybe no structural damage, but a frightening experience for any animal conditioned since a frosty morning at Windfields that humans were his wards, mentors, and protectors. Then various ills precluded his appearing in the Two Thousand Guineas or Derby, or even any prep races. In the summer, it was announced that an American group had purchased him on the basis of the enormous evaluation of $30 million, with Sangster retaining an interest. In most cases, buyers of so ephemeral a commodity as an unbeaten status would retire the attendant horse immediately, but Storm Bird was announced as a candidate for the Prix de l'Arc de Triomphe. He failed in his prep race and was sent to stud at Ashford in Kentucky. (The farm later came under the ownership of the Coolmore complex of Ireland and continues as a major Kentucky farm and stallion operation.)

The prowess of Storm Cat may tend to overshadow Storm Bird himself as one of the many important sons of Northern Dancer at stud. Storm Bird's fifty-nine stakes winners (nine percent)

include the American classic winner Summer Squall, who won the Preakness of 1990 as well as the Hopeful, Blue Grass, and other major stakes. Summer Squall seemed headed toward being a filly sire, with his juvenile champion Storm Song, but in 1999 he was represented by the Kentucky Derby-Preakness winner and Horse of the Year Charismatic. Storm Bird's other top horses include the champion filly Balanchine, winner of the Epsom Oaks over fillies and the Irish Derby over colts. Another Storm Bird filly to defeat colts was Indian Skimmer, who won the Champion Stakes in England and the Irish Champion Stakes, after defeating fillies in the French Oaks and Prix Saint-Alary. Other classic winners and/or champions by Storm Bird include Bluebird, Prince of Birds, Mukaddamah, and Acushla, while his Personal Hope, Classy Mirage, and Pacific Squall have won grade I races in this country.

Fast Ships and Stormy Seas

W. T. Young's Storm Bird—Terlingua colt, named Storm Cat, was foaled and raised at Marshall Jenney's Derry Meeting Farm in Pennsylvania. The mare was boarded there in the spring of 1983, when booked to Northern Dancer in neighboring Maryland. Storm Cat was raised and broken at Derry Meeting, then turned over to trainer Jonathan Sheppard. Although best known as a Hall of Fame steeplechase trainer, Sheppard is no novice at conditioning flat horses. Storm Cat was not impressive as a young foal, but grew into a commanding presence. At two in 1985, he ran six times. He was beaten a head at Saratoga, broke his maiden there, then shipped down to Meadowlands, where he won an allowance race and was second in the World Appeal Stakes. Storm Cat's entrance into the upper echelons, which he has never departed, came when he

Storm Cat

defeated Danzig Connection and Mogambo in a testing, three-horse finish in the grade I Young America Stakes, also at Meadowlands. In the Breeders' Cup Juvenile, he seemed to have a million-dollar race and an Eclipse Award in hand, but Tasso came flying far on the outside. It was conjectured that perhaps Storm Cat did not see Tasso. Whether that was the case or not, the photo finish camera did. Tasso got the Breeders' Cup win, and the championship. (Young later recalled his embarrassment in heading for the winner's circle on the basis of what he, and those around him, hoped they had seen. He vowed not to rush to conclusions, or at least winner's circles, again. Eleven years later, Young waited in his box until he was sure of the result in another hairbreadth affair — his Grindstone's victory in the Kentucky Derby.)

Storm Cat had arthroscopic surgery to remove bone chips in a knee early in his three-year-old season. He came back to race again, but got in only two races, winning one. He was still in training for a campaign at four when he developed inflammation in a foreleg. Although it was too late to make the 1987 breeding season, Young decided to stop on him then rather than risk further injury. He had won four of eight races and earned $570,610. "He had a will to win," Copelan (still a valued adviser to Young) told *The Blood-Horse*. "I think that is a heritable characteristic."

Lukas, too, has spoken of the fire of the Storm Cats. One of the grittiest was Overbrook's Tabasco Cat. Tragically, it was this classy but feisty Storm Cat colt that got loose in the shedrow one morning and collided with Lukas' son and assistant, Jeff Lukas. The young man's life hung in the balance for some time. He recovered and, while unable to be as active in the physical aspects of the stable as he had been, Jeff returned to work, in more of an administrative capacity for his father.

The elder Lukas worked hospital bedside hours into his stable routine. The part of him awash in anguish did not bring down what he — and Jeff — were all about as horsemen. He recognized that Tabasco Cat was no rogue, and he expended the same sort of patience that he had needed in handling the granddam, Terlingua, in taking time in the mornings to settle the colt. Hollywood scriptwriters have no match for what happened. In the spring of 1994, Tabasco Cat (owned in partnership by Young and his friend David Reynolds) won the Preakness Stakes and Belmont Stakes. It was the start of a six-race winning skein in Triple Crown races for Lukas, and Young's Grindstone was a part of that streak in winning the Derby two years later. (Young was also co-owner of the 1995 Preakness winner, Timber Country, also a part of the streak. One race after the streak was broken, Lukas and Young rebounded to win the 1996 Belmont Stakes with Editor's Note!)

Storm Cat twice ranked second on the sire list, in 1994 and 1998, before rising to the top spot in 1999 with a record one-year progeny total of $10,374,436. In 1999, Storm Cat also led the juvenile sire list, for the fifth year. That year, while the Northern Dancer stallion Sadler's Wells had twenty-one stakes winners around the world, the grandson, Storm Cat, had twenty-four. Storm Cat's progeny had earnings of $681,350 million in Europe and of $1,653,564 in Japan in 1999.

Storm Cat's stud fee has increased to $300,000, tops around the world for 2000. The Coolmore group has purchased a packet of lifetime breeding rights in the horse, of whom Young has retained ownership rather than syndicate.

Young's Cat Thief went through part of 1999 not quite getting there in the best company, but in his richest race of all, the Breeders' Cup Classic, the Storm Cat grit took him to the wire in front. In the two-year-old division, Storm Cat's team included Hopeful Stakes winner High Yield. Storm Cat ended 1999 with a rapidly growing total of seventy-nine stakes winners (fifteen percent) at the age of sixteen. In addition to Tabasco Cat, Cat Thief, and High Yield (winner of the 2000 Blue Grass Stakes), his best include:

• *Sharp Cat*, an imposing filly whose demolition of top-class fields almost earned an Eclipse Award and once brought about a walkover in a stakes, before an illness forced her out of the Breeders' Cup Distaff.

• *Mountain Cat*, winner of a Kentucky bonus of $1,000,000 for sweeping a series of Juvenile races, including the Breeders' Futurity.

• *Sardula*, winner of the Kentucky Oaks and as game as any of the tribe.

• *Desert Stormer*, a filly who won the Breeders' Cup Sprint.

• *Vision and Verse*, winner of the Illinois Derby and runner-up in a photo in the 1999 Belmont Stakes.

• *Hennessy*, winner of the Hopeful and Sapling.

• *Catinca*, a consistent filly and a grade I distaff winner.

• *November Snow*, whose mile-and-a-quarter Alabama Stakes win was an early testimony that the Storm Cats could get a distance.

• *Catrail*, twice a division champion in England.

• *Aljabr*, winner of England's group I Sussex Stakes and France's group I Prix de la Salamandre.

Others include Forestry, Aldiza, Tactical Cat, Sir Cat, Tale of the Cat, Giant's Causeway, and Bernstein.

The Storm Cats are off and running as sires as well. The Vosburgh Handicap winner Harlan died young, but sent out Menifee, a grade I winner and runner-up in the 1999 Kentucky Derby. The Storm Cat stallion Storm Boot, not a stakes winner himself, has out the quick graded stakes winner Bourbon Belle, and millionaire Mountain Cat has already sired the millionaire Classic Cat.

The millionaire status may not be what it once was, but it still has a nice ring to it. His millionaires were proliferating as Storm Cat's record of one century merged with that of another. ❖

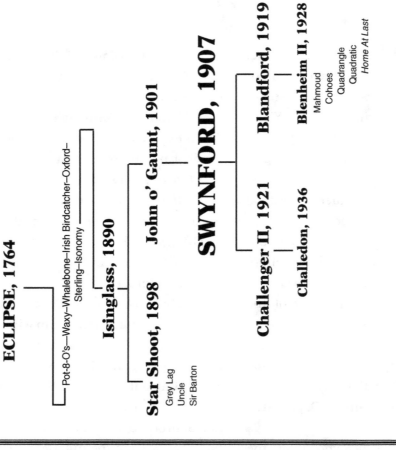

ECLIPSE, 1764

└─Pot-8-O's—Waxy–Whalebone–Irish Birdcatcher–Oxford–
Sterling–Isonomy

Isinglass, 1890

Star Shoot, 1898
Grey Lag
Uncle
Sir Barton

John o' Gaunt, 1901

SWYNFORD, 1907

Challenger II, 1921

Challedon, 1936

Blandford, 1919

Blenheim II, 1928
Mahmoud
Cohoes
Quadrangle
Quadratic
Home At Last

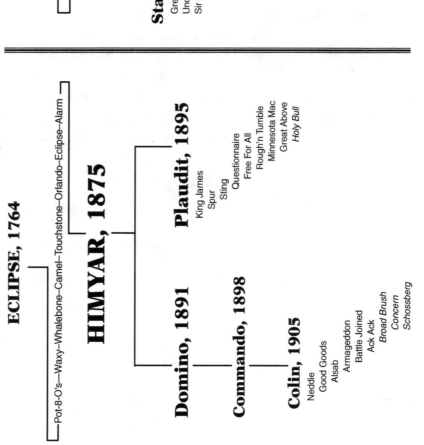

ECLIPSE, 1764

└─Pot-8-O's—Waxy–Whalebone–Camel–Touchstone–Orlando–Eclipse–Alarm

HIMYAR, 1875

Domino, 1891

Plaudit, 1895
King James
Spur
Sting
Questionnaire
Free For All
Rough'n Tumble
Minnesota Mac
Great Above
Holy Bull

Commando, 1898

Colin, 1905
Neddie
Good Goods
Alsab
Armageddon
Battle Joined
Ack Ack
Broad Brush
Concern
Schossberg

Found on these pages are male lines of descent from Eclipse, Herod, and Matchem, the three 18th century English stallions to which all Thoroughbreds today may be traced. Stallions active as of the year 2000 are shown with their names appearing in italic type.

240

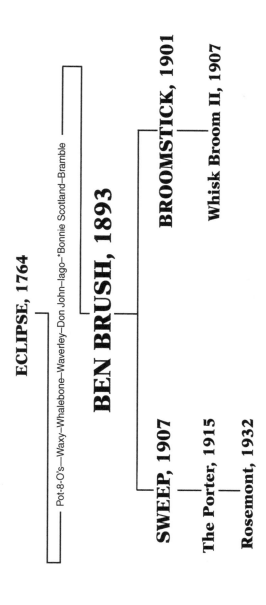

ECLIPSE, 1764

Pot-8-O's—Waxy—Whalebone—Waverley—Don John—Iago—*Bonnie Scotland—Bramble

BEN BRUSH, 1893

BROOMSTICK, 1901

Whisk Broom II, 1907

SWEEP, 1907

The Porter, 1915

Rosemont, 1932

241

ECLIPSE, 1764

Pot-8-O's—Waxy–Whalebone–Sir Hercules–Irish Birdcatcher–The Baron

Stockwell–Doncaster—Bend Or–Ormonde–Orme–Flying Fox–Ajax

TEDDY, 1913

Sun Teddy, 1933
- Sun Again
- Sunglow
- Sword Dancer
- Damascus
- Bailjumper
  - Skip Trial
  - Skip Away
- Crusader Sword
- Cutlass
  - Friendly Lover
- Eastern Echo
  - Swiss Yodeler
  - Western Echo
- Festive
- Marsayas
  - Mister Frisky
  - Frisk Me Now
  - Rod and Staff
- Ogygian
- Ogydoug
- Order
- Private Account
- Brunswick
  - Corporate Report
  - Party Manners
  - Personal Flag
    - Saratoga Sunrise
  - Private Terms
    - Afternoon Deelites
  - Secret Hello
- Sir Leon
- Top Account
  - Unaccounted For
    - Valley Crossing
    - Swiss Trick
  - Time for a Change
    - Fly So Free
    - Technology
  - Timeless Moment
    - Gilded Time

Bull Dog, 1927
Bull Lea, 1935
- Beau Prince
- Bull Page
- Citation
- Coaltown
- Hill Gail
- Iron Liege

Sir Gallahad III, 1920
- Gallant Fox
  - Omaha
- Fighting Fox
  - Crafty Admiral
    - Admiral's Voyage
- Roman
  - Hasty Road

MATCHEM, 1748

Conductor–Trumpeter–Sorcerer–Comos–Humphrey Clinker–Melbourne

West Australian, 1850

Solon, 1861
- Barcaldine
- Marco
- Marcovil
- Hurry On
  - Precipitation
  - Sheshoon
  - Sassafras
  - Baynoun
    - *Sandpit*

Australian, 1858
- Spendthrift
- Hastings
- Fair Play

Man o' War, 1917

War Relic, 1938

Relic, 1945
- Olden Times
- Full Pocket
- *Fighting Fit*
- *Pok Ta Pok*

Intent, 1948
- Intentionally
- In Reality
- *American Standard*
- *Believe It*
- Al Mamoon
- Cost Conscious
- Garthorn
  - *Near the Limit*
  - *Reality Road*
- Dignitas
- Judge Smells
  - *Judge T C*
- Known Fact
  - *Binalong*
- In the Zone
- Kyle's Our Man
- Proper Reality
- *Slice of Reality*
- Relaunch
  - *Bright Launch*
- Canaveral
- Cee's Tizzy
- Honour and Glory
- Skywalker
  - *Bertrando*
- Slew Gin Fizz
- Star of the Crop
- Waquoit
  - *Wa Bert*

- Valid Appeal
  - Kipper Kelly
  - Mister Jolie
- Proud Appeal
  - *Appealing Guy*
  - *Valid Expectations*
- Valid Wager
- World Appeal
  - *The Vid*

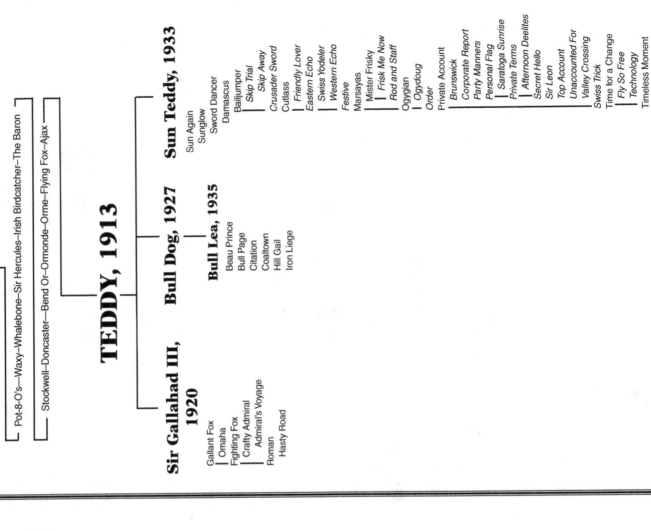
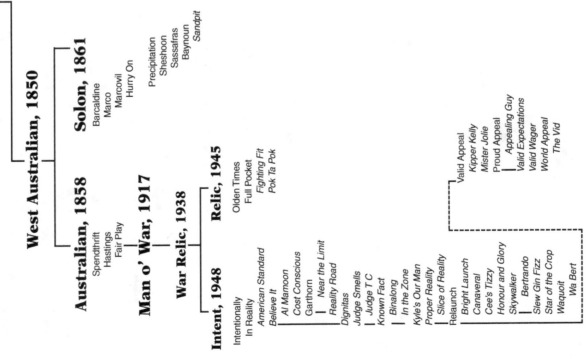

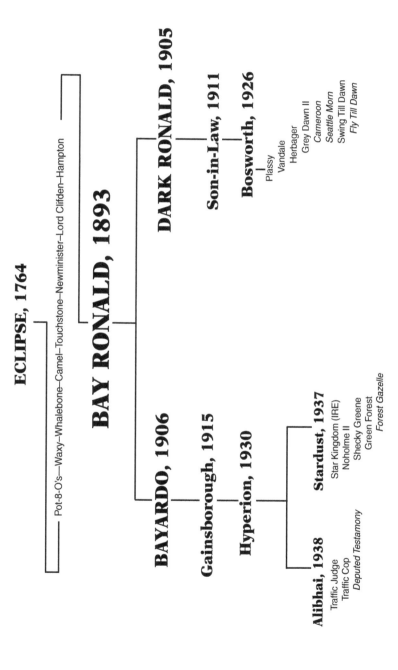

ECLIPSE, 1764

Pot-8-O's—Waxy—Whalebone—Camel—Touchstone—Newminister—Lord Clifden—Hampton

BAY RONALD, 1893

DARK RONALD, 1905

Son-in-Law, 1911

Bosworth, 1926

Plassy
Vandale
Herbager
Grey Dawn II
Cameroon
Seattle Morn
Swing Till Dawn
Fly Till Dawn

BAYARDO, 1906

Gainsborough, 1915

Hyperion, 1930

Stardust, 1937

Star Kingdom (IRE)
Noholme II
Shecky Greene
Green Forest
Forest Gazelle

Alibhai, 1938

Traffic Judge
Traffic Cop
Deputed Testamony

ECLIPSE, 1764

King Fergus–Hambletonian–Whitelock–Blacklock–Voltaire–Voltigeur–Vedette–Galopin

ST. SIMON, 1881

Chaucer, 1900

Prince Chimay
Vatout
Bois Roussel
Migoli
Gallant Man
Gallant Romeo
Elocutionist
Demons Begone
Momsfurrari

Persimmon, 1893

Prince Palatine
Rose Prince
Prince Rose

Prince Bio, 1941

Sicambre
Roi Dagobert
On the Sly
Play Fellow
Western Playboy
Shantung
Felicio
Itajara
Siphon

Princequillo, 1940

Prince John, 1953

Silent Screen
Dusty Screen
Speak John
Hold Your Peace
Meadowlake
Meadow Flight
Meadow Monster
Meadowtime
Undeniable
Thunder Puddles
Thunder Rumble

Go Marching, 1965

Kohoutek
Purple Comet

Round Table, 1954

Advocator
Bert's Bubbleator
Apalachee
Bold Lachee
Grand Circus Park
Flirting Around
Wolf Power (SAF)
Illustrious
Loustrous Bid
Upper Case
Flying Pidgeon

ECLIPSE, 1764

King Fergus—Hambletonian—Whitelock—Blacklock—Voltaire—Voltigeur

VEDETTE, 1854

Galopin, 1872

St. Simon

Rabelais, 1900

Havresac, 1915

Cavaliere d'Arpino
Bellini
Tenerani

Ribot, 1952

Arts and Letters, 1966

Codex
Lost Code

Graustark, 1963

Gregorian
Key to the Mint
Java Gold
Grand Jewel
Rockamundo

His Majesty, 1968

Batonnier
Robannier
Cormorant
Go for Gin
Mighty Magee
Raffie's Majesty
Scarlet Ibis
Country Pine
Rustic Light
Frosty the Snowman
Majesty's Prince
Pleasant Colony
Colonial Affair
Colony Light
Earth Colony
Lac Ouimet
Pleasant Dancer
Pleasant Tap
Roanoke
St. Jovite
Wild Colony
Valiant Nature

Tom Rolfe, 1962

Hoist the Flag
Blue Ensign
Linkage
Salutely
Mr. Zill Bear
Stalwart
Stalwars

Pot-8-O's—Waxy—Whalebone—Sir Hercules—Irish Birdcatcher—The Baron—Stockwell

Doncaster—Bend Or—Bona Vista—Cyllene—Polymelus—Phalaris—Pharos—Nearco

NASRULLAH, 1940 (see also Bold Ruler)

Fleet Nasrullah, 1955
Gummo
Flying Paster
Flying Continental
Flying Victor
Gold Trojan
Gold Spring (ARG)
Golden Act

Grey Sovereign, 1956
Fortino II
Caro (IRE)
Cozzene
Alphabet Soup
Cozy Drive
Hasten To Add
Grand Flotilla
Siberian Express
In Excess (IRE)
Indian Charlie
Tejano
Tejano Run
With Approval
Lasting Approval
Talkin Man
Zeddaan
Kalamoun
Kenmare (FR)
Highest Honor (FR)

Indian Hemp, 1949
T. V. Lark
Romeo
Big Pistol
T. V. Commercial
It's Freezing
Plenty Chilly

Nashua, 1952
Good Manners
Friul (ARG)
Paranoide (ARG)
Mocito Guapo
Memo (CHI)

Nasram, 1960
Naskra
Olympio
Star de Naskra
Carr de Naskra
Moonlight Dancer
Spartan Victory
Dance Floor
Eagle County

Never Bend, 1960
Mill Reef
Shirley Heights (GB)
Darshaan
Mark of Esteem (IRE)
Never Tabled
Smokester
Free House
Proudest Roman
Horatius
Riverman
Bahri
Irish River (FR)
Navarone
Rouse the Louse
Keos
Loup Sauvage
Policeman (FR)
Claramount
River Flyer
Rousillon
Fastness (IRE)

Red God, 1954
Blushing Groom (FR)
Blushing John
Jaggery John
Candy Stripes
Digamist
Groom Dancer
Pursuit of Love
Hazaam
Imperial Gold
Mt. Livermore
Lucky Lionel
Peaks and Valleys
Prince of the Mt.
Pyramid Peak
Same Day Delivery
Subordination
Nashwan
Swain (IRE)
Rahy
Genuine Reward
Rainbow Quest
Urgent Request (IRE)
Runaway Groom
Cherokee Run
Wekiva Springs
Sillery

ECLIPSE, 1764

Pot-8-O's—Waxy—Whalebone—Sir Hercules—Irish Birdcatcher—The Baron—Stockwell

Bend Or—Bona Vista—Cyllene—Polymelus—Phalaris—Pharos—Nearco—Nasrullah

BOLD RULER, 1954

Chieftain, 1961
Fit to Fight
Blare of Trumpets
Key Contender

Dewan, 1965
Glitterman

Raja Baba, 1968
Is It True
Well Decorated
Formal Dinner
Notebook
Pulverizing

Bold Bidder, 1962
Cannonade
Caveat
Awad
Ops Smile
Spectacular Bid

Cornish Prince, 1962
Zuppardo's Prince

What a Pleasure, 1965
Foolish Pleasure
Foligno
Kiri's Clown
Marfa
Farma Way
Cobra King
Maudlin
Mecke

Secretariat, 1970
Academy Award
D'Accord
Montreal Red
General Assembly
Presidium (GB)
Mighty Forum (GB)
Medaille d'Or
Tour d'Or
Pancho Villa

Boldnesian, 1963
Bold Reasoning
Seattle Slew
A.P. Indy
A P Ruler
Accelerator
Admiral Indy
Cromwell
General Royal
Indy Mood
Malibu Moon
Old Trieste
Pulpit
Avenue of Flags
Capote
Acceptable
Boston Harbor
Capote's Prospect
Matty G
Thisnearlywasmine
Carolina Kid
Corslew
Dr. Caton
Eastover Court
Event of the Year
Fast Play
General Meeting
Gold Legend
Dr J
Harry the Hat

Hickman Creek
Houston
Metfield
Nelson
Ocala Slew
Seattle Proud
Seattle Sleet
Seattle Song
Whadjathink
Slew City Slew
Evansville Slew
Slew o' Gold
Slew the Coup
Slew the Knight
Slewacide
Slewpy
Slewvescent
Stately Slew
Williamstown
Super Concorde
Concorde Bound
Concorde's Tune
Bold Ruckus
Beau Genius
Bold Executive
Demaloot Demashoot
John the Magician
Kiridashi

Irish Castle, 1967
Bold Forbes
Air Forbes Won
Irish Tower
Irish Open

ECLIPSE, 1764

Pot-8-O's—Waxy—Whalebone—Sir Hercules—Irish Birdcatcher—The Baron—Stockwell

Doncaster—Bend Or—Bona Vista—Cyllene—Polymelus—Phalaris—Pharos—Nearco

ROYAL CHARGER, 1942

Turn-to, 1951

Cyane, 1959

Roanoke Island
Willard Scott
Smarten
Prenup
Smart Alec

Best Turn, 1957

Cox's Ridge
Eltish
Out of Place
Sultry Song
Trapp Mountain
High Brite

First Landing, 1956

Riva Ridge
The Red Rolls

Hail to Reason, 1958

Halo
Devil's Bag
Abaginone
Devil His Due
Holy Mountain
Kerosene
Lived It Up
Twilight Agenda
Halo's Image
Hay Halo
Heaven's Wish
Hurontario
D. J. Cat
Saint Ballado
Captain Bodgit
Sanctuary
Southern Halo
Star of Halo
Stauder
Strodes Creek
Sunny's Halo
Dispersal
Hesabull
Irgun
Mr. Leader
Doc's Leader
Proud Clarion
Proud Birdie
Birdonthewire

Roberto
Darby Creek Road
Salem Drive
Dynaformer
Blumin Affair
Kris S.
Arch
Kissin Kris
Prized
Thug
To a Wild Kris
You and I
Lear Fan
Fantastic Fellow
Labeeb (GB)
Major Impact
Red Ransom
Hold for Gold
Repriced
Robellino
Mister Baileys (GB)
Royal Roberto
Shuailaan
Silver Hawk
Benny the Dip
Wistful Roberto
Stop the Music
Cure the Blues
American Chance
Dr. Adagio
Incurable Optimist
Prudent Manner (IRE)
Take Me Out
Tethra

Sir Gaylord, 1959

Habitat
Dalsaan
Raykour (IRE)
Habitony
Richter Scale
Lord Gaylord
Lord Avie
Sir Ivor
Bates Motel
Private School
Sir Ivor Again
Ten Keys
Sir Tristram
Zabeel
Octagonal
Sir Wimborne
My Prince Charming

248

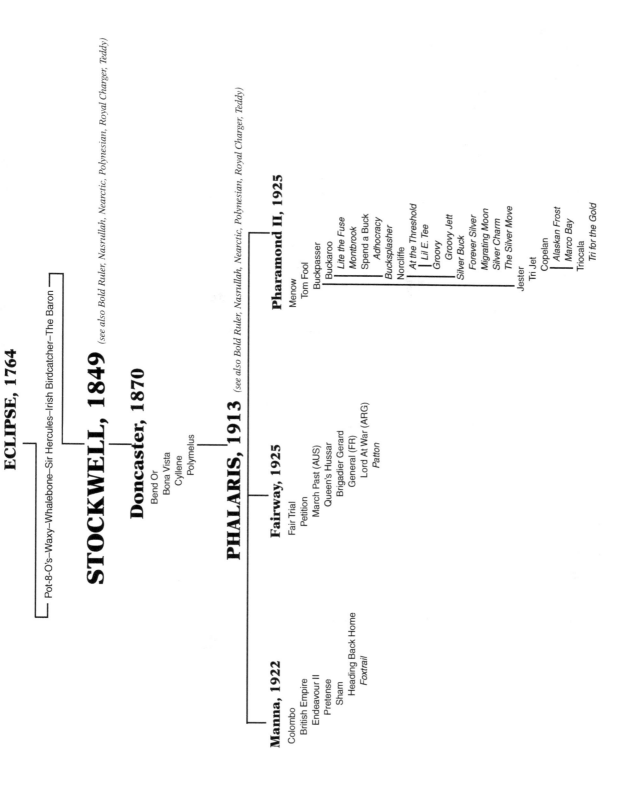

ECLIPSE, 1764

Pot-8-O's–Waxy–Whalebone–Sir Hercules–Irish Birdcatcher–The Baron

STOCKWELL, 1849 *(see also Bold Ruler, Nasrullah, Nearctic, Polynesian, Royal Charger, Teddy)*

Doncaster, 1870

Bend Or
Bona Vista
Cyllene
Polymelus

PHALARIS, 1913 *(see also Bold Ruler, Nasrullah, Nearctic, Polynesian, Royal Charger, Teddy)*

Fairway, 1925

Fair Trial
Petition
March Past (AUS)
Queen's Hussar
Brigadier Gerard
General (FR)
Lord At War (ARG)
Patton

Manna, 1922

Colombo
British Empire
Endeavour II
Pretense
Sham
Heading Back Home
Foxtrail

Pharamond II, 1925

Menow
Tom Fool
Buckpasser
Buckaroo
Lite the Fuse
Montbrook
Spend a Buck
Adhocracy
Bucksplasher
Norcliffe
At the Threshold
Lil E. Tee
Groovy
Groovy Jett
Silver Buck
Forever Silver
Migrating Moon
Silver Charm
The Silver Move
Jester
Tri Jet
Copelan
Alaskan Frost
Marco Bay
Triocala
Tri for the Gold

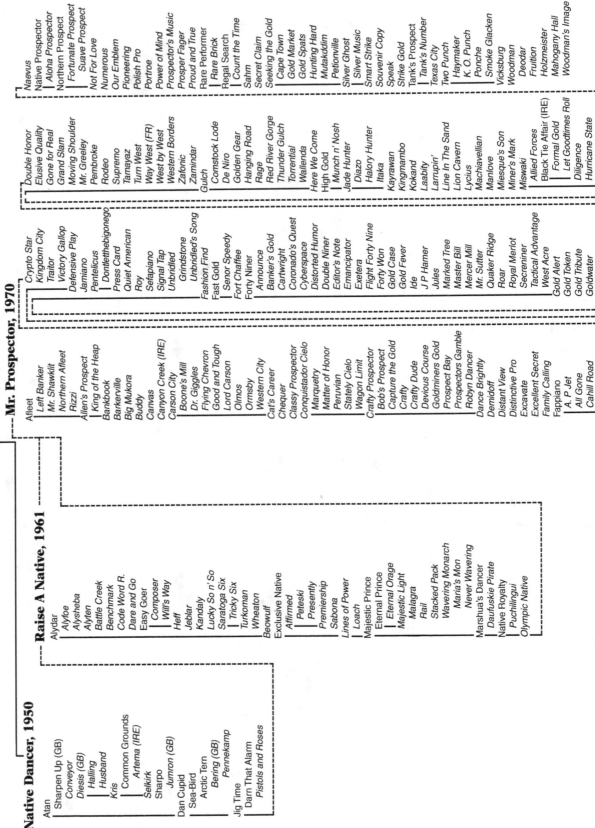

ECLIPSE, 1764

Pot-8-O's—Waxy—Whalebone—Sir Hercules—Irish Birdcatcher—The Baron—Stockwell

Doncaster—Bend Or—Bona Vista—Cyllene—Polymelus—Phalaris—Sickle—Unbreakable

POLYNESIAN, 1942

Mr. Prospector, 1970

Naevus
Native Prospector
Aloha Prospector
Northern Prospect
Fortunate Prospect
Suave Prospect
Not For Love
Numerous
Our Emblem
Pioneering
Polish Pro
Portroe
Power of Mind
Prospector's Music
Prosper Fager
Proud and True
Rare Performer
Rare Brick
Regal Search
Count the Time
Sahm
Secret Claim
Seeking the Gold
Cape Town
Gold Market
Gold Spats
Hunting Hard
Mutakddim
Petionville
Silver Ghost
Silver Music
Smart Strike
Souvenir Copy
Speak
Strike Gold
Tank's Prospect
Tank's Number
Texas City
Two Punch
Haymaker
K. O. Punch
Ponche
Smoke Glacken
Vicksburg
Woodman
Deodar
Fruition
Holzmeister
Mahogany Hall
Woodman's Image

Double Honor
Elusive Quality
Gone for Real
Grand Slam
Moving Shoulder
Mr. Greeley
Pembroke
Rodeo
Supremo
Tamayaz
Turn West
Way West (FR)
West by West
Western Borders
Zafonic
Zamindar
Gulch
Comstock Lode
De Niro
Golden Gear
Hanging Road
Rage
Red River Gorge
Thunder Gulch
Torrential
Wallenda
Here We Come
High Gold
Munch n' Nosh
Jade Hunter
Diazo
Halory Hunter
Itaka
Kayrawan
Kingmambo
Kokand
Laabity
Larrupin'
Line In The Sand
Lion Cavern
Lycius
Machiavellian
Manlove
Miesque's Son
Miner's Mark
Miswaki
Allied Forces
Black Tie Affair (IRE)
Formal Gold
Let Goodtimes Roll
Diligence
Hurricane State
Muskoka Music
Waki Warrior

Crypto Star
Kingdom City
Traitor
Victory Gallop
Defensive Play
Jamiano
Pentelicus
Dontletthebigonego
Press Card
Quiet American
Roy
Sefapiano
Signal Tap
Unbridled
Grindstone
Unbridled's Song
Fashion Find
Fast Gold
Senor Speedy
Fort Chaffee
Forty Niner
Announce
Banker's Gold
Cartwright
Coronado's Quest
Cyberspace
Distorted Humor
Double Niner
Editor's Note
Emancipator
Exetera
Flight Forty Nine
Forty Won
Gold Case
Gold Fever
Ide
J P Hamer
Jules
Marked Tree
Master Bill
Mercer Mill
Mr. Sutter
Quaker Ridge
Roar
Royal Merlot
Secreniner
Tactical Advantage
West Acre
Gold Alert
Gold Token
Goldwater
Gone West

Afleet
Left Banker
Mr. Shawklit
Northern Afleet
Rizzi
Allen's Prospect
King of the Heap
Bankbook
Barkerville
Big Mukora
Buddy
Canvas
Canyon Creek (IRE)
Carson City
Boone's Mill
Dr. Giggles
Flying Chevron
Good and Tough
Lord Carson
Olmos
Ormsby
Western City
Cat's Career
Chequer
Classy Prospector
Conquistador Cielo
Marquetry
Matter of Honor
Peruvian
Stately Cielo
Wagon Limit
Crafty Prospector
Bob's Prospect
Capture the Gold
Crafty
Crafty Dude
Devious Course
Goldminers Gold
Prospect Bay
Prospectors Gamble
Robyn Dancer
Dance Brightly
Demidoff
Distant View
Distinctive Pro
Excavate
Excellent Secret
Family Calling
Fappiano
A. P Jet
All Gone
Cahill Road
Cryptoclearance

Raise A Native, 1961

Alydar
Alyfoe
Alysheba
Alyten
Battle Creek
Benchmark
Code Word R.
Dare and Go
Easy Goer
Composer
Will's Way
Heff
Jeblar
Kandaly
Lucky So n' So
Saratoga Six
Tricky Six
Turkoman
Wheaton
Beowulf
Exclusive Native
Affirmed
Peteski
Presently
Premiership
Sabona
Lines of Power
Loach
Majestic Prince
Eternal Prince
Eternal Orage
Majestic Light
Malagra
Rail
Stacked Pack
Wavering Monarch
Maria's Mon
Never Wavering
Marshua's Dancer
Daufuskie Pirate
Native Royalty
Puchilingui
Olympic Native

Native Dancer, 1950

Atan
Sharpen Up (GB)
Conveyor
Diesis (GB)
Halling
Husband
Kris
Common Grounds
Artema (IRE)
Selkirk
Sharpo
Jumron (GB)
Dan Cupid
Sea-Bird
Arctic Tern
Bering (GB)
Pennekamp
Jig Time
Darn That Alarm
Pistols and Roses

ECLIPSE, 1764

Pot-8-O's—Waxy—Whalebone—Sir Hercules—Irish Birdcatcher—The Baron—Stockwell

Doncaster—Bend Or—Bona Vista—Cyllene—Polymelus—Phalaris—Pharos—Nearco

NEARCTIC, 1954

Northern Dancer, 1961

Explodent
Expelled
Explosive Bid
Expensive Decision
Explosive Red
Time to Explode
Icecapade
Clever Trick
Anet
Grim Reaper
Hadif
Matchlite
Phone Trick
Caller I. D.
Confide
Favorite Trick
Mazel Trick
Not Tricky
Semoran
Star of Valor
Tricky Fun
Tricky Creek
Wild Again
El Amante
Free At Last
Nines Wild
Vicar
Whiskey Wisdom
Wild Deputy
Wild Escapade
Wild Event
Wild Gold
Wild Rush
Wild Syn
Wild Wonder
Wild Zone

Be My Guest
Media Starguest (IRE)
Carnivalay
Danzatore
Danzig
Ago
Always Fair
Anabaa
Anziyan
Ascot Knight
Belong to Me
Bianconi
Boundary
Brooklyn Nick
Bugatti Reef (IRE)
Burooj (GB)
Chief's Crown
Concerto
Erhaab
Vermont
Crimson Guard
Danzatame
Dayjur
Danjur
Elajjud
Deerhound
Dove Hunt
Dumaani
Eqtesaad
Furiously
Game Plan
Green Desert
Cape Cross (IRE)
Honor Grades
Langfuhr
Lost Soldier
Lure
Military
New Way
Nicholas
Outflanker
Partner's Hero
Pine Bluff
Lil's Lad
Polish Navy
Ghazi
Pollock's Luck
Prussian Blue
Sea Hero

Polish Numbers
Polish Precedent
Peace Prize (IRE)
Presidential Order
Safely's Mark
Sea Salute
Slavic
Stephene Mon Amour
Truckee
Dixieland Band
Capitalimprovement
Chimes Band
Citidancer
Dixie Brass
Dixie Connection
Dixie Power
Dixieland Brass
Toolighttoquit
Dixieland Heat
Jambalaya Jazz
Southern Rhythm
Swear by Dixie
El Gran Senor
El Angelo
Helmsman
Lit de Justice
Stylish Senor
Eskimo
Fire Dancer
Fire Maker
Imperial Falcon
Incinderator
Lucky North
Lyphard
Bellypha (IRE)
Mendez
Linamix (FR)
Dahar
Buckhar
Falstaff
Apollo
Lyphard's Wish (FR)
Spellbound
Spiritbound
Lypheor (GB)
Chenin Blanc
Manila
Bien Bien
Secretto

Magesterial
Tossofthecoin
Night Shift
Struggler (GB)
Nijinsky II
Baldski
Appealing Skier
Once Wild
Encino
The Name's Jimmy
Ferdinand
Clearly Awesome
Fred Astaire
Free and Equal
Gorytus
Gorky Park (FR)
Green Dancer
Fabulous Frolic
Kanjinsky
Manzotti
Moscow Ballet
Royal Academy
Russian Courage
Shadeed
Alydeed
Shahrastani
Kazabaiyn
Sky Classic
Stack
Sword Dance (IRE)
Marlin
Whiskey Road
Strawberry Road (AUS)
Chilito
Mud Route
Northern Baby
Deposit Ticket
Cash Deposit
Northern Flagship
Limit Out
Northern Jove
Jovial Turn
Northern Park
Northern Score
Score Quick
Nureyev
Anjiz
Atticus
Goldneyev

Gold Away (IRE)
Joyeux Danseur
Private Interview
Rinka Das
Robin des Bois
Gentlemen (ARG)
Romanov (IRE)
Russian Connection
Soviet Star
Bon Point (GB)
Stravinsky
Theatrical (IRE)
Noactor
Vaudeville
Zocor
Zilzal
Pilgrim
Sadler's Wells
Desert Secret (IRE)
El Prado (IRE)
Imperial Ballet (IRE)
In the Wings (GB)
Singspiel (IRE)
King of Kings (IRE)
Northern Spur (IRE)
Theatre Critic (IRE)
Wayne County (IRE)
World Stage (IRE)
Secreto
Secret Odds
Sovereign Dancer
Gate Dancer
Green Alligator
Leo Castelli
Louis Quatorze
Reign Road
Storm Bird
Cat in Town
Circus Surprise
Islefaxyou
King's Arrow
Mystery Storm
Ocean Crest
Sea Wall
Squadron Leader
Storm Cat
Bustopher Jones
Category Five
Cloud Cover

Crown Ambassador
Exploit
Forestry
Forest Wildcat
Future Storm
S. L. Top Cat
Goodbye Doeny
Hennessy
In Case
Iron Cat
Just a Cat
Level Sands
Mountain Cat
Noble Cat
Notable Cat
Perfect Vision
Scatmandu
Sir Cat
Storm Ashore
Storm Boot
Storm Broker
Storm Creek
Storm of Angels
Stormin Fever
Stormy Atlantic
Tabasco Cat
Tale of the Cat
Tomorrows Cat
Summer Squall
Charismatic
Othello
Whitney Tower
The Minstrel
Opening Verse
Topsider
Suggest
Try My Best
Last Tycoon (IRE)
Tychonic (GB)
Unfuwain
Vice Regent
Crown's Wish
Deputy Minister
Awesome Again
Bombardier
Byars
Coordinator
Defrere
Deputy Commander
Flag Down

French Deputy
Minister's Mark
Mongol Warrior
Open Forum
Preacherman
Run Softly
Salt Lake
Ordway
Service Stripe
Silver Deputy
Archers Bay
Etbauer
Statesmanship
State Craft
The Prime Minister
Touch Gold
Tough Call
Treasury
Victory Speech
War Deputy
Westminster
Yarrow Brae
En Tete
King's Grant
Lake George
Native Regent
Northern No Trump
Once a Sailor
Regal Classic
Regal Discovery
Regal Remark
Regent Act

References

COMMANDO

1. Hollingsworth, Kent (Ed.). (1970). *The Great Ones*. Lexington, KY: The Blood-Horse, Inc.
2. Hewitt, Abram S. (1977). *Sire Lines*. Lexington, KY: Thoroughbred Owners and Breeders Association.
3. Ulbrich, Richard. (1986). *The Great Stallion Book*. Hobart, Australia: Libra Books.

STAR SHOOT

1. Palmer, Joe H. (1977). *Names in Pedigrees*. Lexington, KY: The Blood-Horse, Inc.

CHALLENGER

1. "William L. Brann Is Taken by Death." (April 12, 1951). *Daily Racing Form*.
2. Hewitt, Abram S. *Sire Lines*.

BLENHEIM II

1. Burnet, Alastair. (1993). *The Derby*. London: Michael O'Mara Books.

HYPERION

1. Seth-Smith, Michael. (1974). *International Stallions and Studs*. New York: The Dial Press.

BULL LEA

1. Fitzgerald, Arthur. (1997). *The Grand History of the Prix de l'Arc de Triomphe*. London: Genesis Publications Ltd.

NEARCO

1. Hewitt, Abram S. *Sire Lines*.

NASRULLAH

1. *The Bloodstock Breeders' Review* of 1959 gives a slightly different version of the transaction. It suggests that it was not until after Nasrullah had stood a season that McGrath bought him for his Irish stud. This version has the British Bloodstock Agency buying him on behalf of Gerald McElligott and Bert Kerr, they doing business for the moment as "Nasrullah Syndicate." That pair then sold him to McGrath for approximately $75,000.
2. Seth-Smith, Michael. *International Stallions and Studs*.

BOLD RULER

1. Shropshire, Laurence K. (1971). "The Death of Bold Ruler." *The Blood-Horse*.

Index

Index

Index

Index

Index

LIST OF *Illustrations*

Commando (*The Blood-Horse*); Colin (*The Blood-Horse*); Broad Brush (*Anne M. Eberhardt*); Star Shoot (*The Blood-Horse*); Sir Barton (*Keeneland-Cook*); Sweep (*L.S. Sutcliffe*); Fair Play (*The Blood-Horse*); Man o' War (*James W. Sames III*); War Admiral (*The Blood-Horse*); Display (*Keeneland-Morgan*); In Reality (*Jim Jernigan*); Honour and Glory (*Bill Straus-Keeneland*); Sir Gallahad III (*J.A. Estes*); Gallant Fox (*The Blood-Horse*); Roman (*The Blood-Horse*); Challenger II (*The Blood-Horse*); Challedon (*The Blood-Horse*); Gallorette (*Bert Morgan*); Blenheim II (*The Blood-Horse*); Mahmoud (*H.A. Rouch*); Whirlaway (*C.C. Cook*); Hyperion (*The Blood-Horse*); Khaled (*Bob Hopper*); Vaguely Noble (*J. Noye*).

Bull Lea (*Jimmie Sames Studio*); Citation (*Bert Clark Thayer*); Majestic Prince (*The Blood-Horse*); Twilight Tear (*Bert Morgan*); Damascus (*Paul Schafer/New York Racing Association*); Princequillo (*The Blood-Horse*); Apalachee (*Ruth Rogers*); Meadowlake (*Louise Reinagel*); Rough'n Tumble (*The Blood-Horse*); Dr. Fager (*Bob Coglianese/New York Racing Association*); Holy Bull (*Barbara D. Livingston*); Nearco (*British Racehorse*); Nearctic (*The Blood-Horse*); Amerigo (*Marshall Hawkins*); Nasrullah (*The Blood-Horse*); Nashua (*The Blood-Horse*); Never Bend (*The Blood-Horse*); Hail to Reason (*John C. Wyatt*); Halo (*Barbara D. Livingston*); Sunday Silence (*Four Footed Photos*); Roberto (*The Blood-Horse*); Straight Deal (*The Blood-Horse*).

Bold Ruler (*The Blood-Horse*); Secretariat (*Anne M. Eberhardt*); Seattle Slew (*Barbara D. Livingston*); Blushing Groom (*Tony Leonard*); Rahy (*Barbara D. Livingston*); Rainbow Quest (*W.W. Rouch & Co.*); Cherokee Run (*Tony Leonard*); Sky Beauty (*Barbara D. Livingston*); Swain (*Barbara D. Livingston*); Ribot (*The Blood-Horse*); Arts and Letters (*Tony Leonard*); Graustark (*J. Noye*); Native Dancer (*Peter Winants*); Natalma (*The Blood-Horse*); Darn That Alarm (*Jim Raftery*); Sea-Bird (*W.W. Rouch & Co.*); Diesis (*John Crofts*); Arctic Tern (*The Blood-Horse*); Mr. Prospector (*Tony Leonard*); Woodman (*Anne M. Eberhardt*); Gulch (*Barbara D. Livingston*); Raise a Native (*The Blood-Horse*); Alydar (*Anne M. Eberhardt*); Affirmed (*Kevin Ellsworth*).

Northern Dancer (*Tony Leonard*); El Gran Senor (*Tony Leonard*); Deputy Minister (*Tony Leonard*); Lyphard (*Anne M. Eberhardt*); Dixieland Band (*The Blood-Horse*); Storm Bird (*E. Martin Jessee*); Nijinsky II (*Dell Hancock*); Caerleon (*Tony Leonard*); Royal Academy (*The Blood-Horse*); Nureyev (*Tony Leonard*); Miesque (*Steve Stidham*); Theatrical (*Skip Dickstein*); Danzig (*Dell Hancock*); Dance Smartly (*Skip Dickstein*); Danehill (*Mary Pitt*); Sadler's Wells (*Anne M. Eberhardt*); Salsabil (*John Crofts*); Montjeu (*John Crofts*); El Prado (*Bill Straus*); Singspiel (*John Crofts*); In the Wings (*Anne M. Eberhardt*); Storm Cat (*Tony Leonard*); Sharp Cat (*Barbara D. Livingston*); Hennessy (*Barbara D. Livingston*).

Edward L. Bowen (*Dell Hancock*)

Acknowledgments

DYNASTIES: GREAT THOROUGHBRED STALLIONS was produced with assistance from editor Jacqueline Duke, assistant editor Judy L. Marchman, artist Brian Turner, copy editors Tom Hall, Diane L. Viert, and Jill Williams, research director James A. Cox, and researchers Jo McKinney, Linda Manley, and Jay Wallace. Pedigree information was provided by The Jockey Club Information Systems.

A B O U T   T H E   *Author*

EDWARD L. BOWEN is considered one of Thoroughbred racing's most insightful and erudite writers. A native of West Virginia, Bowen grew up in South Florida where he became enamored of racing while watching televised stakes from Hialeah.

Bowen entered journalism school at the University of Florida in 1960. The next summer he worked at Ocala Stud Farm, then spent the following summer working for trainer Kenny Noe at Monmouth Park and Atlantic City. Bowen transferred to the University of Kentucky in 1963 so he could work as a writer for *The Blood-Horse*, the leading weekly Thoroughbred magazine. From 1968 to 1970, he served as editor of *The Canadian Horse*, then returned to *The Blood-Horse* as managing editor. He rose to the position of editor-in-chief before leaving the publication in 1993.

Bowen served as president (1994–2018) of the Grayson-Jockey Club Research Foundation, which raises funds for equine research. In addition to Dynasties, he has written more than twenty other books, including *Man o' War, Legacies of the Turf, The Lucky Thirteen: The Winners of America's Triple Crown of Horse Racing*, and *Matriarchs: Great Mares of the 20th Century*. Bowen has won the Eclipse Award for magazine writing, the Charles Engelhard Award, the Old Hilltop Award, the Walter Haight Award, and the gold medal designation in *Foreword*'s sports category. He lives in Versailles, Kentucky, with his wife, Ruthie, and has three grown children: George Bowen, Tracy Bowen, and Jennifer Schafhauser.

www.ingramcontent.com/pod-product-compliance
Lightning Source LLC
Chambersburg PA
CBHW081207120325
23301CB00003B/3